Origami Symphony No. 9

Ode to Australia

Books by John Montroll
www.johnmontroll.com
Instagram: @montrollorigami

Origami Symphonies

Origami Symphony No. 1: The Elephant's Trumpet Call
Origami Symphony No. 2: Trio of Sharks & Playful Prehistoric Mammals
Origami Symphony No. 3: Duet of Majestic Dragons & Dinosaurs
Origami Symphony No. 4: Capturing Vibrant Coral Reef Fish
Origami Symphony No. 5: Woodwinds, Horns, and a Moose
Origami Symphony No. 6: Striped Snakes Changing Scales
Origami Symphony No. 7: Musical Monkeys
Origami Symphony No. 8: An Octet of Cats
Origami Symphony No. 9: Ode to Australia

General Origami

Origami Fold-by-Fold
DC Super Heroes Origami
Origami Worldwide
Teach Yourself Origami: Third Edition
Christmas Origami: Second Edition
Storytime Origami
Origami Inside-Out: Third Edition

Animal Origami

Arctic Animals in Origami
Origami Aquarium
Dogs in Origami
Perfect Pets Origami
Dragons and Other Fantastic Creatures in Origami
Bugs in Origami
Horses in Origami: Second Edition
Origami Birds: Second Edition
Origami Gone Wild
Dinosaur Origami
Origami Dinosaurs for Beginners
Prehistoric Origami: Dinosaurs and other Creatures: Third Edition
Mythological Creatures and the Chinese Zodiac Origami
Origami Sea Life: Third Edition
Bringing Origami to Life: Second Edition
Origami Sculptures: Fourth Edition
African Animals in Origami: Third Edition
North American Animals in Origami: Third Edition
Origami for the Enthusiast: Second Edition
Animal Origami for the Enthusiast: Second Edition

Geometric Origami

Origami Stars: Second Edition
Galaxy of Origami Stars: Second Edition
Origami and Math: Simple to Complex: Second Edition
Origami & Geometry
3D Origami Platonic Solids & More: Second Edition
3D Origami Diamonds
3D Origami Antidiamonds
3D Origami Pyramids
A Plethora of Polyhedra in Origami: Third Edition
Classic Polyhedra Origami
A Constellation of Origami Polyhedra
Origami Polyhedra Design

Dollar Bill Origami

Dollar Origami Treasures: Second Edition
Dollar Bill Animals in Origami: Second Revised Edition
Dollar Bill Origami
Easy Dollar Bill Origami

Simple Origami

Fun and Simple Origami: 101 Easy-to-Fold Projects: Second Edition
Origami Twelve Days of Christmas: And Santa, Too!
Super Simple Origami
Easy Dollar Bill Origami
Easy Origami
Easy Origami 2
Easy Origami 3
Easy Origami Coloring Book
Easy Origami Animals
Easy Origami Polar Animals
Easy Origami Ocean Animals
Easy Origami Woodland Animals
Easy Origami Jungle Animals
Meditative Origami

Origami Symphony No. 9

Ode to Australia

John Montroll

Antroll Publishing Company

To Kimmy and Charley

Origami Symphony No. 9: *Ode to Australia*

ISBN-10: 1-877656-63-1
ISBN-13: 978-1-877656-63-7

Antroll Publishing Company

Introduction

Welcome to the world premier of the Ninth Origami Symphony! Modeled after a musical symphony in four movements, many themes reveal the possibilities of origami. Australian mammals and birds along with colorful cubes and backyard bugs are explored in beautiful detail.

The four movements contain diagrams for 35 models ranging from simple to very complex. Many unusual Australian mammals and birds are shown in the first two movements. Three kangaroos including the familiar Red Kangaroo are diagrammed in the first movement along with a cute Koala and Rabbit-Bandicoot. Many of Australian birds of the second movement come to life with color-change patterns. Some of the duo-colored birds are the Brahminy Kite, Magpie Goose and Black Butcherbird. The third movement begins with a Cube followed by cubes with color-change patterns. A trio of polyhedra based on the cube includes the stunning Stella Octangula. The symphony concludes with the fourth movement of complex backyard bugs. An Ant, Cicada, Katydid, Mosquito, Hornet and four-winged Dragonfly add variety and challenges to the enjoyment of origami.

The models were designed to be easily foldable from standard origami paper. Each is from one sheet and explores interesting structures, styles, and techniques. Many of the models use elegant design methods so they can be folded in far fewer steps than imagined. The cute Red Kangaroo with such details as the long, open ears is accomplished in 21 steps. All the cubes with colorful patterns are diagrammed in under 25 steps. Even the bugs use fewer steps than usual, such as the Hornet in 49 steps. Realizing these complex subjects in fewer steps adds elegance and a life-force to them.

The diagrams are drawn in the internationally approved Randlett-Yoshizawa style. You can use any kind of square paper for these models, but the best results will be achieved with standard origami paper, which is colored on one side and white on the other (in the diagrams in this book, the shading represents the colored side). Large sheets, such as nine inches squared, are easier to use than small ones.

Origami supplies can be found in arts and craft shops, or at Dover Publications online: www.doverpublications.com. You can also visit OrigamiUSA at www.origamiusa.org for origami supplies and other related information including an extensive list of local, national, and international origami groups.

Please follow me on Instagram @montrollorigami to see posts of my origami.

I thank my editor, Charley Montroll. I also thank the folders who proof-read the diagrams and continued to encourage me to present origami in symphonic form.

I hope you enjoy this Ode to Australia, the colorful cubes and the beautiful backyard bugs from Origami Symphony No. 9.

John Montroll
www.johnmontroll.com

Contents

★ Simple
★★ Intermediate
★★★ Complex
★★★★ Very Complex

First Movement
Allegro: Australian Mammals Hopping Around

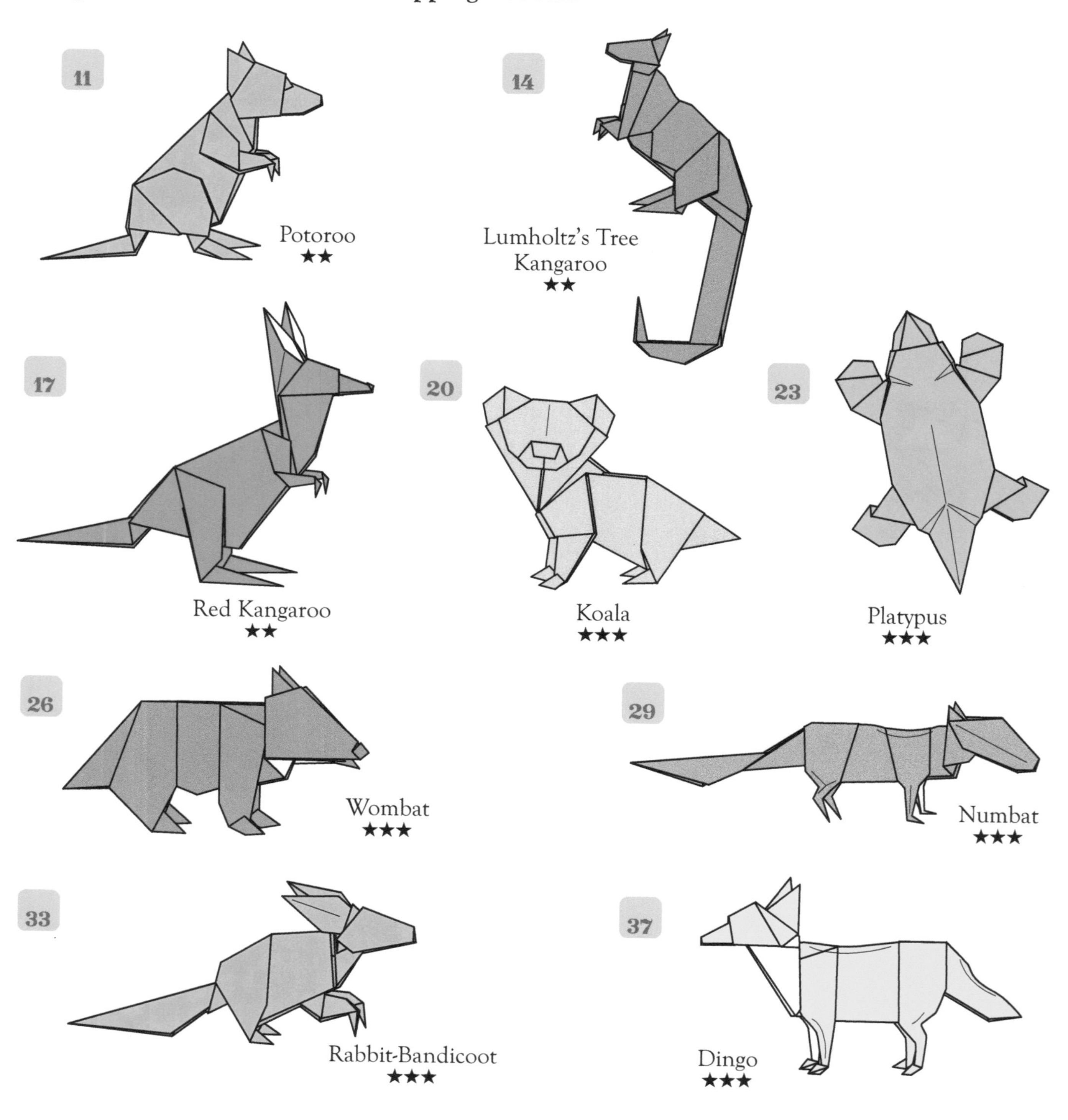

Second Movement
Andante: Australian Birds Hopping Around

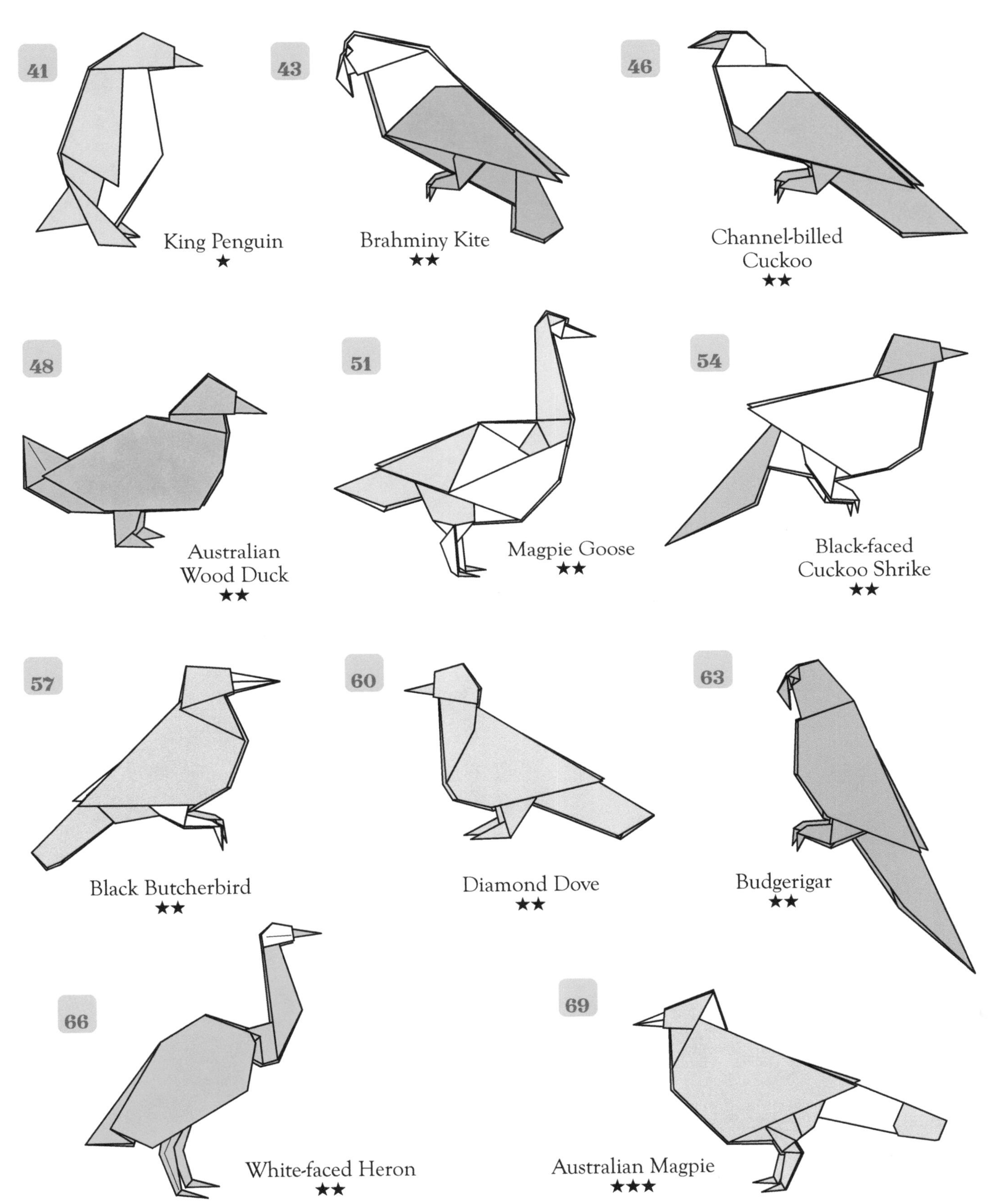

Third Movement
Minuet of Colorful Cubes with a Trio of Shapes Based on Cubes

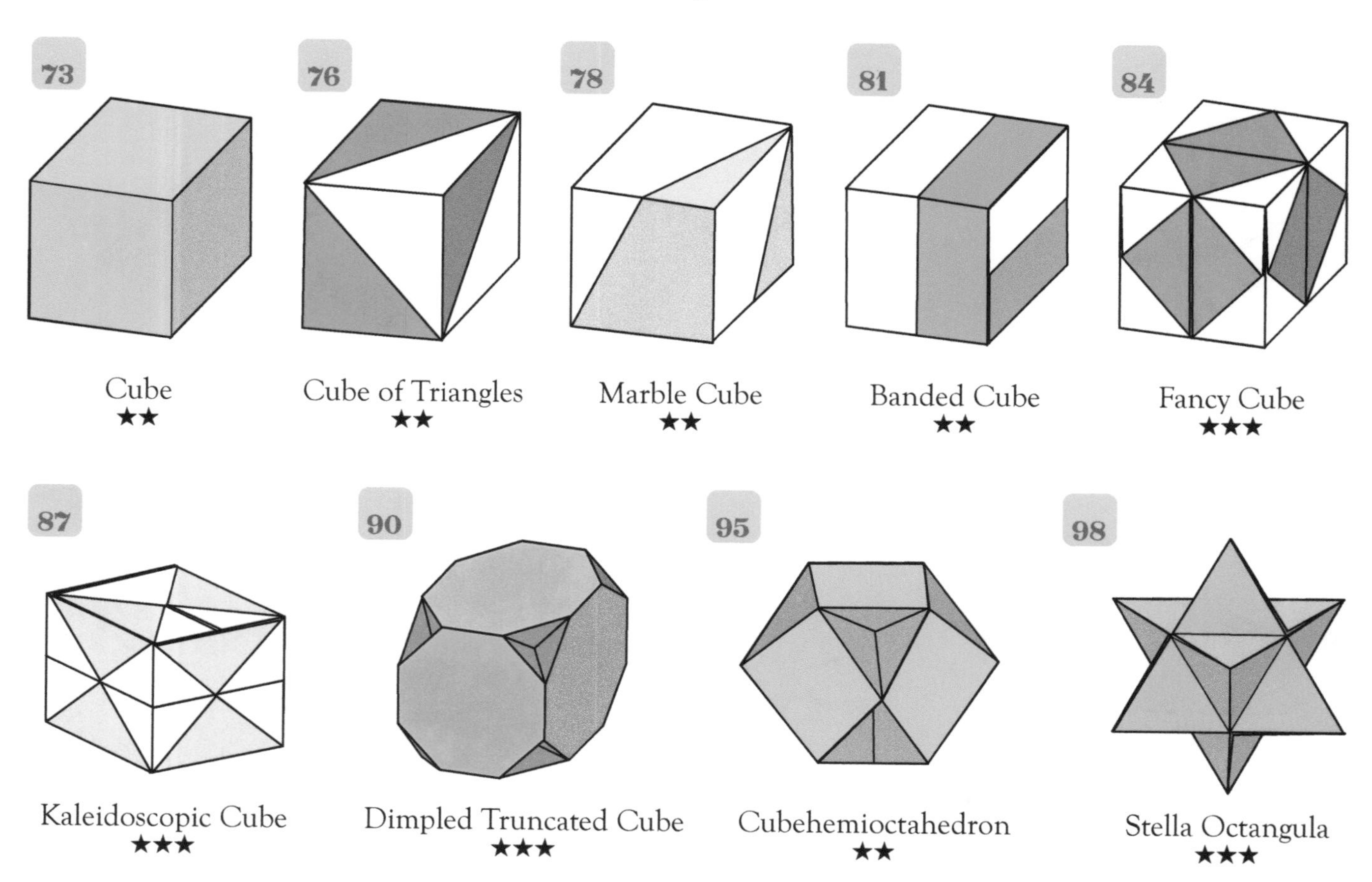

Fourth Movement
Allegro: The Buzzing of Backyard Bugs

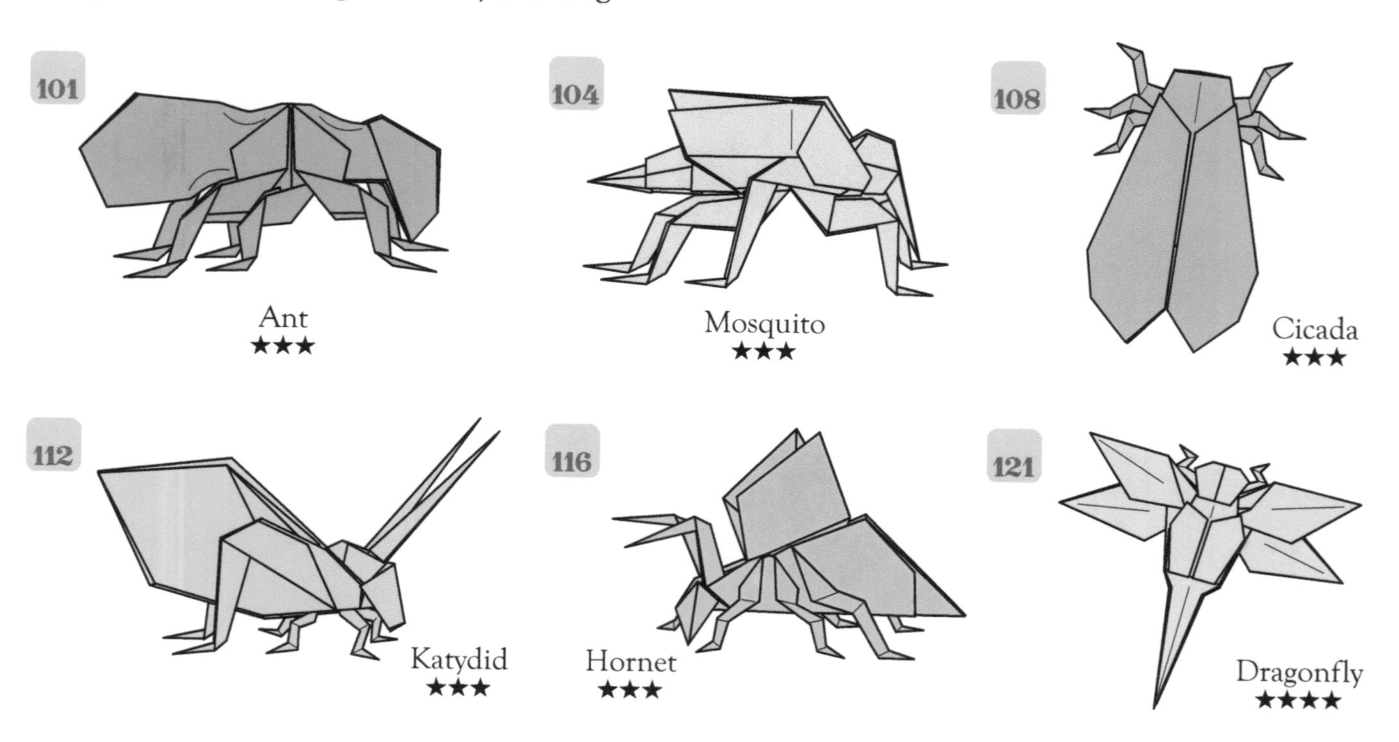

Symbols

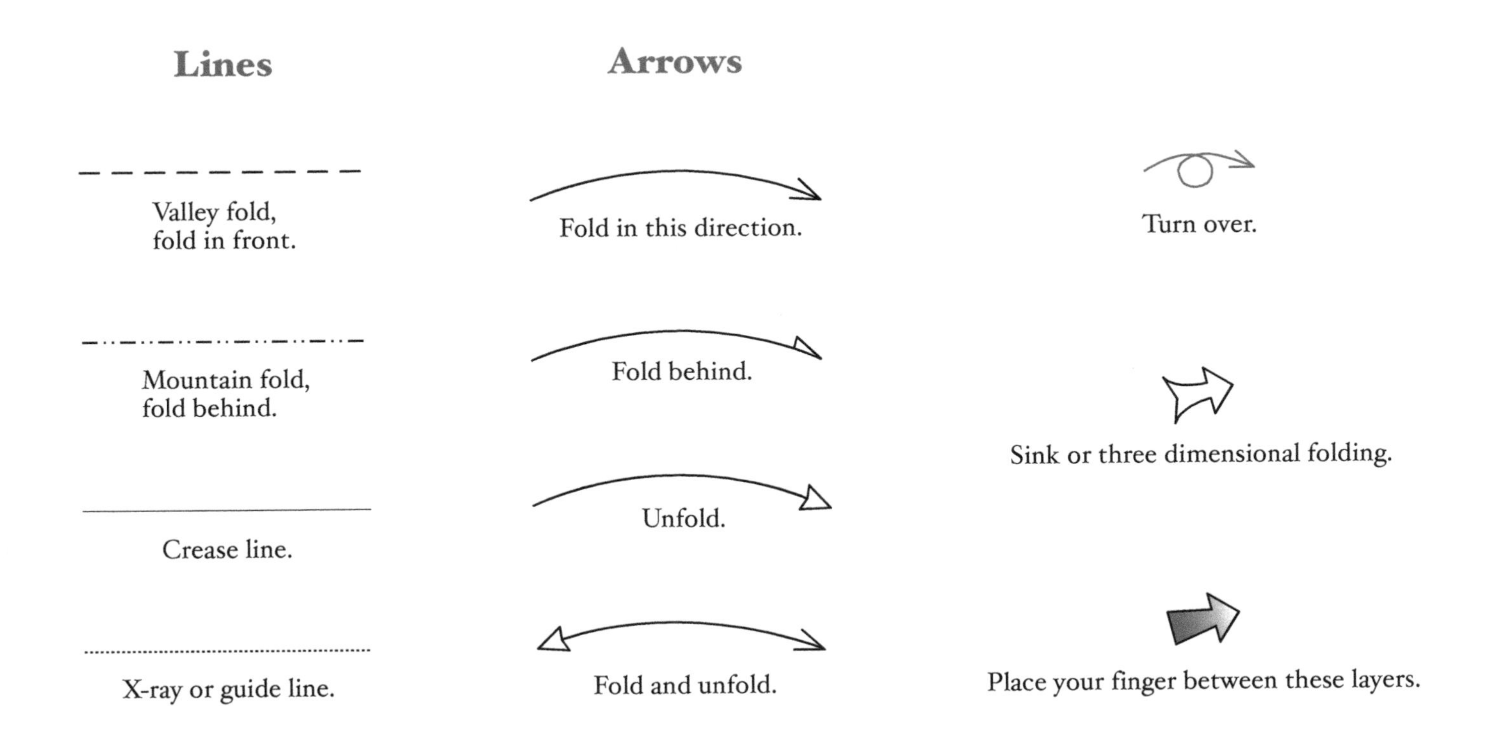

The Beethoven Nine Symphonies

While finishing this 9th origami symphony, I am reflecting on Beethoven's nine symphonies, which were composed in the early 19th century.

Prior to Beethoven, Mozart and Haydn established the symphony to be a structured work in typically four movements. Mozart wrote over 40 symphonies, though several were shorter works written as a child, and Haydn wrote over 104, and symphonies were written to entertain the nobility.

Beethoven wrote his first two symphonies modeled after Haydn's work though he added musical jokes throughout. His third symphony, the Eroica, took a much larger and grander form, forever changing the notion of a symphony. His famous fifth symphony, opening with four notes of despair "G G G E-flat" and ending triumphantly with piccolo fanfare, was revolutionary. He created emotions and depth beyond anyone else's musical expression. His ninth and last symphony introduced vocalists in the fourth movement as they sang about brotherhood in his Ode to Joy.

Beethoven changed the world through the depth of his symphonies. Composers after him realized their work must also be grand, too, and most could write no more than nine symphonies, if even close to that.

I know Beethoven's work well and it inspires me as I write my origami symphonies. As I am finishing this 9th origami symphony, I am reflecting on Beethoven's 9th. His Ode to Joy is my Ode to Australia. I was contemplating how grand I could make the fourth movement to match his chorus singing about brotherhood, and all I could come up with was The Buzzing of Backyard Bugs. Well, I hope the bugs at least inspire peace.

Origami Symphony No. 9

The first half of this symphony celebrates unusual birds and mammals from Australia. The second half complements them with colorful cubes and backyard bugs. Many unusual origami subjects are explored.

The first movement, Allegro: Australian Mammals Hopping Around, begins with a trio of kangaroos: the small Potoroo, the tree dwelling Lumholtz's Tree Kangaroo and the familiar Red Kangaroo. Capturing the detail and distinct shape of the Red Kangaroo in 21 steps adds elegance to the design. A cute Koala, Platypus and Wombat add to the variety of Australian mammals. The movement ends with the lesser known Numbat, Rabbit-Bandicoot and Dingo, each wandering around in their own rhythm.

Most of the birds in the second movement, Andante: Australian Birds Hopping Around, are lesser known birds. Many have color-change patterns. Opening with a seemingly out-of-place penguin, the King Penguin is native to Australia. A Brahminy Kite, Magpie Goose and Black-faced Cuckoo Shrike fly around in splendid color. The songs of the White-faced Heron and Australian Magpie end the movement.

After the Australian visit, we reach the land of cubes in the Minuet of Colorful Cubes with a Trio of Shapes based on Cubes. In theme and variation format, a solid colored cube is introduced, followed by five cubes with color-change patterns. Elegant folding methods are used so these mind-boggling shapes and patterns are all accomplished in under 25 steps. The trio of shapes based on cubes ends with the spectacular Stella Octangula, which looks like intersecting tetrahedra.

The fourth movement, Allegro: The Buzzing of Backyard Bugs, takes us home where we watch beauty in its tiniest and most detailed form. An Ant, Mosquito, Cicada and Katydid march and fly around the yard. A Hornet in 49 steps highlights the possibilities of complex origami. The symphony closes with a beautiful and delicate four-winged Dragonfly with six legs.

Mammals, birds, bugs and polyhedra based on cubes all weave a song and story showing the variety and possibilities of origami. I hope you enjoy the beauty, elegance, and complexity of this origami symphony.

First Movement

Allegro: Australian Mammals Hopping Around

With a Red Kangaroo as our guide, let's hop around Australia to meet strange and wonderful mammals. The cuteness of the Koala and Rabbit-Bandicoot are captured through origami. While the Numbat sneaks around, the Dingo is keeping watch. A Potoroo, Lumholtz's Tree Kangaroo, Platypus, and Wombat highlight the majestic and mysterious Australian mammals.

Potoroo

These small marsupials are relatives of kangaroos and wallabies and have also been called "Rat Kangaroos". Like many marsupials, Potoroos are nocturnal and their long noses help them sniff out and find food. They can carry sticks and other nesting materials in their tails.

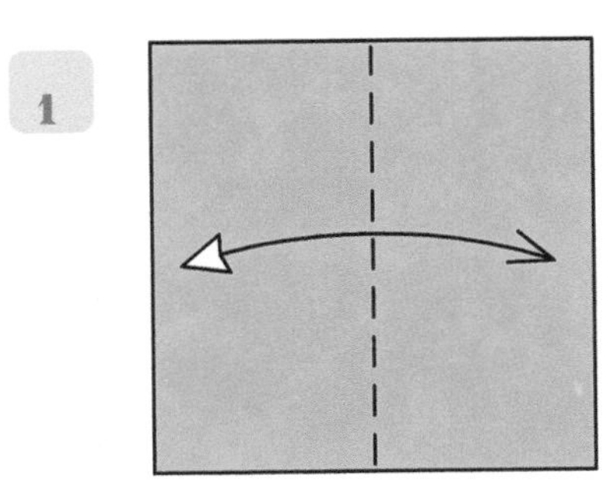

Fold and unfold.

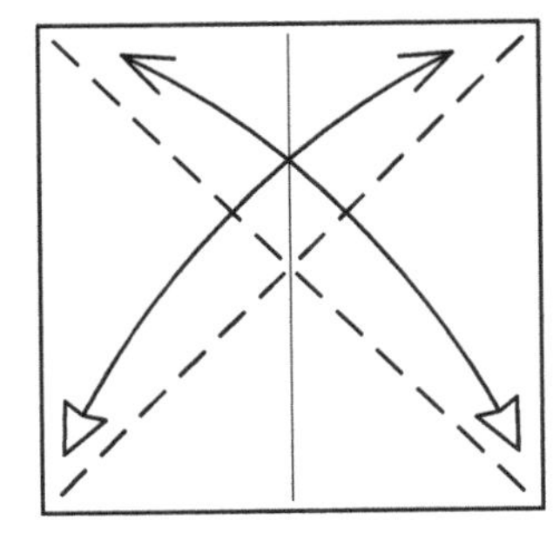

Fold and unfold.

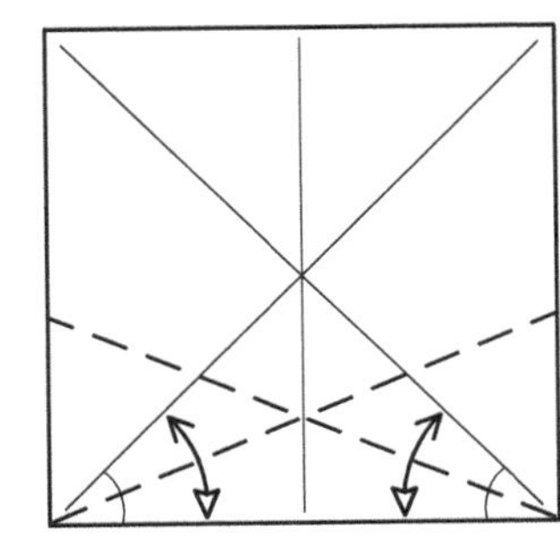

Fold and unfold.

4

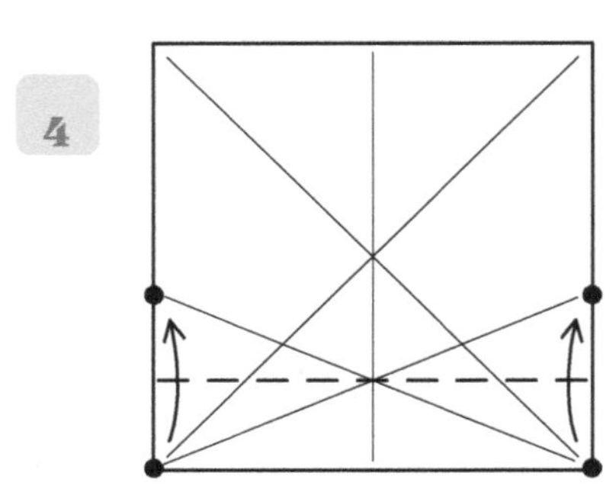

5

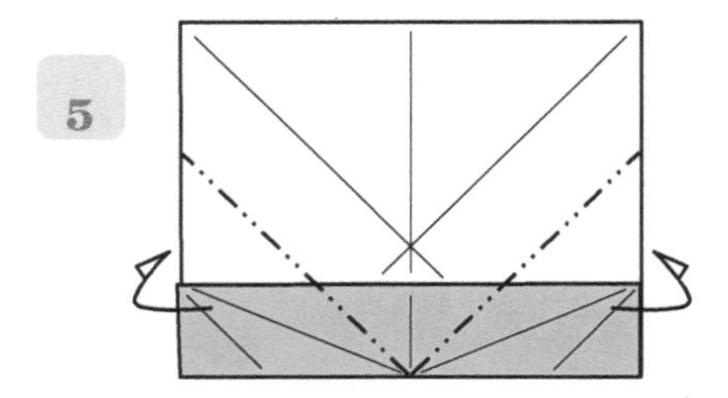

Fold to the center.

6

Fold to the center and swing out from behind.

7

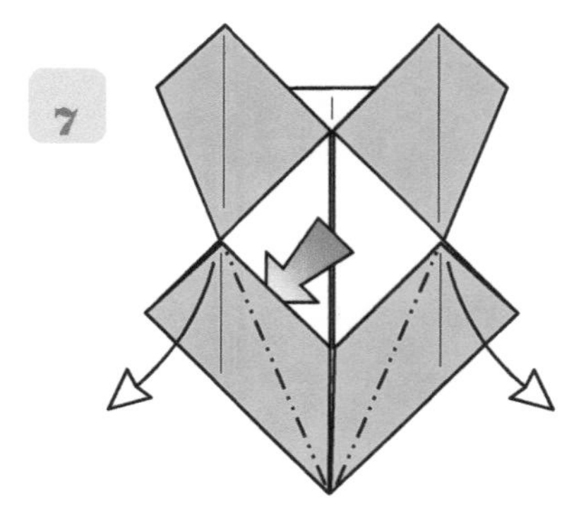

Unlock the paper.

8

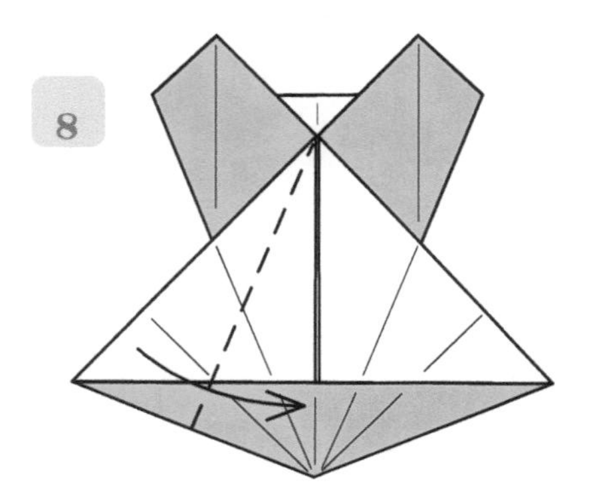

9

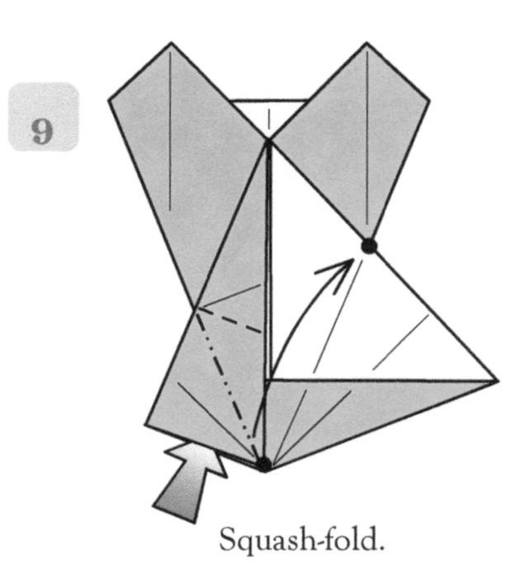

Squash-fold.

10

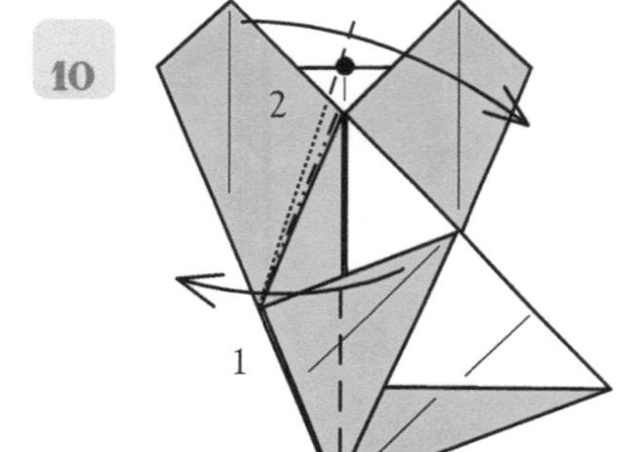

1. Valley-fold.
2. Reverse-fold.

11

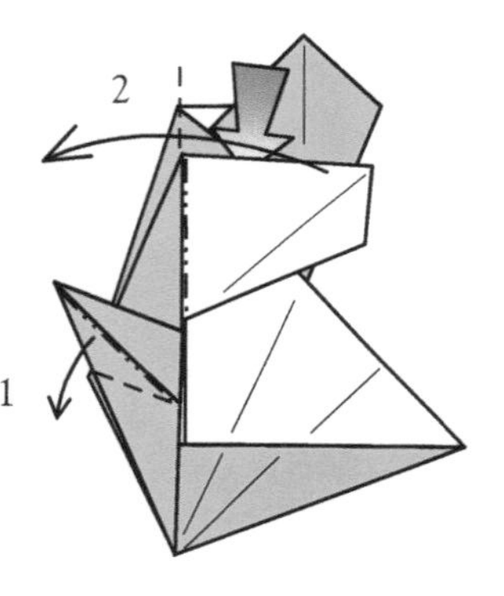

1. Squash-fold.
2. Reverse-fold.

12

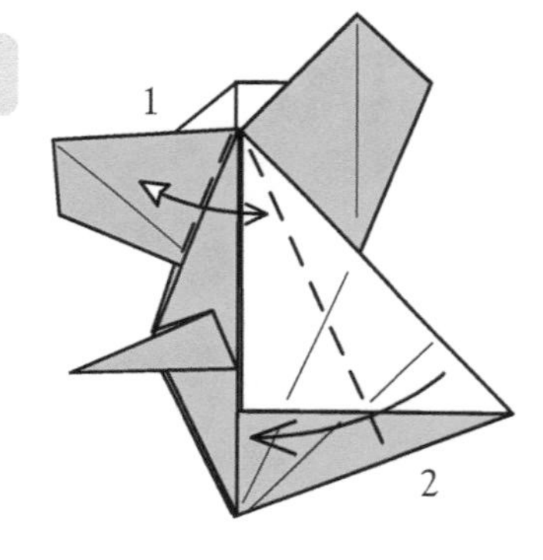

1. Fold and unfold the top layer.
2. Repeat steps 8–12 on the right.

13

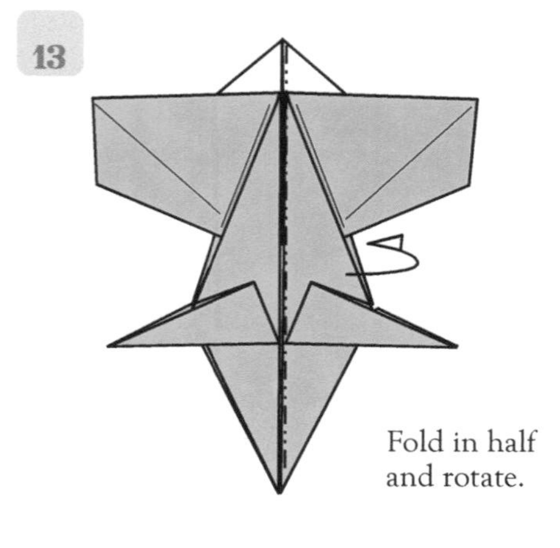

Fold in half and rotate.

14

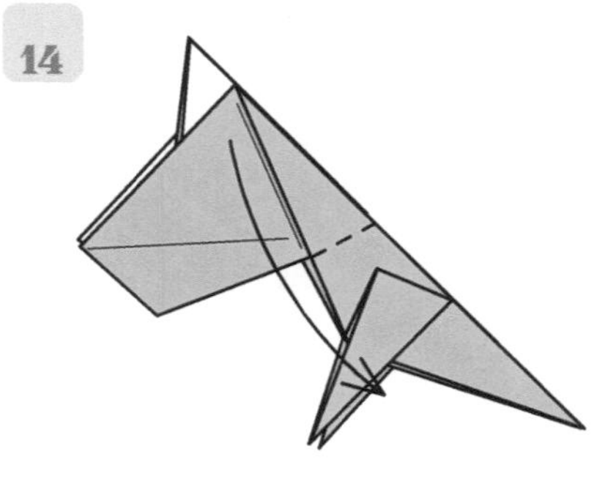

Repeat behind.

15

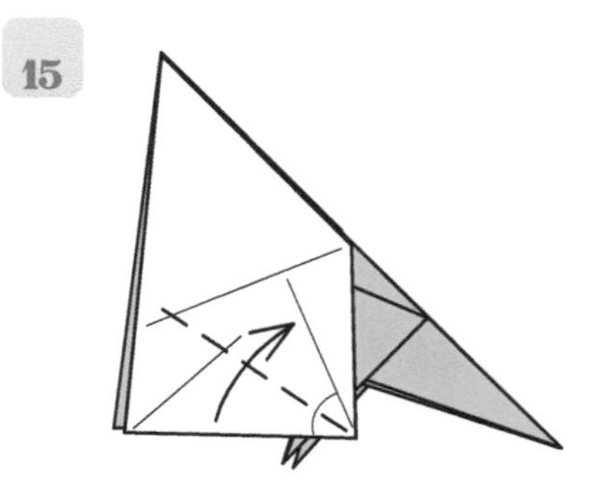

Repeat behind.

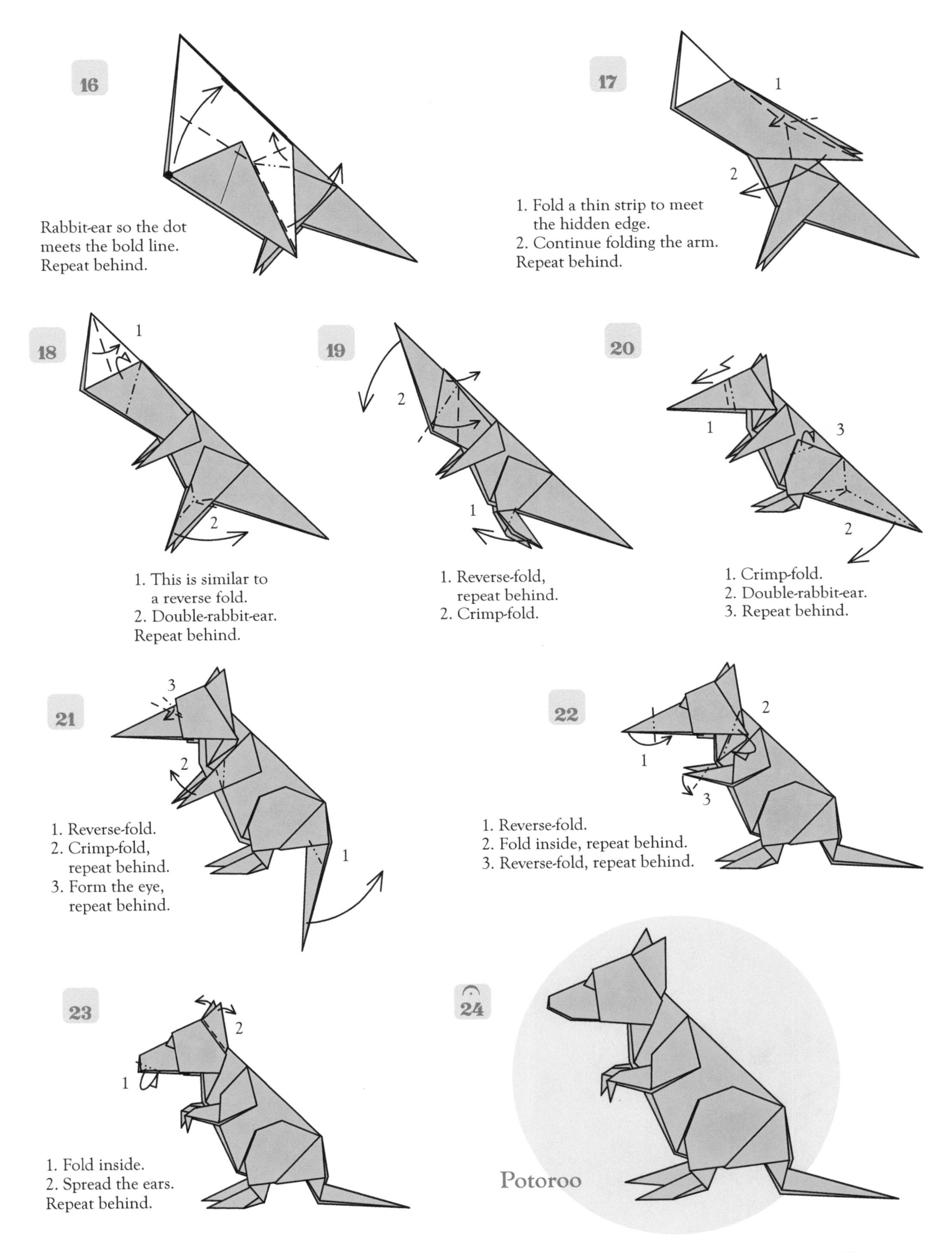
16
Rabbit-ear so the dot meets the bold line.
Repeat behind.
17
1
2
1. Fold a thin strip to meet the hidden edge.
2. Continue folding the arm.
Repeat behind.
18
1
2
1. This is similar to a reverse fold.
2. Double-rabbit-ear.
Repeat behind.
19
2
1
1. Reverse-fold, repeat behind.
2. Crimp-fold.
20
1
3
2
1. Crimp-fold.
2. Double-rabbit-ear.
3. Repeat behind.
21
3
2
1
1. Reverse-fold.
2. Crimp-fold, repeat behind.
3. Form the eye, repeat behind.
22
2
1
3
1. Reverse-fold.
2. Fold inside, repeat behind.
3. Reverse-fold, repeat behind.
23
2
1
1. Fold inside.
2. Spread the ears.
Repeat behind.
24
Potoroo

Lumholtz's Tree Kangaroo

These scarce marsupials look like a squat kangaroo that jumped into a tree and decided to live there. Long tailed and solitary, they feed on vegetation and like kangaroos carry their young in a pouch.

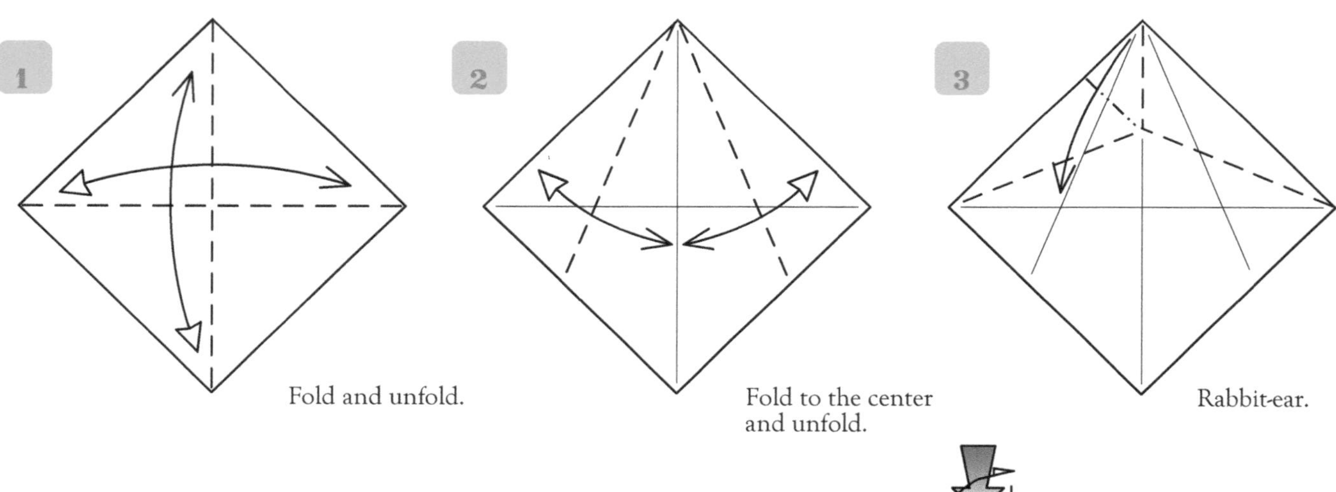

1. Fold and unfold.
2. Fold to the center and unfold.
3. Rabbit-ear.

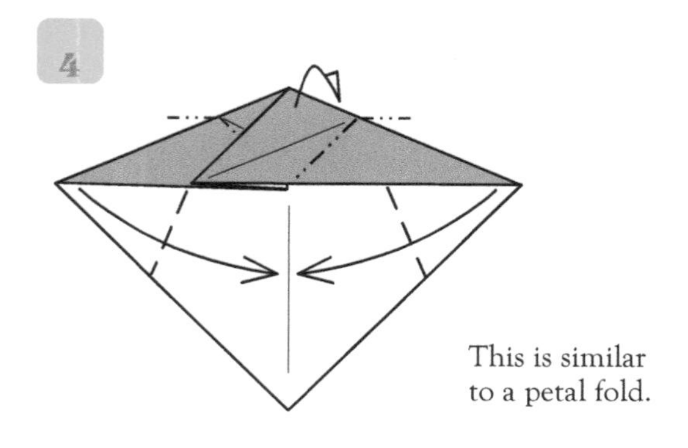

4. This is similar to a petal fold.

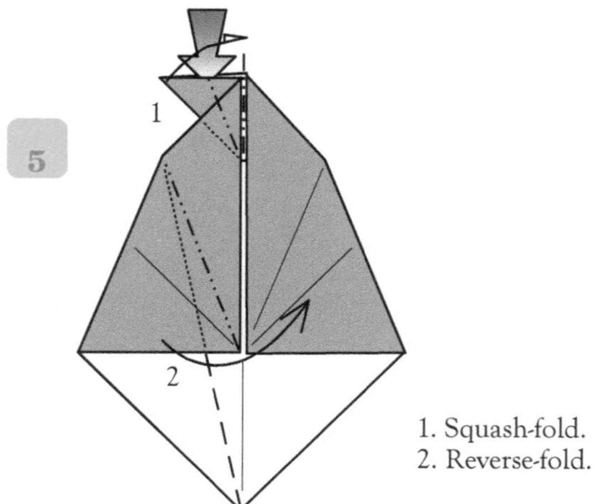

5. 1. Squash-fold.
   2. Reverse-fold.

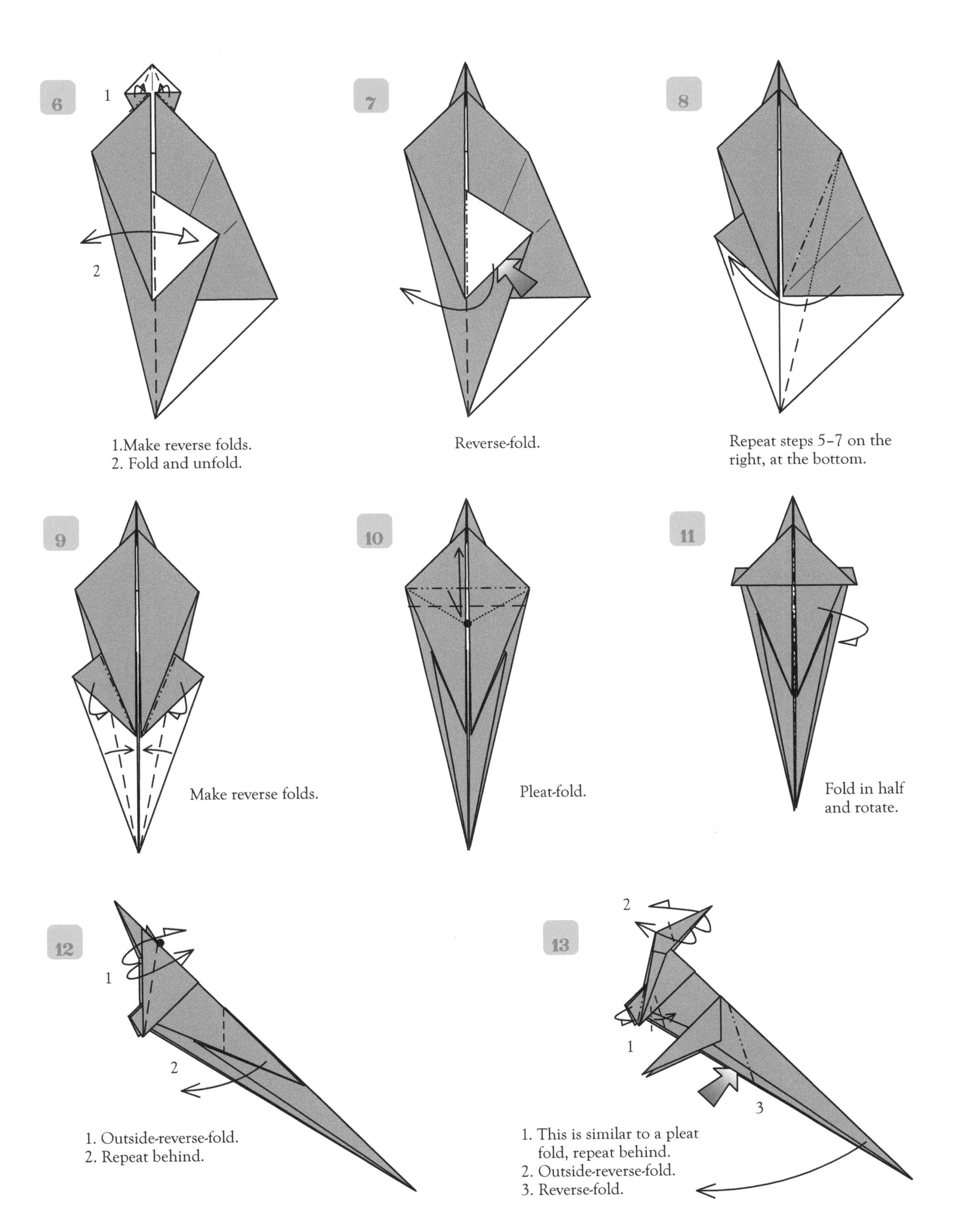
6
1
2
1.Make reverse folds.
2. Fold and unfold.
7
Reverse-fold.
8
Repeat steps 5–7 on the
right, at the bottom.
9
Make reverse folds.
10
Pleat-fold.
11
Fold in half
and rotate.
12
1
2
1. Outside-reverse-fold.
2. Repeat behind.
13
2
1
3
1. This is similar to a pleat
fold, repeat behind.
2. Outside-reverse-fold.
3. Reverse-fold.

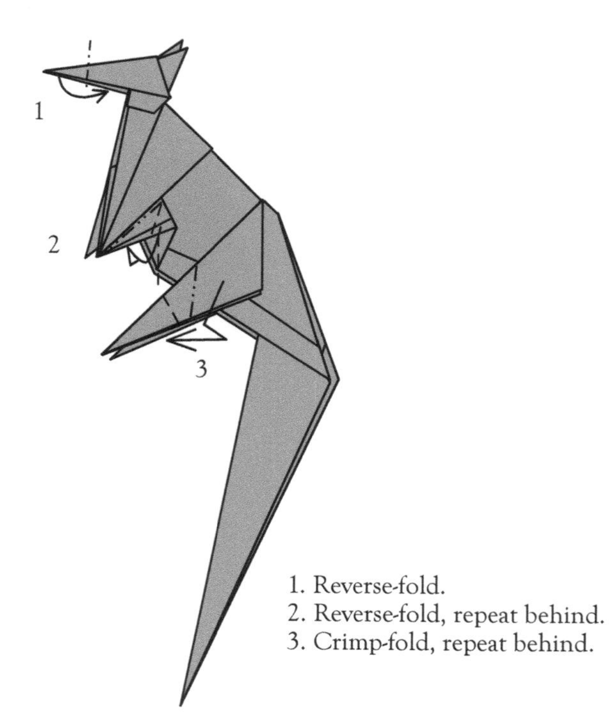

1. Reverse-fold.
2. Reverse-fold, repeat behind.
3. Crimp-fold, repeat behind.

15

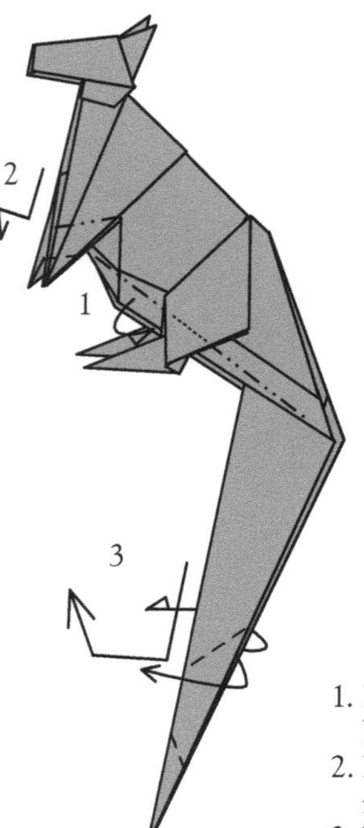

1. Fold inside, repeat behind.
2. Make reverse folds, repeat behind.
3. Make reverse folds, beginning with an outside-reverse fold.

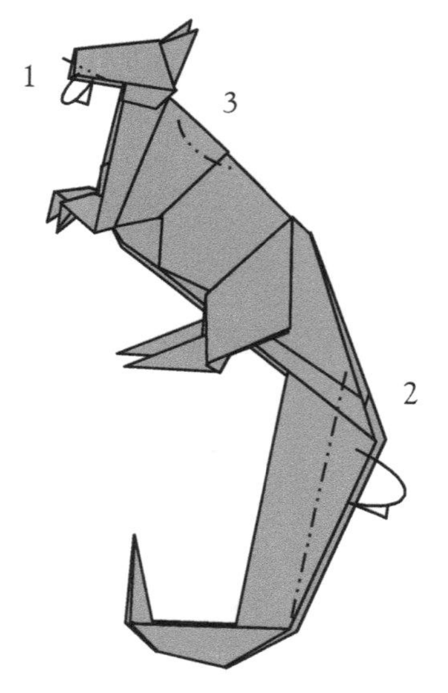

1. Fold inside.
2. Fold inside.
3. Shape the back.
Repeat behind.

17

Red Kangaroo

The largest of the kangaroos and also the world's largest marsupial, Red Kangaroos are very muscular and strong. Although they may become aggressive when threatened or very hungry, they are normally shy and can be gentle with humans.

1

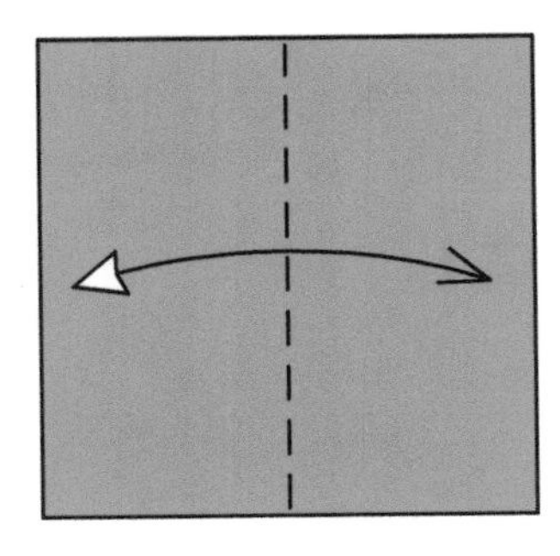

Fold and unfold.

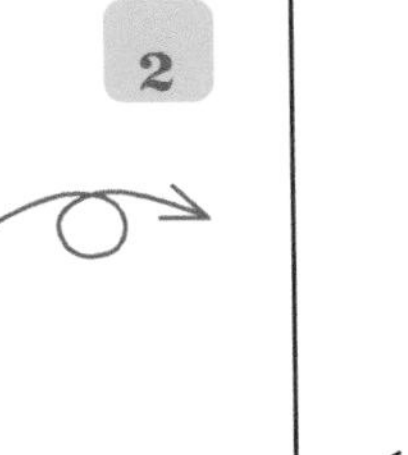

2

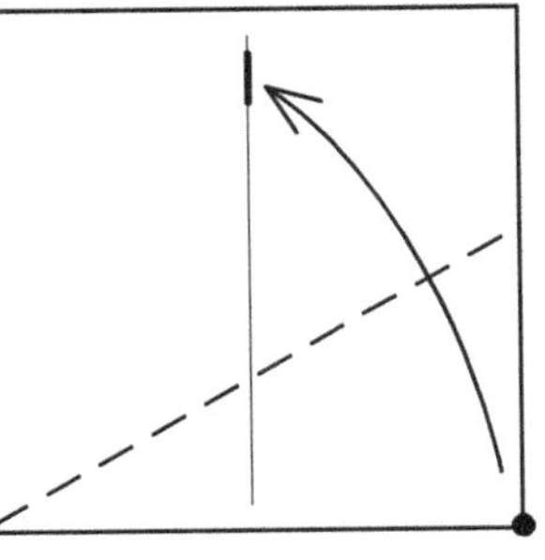

Bring the corner to the line.

3

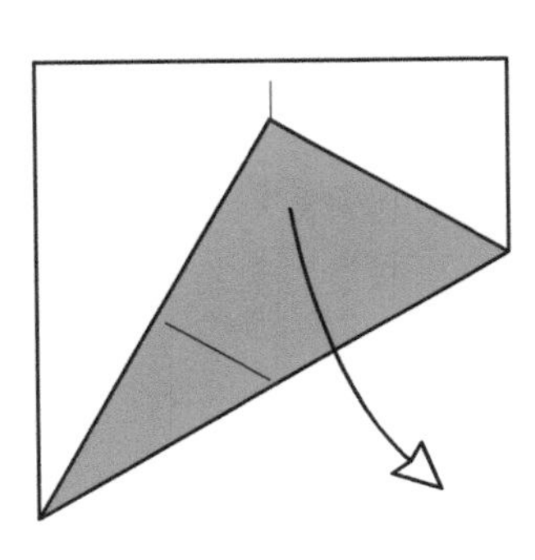

Unfold.

4

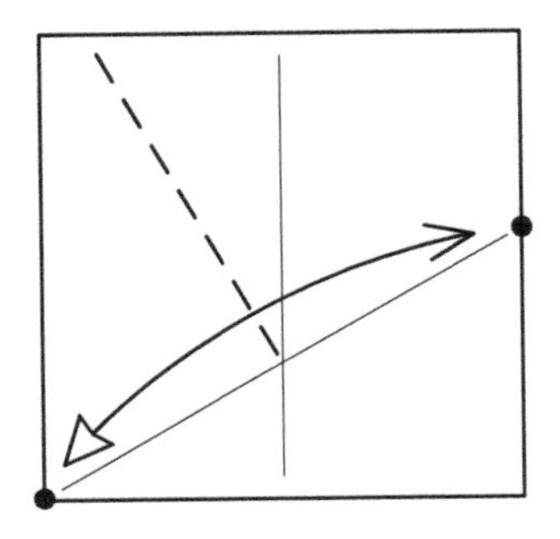

Fold and unfold.

5

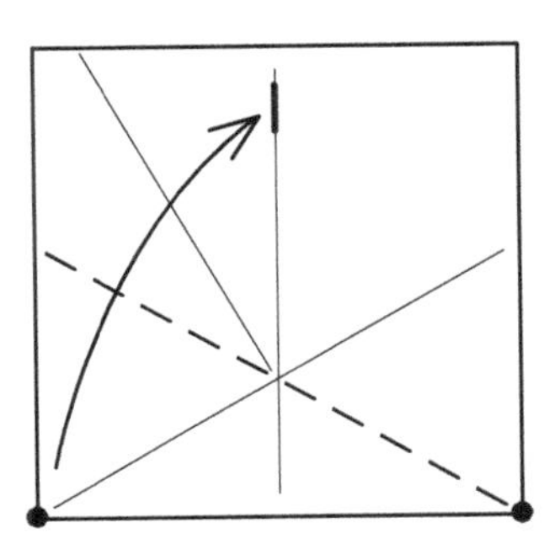

Repeat steps 2–4 in the opposite direction.

6

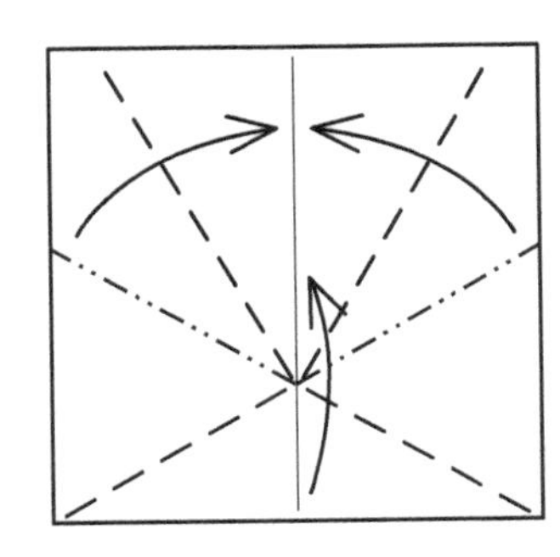

Fold along the creases.

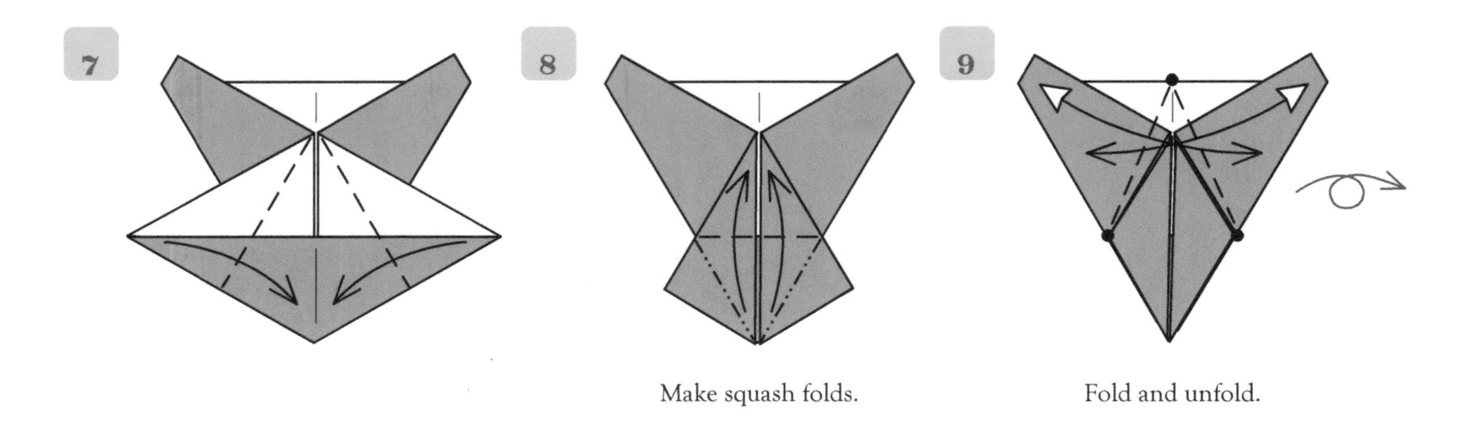

Make squash folds.

Fold and unfold.

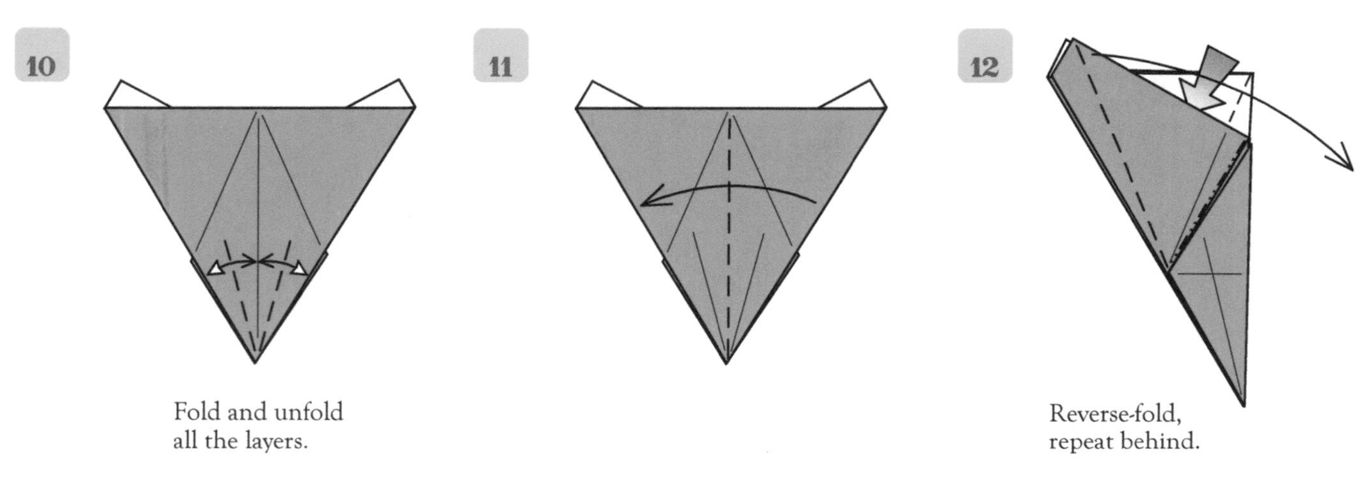

Fold and unfold
all the layers.

Reverse-fold,
repeat behind.

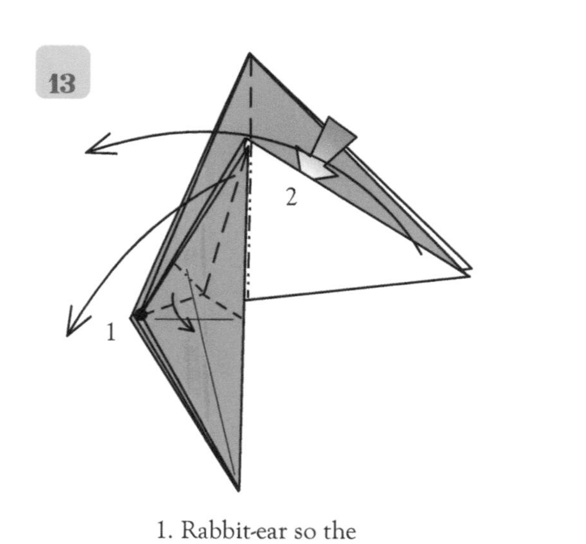

1. Rabbit-ear so the
   edge meets the dot.
2. Reverse-fold.
Repeat behind.

Reverse-fold,
repeat behind.

Reverse-fold,
repeat behind.

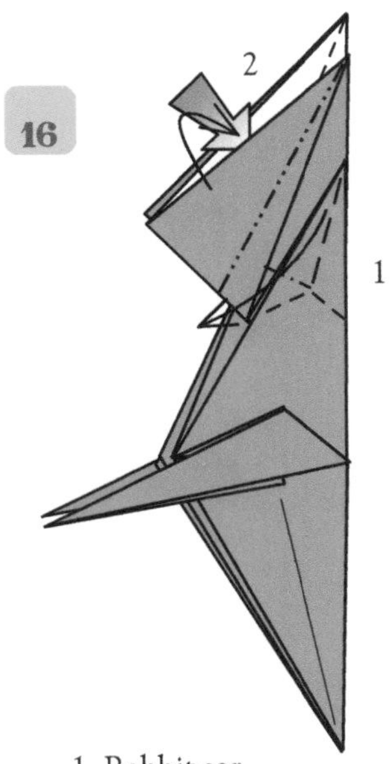

1. Rabbit-ear.
2. Reverse-fold.
Repeat behind and rotate.

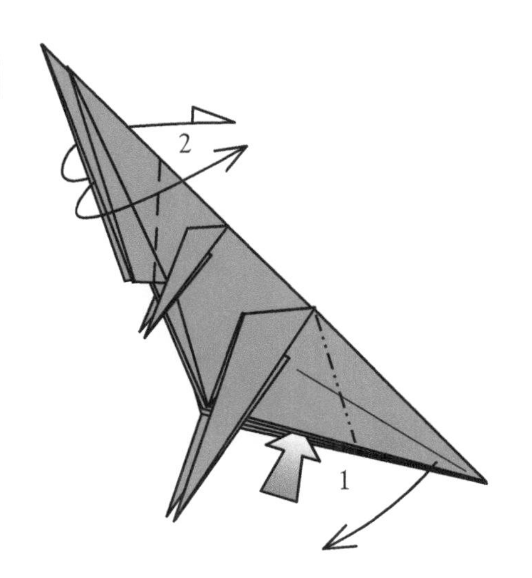

1. Reverse-fold.
2. Outside-reverse-fold.

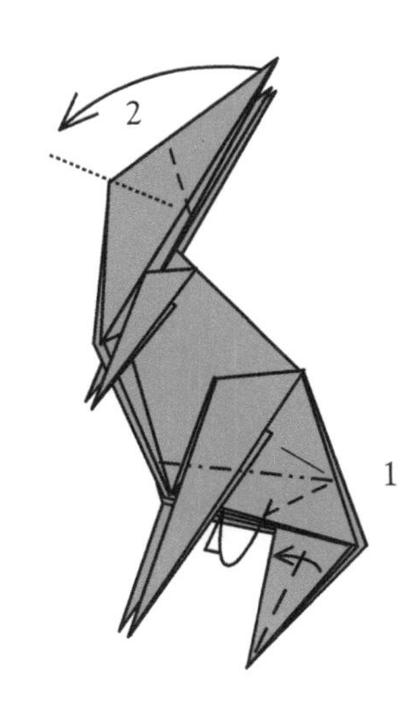

1. Thin the tail and shape the bottom, repet behind.
2. Outside-reverse-fold to the dotted line.

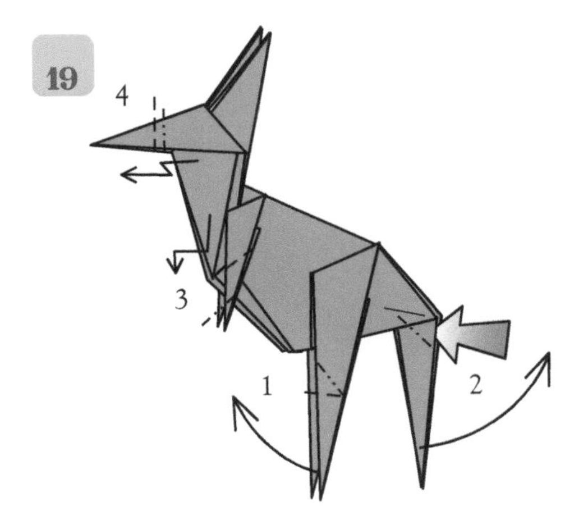

1. Crimp-fold, repeat behind.
2. Reverse-fold.
3. Shape the arm with outside reverse folds, repeat behind.
4. Crimp-fold.

1. Outside-reverse-fold.
2. Fold inside, repeat behind.
3. Open the ears, repeat behind.

Red Kangaroo

Koala

Despite their often being called "Koala Bears", Koalas are in fact marsupials and are closely related to Wombats. Koalas prefer to be alone and like most wild animals can become aggressive when threatened.

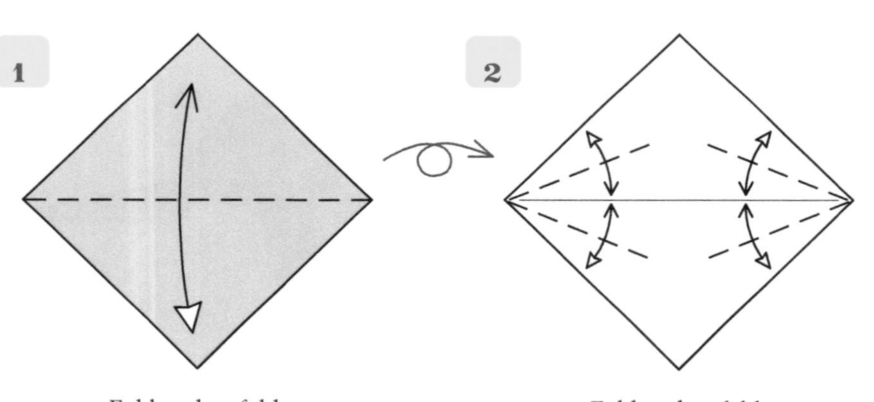

Fold and unfold.

Fold and unfold.

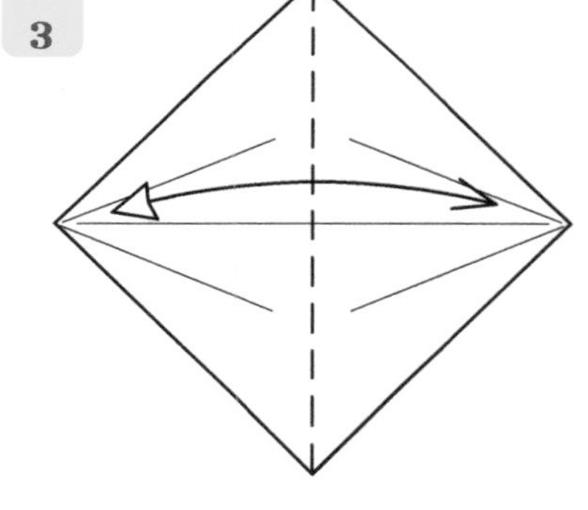

Fold and unfold.

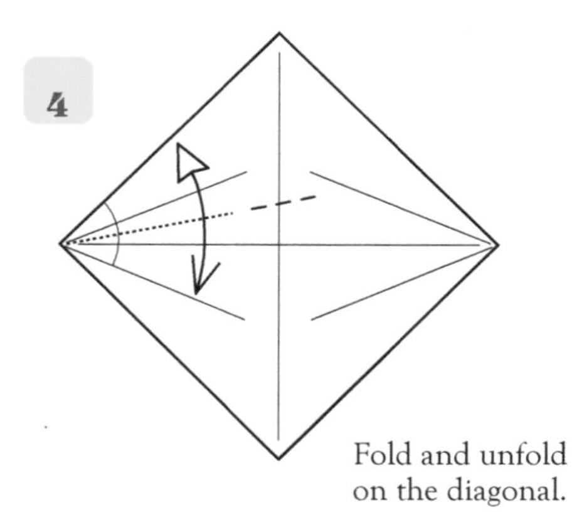

Fold and unfold on the diagonal.

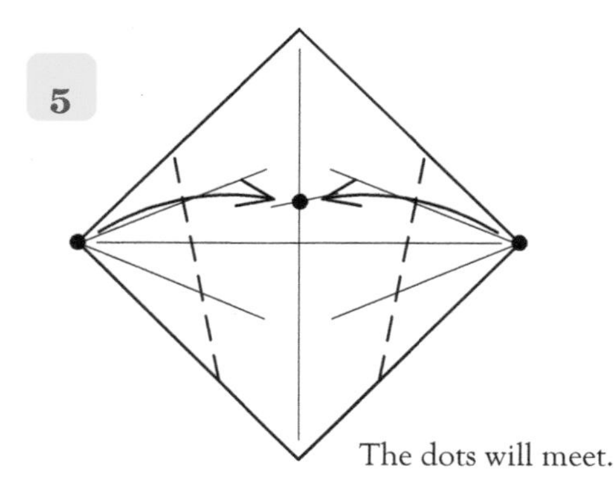

The dots will meet.

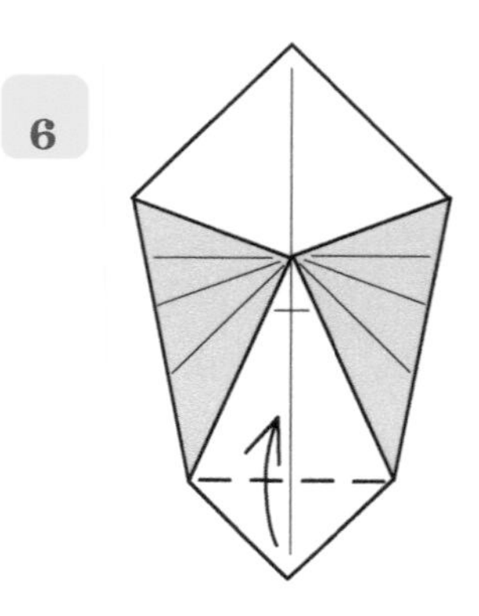

7

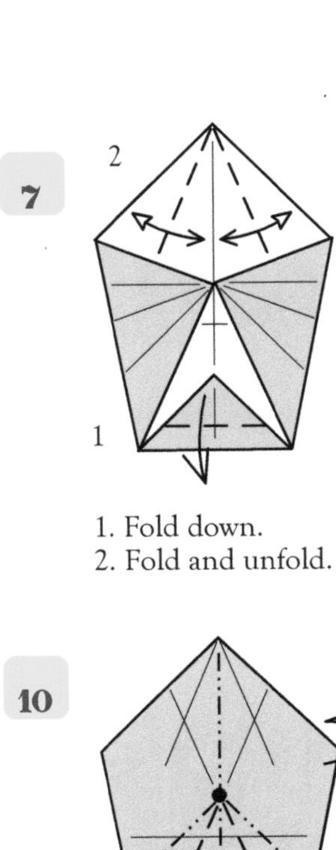

1. Fold down.
2. Fold and unfold.

8

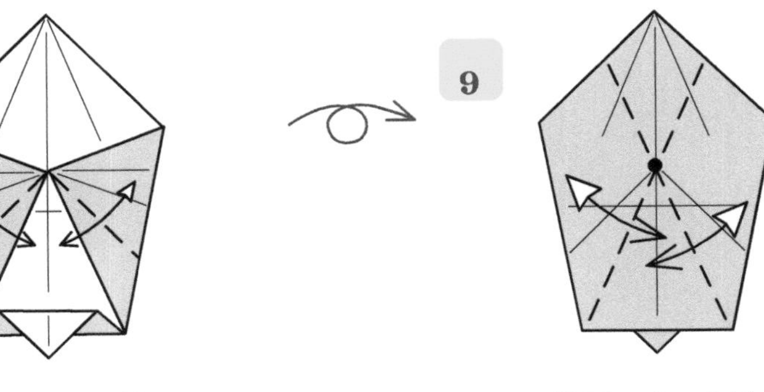

Fold and unfold along the creases.

9

Fold and unfold.

10

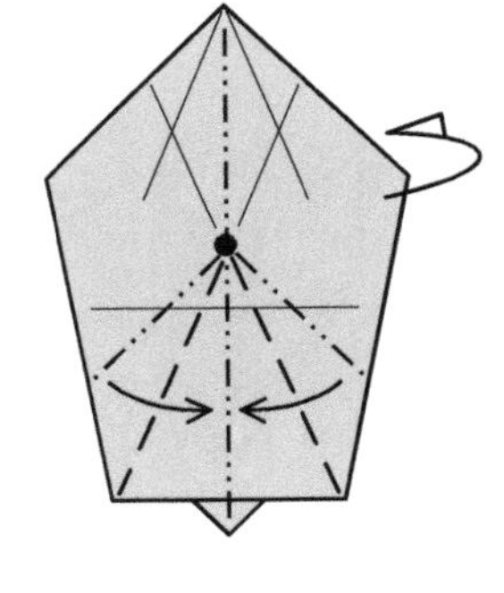

Fold along the creases. Puff out at the dot and flatten.

11

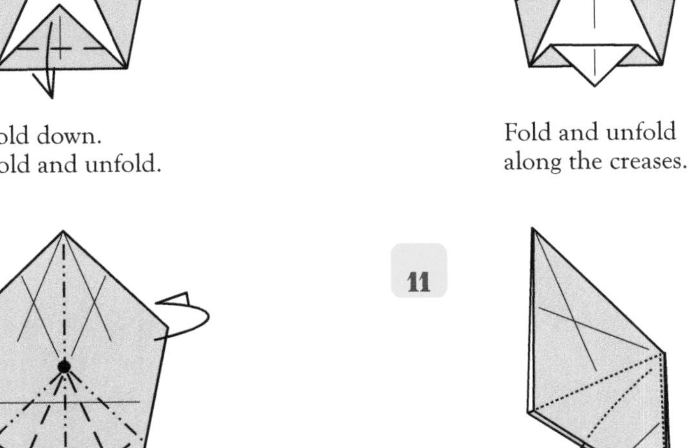

Pull out the hidden paper. Repeat behind.

12

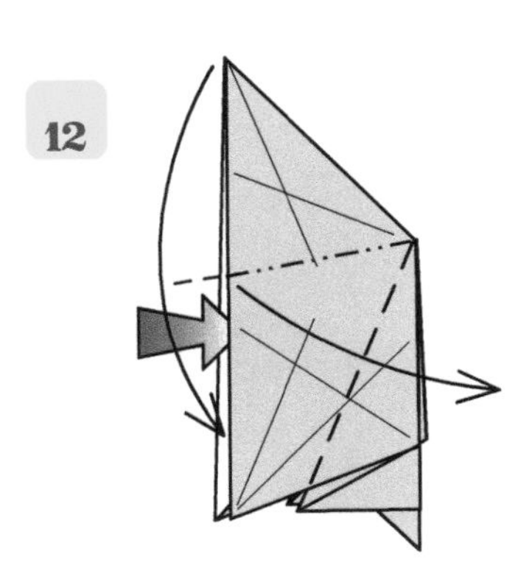

Squash-fold and rotate slightly.

13

14

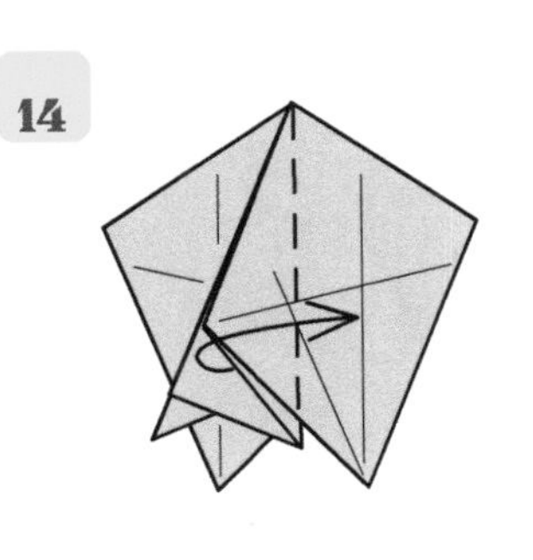

15

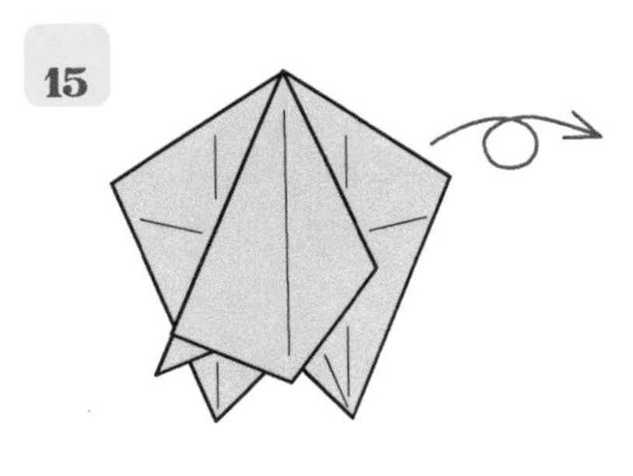

16

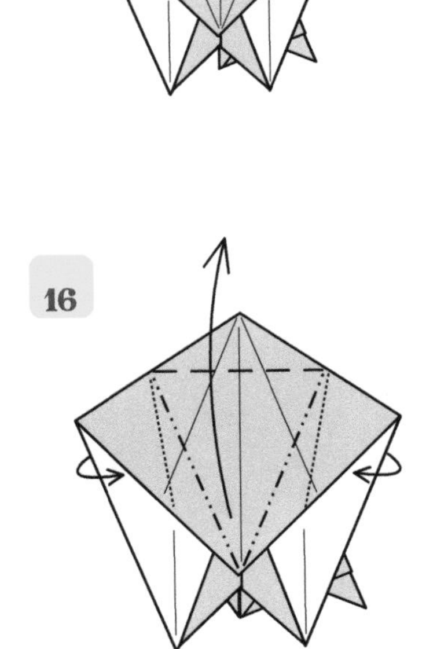

Begin a petal fold.

17

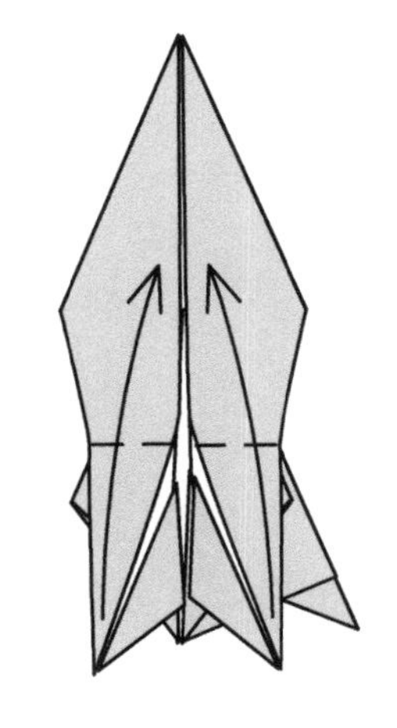

The bottom is 3D. Fold up and flatten.

18

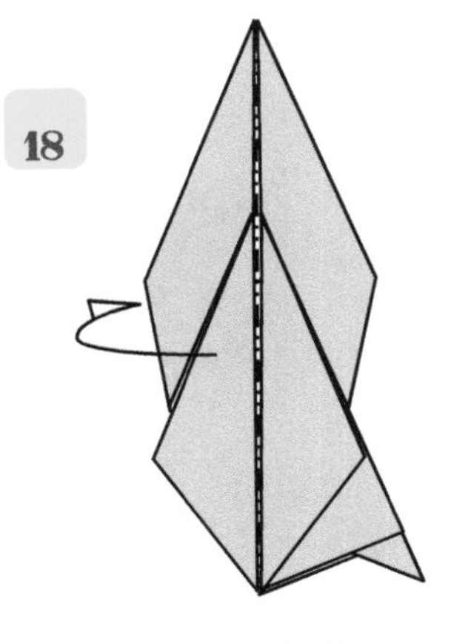

Fold in half and rotate.

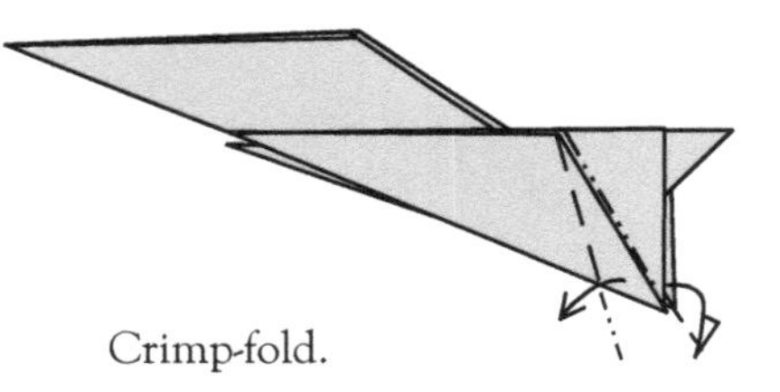

Crimp-fold.

20

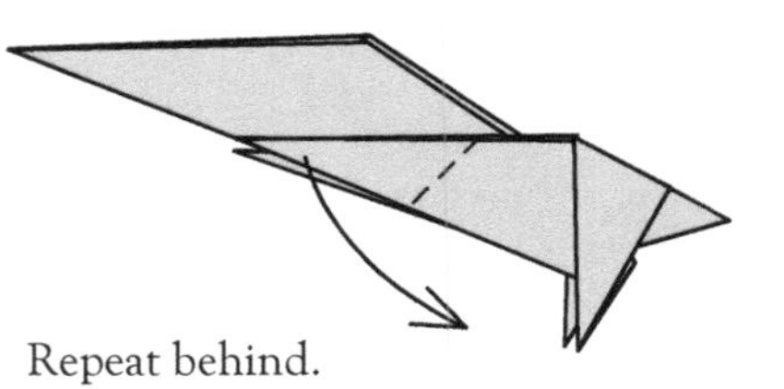

Repeat behind.

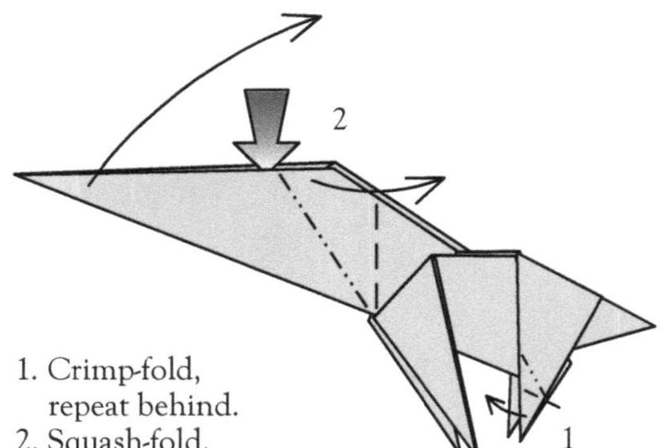

1. Crimp-fold, repeat behind.
2. Squash-fold.

22

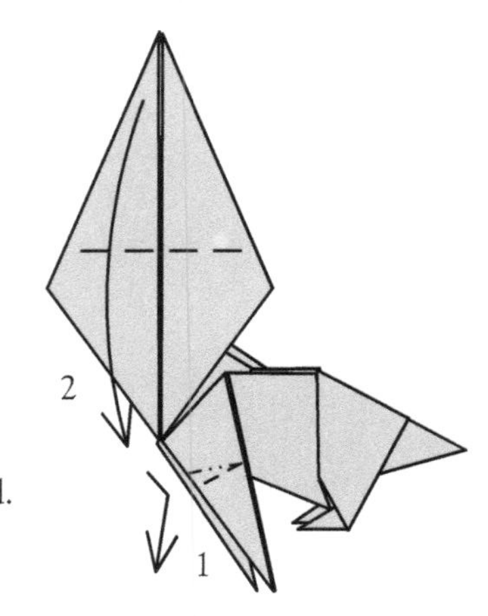

1. Crimp-fold, repeat behind.
2. Fold down.

23

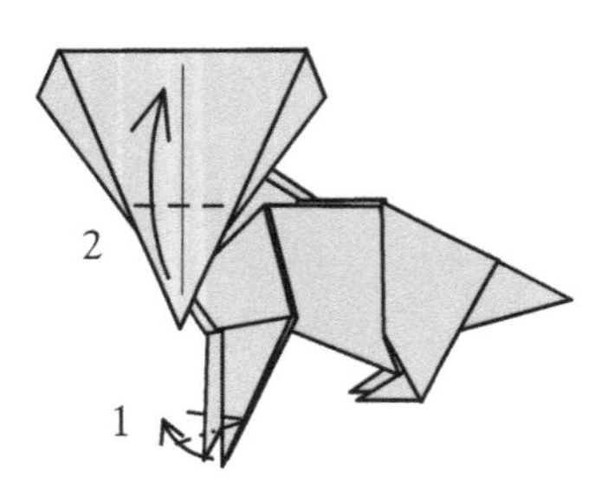

1. Spread and outside-reverse-fold. Repeat behind.
2. Fold up.

24

25

1. Fold down.
2. Make pleat folds.

26

27

Platypus

Although it looks like an odd mix of multiple water creatures such as a duck and a beaver, the Platypus is well-suited to its environment with a bill, webbed feet and long tail that aids in swimming. Classified as a mammal, the Platypus shares common genes with birds and reptiles.

1

Fold and unfold.

2

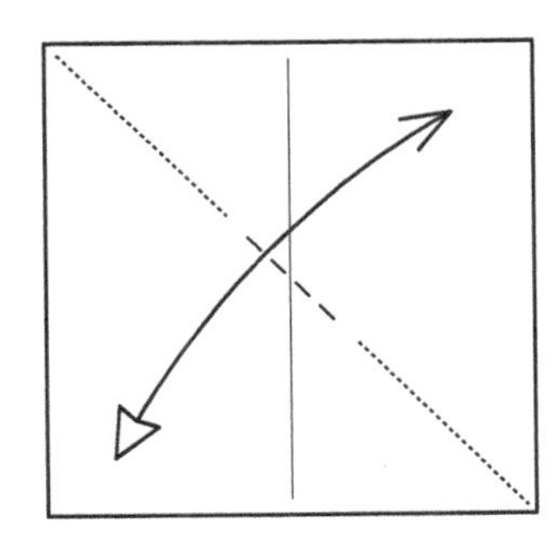

Fold and unfold in the center.

3

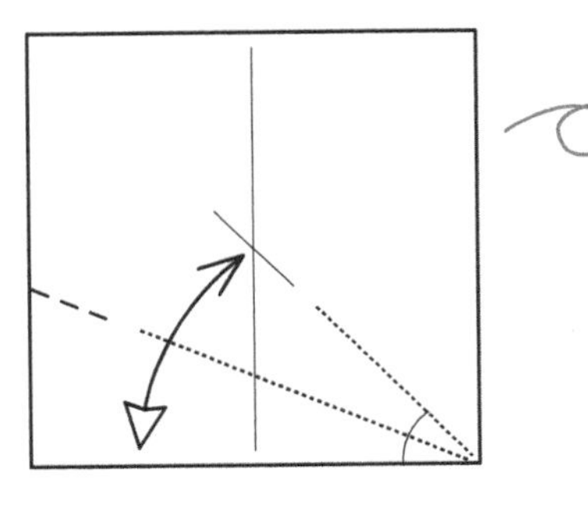

Fold and unfold on the left.

4

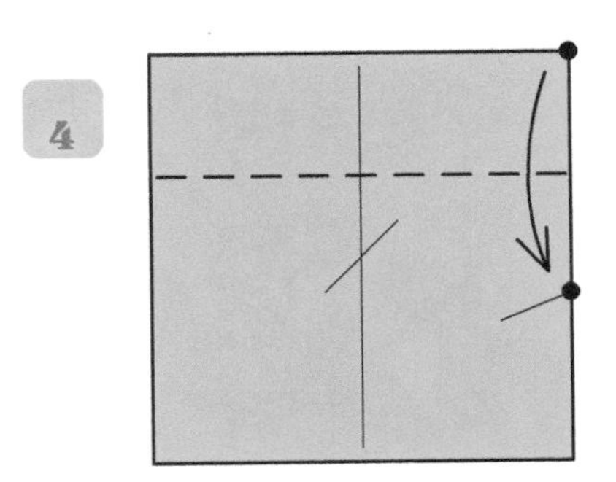

5

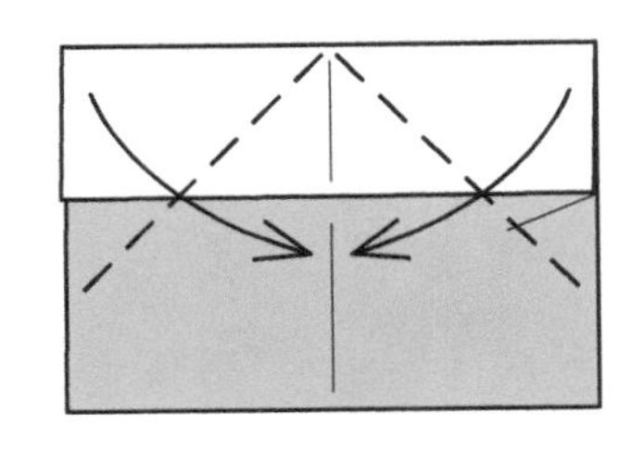

Fold to the center.

6

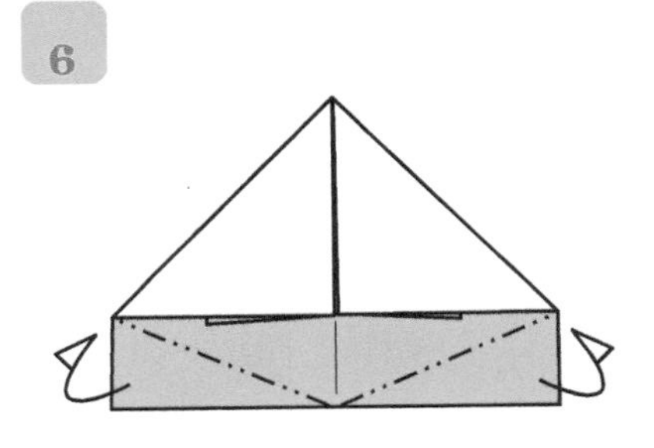

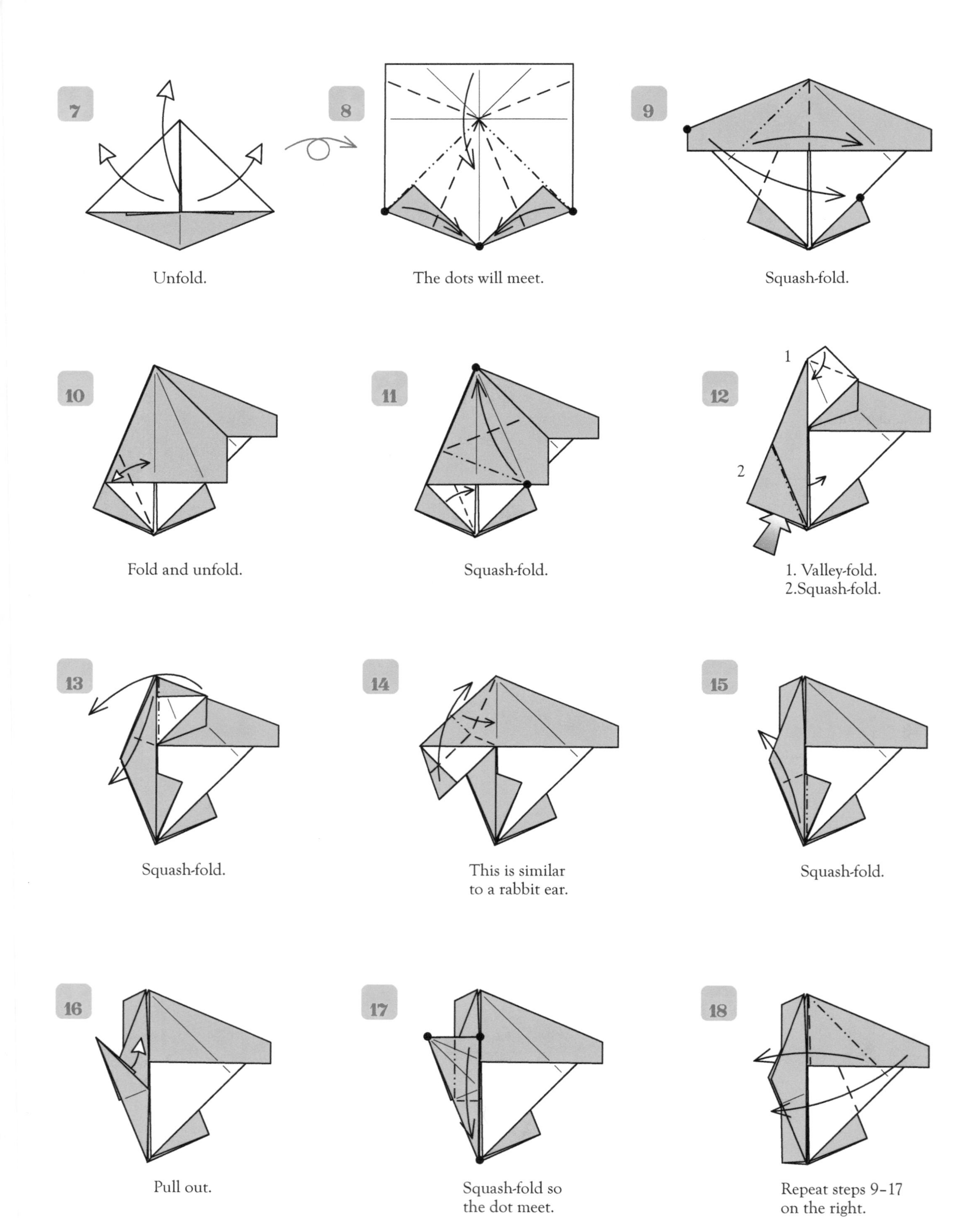
7
Unfold.
8
The dots will meet.
9
Squash-fold.
10
Fold and unfold.
11
Squash-fold.
12
1
2
1. Valley-fold.
2.Squash-fold.
13
Squash-fold.
14
This is similar
to a rabbit ear.
15
Squash-fold.
16
Pull out.
17
Squash-fold so
the dot meet.
18
Repeat steps 9–17
on the right.

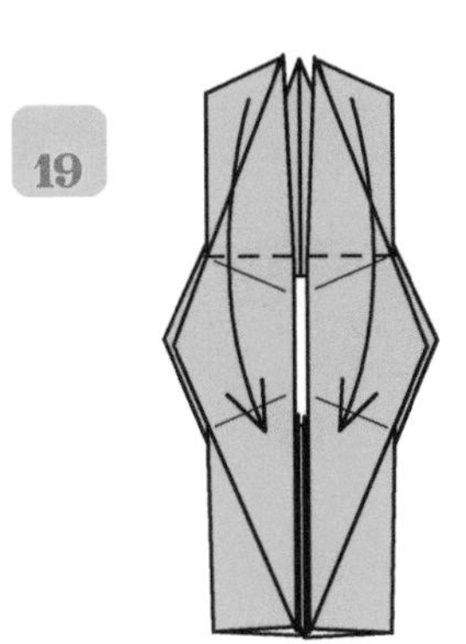

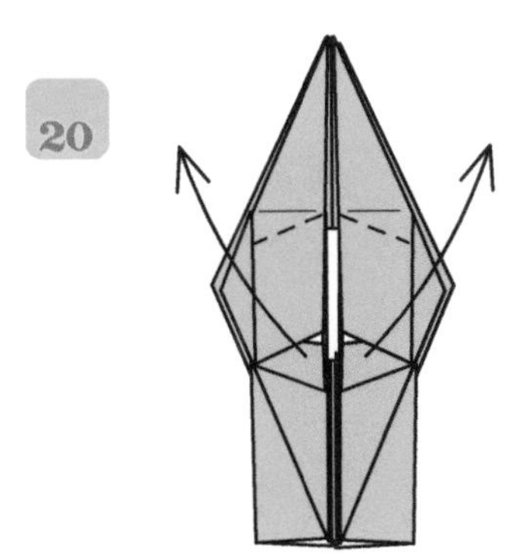

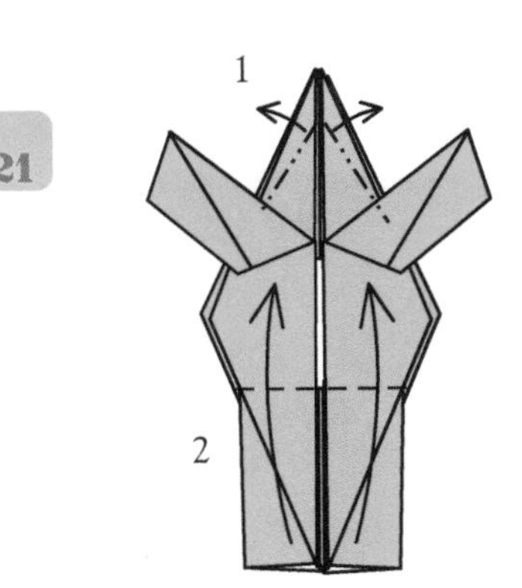

1. Spread the top layer.
2. Fold up.

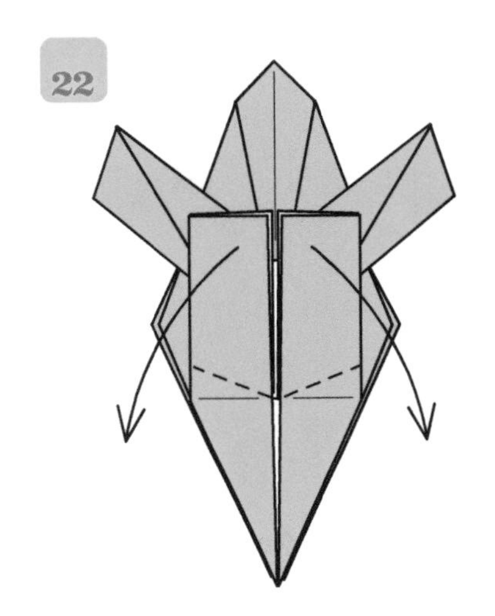

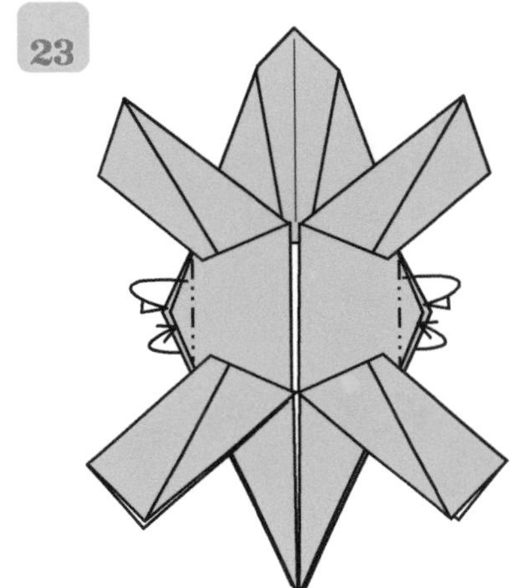

Fold inside, repeat behind.

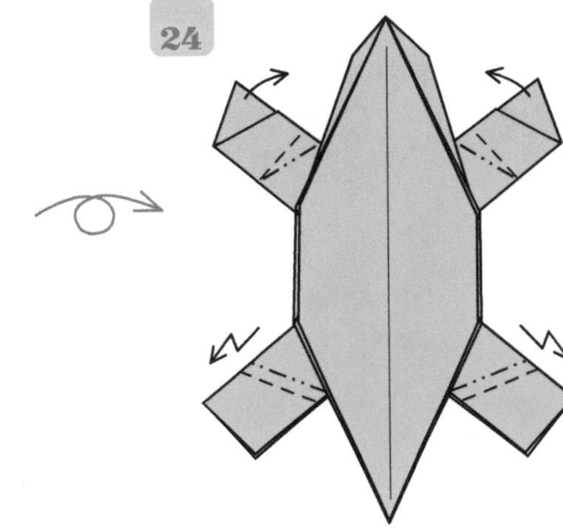

Make pleat folds.

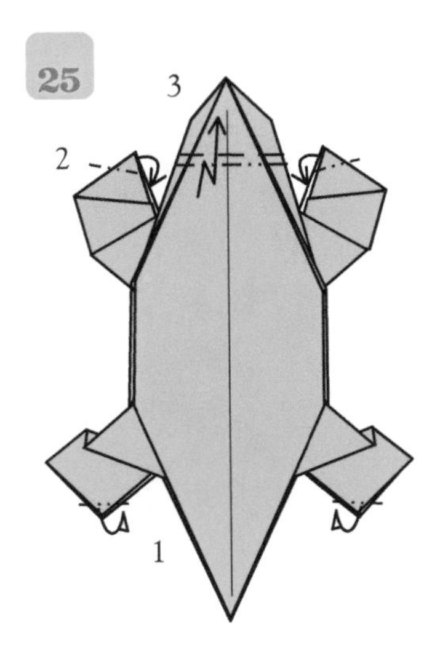

1. Fold behind.
2. Reverse-fold.
3. Pleat-fold.

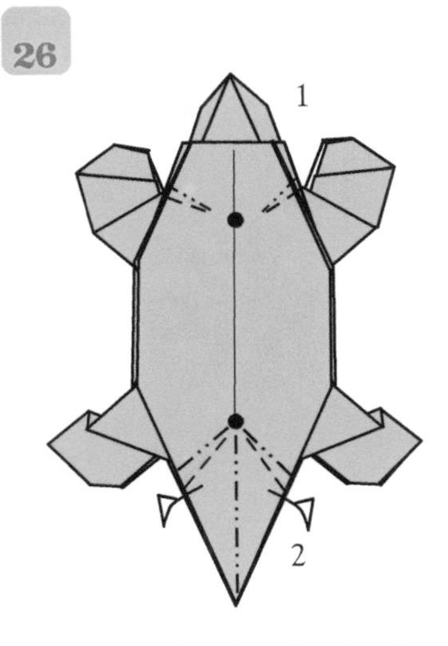

Shape the head and tail with pleat folds. Puff out at the dots so the Platypus will be 3D.

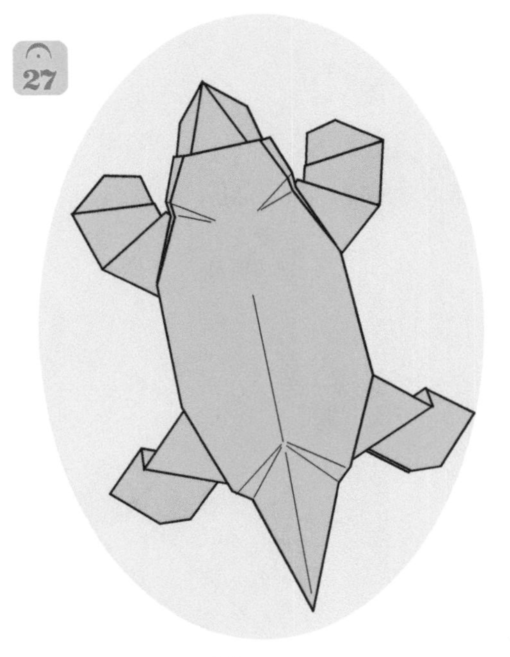

Platypus

Wombat

Looking like very small bears or very large rodents, Wombats are marsupials and can grow to approximately three feet long. Usually quiet, they will vocalize with what sounds like hisses and shrieks when protecting their territory. All Wombats are protected in Australia and are considered endangered.

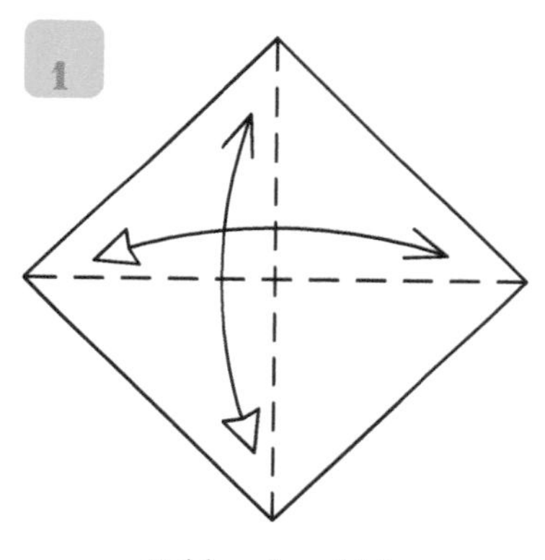

Fold and unfold.

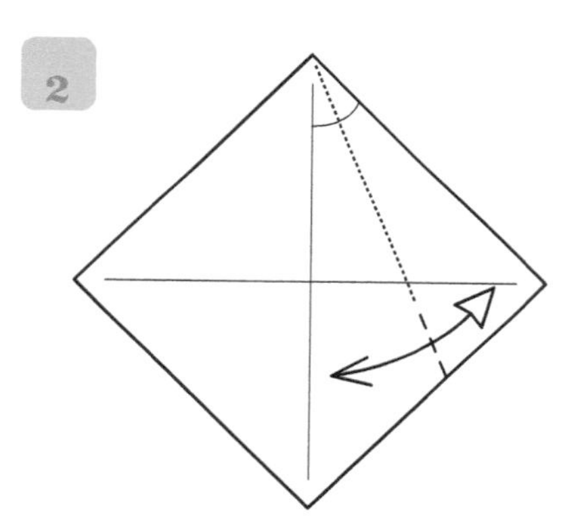

Fold and unfold by the edge.

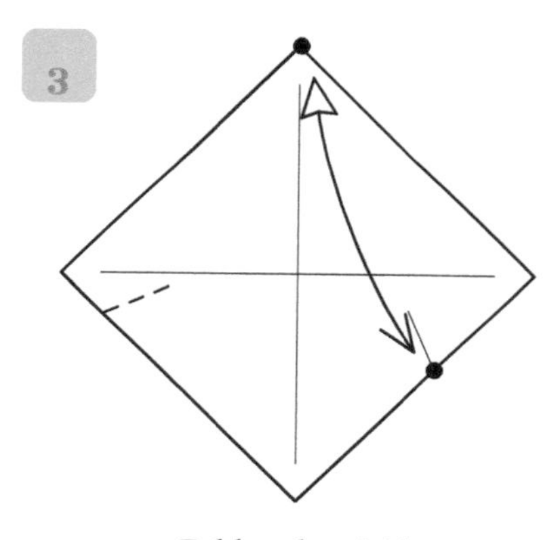

Fold and unfold by the edge.

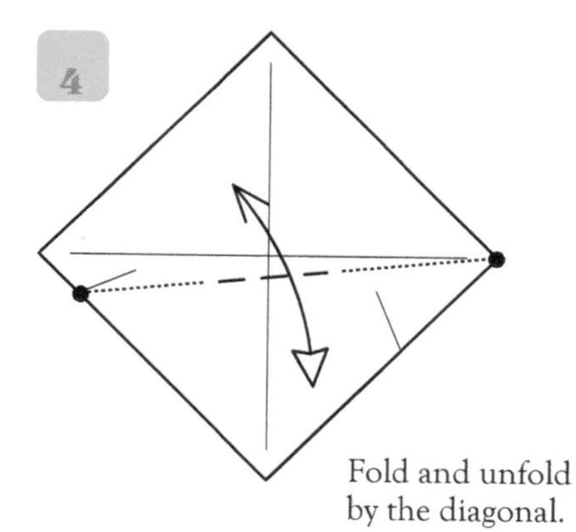

Fold and unfold by the diagonal.

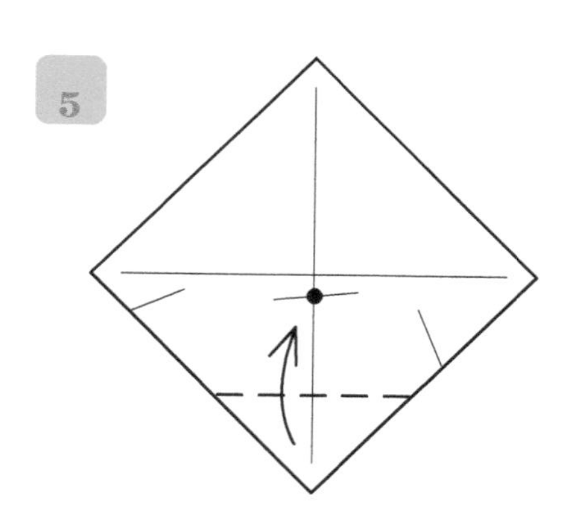

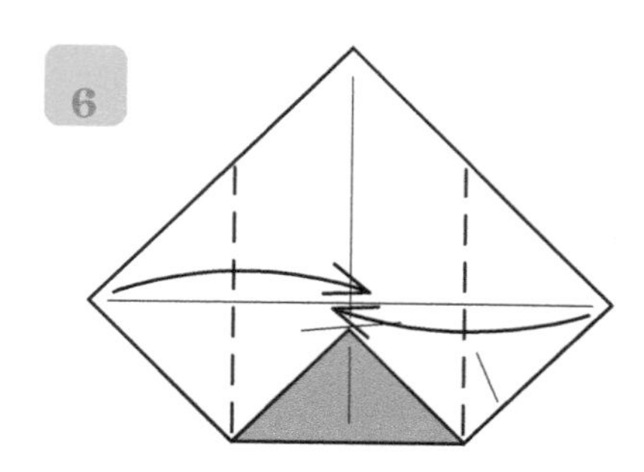

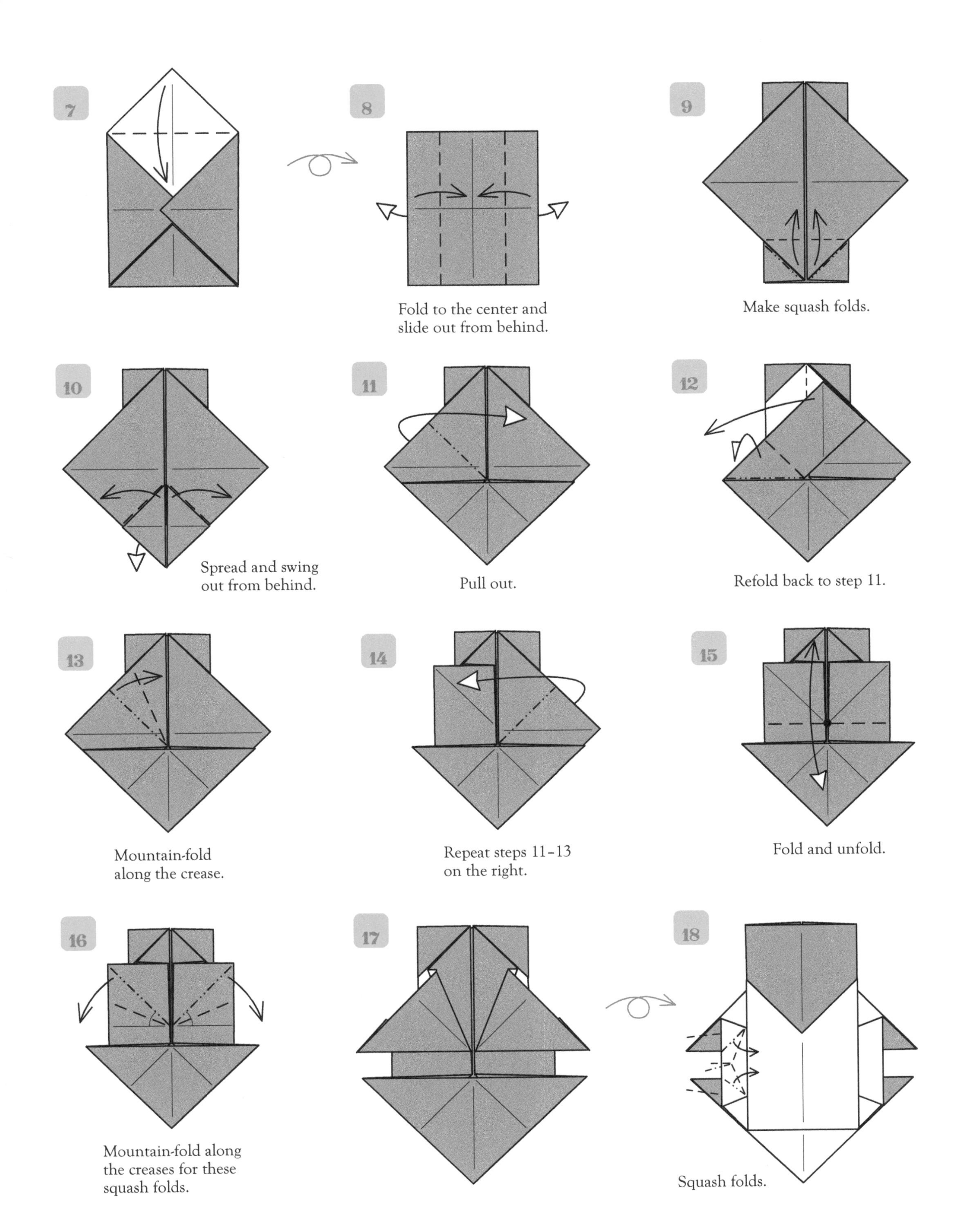
7
8
Fold to the center and slide out from behind.
9
Make squash folds.
10
Spread and swing out from behind.
11
Pull out.
12
Refold back to step 11.
13
Mountain-fold along the crease.
14
Repeat steps 11–13 on the right.
15
Fold and unfold.
16
Mountain-fold along the creases for these squash folds.
17
18
Squash folds.

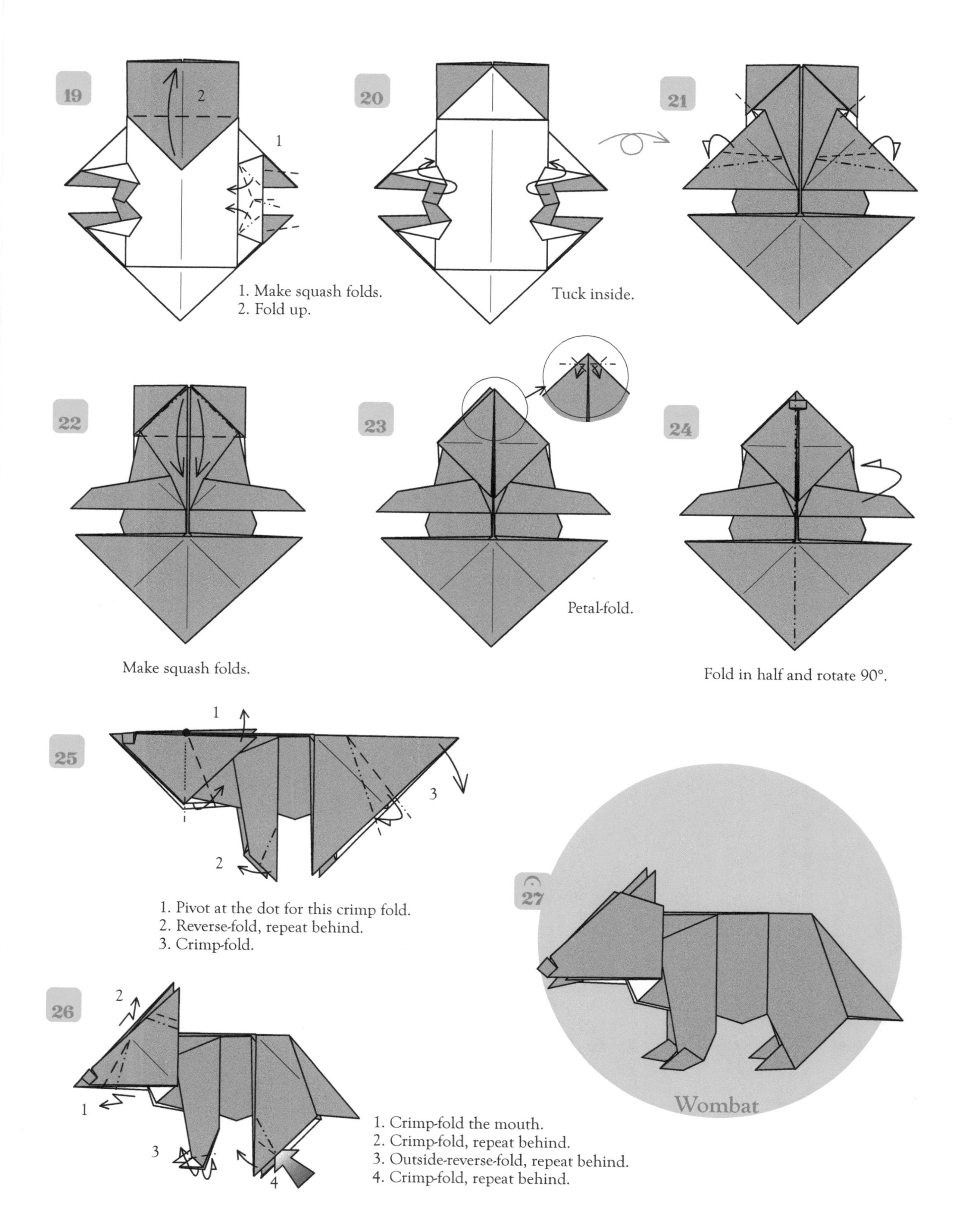
19
2
1
1. Make squash folds.
2. Fold up.
20
Tuck inside.
21
22
Make squash folds.
23
Petal-fold.
24
Fold in half and rotate 90°.
25
1
2
3
1. Pivot at the dot for this crimp fold.
2. Reverse-fold, repeat behind.
3. Crimp-fold.
26
2
1
3
4
1. Crimp-fold the mouth.
2. Crimp-fold, repeat behind.
3. Outside-reverse-fold, repeat behind.
4. Crimp-fold, repeat behind.
27
Wombat

Numbat

These small marsupials mainly eat termites and resemble a squirrel with a striped back and a very pointed nose. Once plentiful, it's estimated that less than 1,000 mature Numbats exist due to loss of their habitats and being preyed upon by foxes. Unlike most marsupials, which tend to be nocturnal, they are awake and active during the daytime.

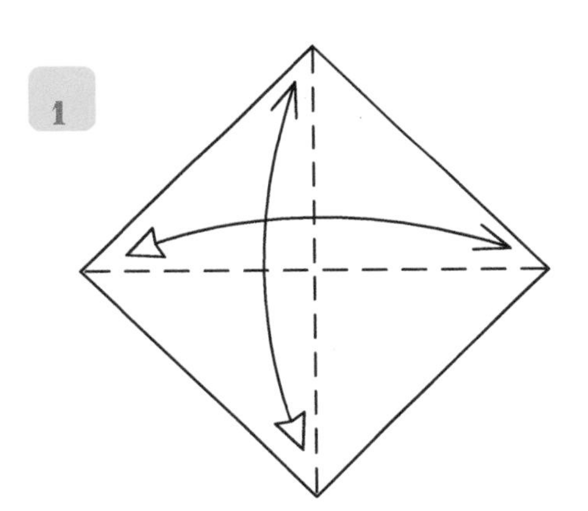

Fold and unfold.

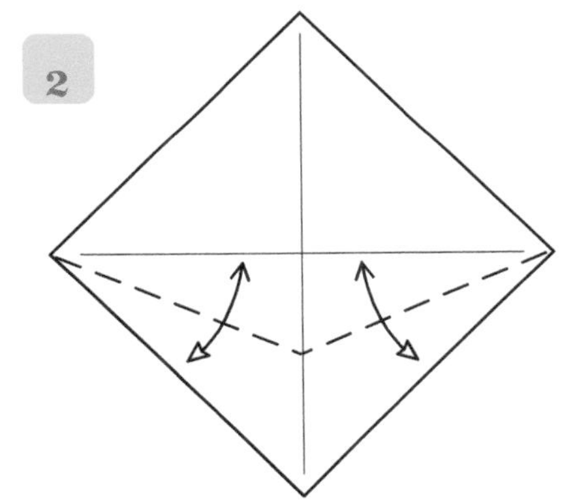

Fold and unfold.
Rotate 180°.

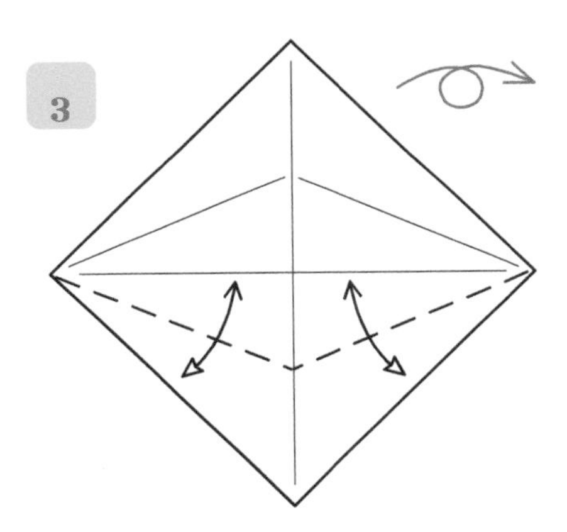

Fold and unfold.

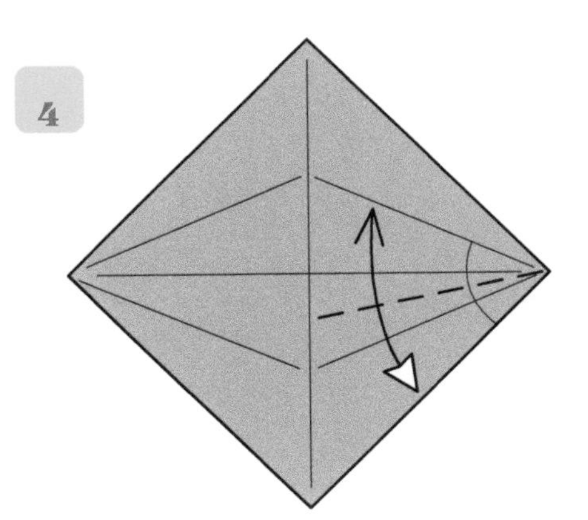

Fold and unfold.

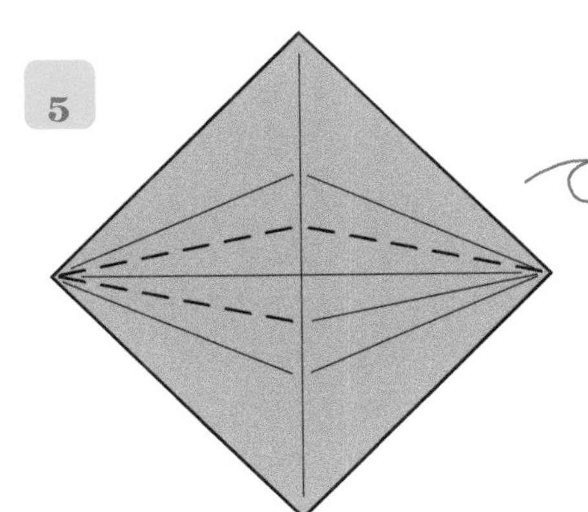

Repeat step 4 three times, on the left and above.

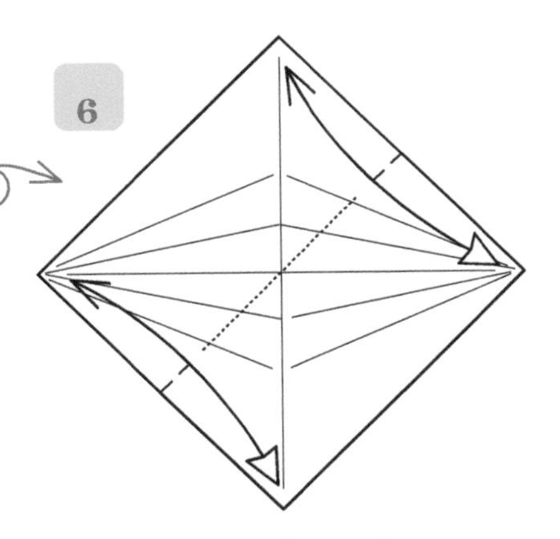

Fold and unfold on the edges.

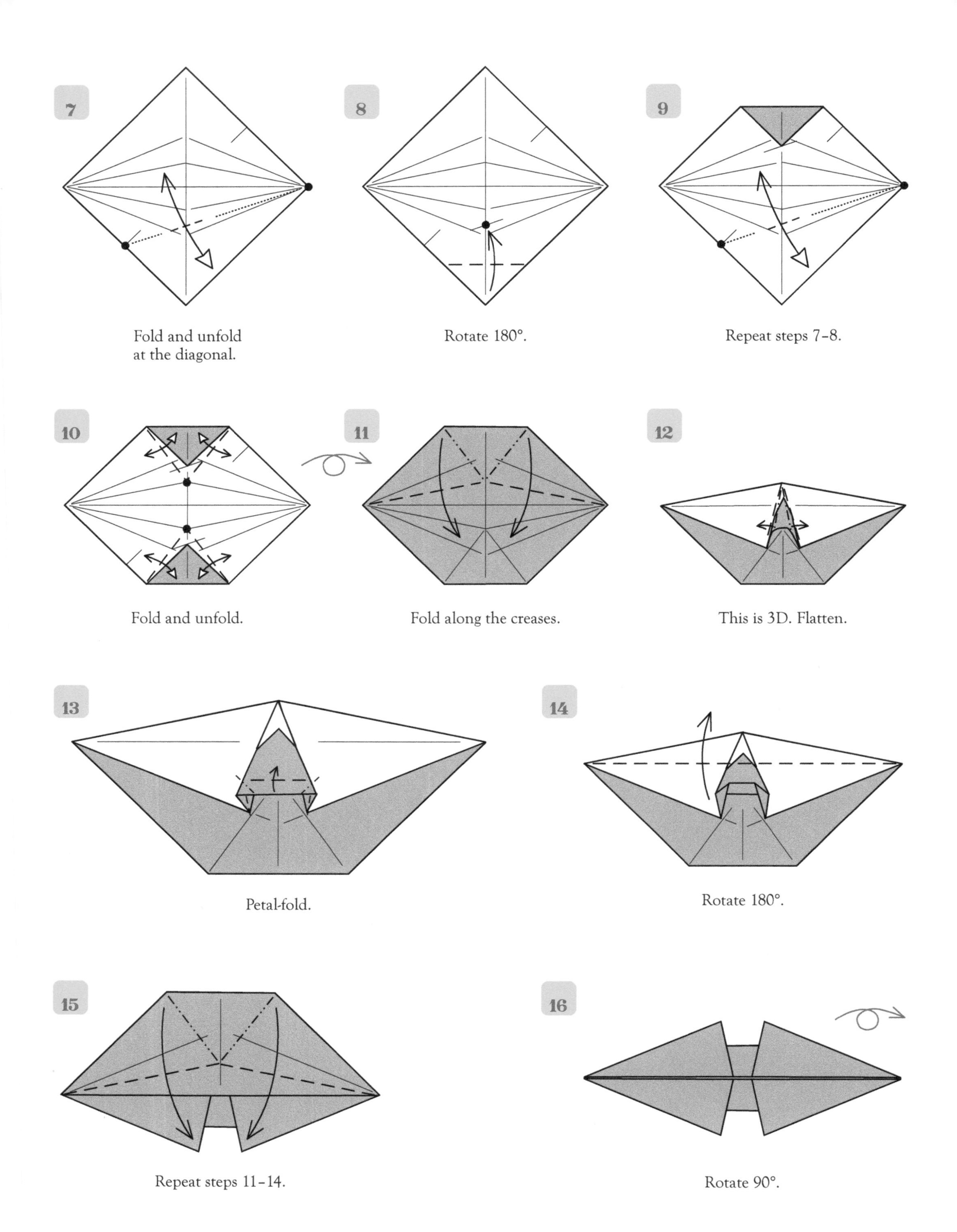
7
8
9
Fold and unfold
at the diagonal.
Rotate 180°.
Repeat steps 7–8.
10
11
12
Fold and unfold.
Fold along the creases.
This is 3D. Flatten.
13
14
Petal-fold.
Rotate 180°.
15
16
Repeat steps 11–14.
Rotate 90°.

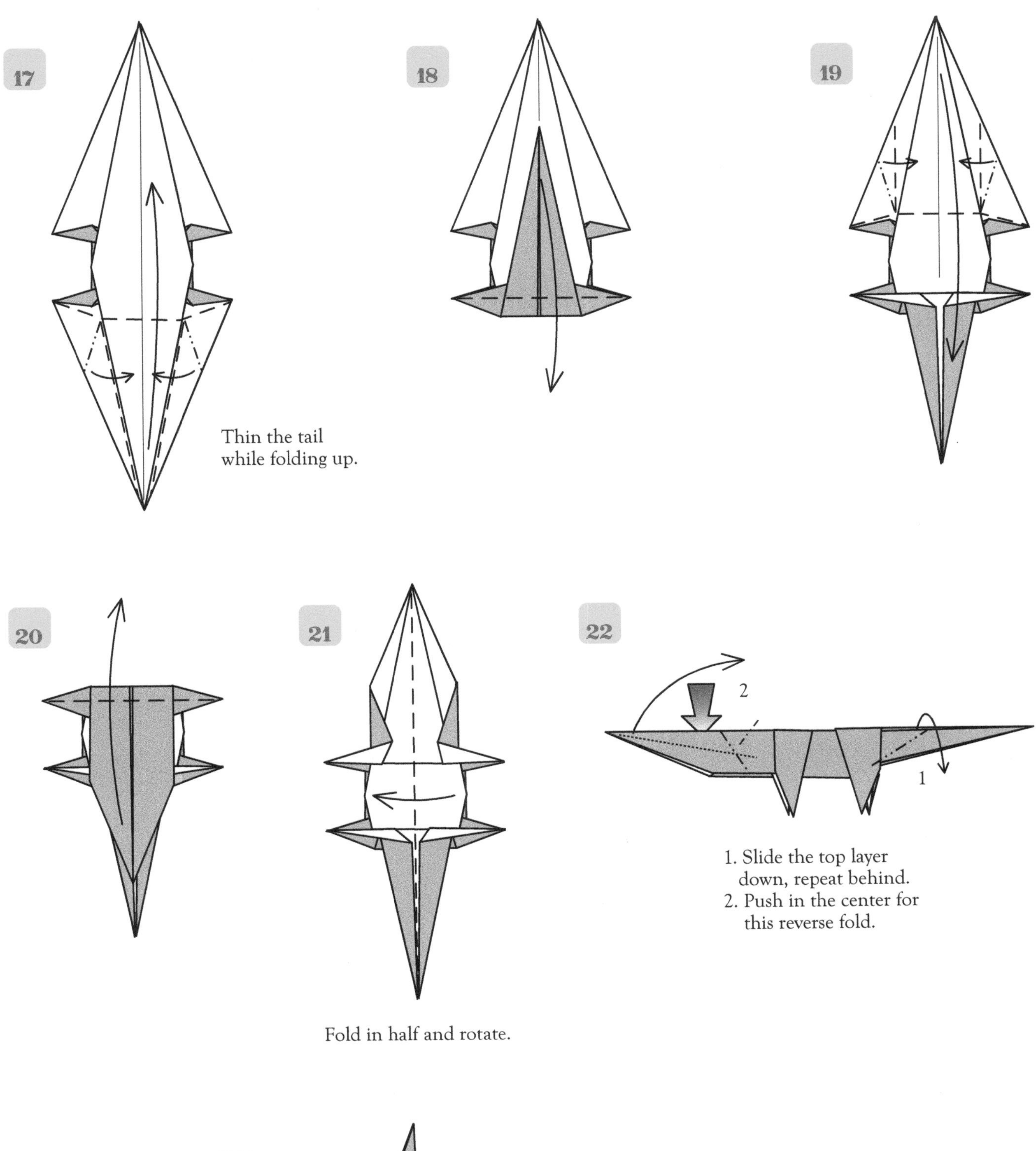

Thin the tail while folding up.

Fold in half and rotate.

1. Slide the top layer down, repeat behind.
2. Push in the center for this reverse fold.

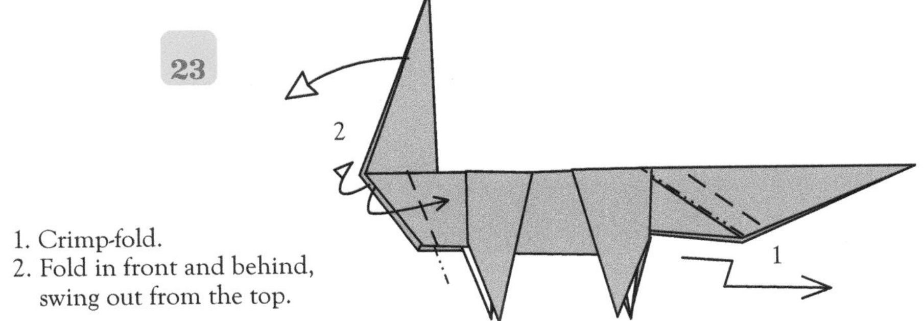

1. Crimp-fold.
2. Fold in front and behind, swing out from the top.

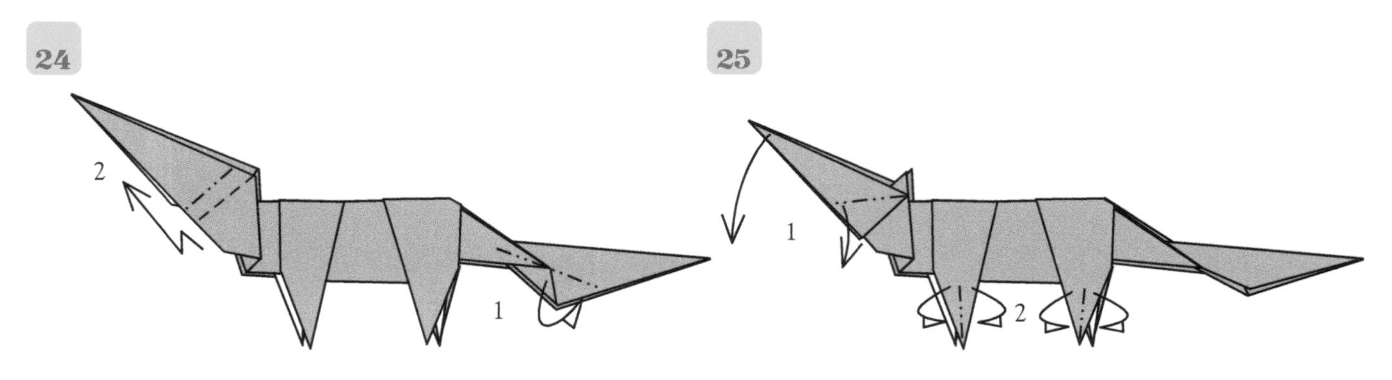

1. Fold inside, repeat behind.
2. Crimp-fold.

1. Spread the paper to form the head.
2. Thin the legs, repeat behind.

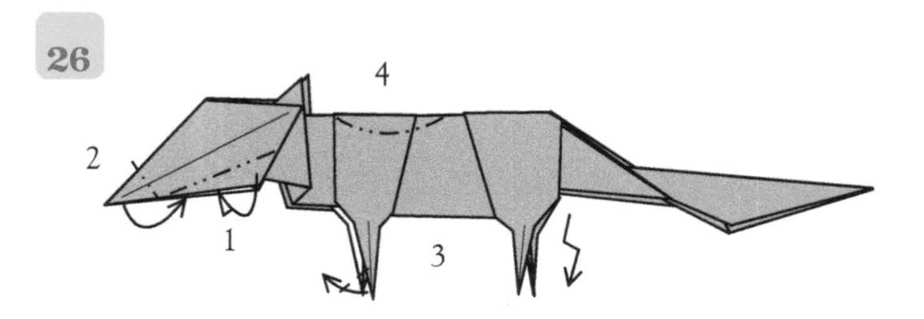

1. Fold inside, repeat behind.
2. Reverse-fold.
3. Shape the legs, repeat behind.
4. Shape the back.

Numbat

Rabbit-Bandicoot

These small nocturnal marsupials look like round mice with long rabbit-like ears. They live in burrows and will feed on fruits, fungi and insects. Like the Numbat, their numbers have also decreased and they are now considered an endangered species.

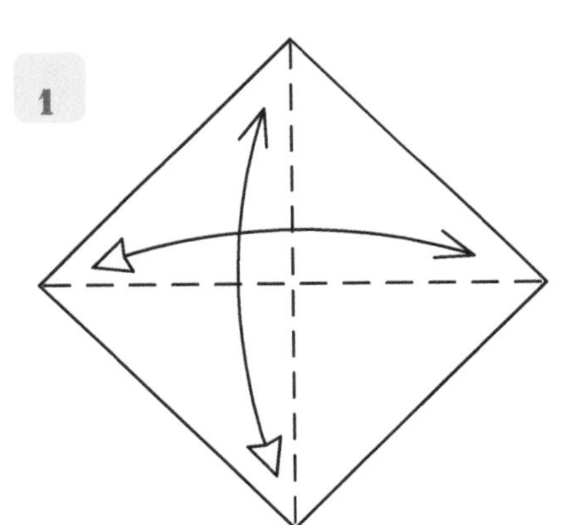

Fold and unfold.

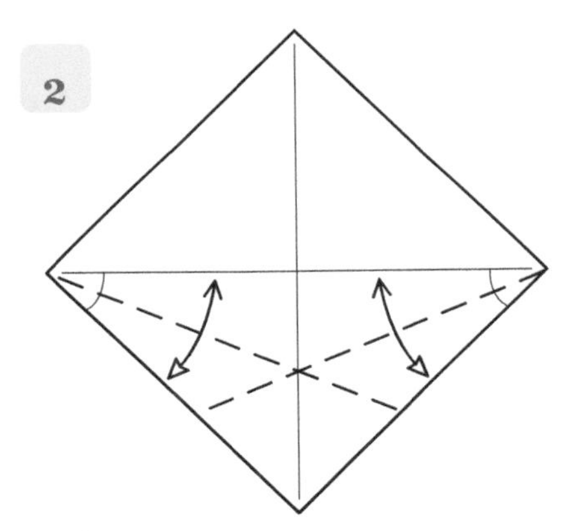

Fold to the center and unfold.

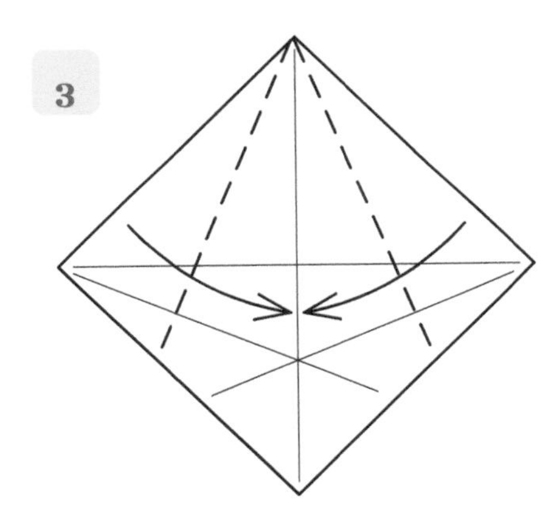

Fold to the center.

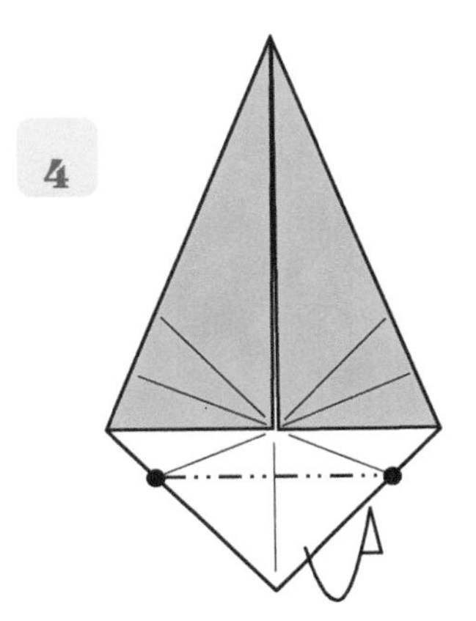

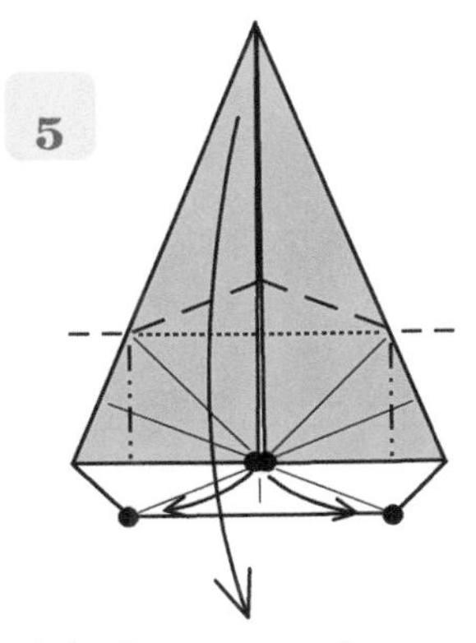

Slide the paper so the upper dots meet the lower dots. Fold down along a hidden crease.

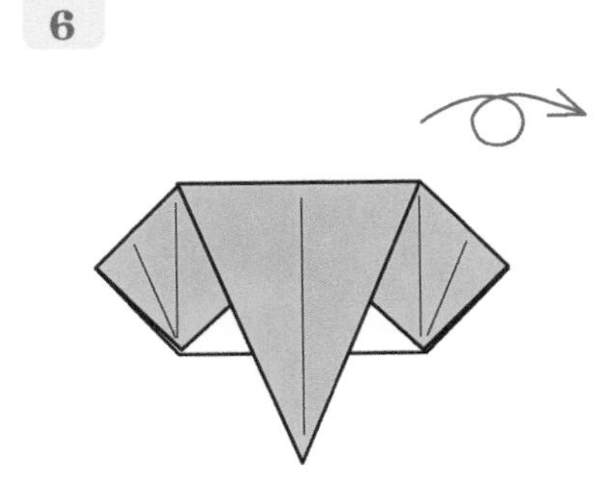

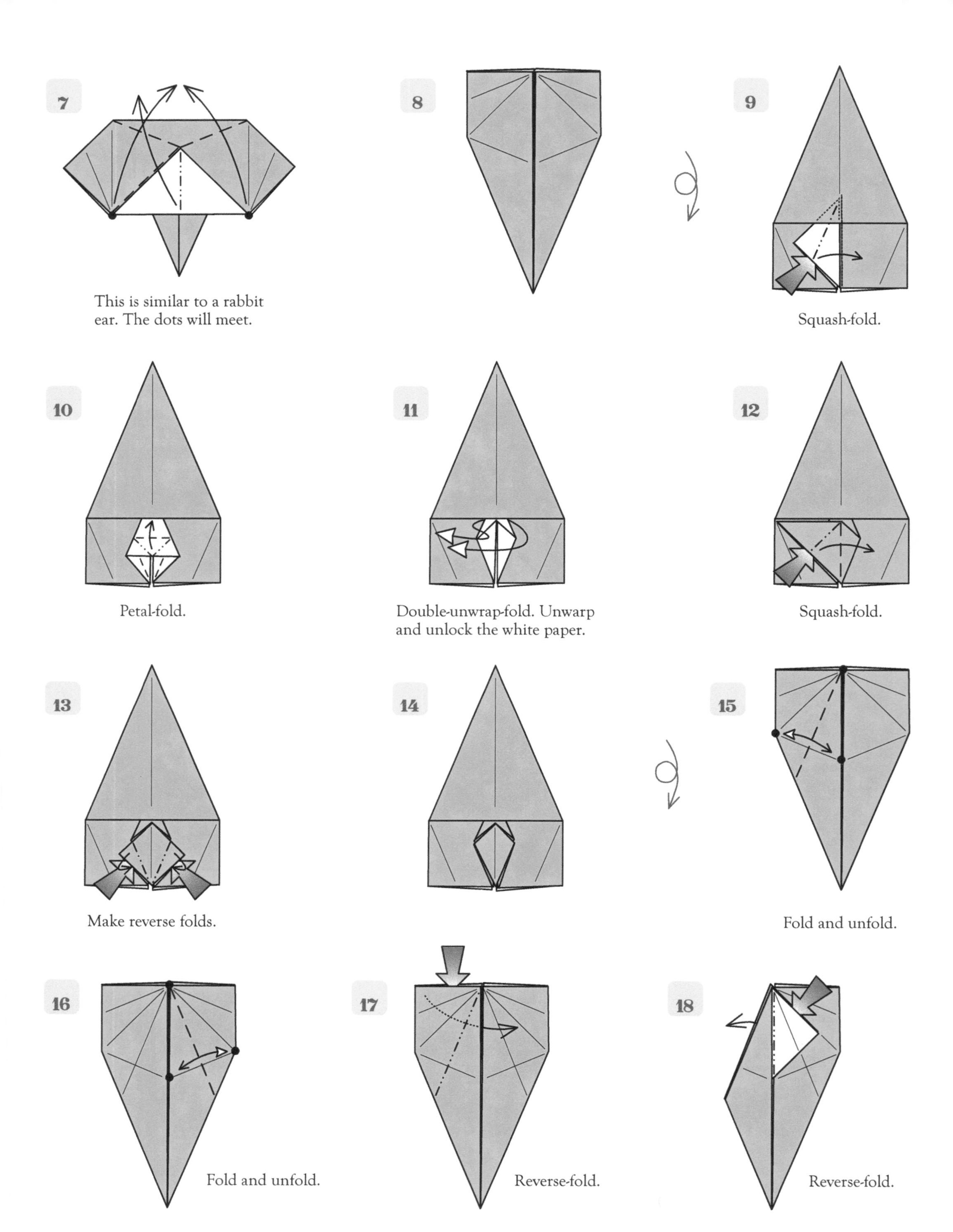

This is similar to a rabbit ear. The dots will meet.

Squash-fold.

Petal-fold.

Double-unwrap-fold. Unwarp and unlock the white paper.

Squash-fold.

Make reverse folds.

Fold and unfold.

Fold and unfold.

Reverse-fold.

Reverse-fold.

19

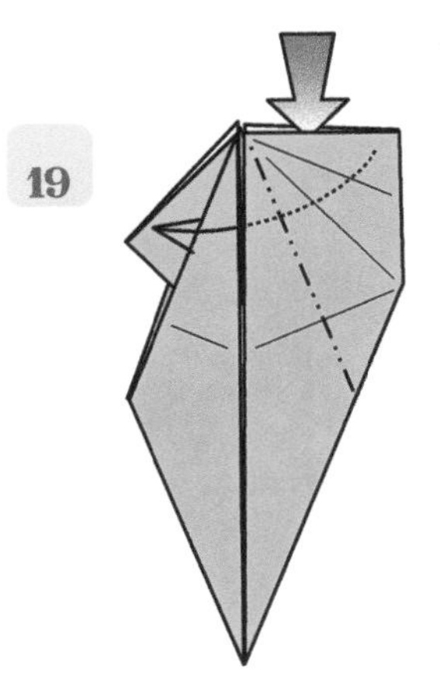

Repeat steps 17–18 on the right.

20

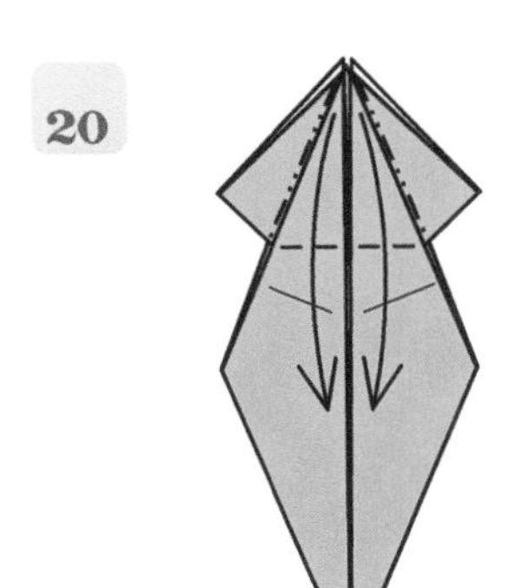

Make squash folds.

21

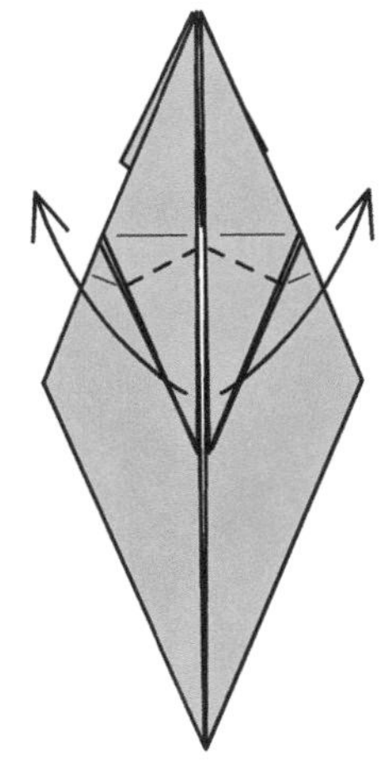

Make valley folds.

22

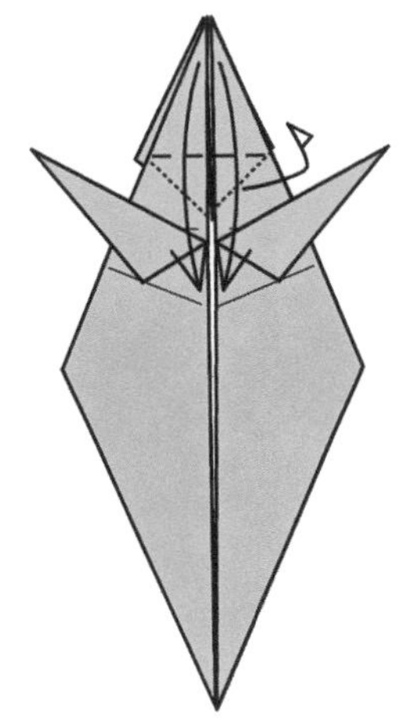

Fold two flaps down while folding the hidden triangle up.

23

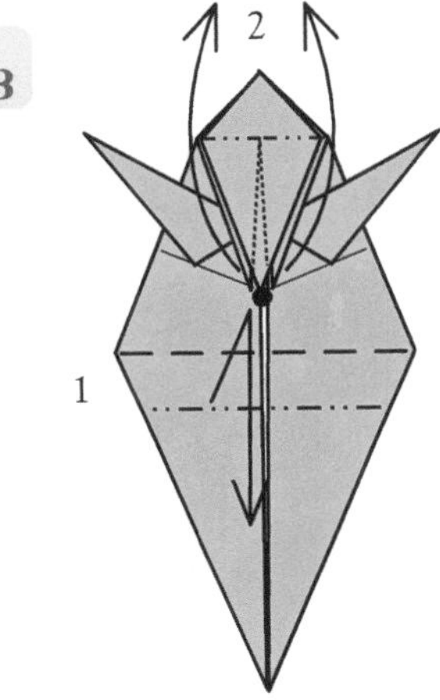

1. Pleat-fold to the dot.
2. Make reverse folds.

24

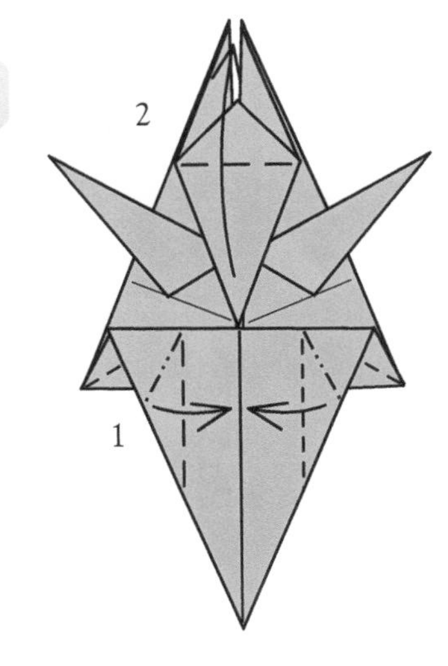

1. Make squash folds.
2. Fold up.

25

This is the same as folding in half and making an outside-reverse fold for the head.

26

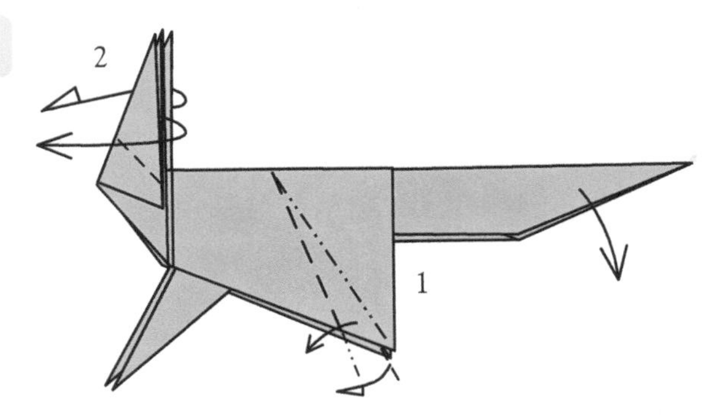

1. Crimp-fold.
2. Outside-reverse-fold.

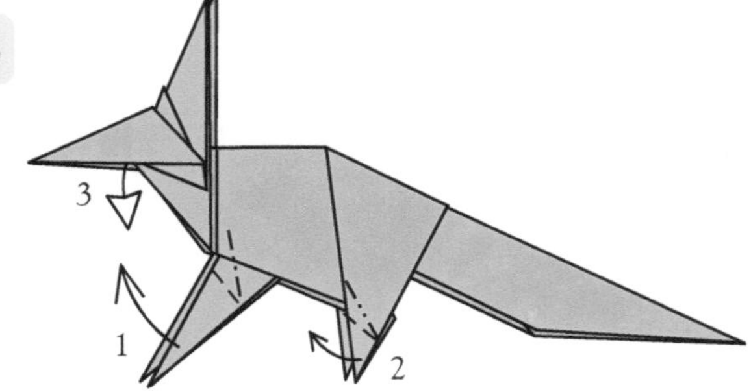

1. Crimp-fold.
2. Crimp-fold.
3. Pull out.

Repeat behind.

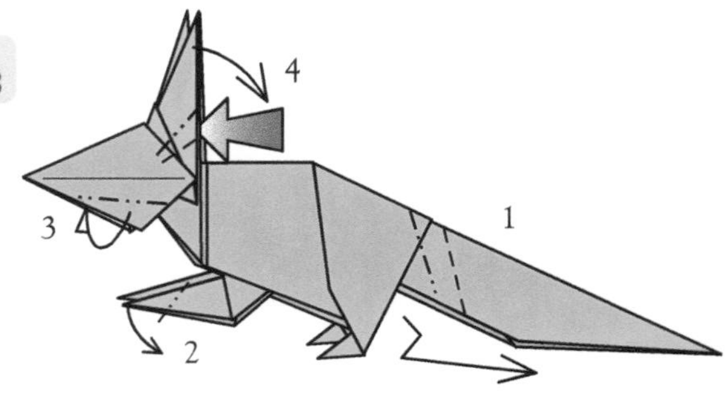

1. Crimp-fold.
2. Reverse-fold.
3. Fold inside.
4. Squash-fold.

Repeat behind at 2–4.

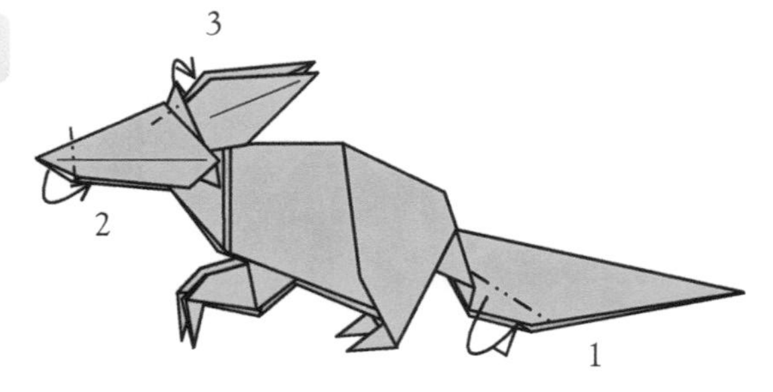

1. Fold inside, repeat behind.
2. Reverse-fold.
3. Reverse-fold.

30

Rabbit-Bandicoot

Dingo

Dingoes are part of the canine family and are related to wolves. They have strong, lean bodies that are suited to their predatory nature, which helps make them fast and agile. Dingoes will hunt both alone and in packs. They have been known to eat large water buffaloes as well as insects and other animals in between.

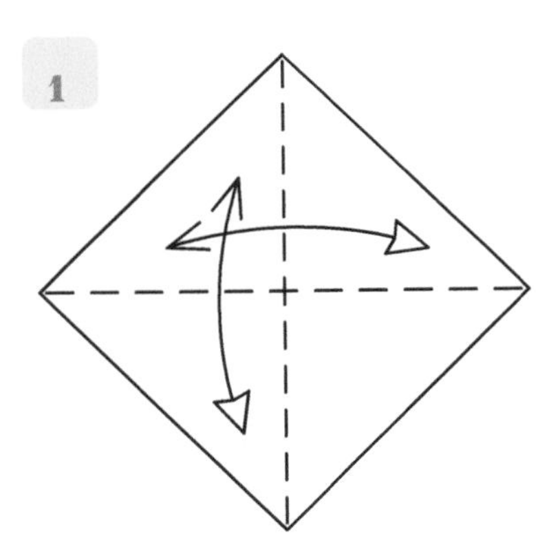

Fold and unfold.

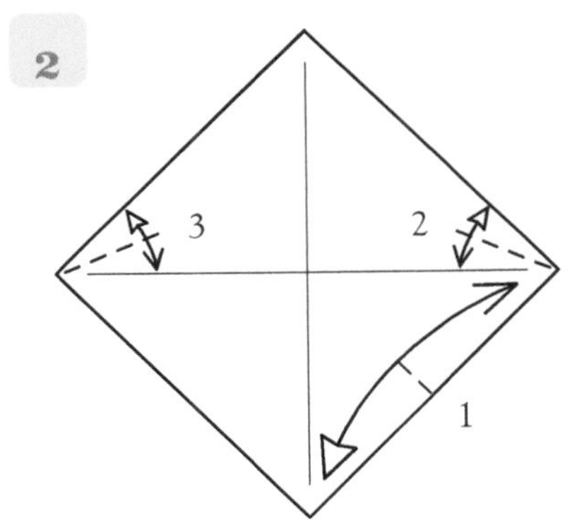

Fold and unfold..

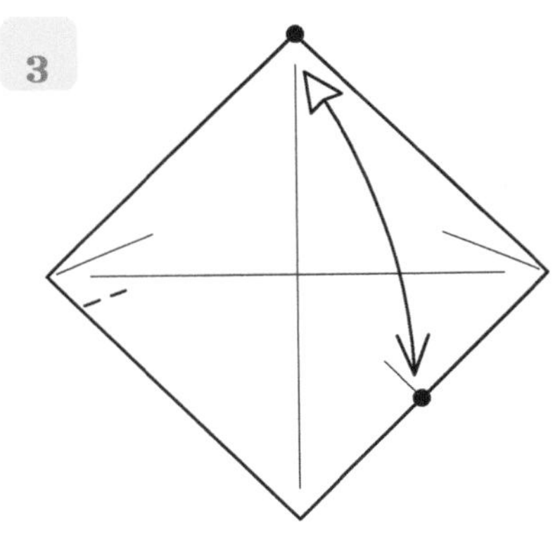

Fold and unfold on the left so the dots meet.

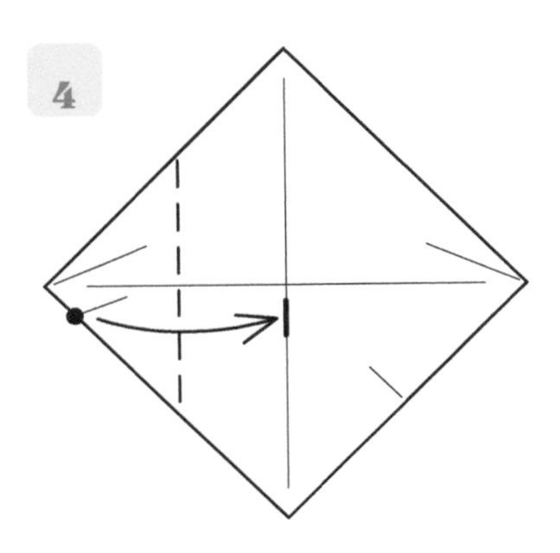

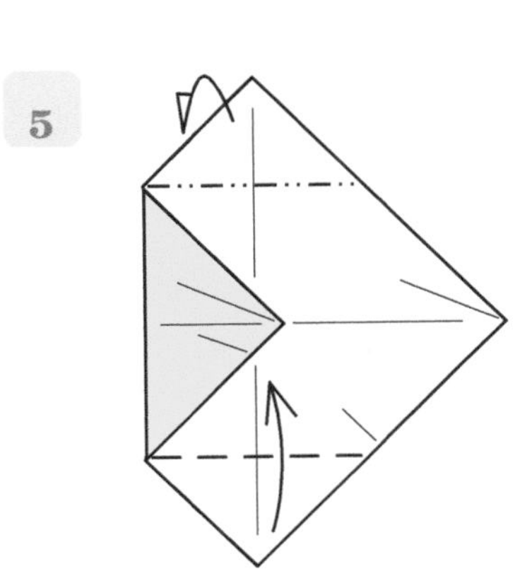

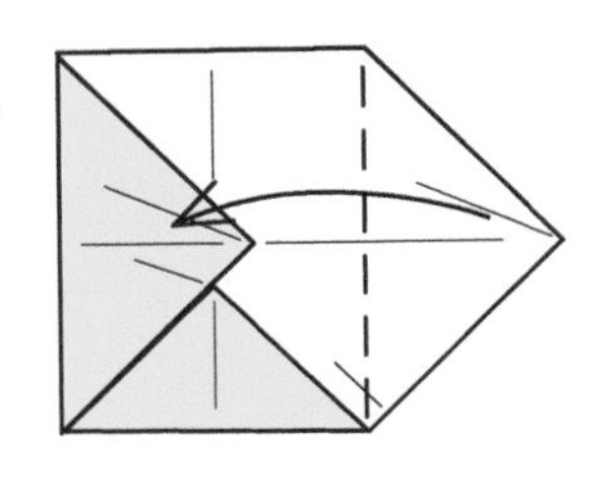

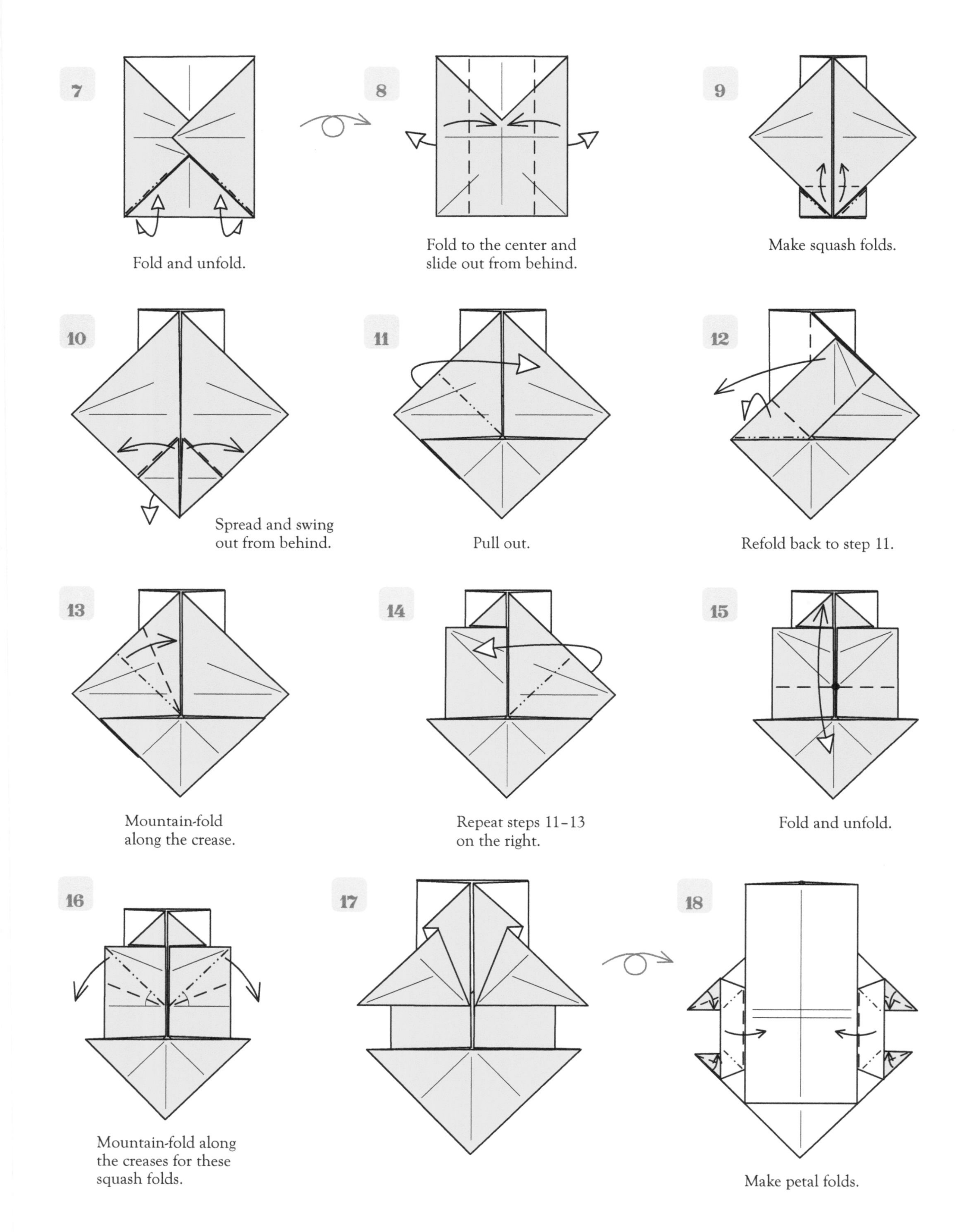
7
Fold and unfold.
8
Fold to the center and
slide out from behind.
9
Make squash folds.
10
Spread and swing
out from behind.
11
Pull out.
12
Refold back to step 11.
13
Mountain-fold
along the crease.
14
Repeat steps 11–13
on the right.
15
Fold and unfold.
16
Mountain-fold along
the creases for these
squash folds.
17
18
Make petal folds.

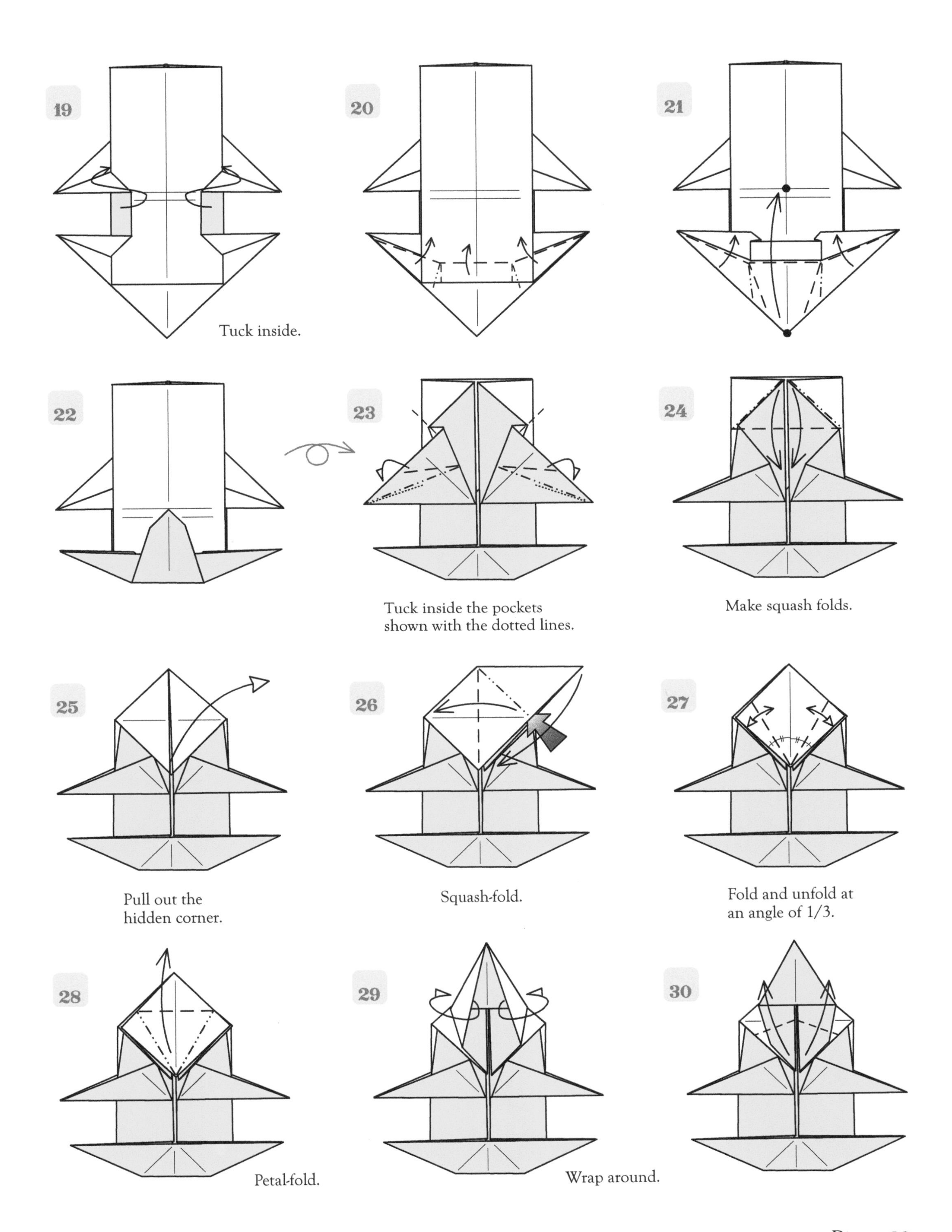
19
Tuck inside.
20
21
22
23
Tuck inside the pockets
shown with the dotted lines.
24
Make squash folds.
25
Pull out the
hidden corner.
26
Squash-fold.
27
Fold and unfold at
an angle of 1/3.
28
Petal-fold.
29
Wrap around.
30

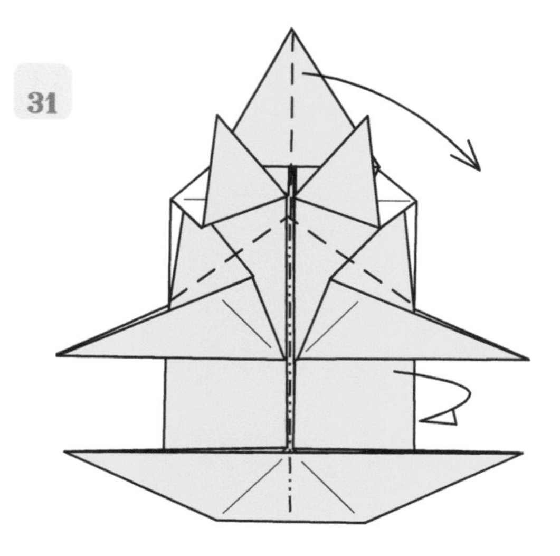

Fold the head up while folding in half. Rotate.

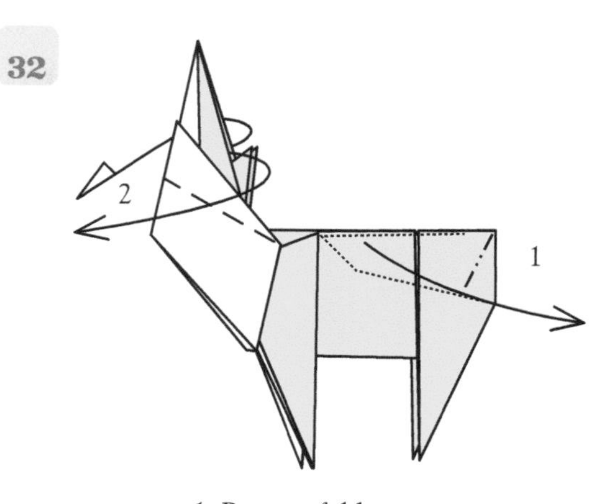

1. Reverse-fold.
2. Outside-reverse-fold.

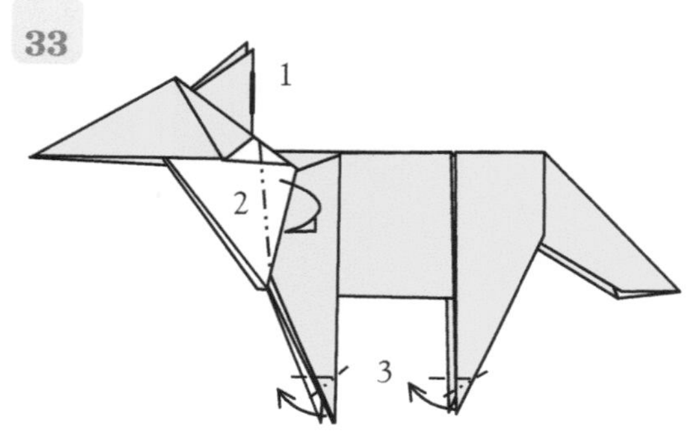

1. Adjust the ears so the bold line is vertical.
2. Fold inside.
3. Make small squash folds.
Repeat behind.

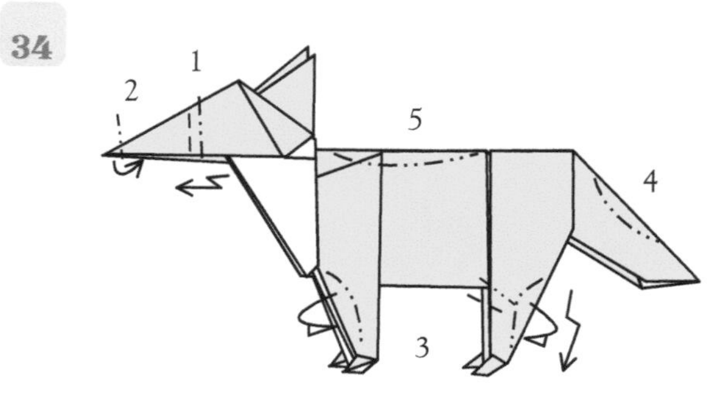

1. Crimp-fold.
2. Reverse-fold.
3. Shape the legs, repeat behind.
4. Shape the tail.
5. Shape the back.

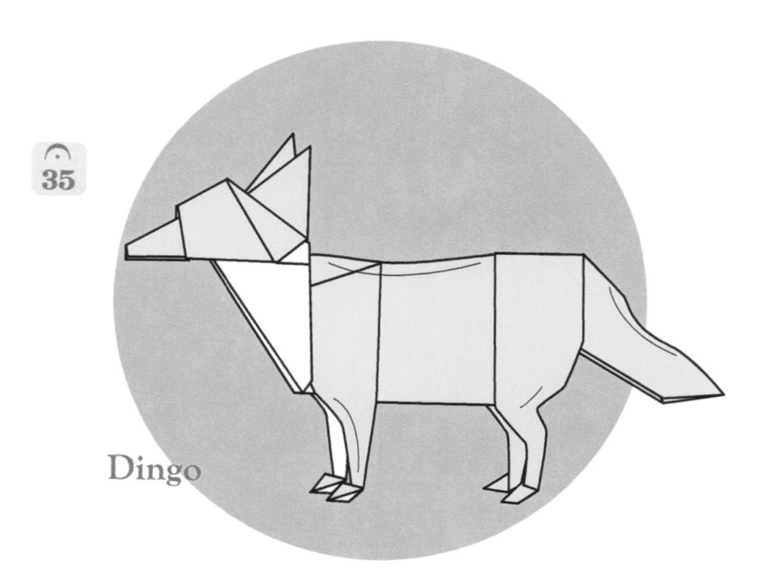

Second Movement

Andante: Australian Birds Hopping Around

Australian birds fill the land, trees, and sky with color. Most shown here have color-change patterns such as the Brahminy Kite, Magpie Goose, and Australian Magpie. Interesting folding structures add elegance and simplicity to these birds. Listen to the songs of the Channel-billed Cuckoo, Black-faced Cuckoo Shrike, Black Butcherbird, and the Australian Wood Duck's quacks.

King Penguin

Surpassed in size only by the larger Emperor Penguins, these penguins have a diet of squid, small fish and krill and live on temperate islands such as the Prince Edward Islands, the Falkland Islands, and also in Western Australia. They time their breeding so their chicks will be mature enough to leave their parents during the Summer months when food is plentiful and it is safer for them to venture out alone.

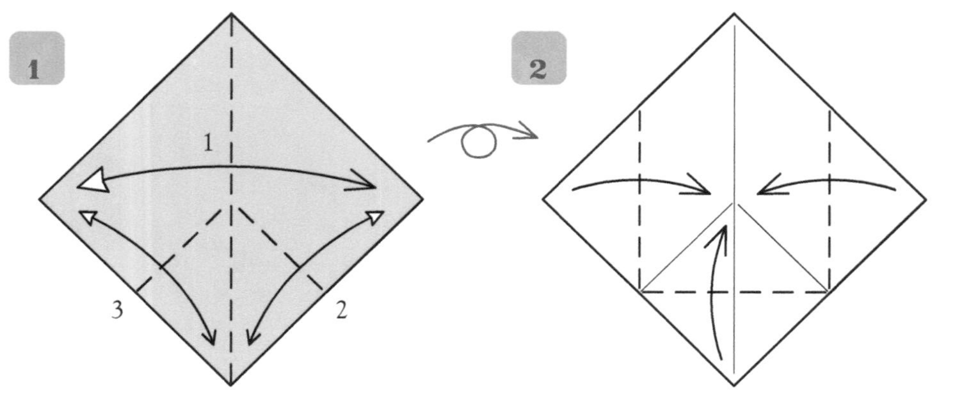

Fold and unfold.

Fold three corners
to the center.

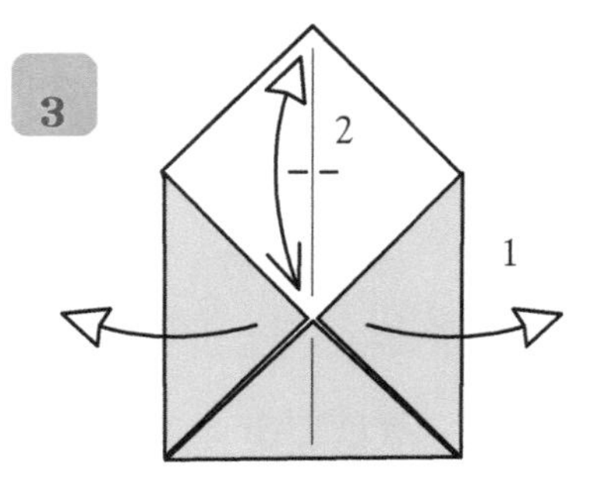

1. Unfold on the left and right.
2. Fold and unfold to the center.

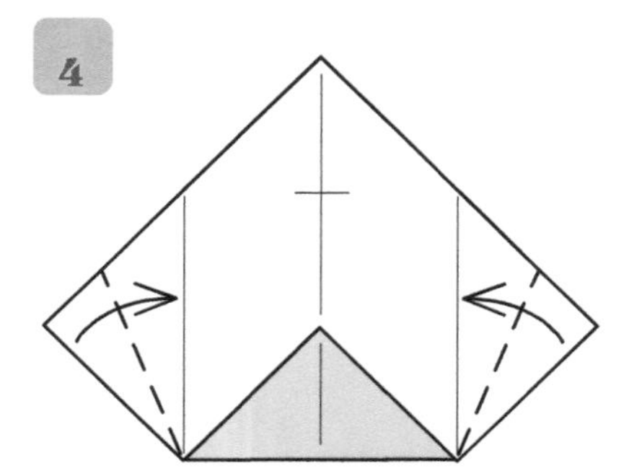

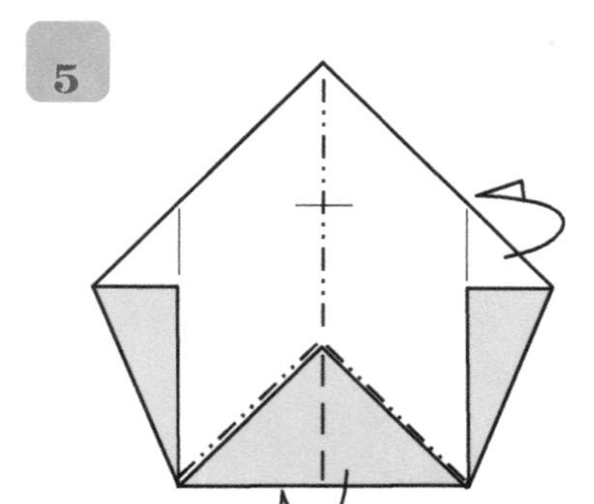

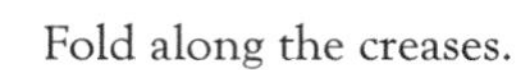

Fold along the creases.

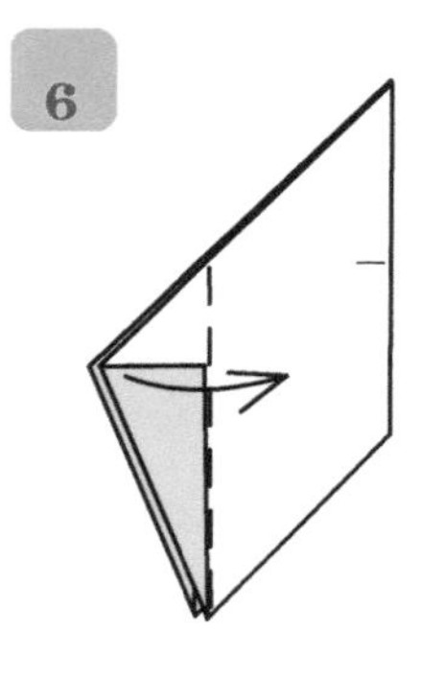

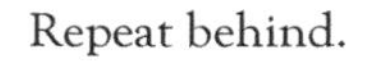

Repeat behind.

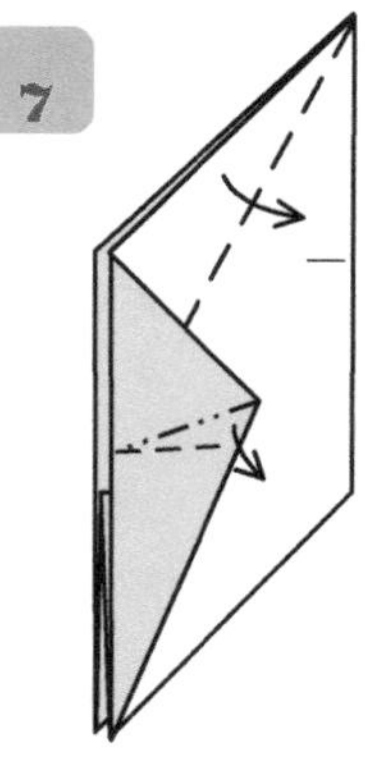

Squash-fold,
repeat behind.

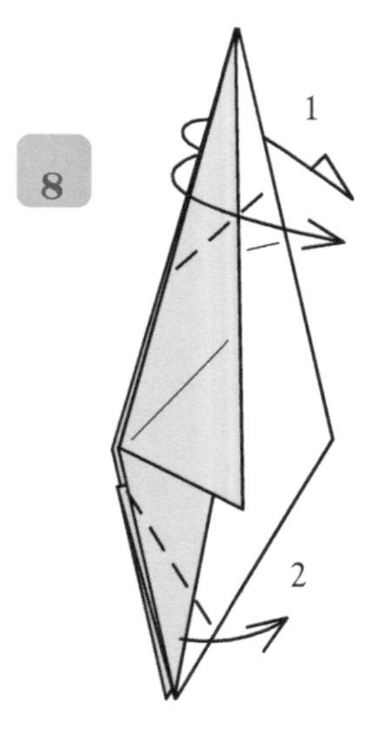

1. Outside-reverse-fold
   above the crease.
2. Valley-fold, repeat behind.

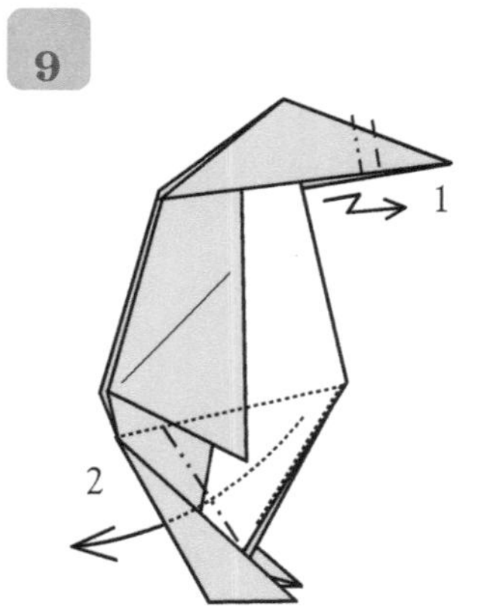

1. Crimp-fold.
2. Reverse-fold the
   hidden flap.

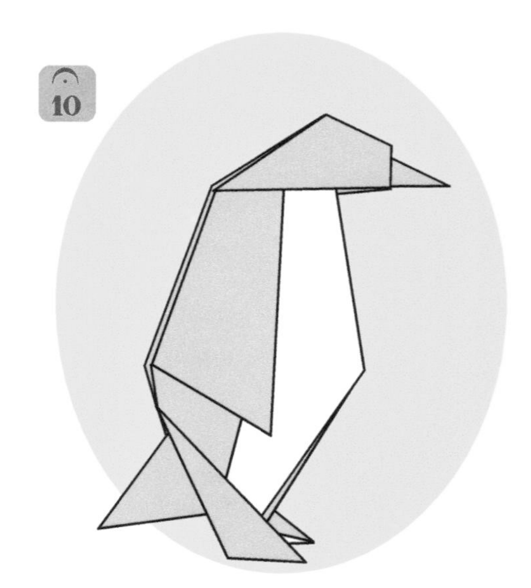

King Penguin

Brahminy Kite

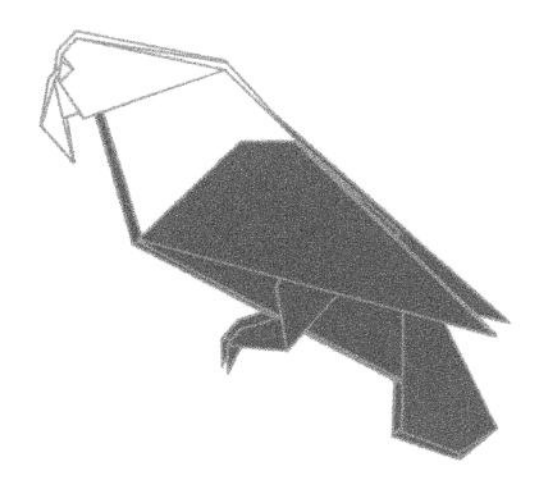

Also called Red Backed Kite and Rufous Eagle, these large birds resemble Bald Eagles with their white heads. They have long been considered sacred and live on the Indian Subcontinent, Southeast Asia and Australia. They are birds of prey, related to Eagles and Buzzards.

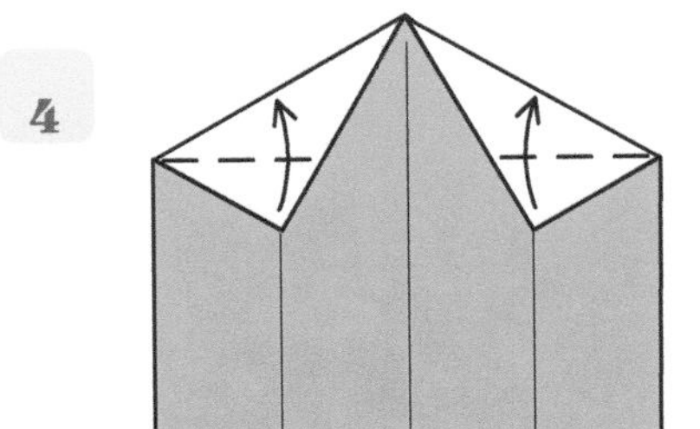

Fold and unfold.

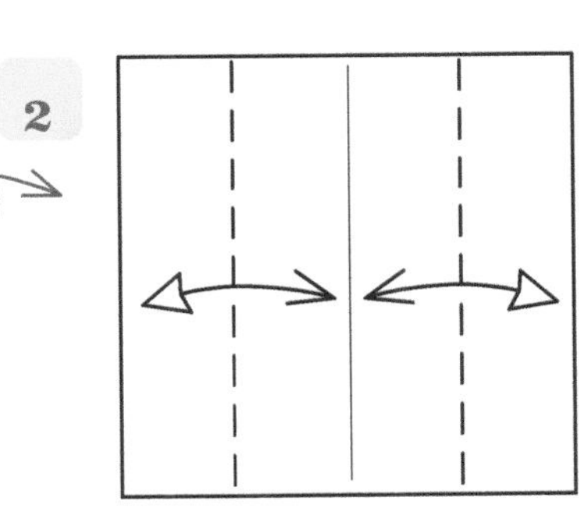

Fold and unfold to the center.

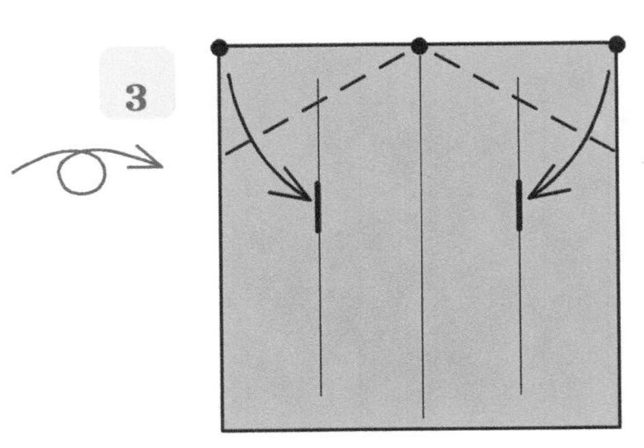

Bring the corners to the lines.

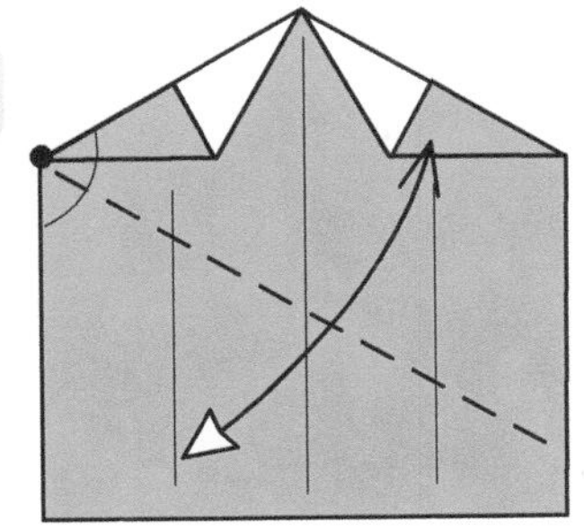

Fold and unfold.

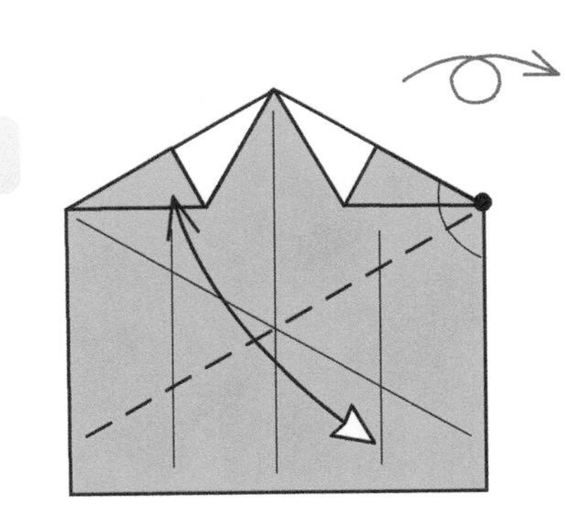

Fold and unfold.

7

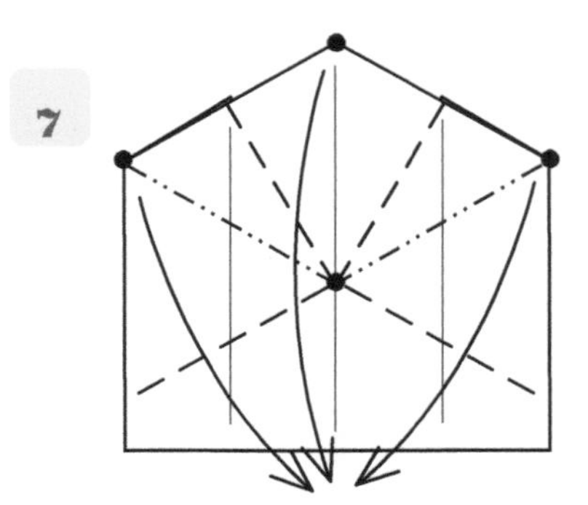

Push in at the lower dot.
The upper dots will meet.

8

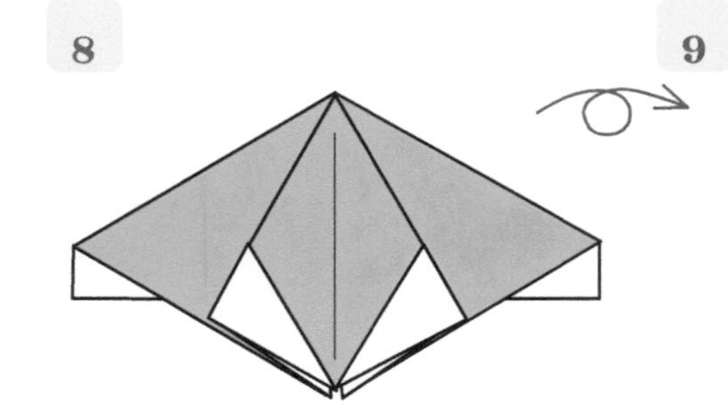

Rotate 180°.

9

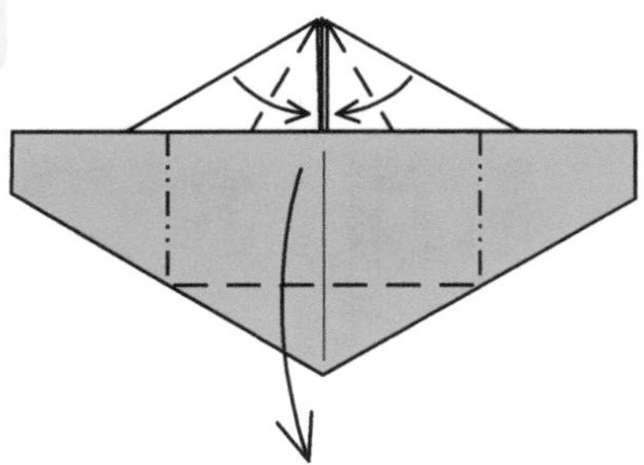

Petal-fold.

10

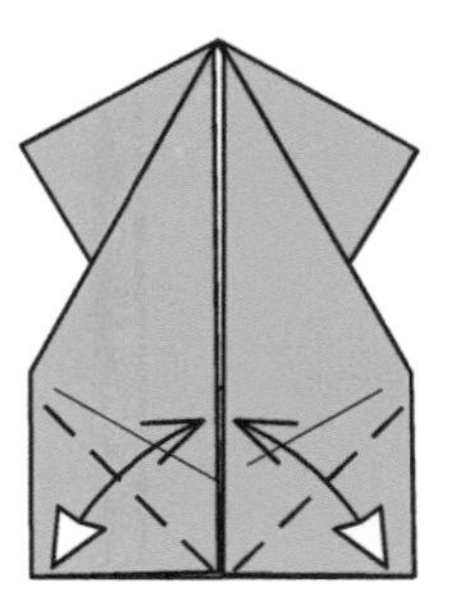

Fold and unfold.

11

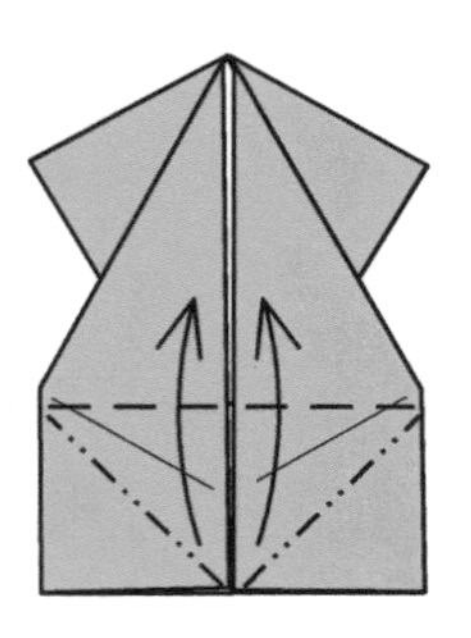

Make squash folds.

12

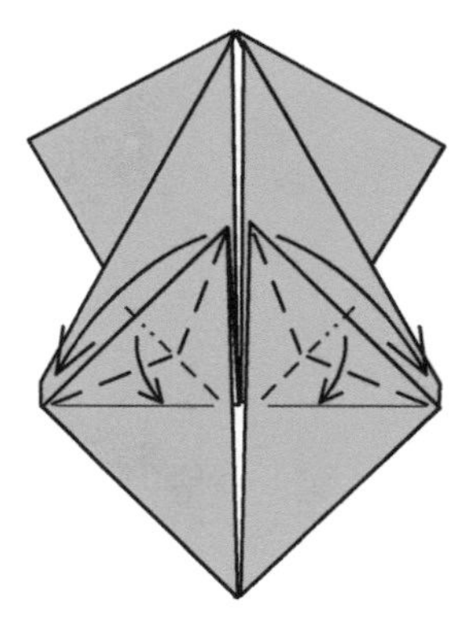

Make rabbit ears.

13

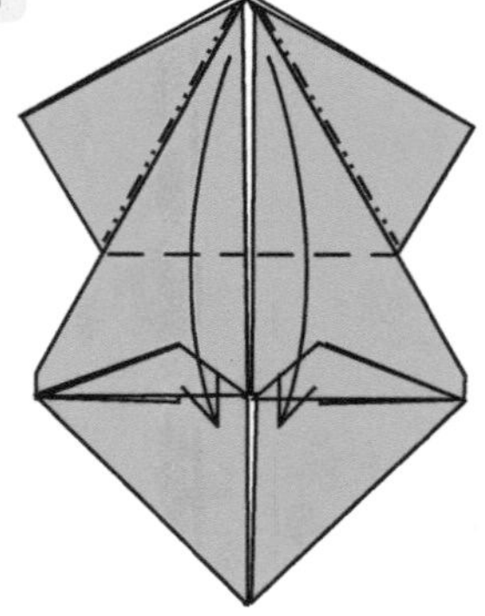

Make squash folds.

14

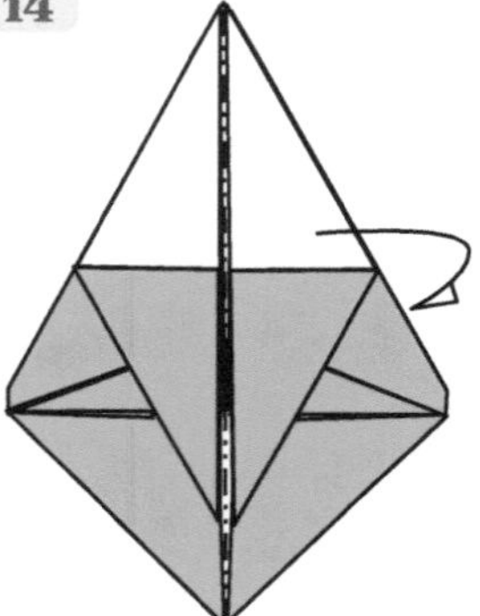

Fold in half and rotate.

15

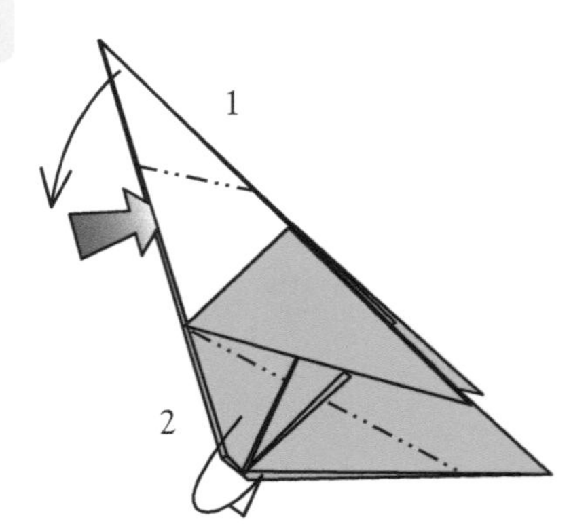

1. Reverse-fold.
2. Repeat behind.

16

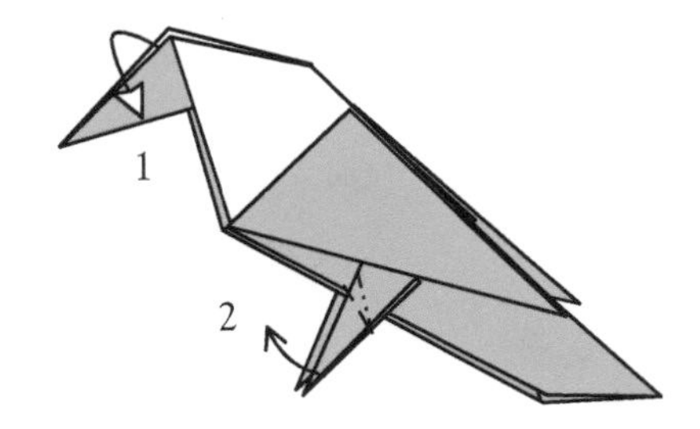

1. Wrap around.
2. Crimp-fold.
Repeat behind.

17

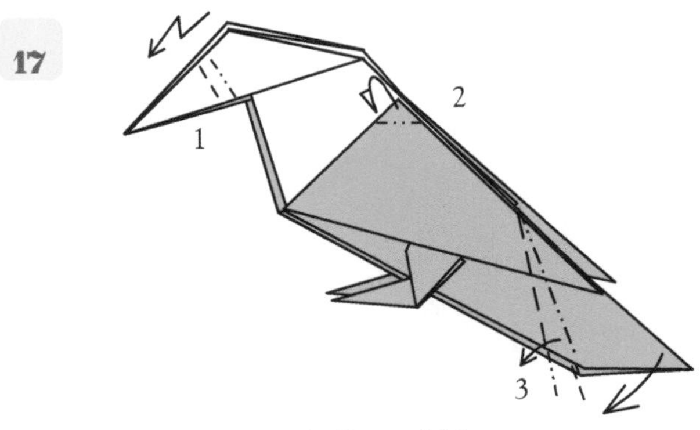

1. Crimp-fold.
2. Repeat behind.
3. Crimp-fold.

18

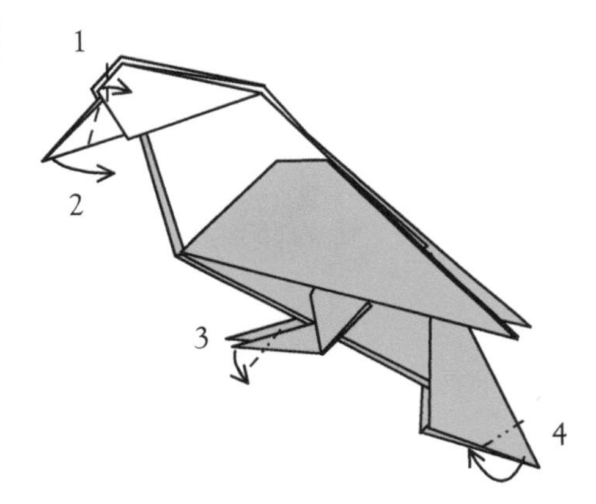

1. Form the eye, repeat behind.
2. Outside-reverse-fold.
3. Crimp-fold, repeat behind.
4. Reverse-fold.

19

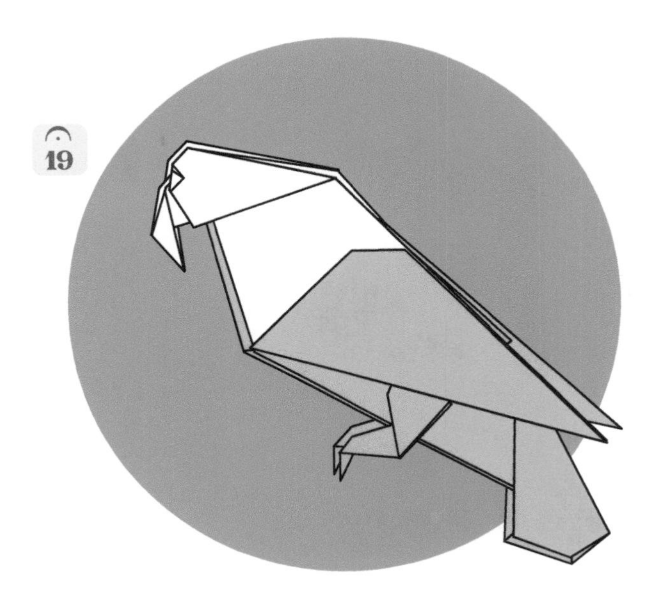

Brahminy Kite

Channel-billed Cuckoo

The largest of the Cuckoos, this bird tends to be shy, but can also get very loud. Unlike most Cuckoos that have a diet mainly consisting of insects, the Channel-Billed Cuckoo also eats a variety of fruits, such as figs and black mulberries. These birds get their name from the distinctive groove in their bills.

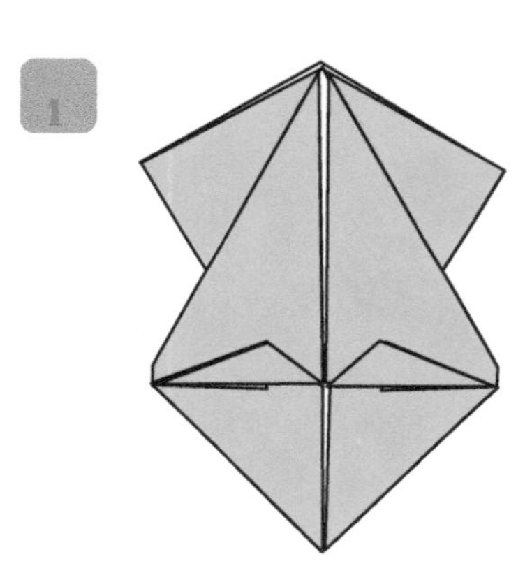

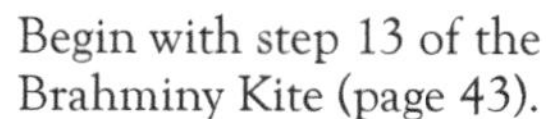
Begin with step 13 of the Brahminy Kite (page 43).

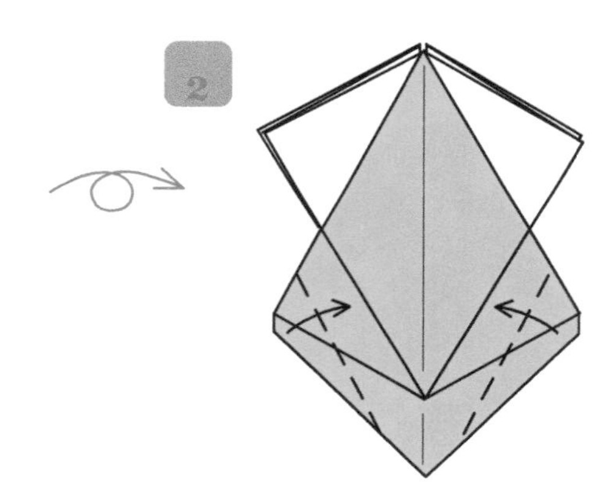

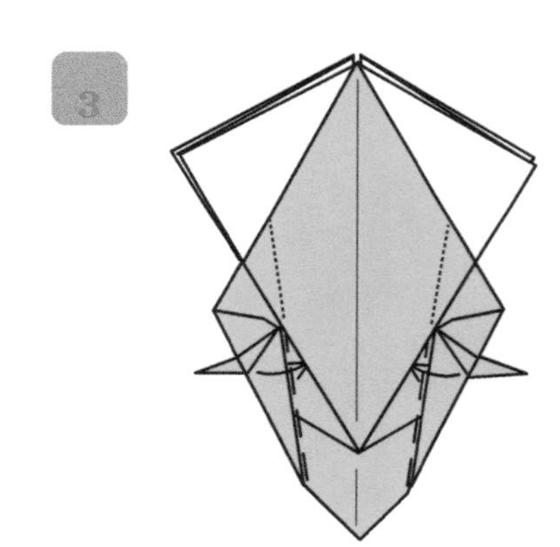

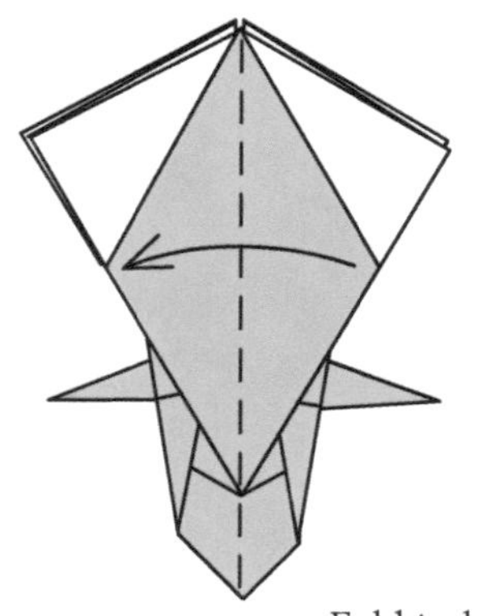

Fold in half and rotate.

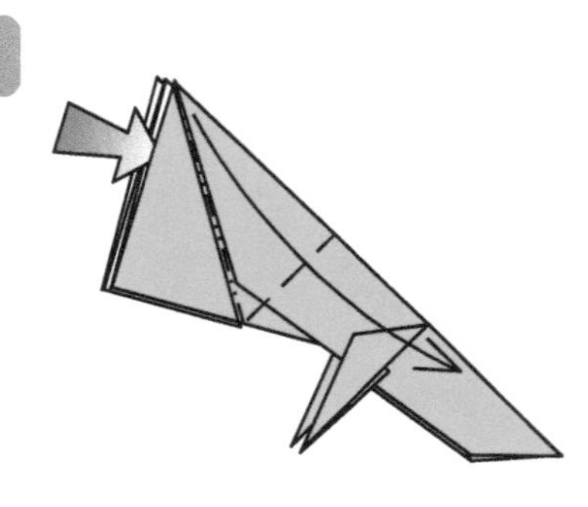

Squash-fold, repeat behind.

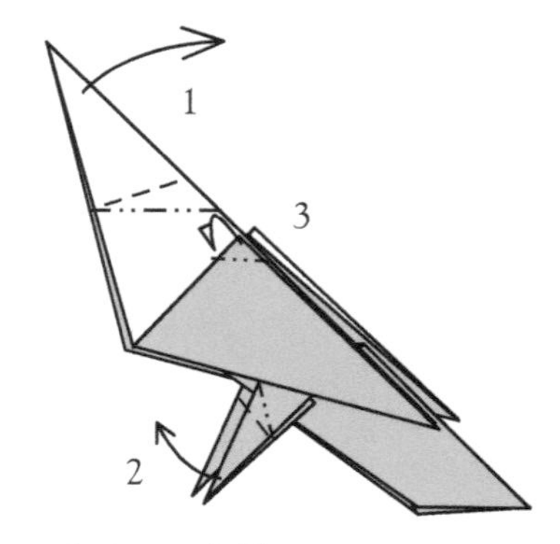

1. Crimp-fold.
2. Crimp-fold, repeat behind.
3. Repeat behind.

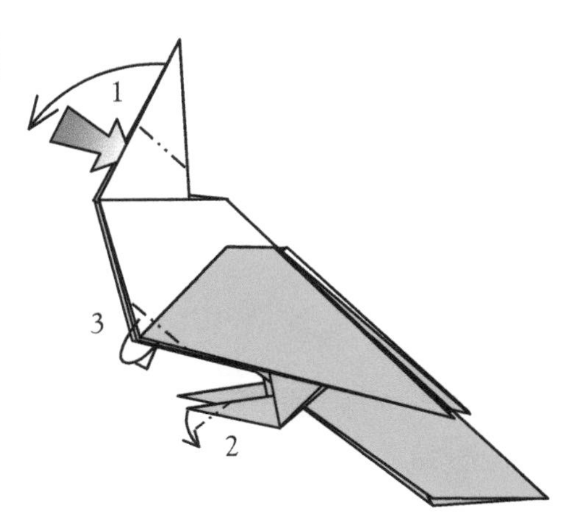

1. Reverse-fold.
2. Reverse-fold, repeat behind.
3. Reverse-fold.

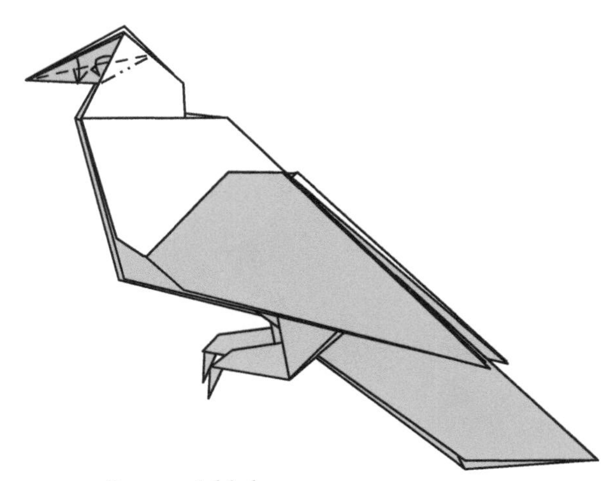

Reverse-fold the top flap. Repeat behind.

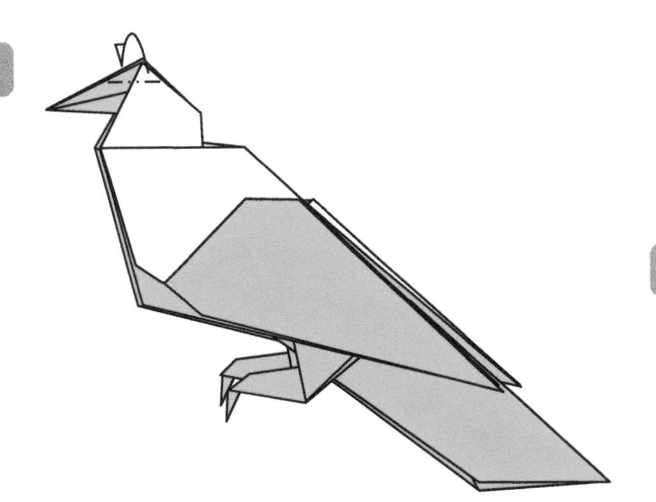

Repeat behind.

Channel-billed Cuckoo

Australian Wood Duck

Also called the Maned Duck and Maned Goose, these ducks do bear a very strong resemblance to geese. Wood Ducks are a common sight in urban areas throughout Australia and can be found where there are permanent bodies of water such as near dams and pools.

1

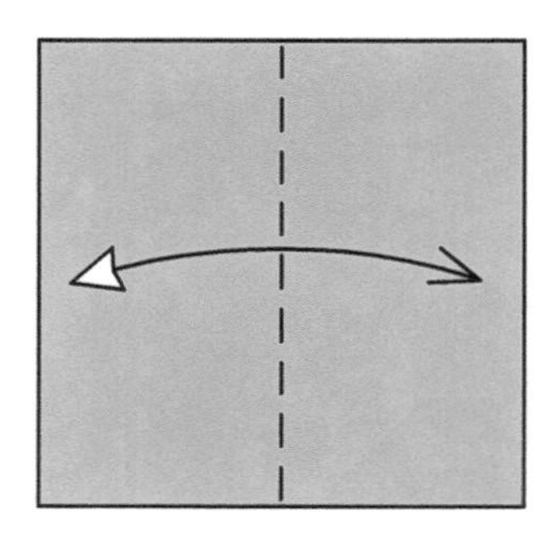

Fold and unfold.

2

Bring the corner to the line.

3

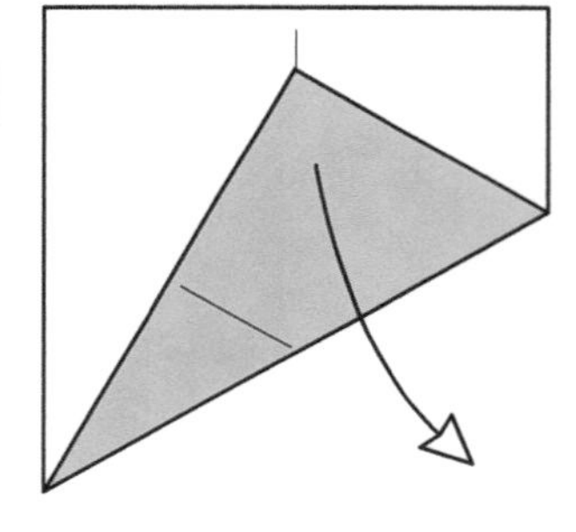

Unfold.

4

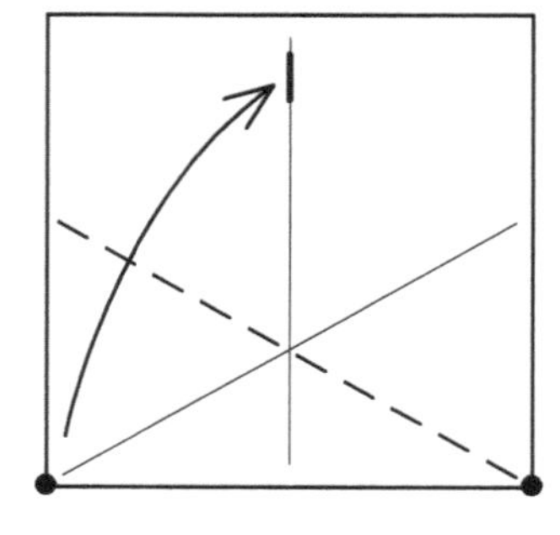

Repeat steps 2–3 in the opposite direction.

5

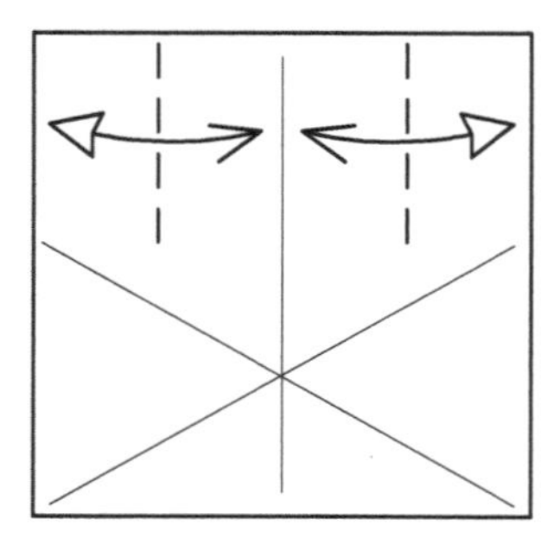

Fold to the center and unfold.

6

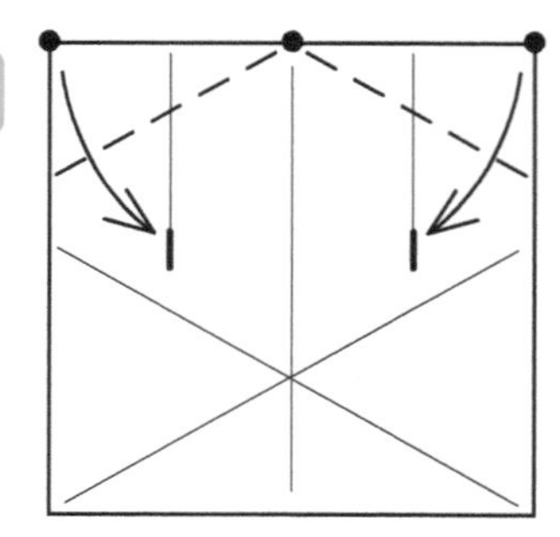

Bring the corners to the lines.

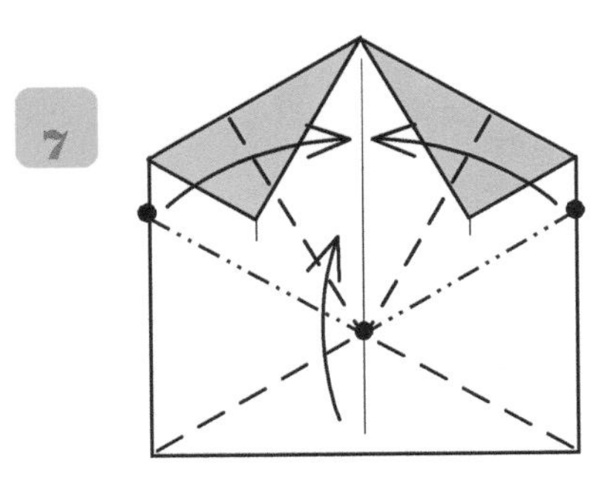

Push in at the lower dot.
The upper dots will meet.

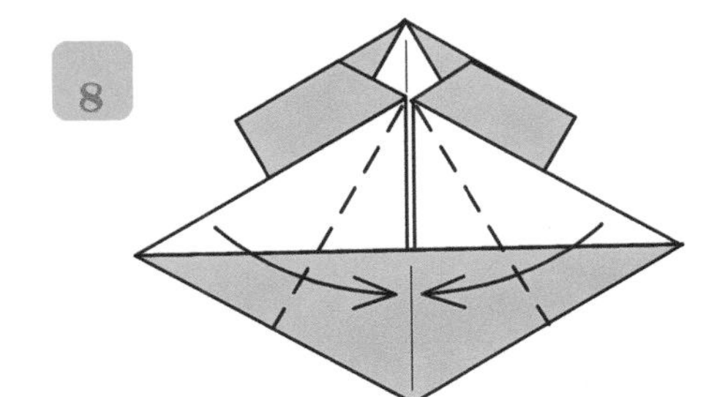

9

Make squash folds.

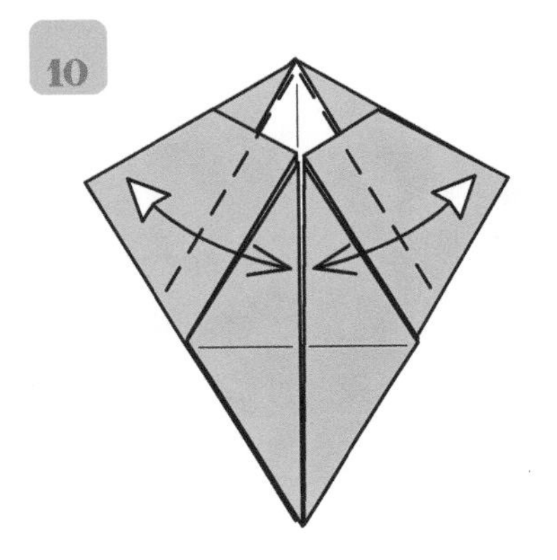

Fold and unfold.

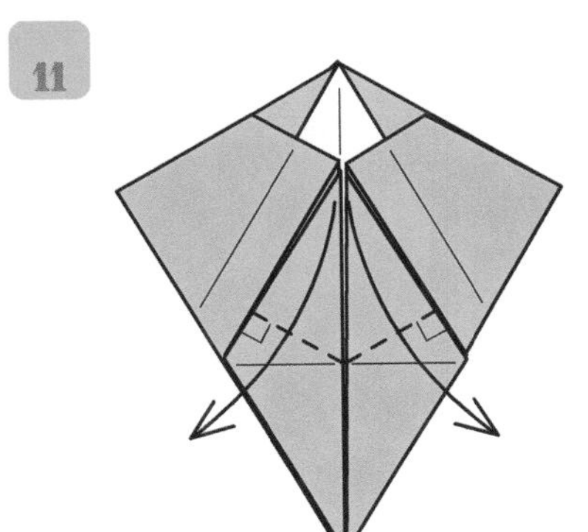

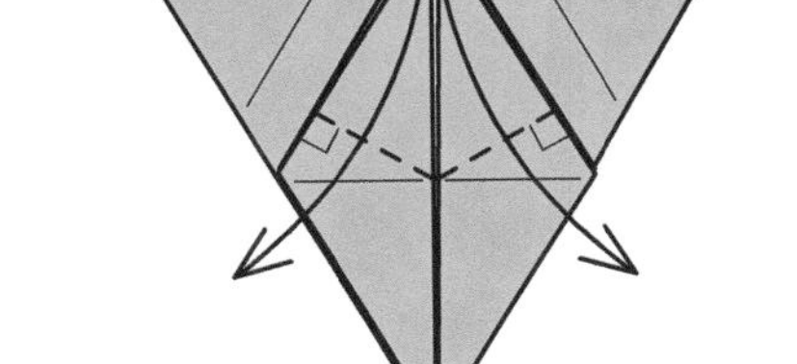

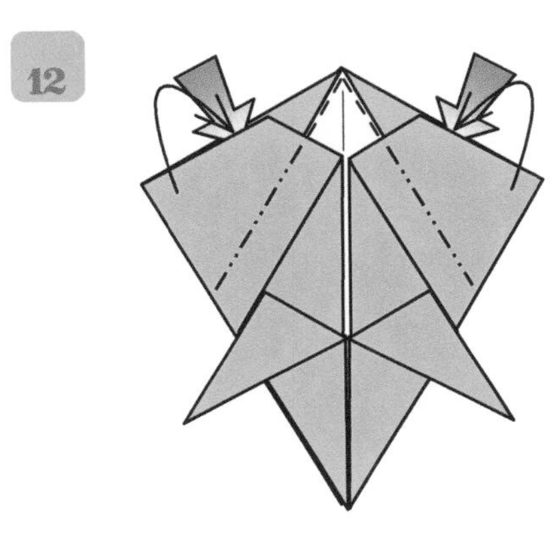

Make reverse folds.

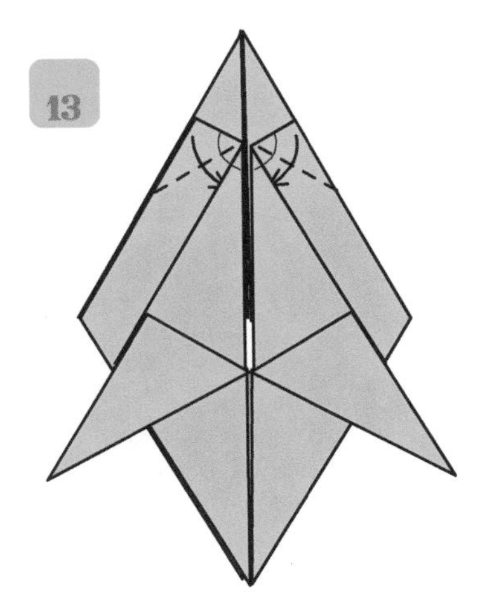

Tuck inside.

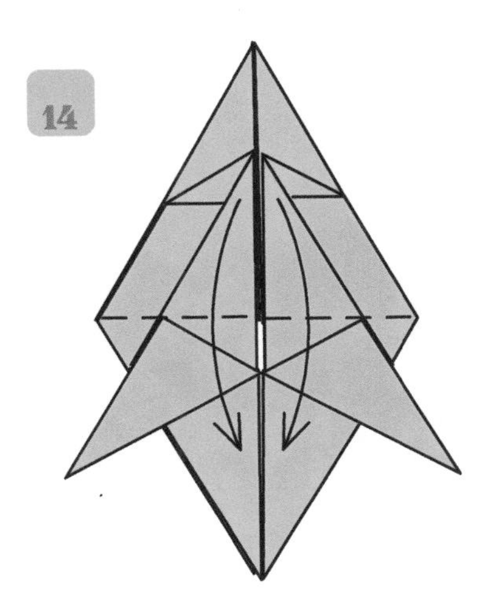

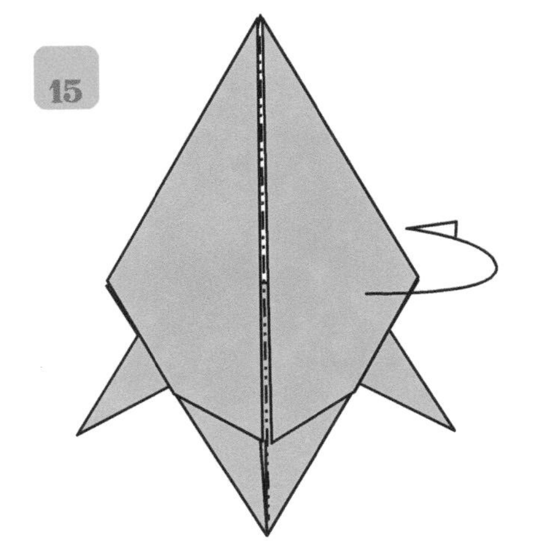

Fold in half and rotate.

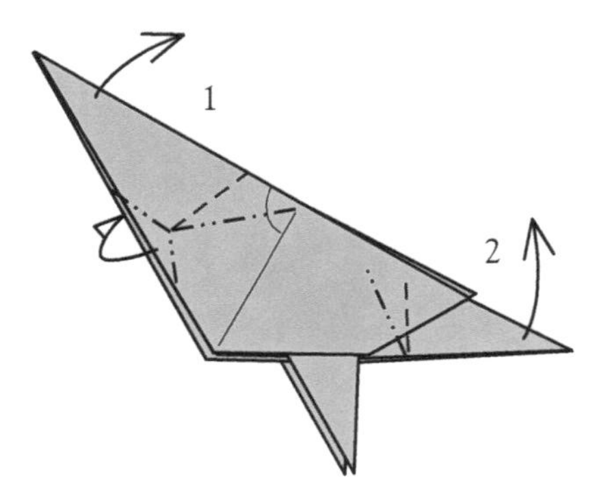

1. Crimp-fold and push in on the left.
2. Crimp-fold.

17

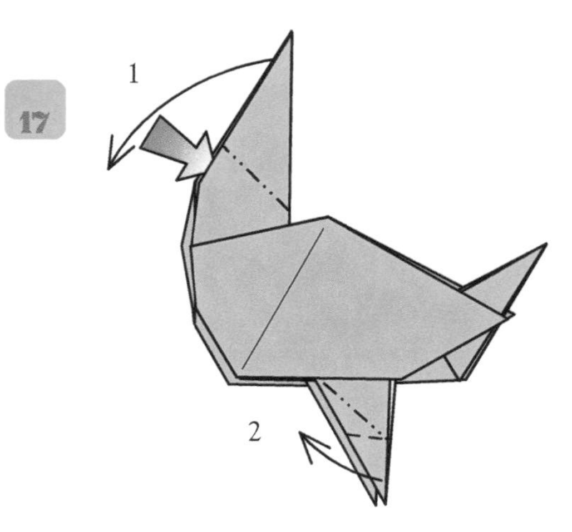

1. Reverse-fold.
2. Crimp-fold, repeat behind.

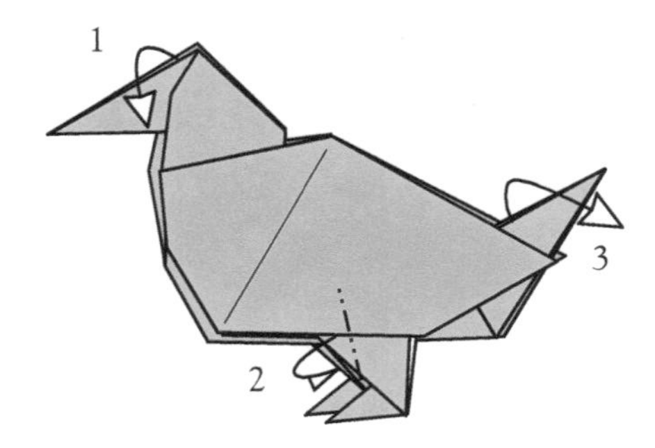

1. Wrap around.
2. Reverse-fold the inner layers.
3. Pull out.
Repeat behind.

19

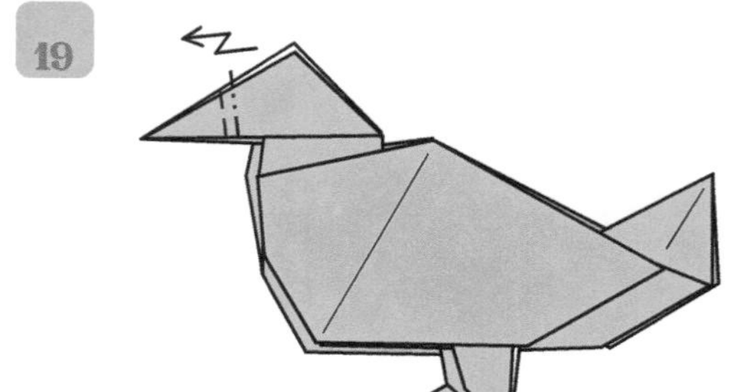

Crimp-fold.

20

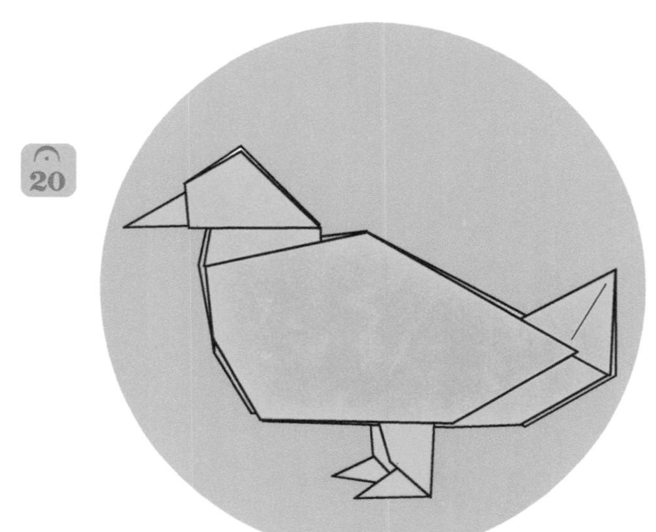

Australian Wood Duck

Magpie Goose

Found in Northern Australia and Southern New Guinea, these geese often tend to wander outside of their home territories. They feed on vegetation on land and in the water. Unlike other geese, they have strongly clawed toes and only partially webbed feet.

1

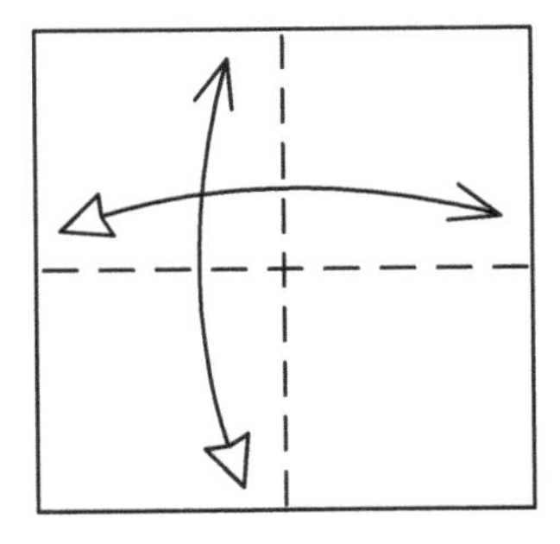

Fold and unfold.

2

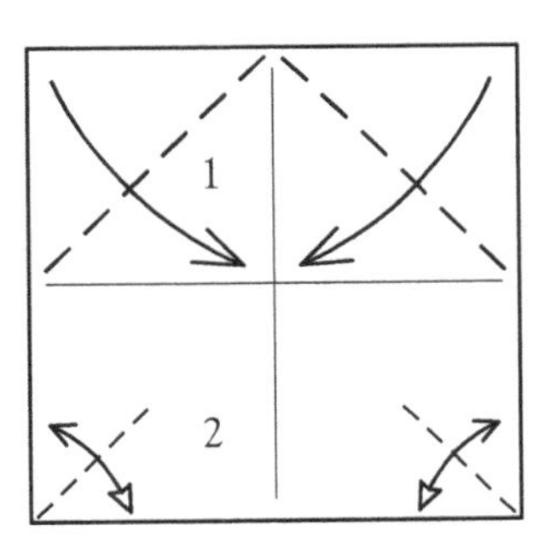

1. Fold to the center.
2. Fold and unfold.

3

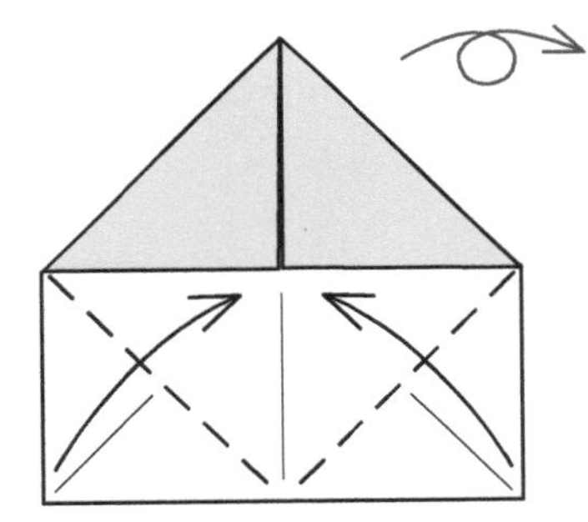

Fold to the center.

4

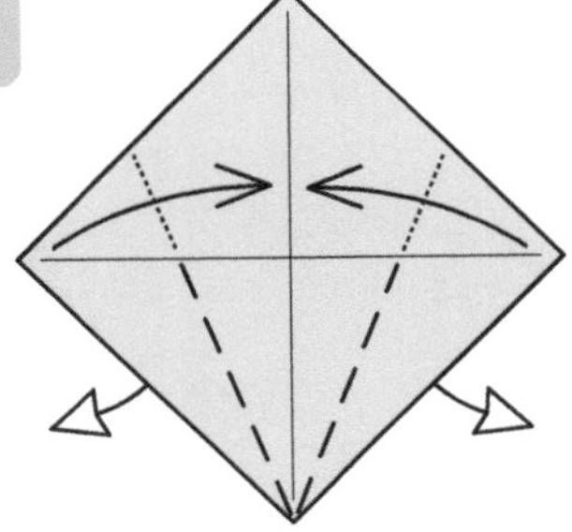

Fold to the center and swing out from behind. Do not crease at the top.

5

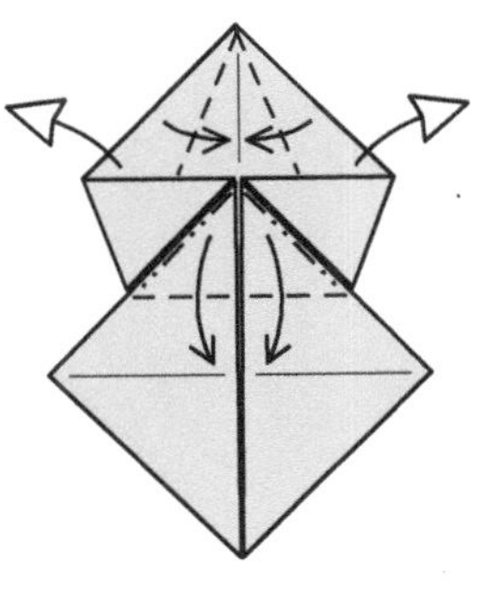

Squash-fold and swing out from behind.

6

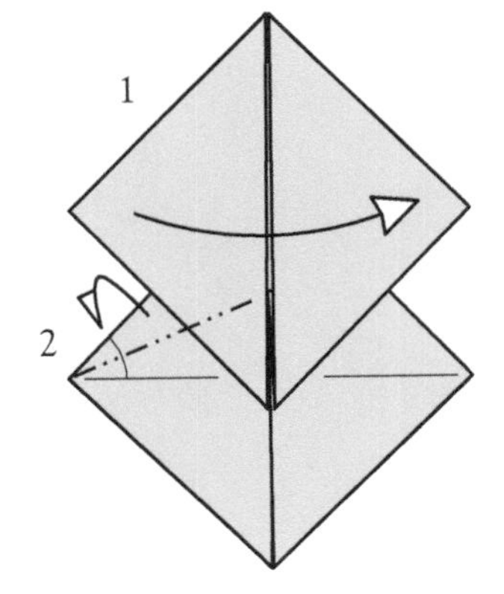

1. Unfold.
2. Fold behind.

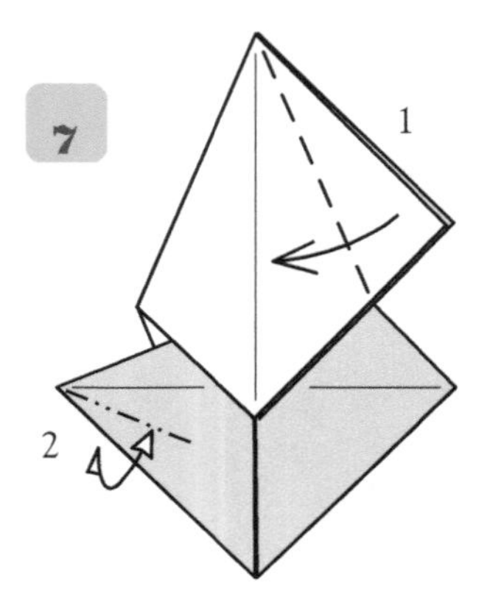

1. Fold the top layer.
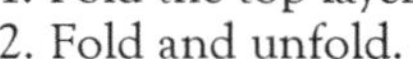
2. Fold and unfold.

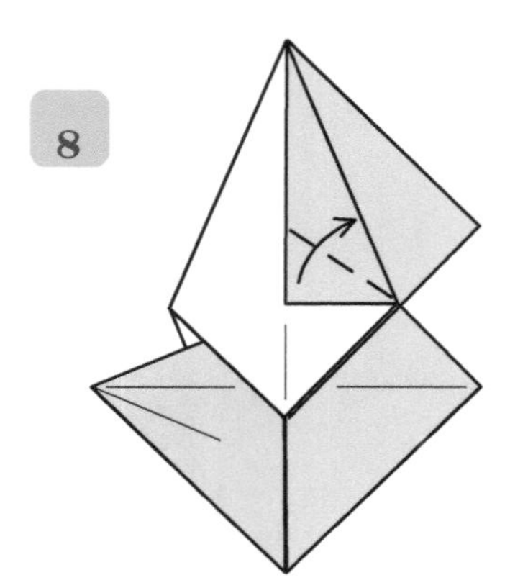

9

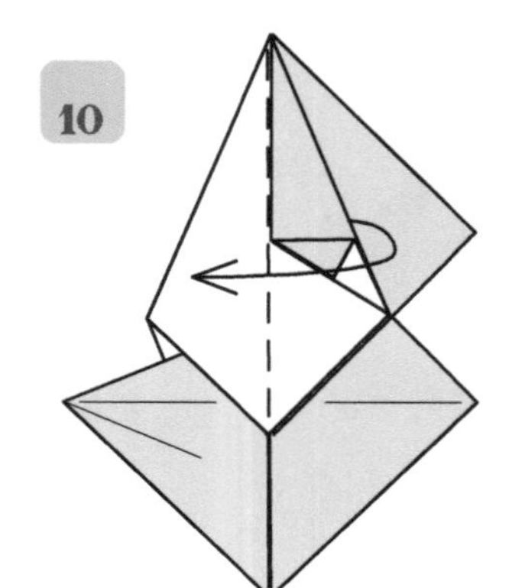

11

Repeat steps 7–10 on the right.

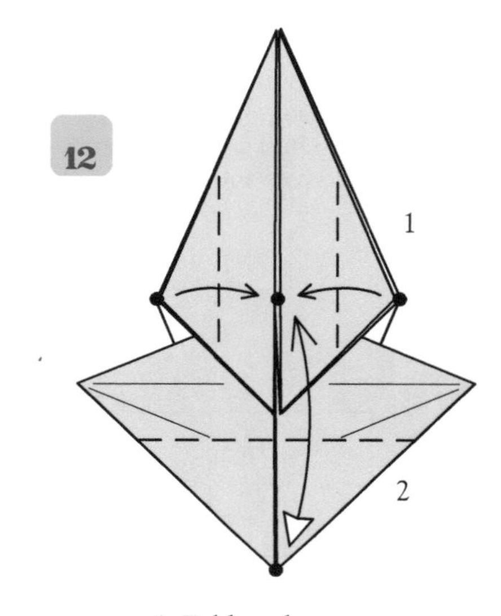

1. Fold to the center.
2. Fold and unfold.

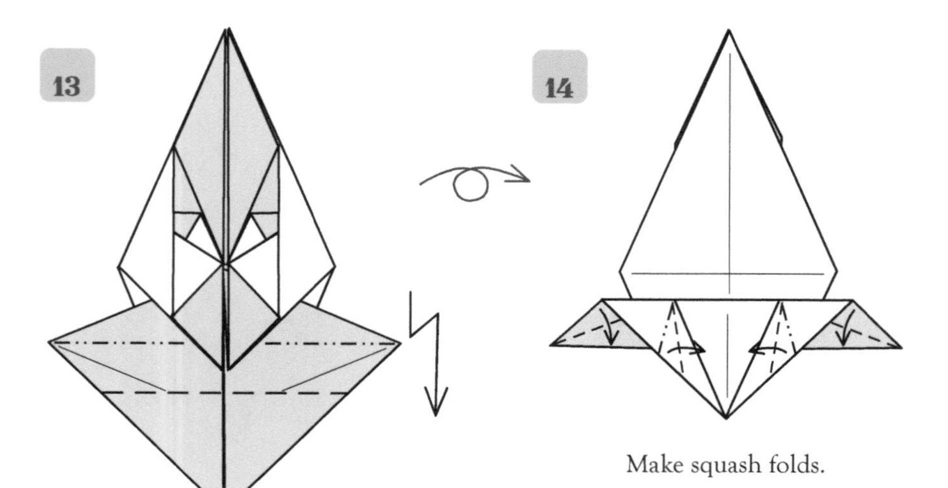

Pleat-fold along the creases.

Make squash folds.

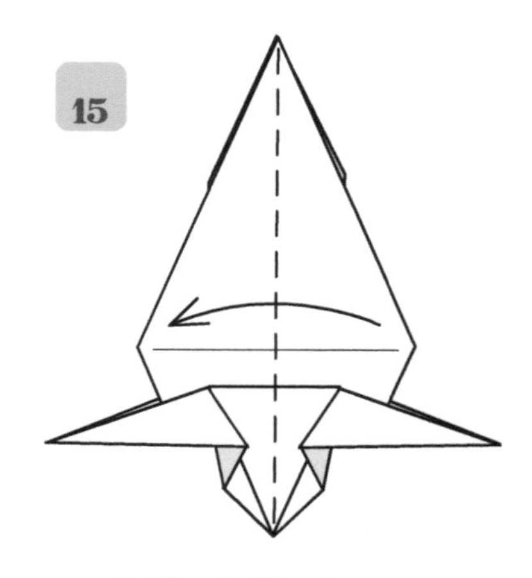

Fold in half and rotate.

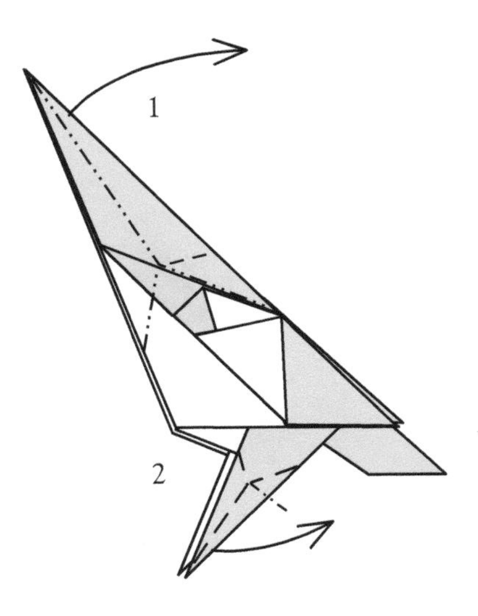

1. Double-rabbit-ear.
2. Rabbit-ear, repeat behind.

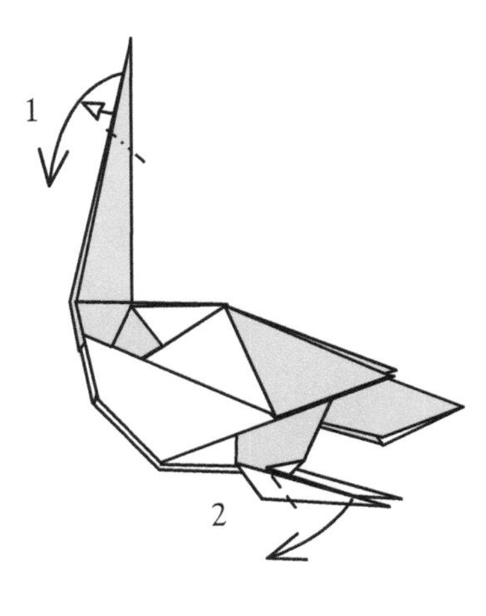

1. Reverse-fold and spread.
2. Repeat behind.

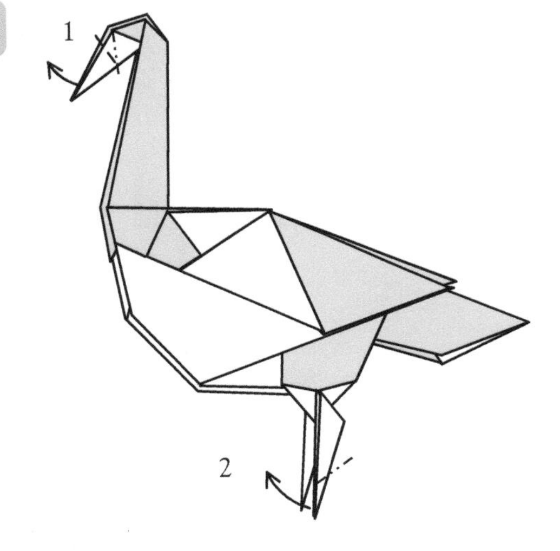

1. Crimp-fold.
2. Reverse-fold, repeat behind.

Magpie Goose

Black-faced Cuckoo-Shrike

Native to Australia and southern New Guinea, these birds can be found in almost every wooded habitat except the rainforest. They have a rather shrill call and tend to move very slowly.

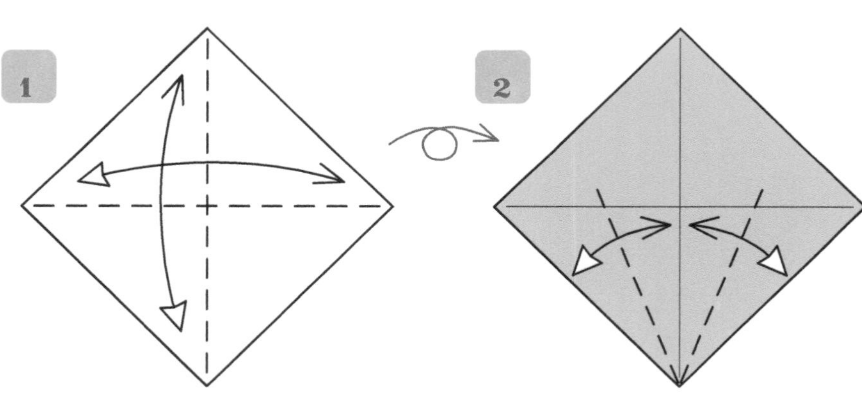

Fold and unfold.

Fold and unfold.

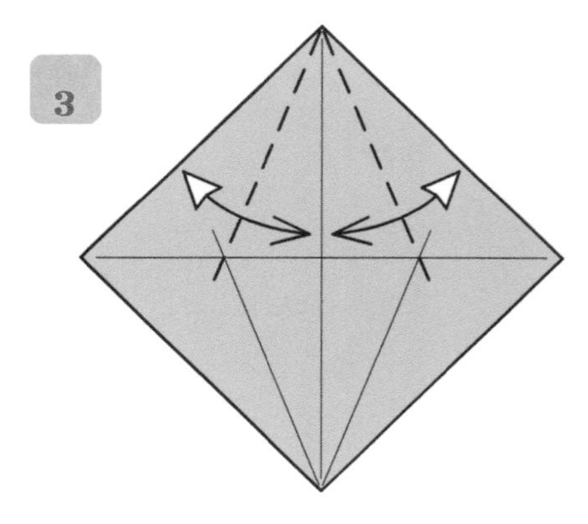

Fold and unfold.

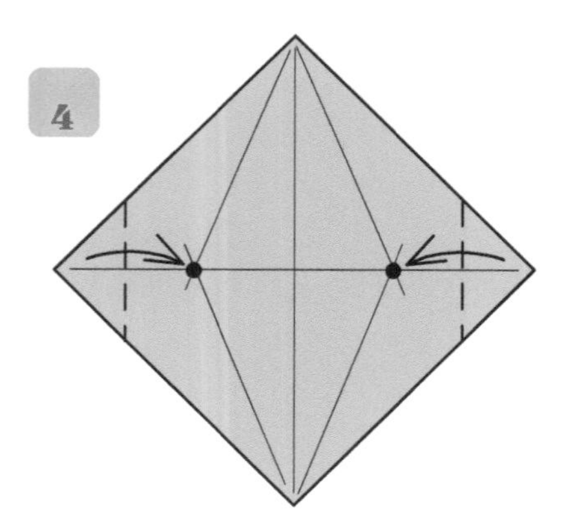

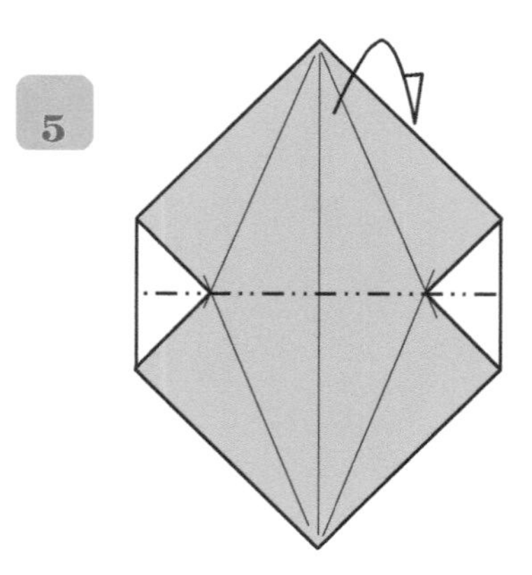

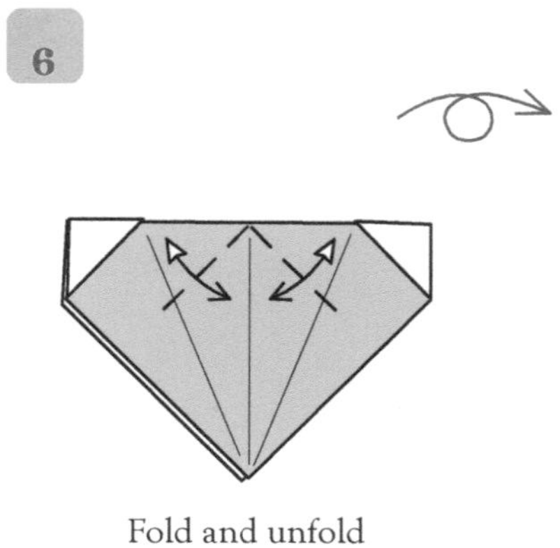

Fold and unfold all the layers.

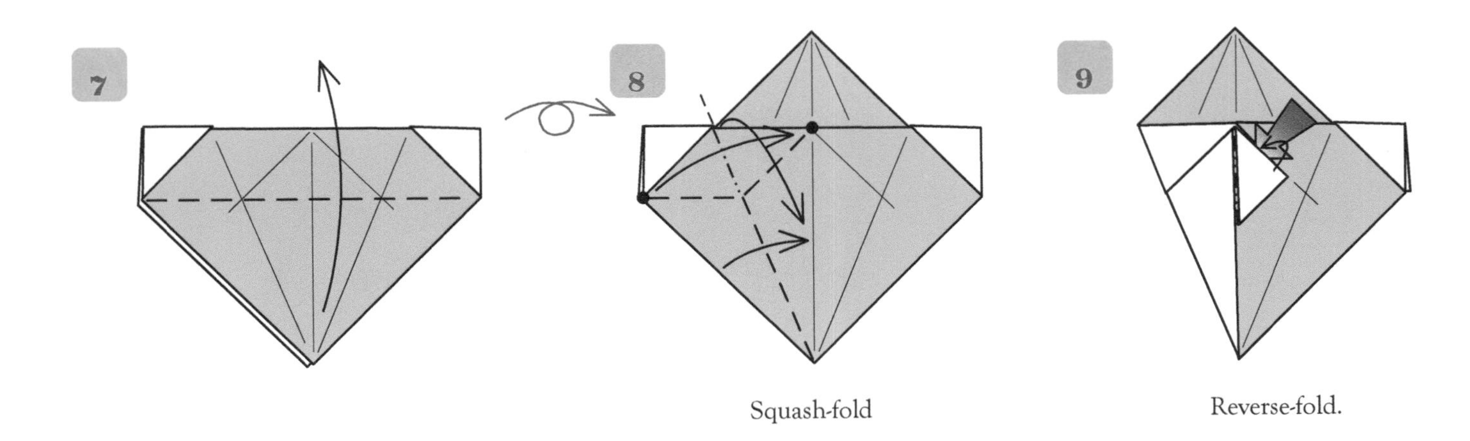

Squash-fold

Reverse-fold.

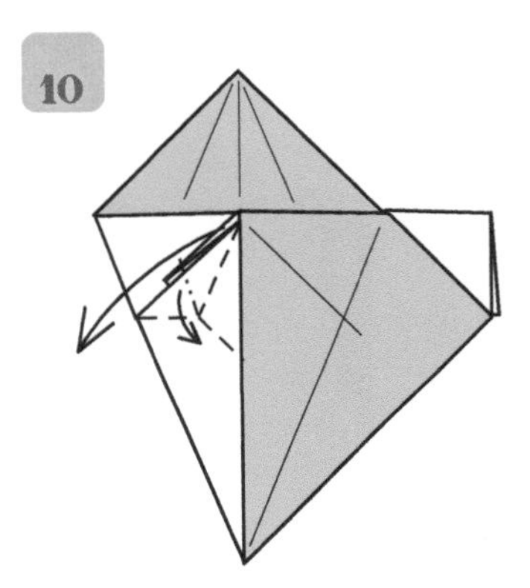

Fold a layer in half
while folding down.

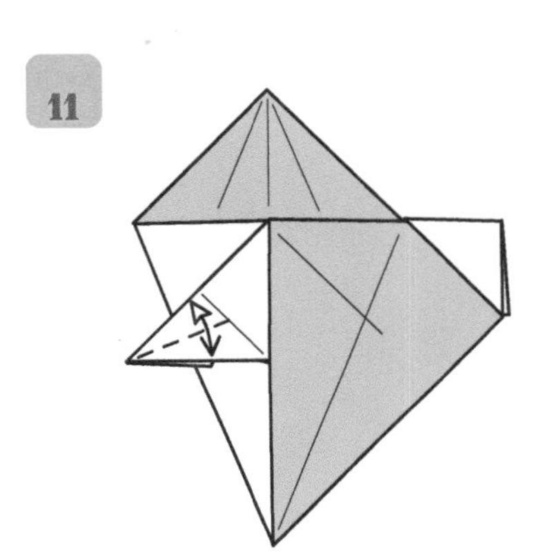

Fold and unfold.

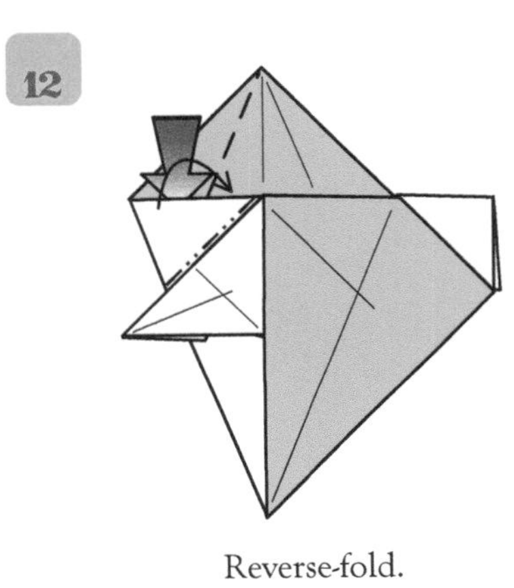

Reverse-fold.

13

14

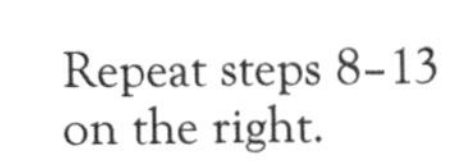

Repeat steps 8–13
on the right.

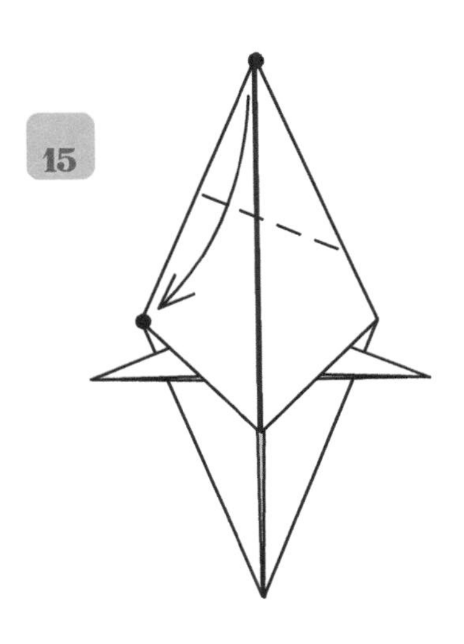

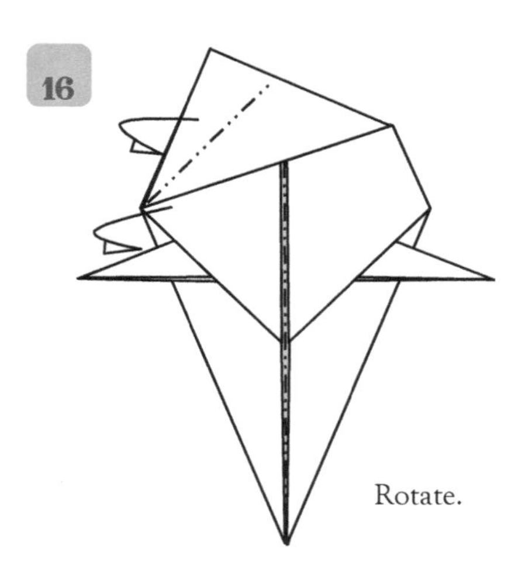

Rotate.

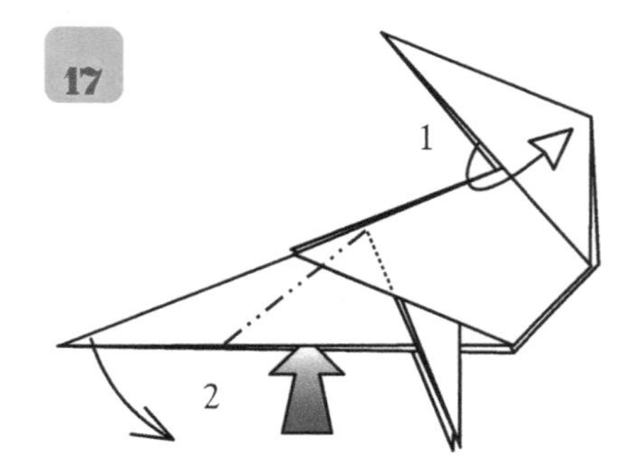

1. Wrap around, repeat behind.
2. Reverse-fold.

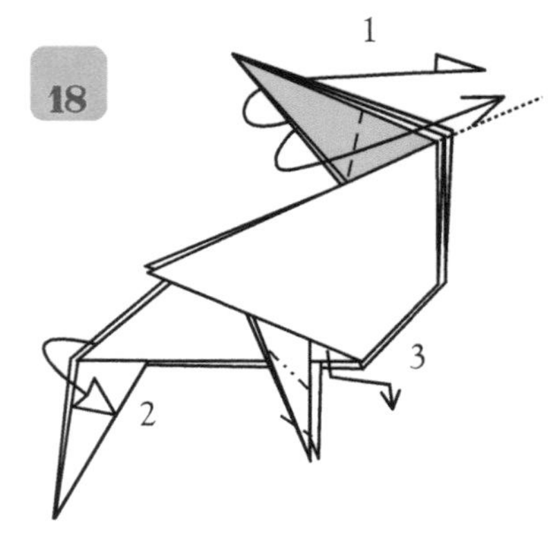

1. Outside-reverse-fold.
2. Wrap around, repeat behind.
3. Make reverse folds, repeat behind.

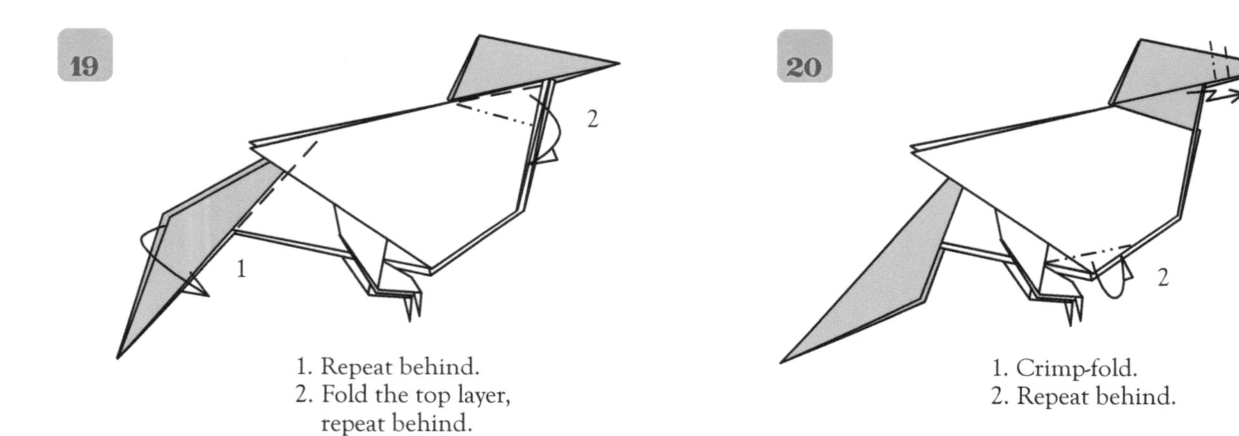

1. Repeat behind.
2. Fold the top layer, repeat behind.

1. Crimp-fold.
2. Repeat behind.

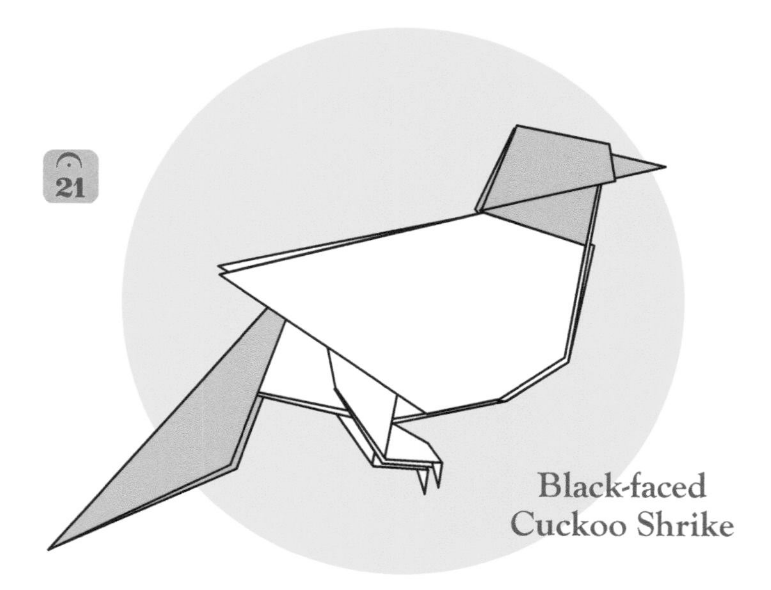

Black-faced
Cuckoo Shrike

Black Butcherbird

Black with a white striped beak, these aggressive birds are active predators and their diet ranges from small lizards and birds to seeds and fruits. They live in the far northern areas of the Australian continent.

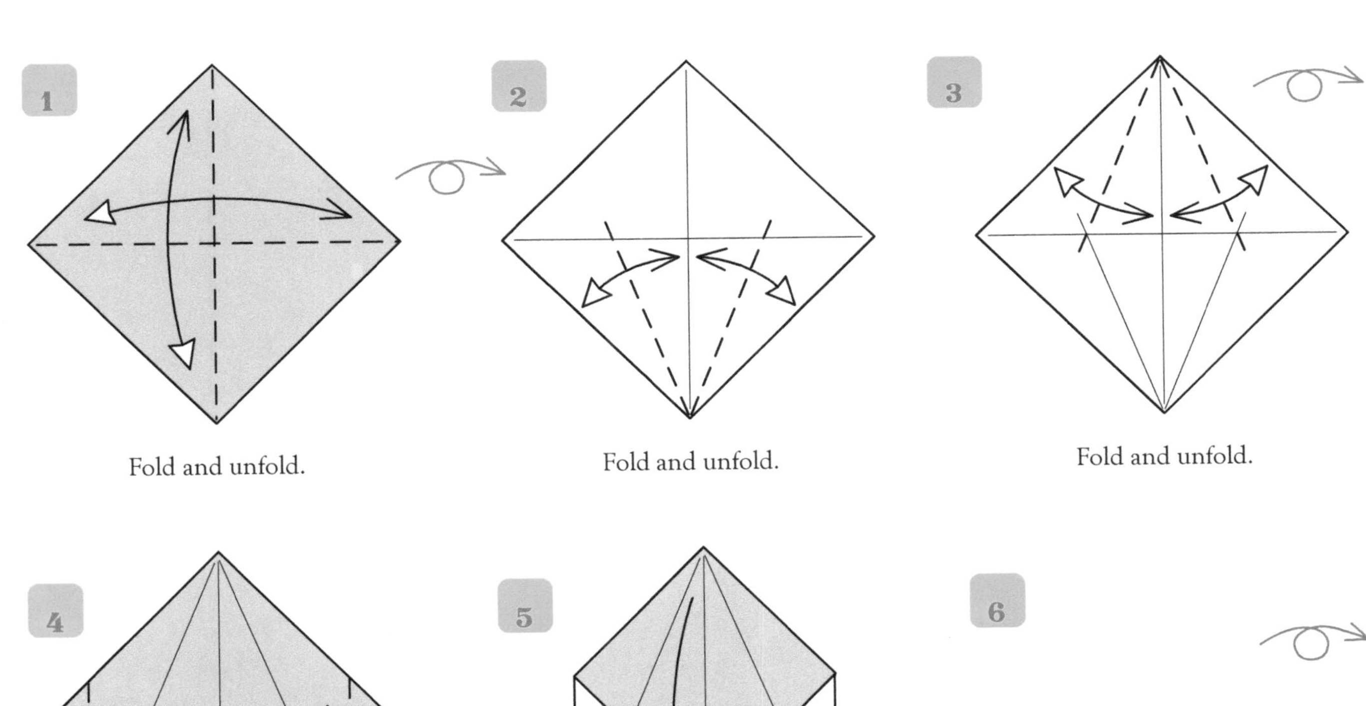

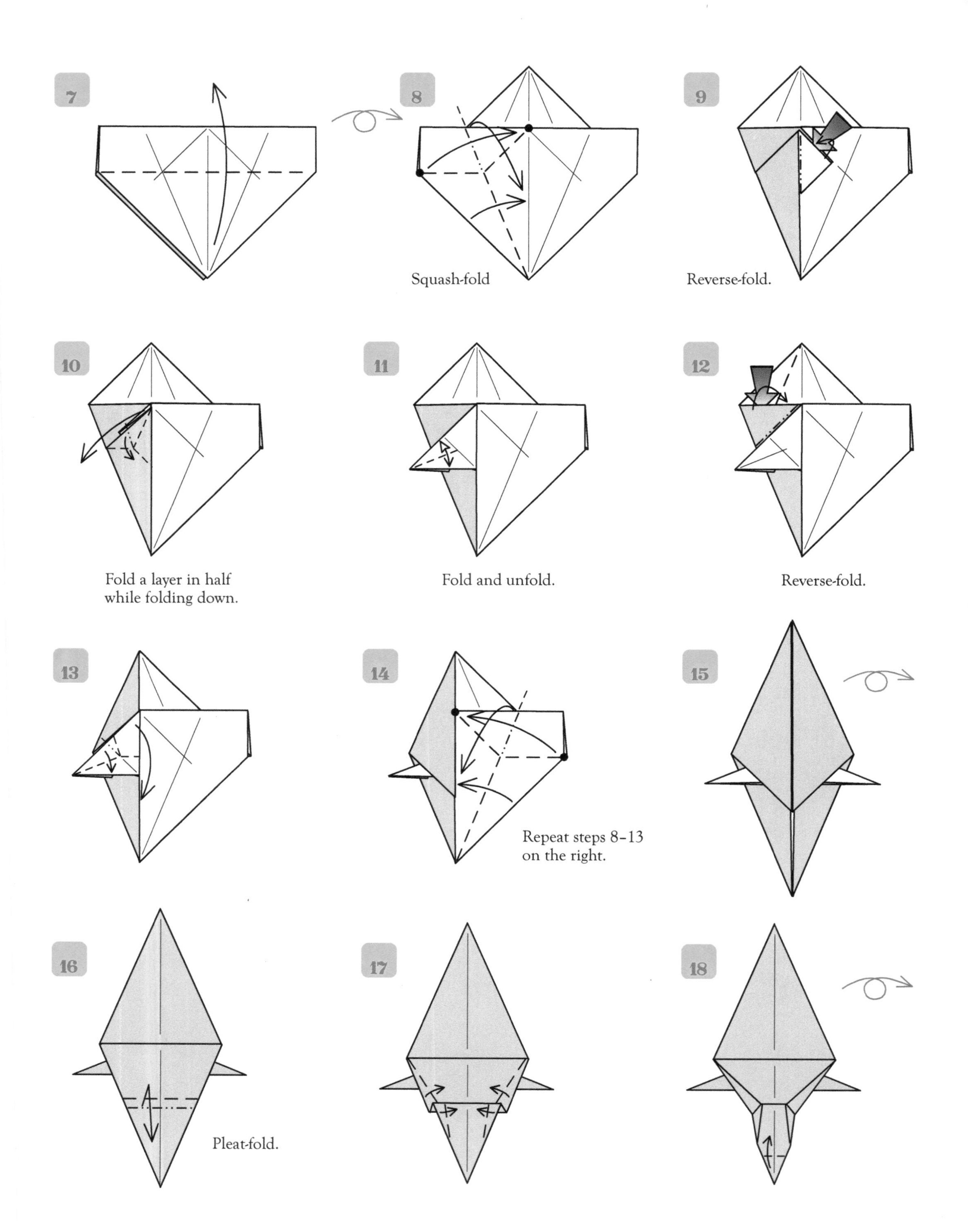
7
8
Squash-fold
9
Reverse-fold.
10
Fold a layer in half
while folding down.
11
Fold and unfold.
12
Reverse-fold.
13
14
Repeat steps 8–13
on the right.
15
16
Pleat-fold.
17
18

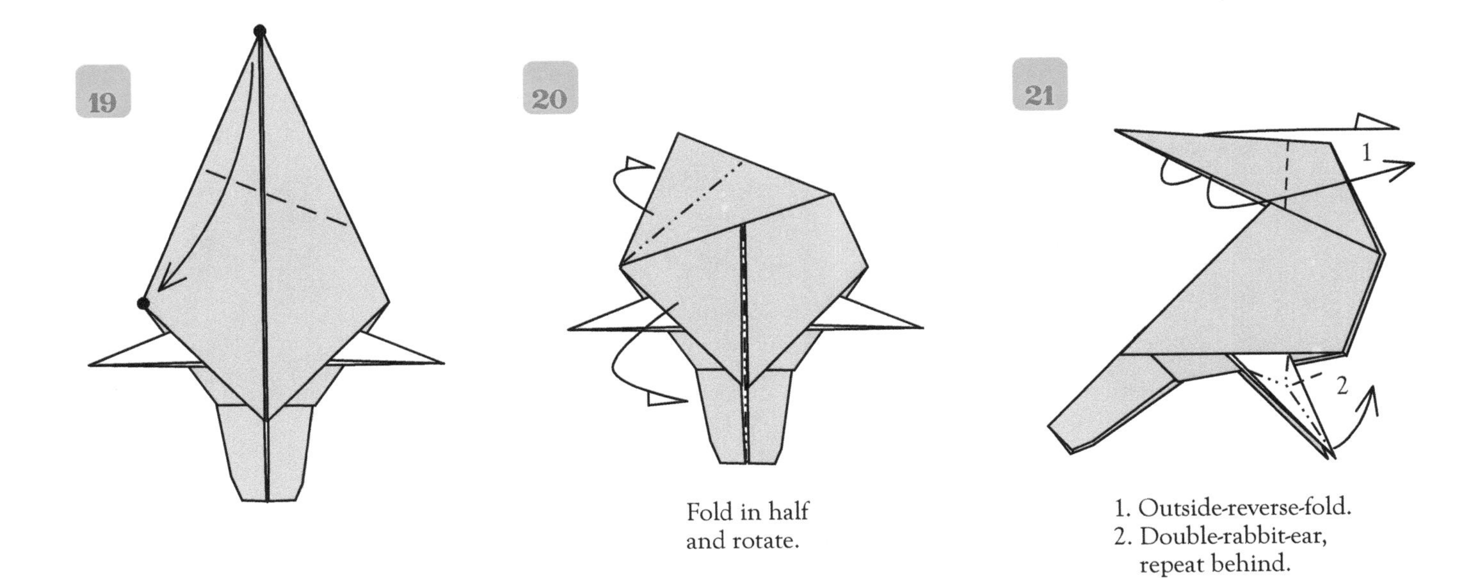

Fold in half
and rotate.

1. Outside-reverse-fold.
2. Double-rabbit-ear,
   repeat behind.

22

1. Crimp-fold.
2. Repeat behind.

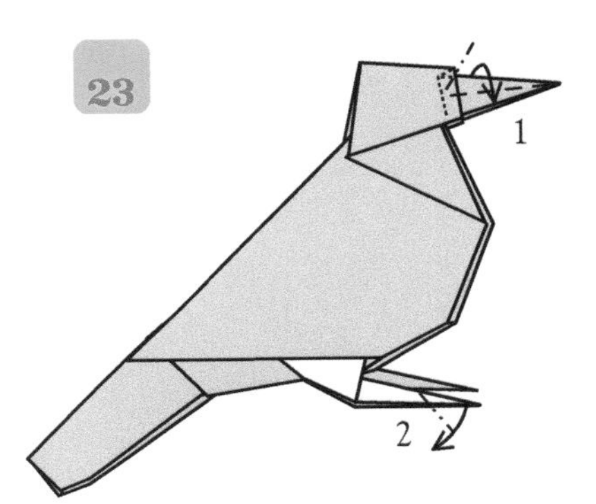

1. Fold the top layer in half.
2. Reverse-fold.
Repeat behind.

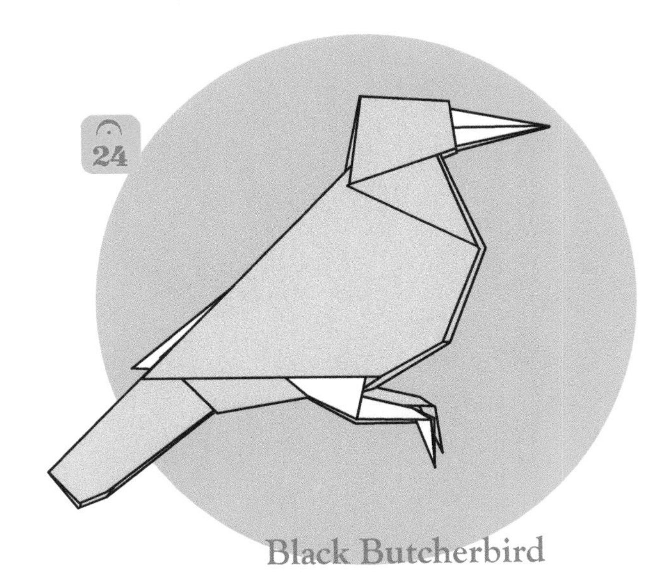

Diamond Dove

With their distinct red eyes and a grey blue coat of feathers, these birds rank amongst the smallest of Australian pigeons along with the Peaceful Doves. They get their name from the small white speckles on their wings.

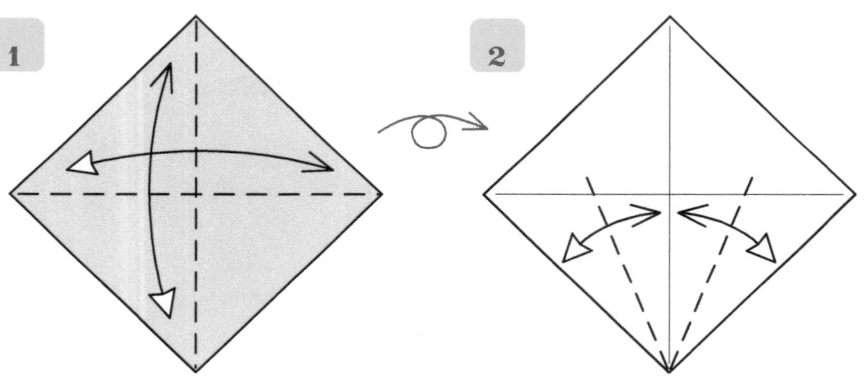

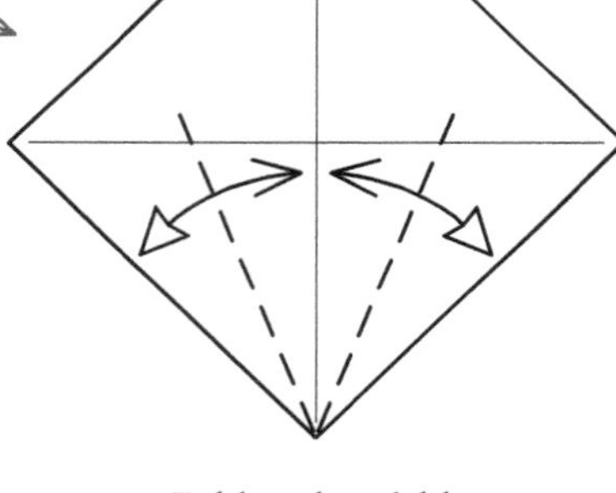

1

Fold and unfold.

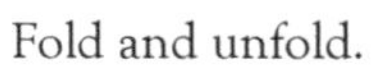

2

Fold and unfold.

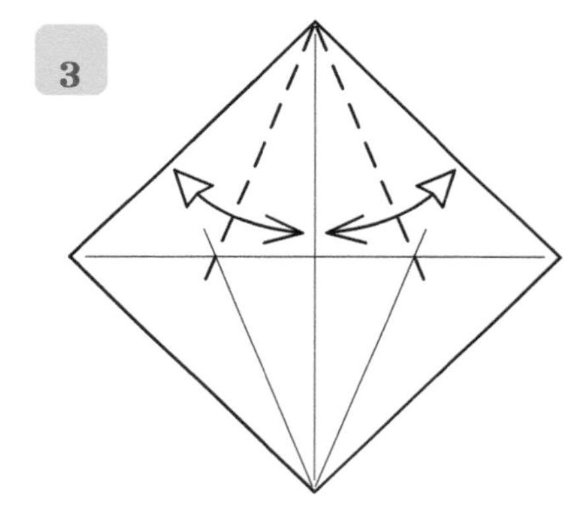

3

Fold and unfold.

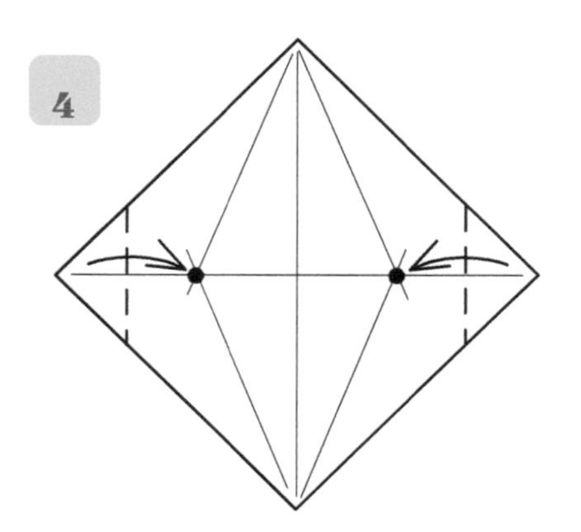

4

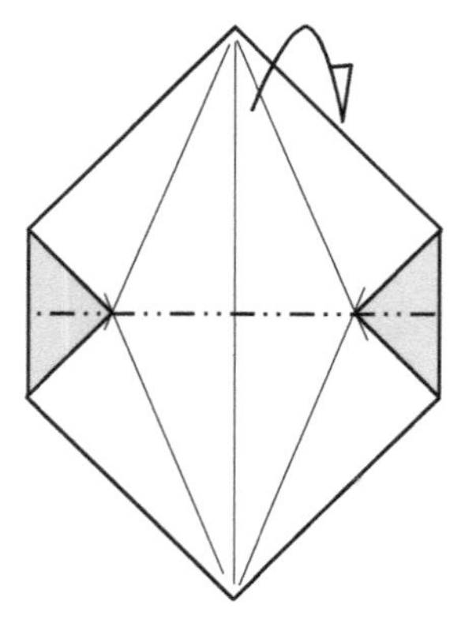

5

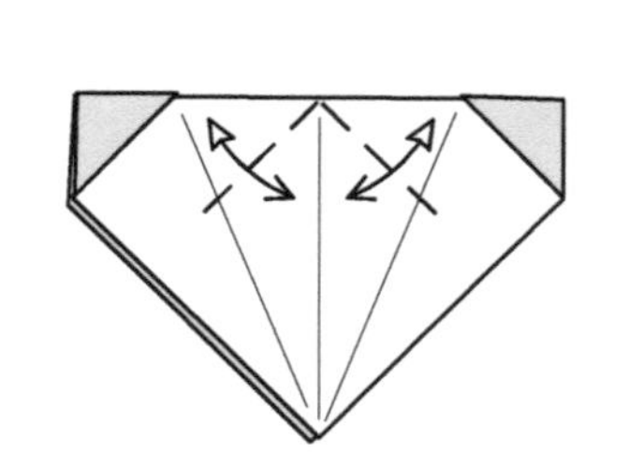

6

Fold and unfold all the layers.

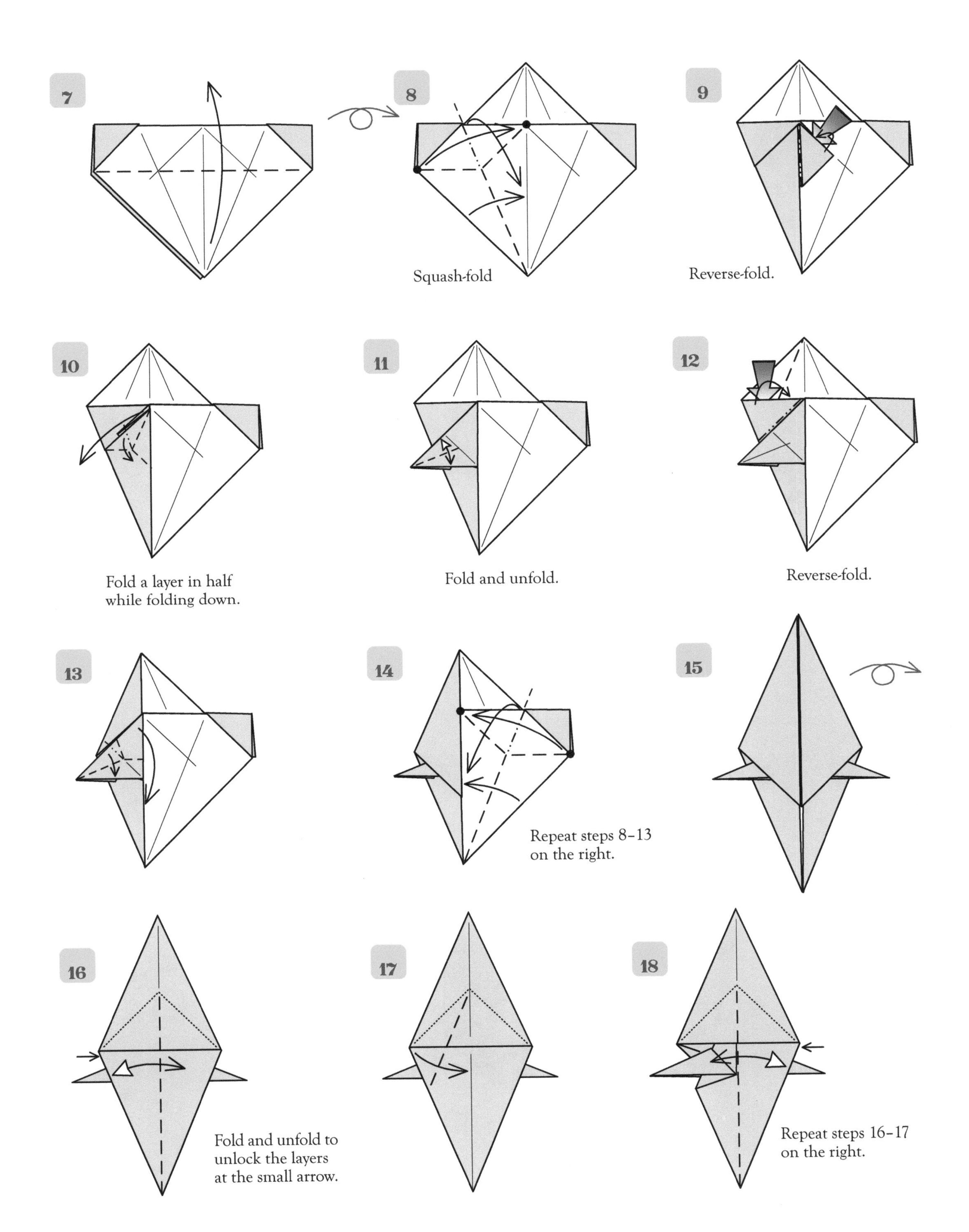
7
8
Squash-fold
9
Reverse-fold.
10
Fold a layer in half
while folding down.
11
Fold and unfold.
12
Reverse-fold.
13
14
Repeat steps 8–13
on the right.
15
16
Fold and unfold to
unlock the layers
at the small arrow.
17
18
Repeat steps 16–17
on the right.

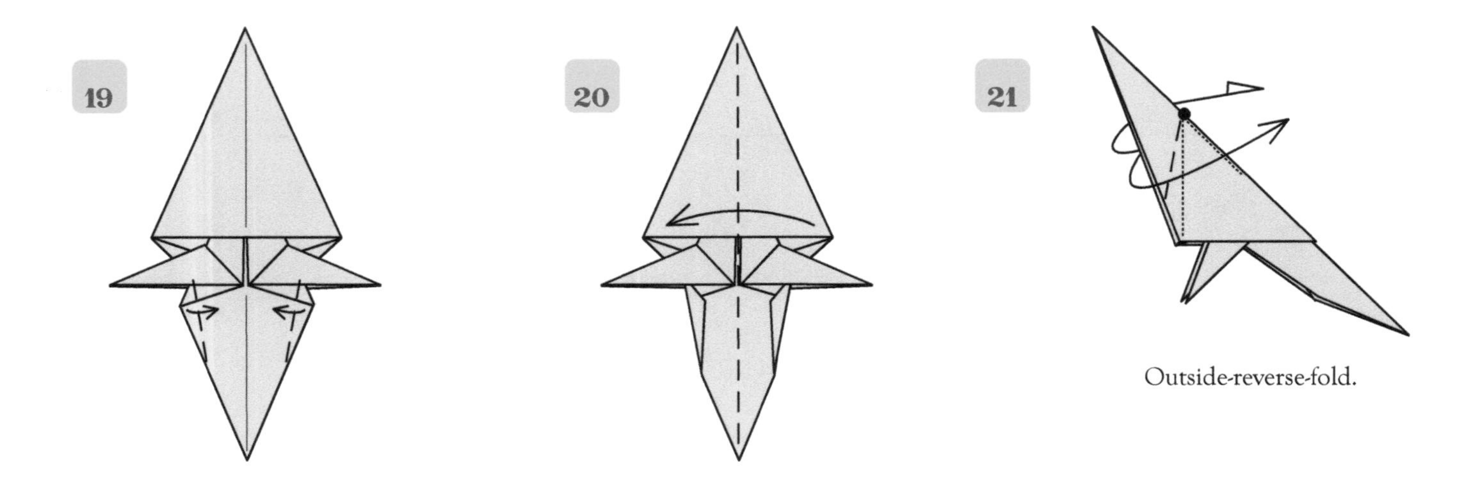

Outside-reverse-fold.

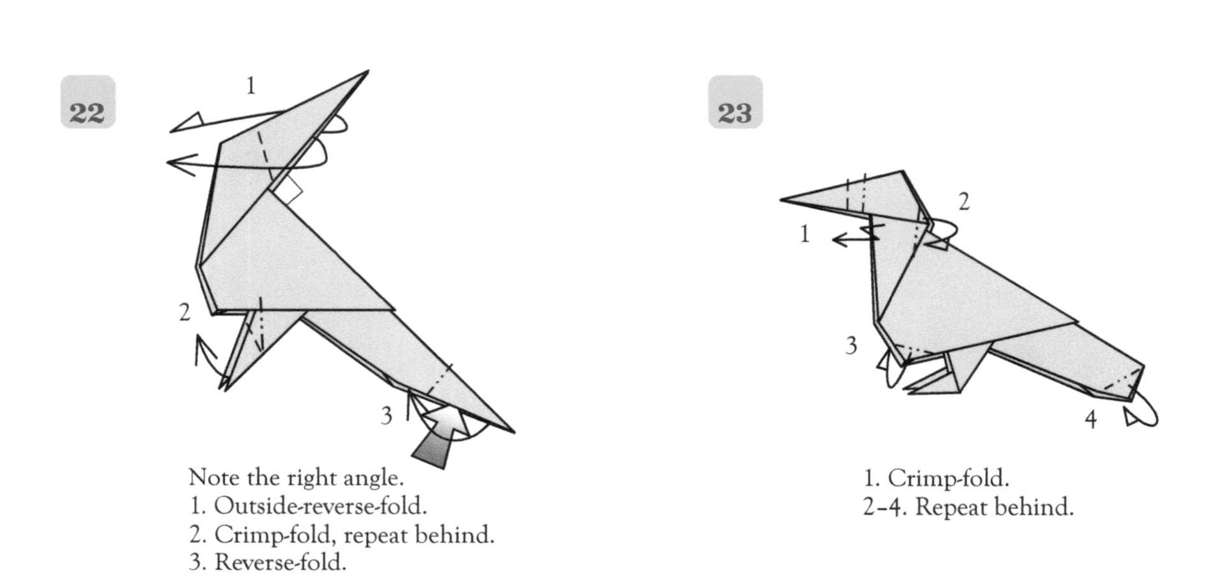

Note the right angle.
1. Outside-reverse-fold.
2. Crimp-fold, repeat behind.
3. Reverse-fold.

1. Crimp-fold.
2–4. Repeat behind.

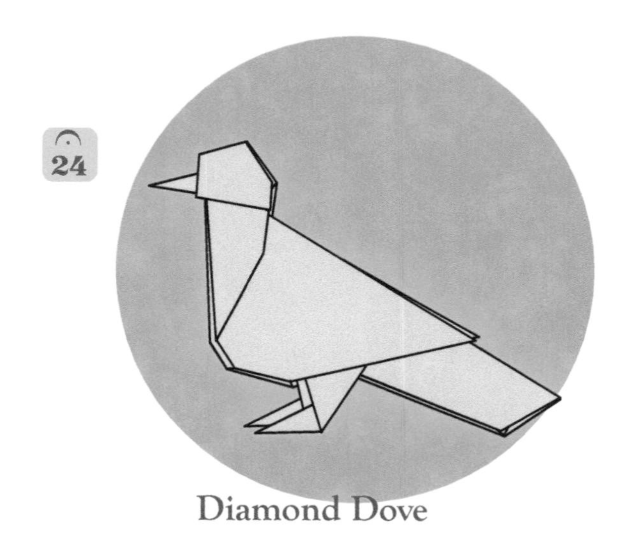

Diamond Dove

Budgerigar

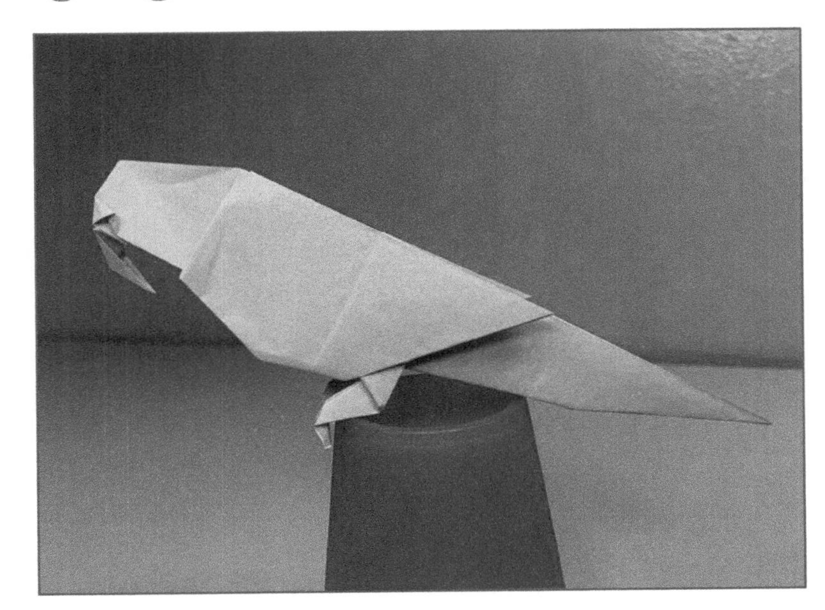

Many know this bird as the Common Parakeet, almost as popular a pet as dogs and cats. Their diet consists mainly of grass seeds, and they have been bred as pets since the mid 19th Century. The males can often mimic human speech.

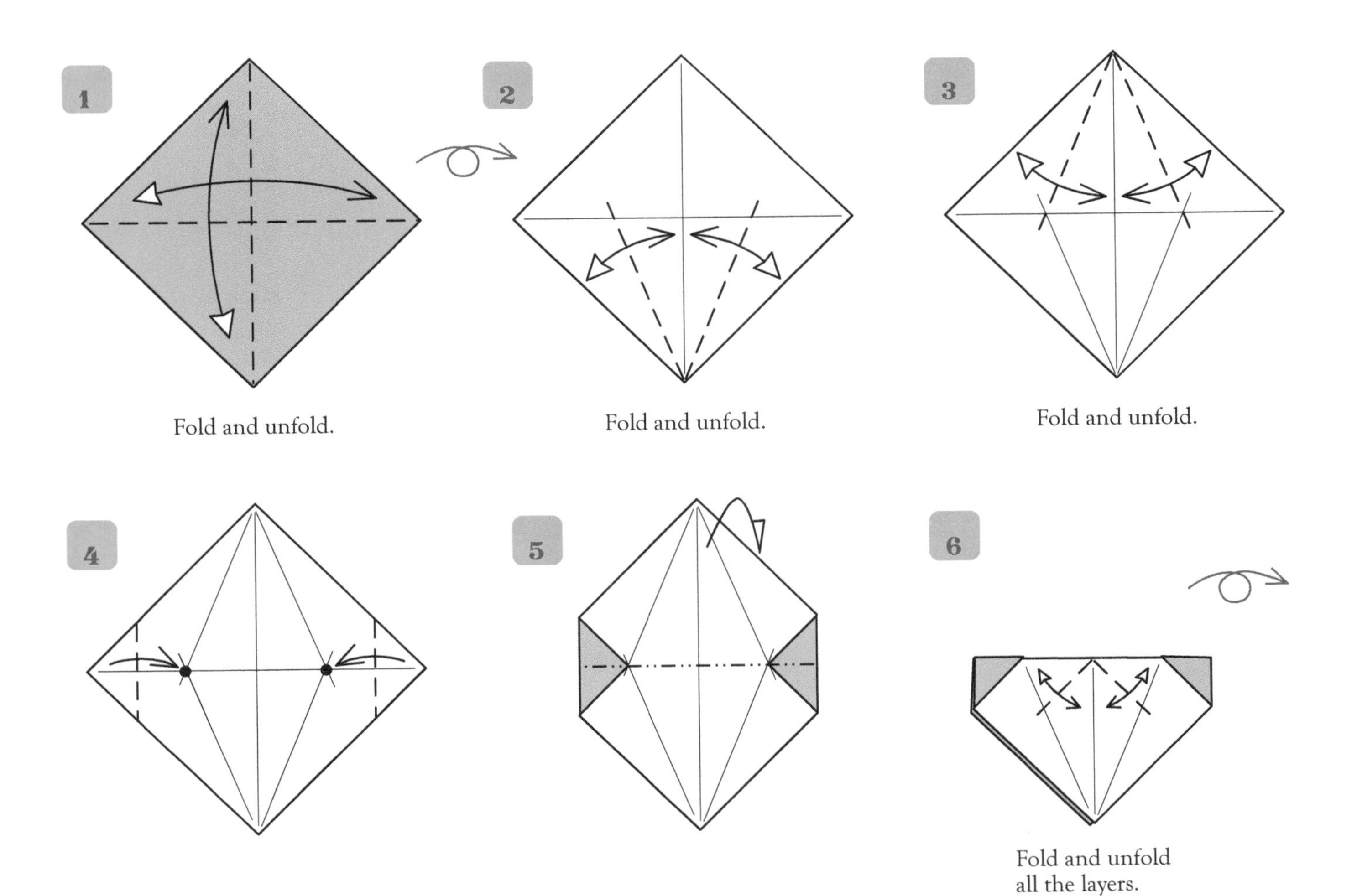

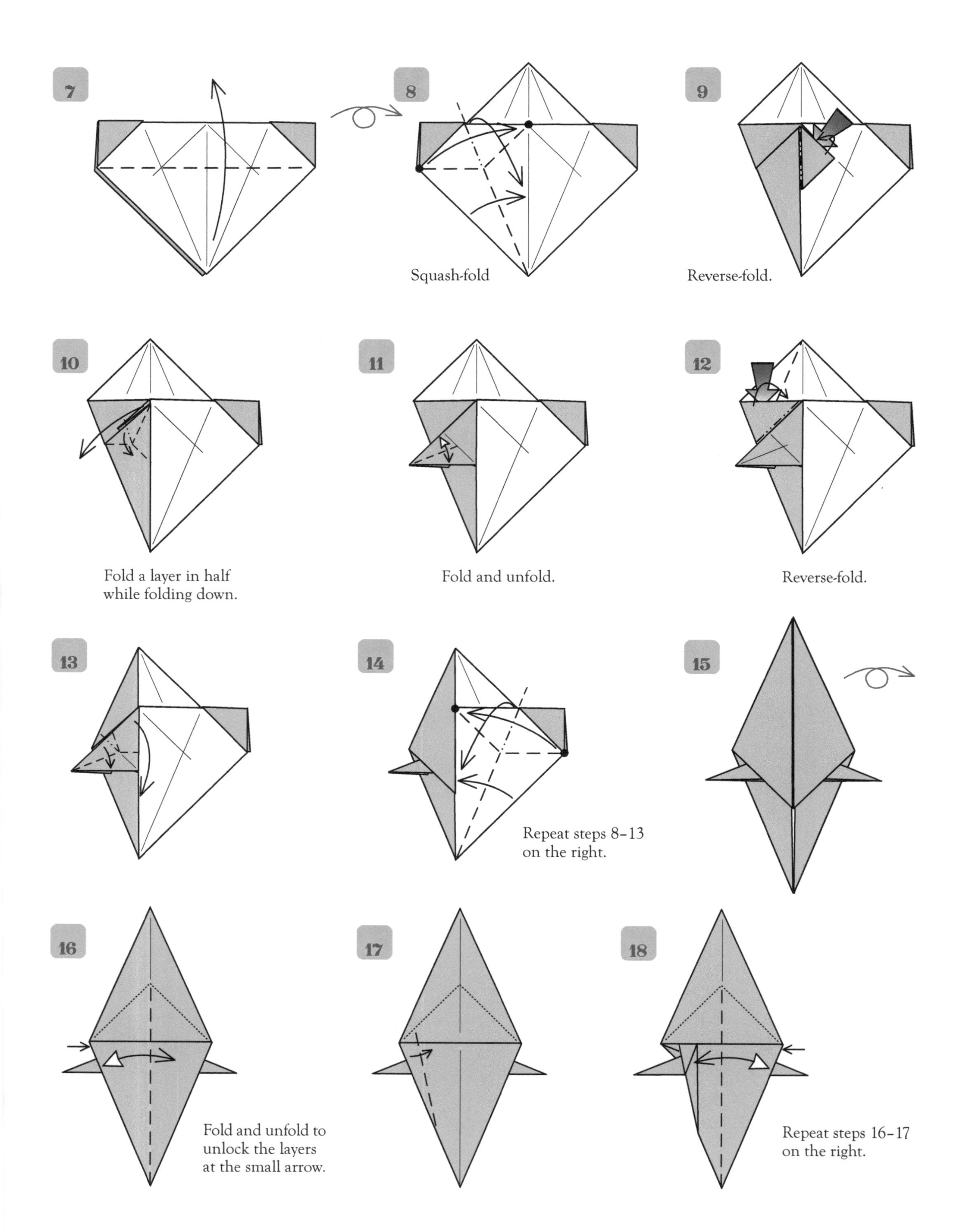
7
8
Squash-fold
9
Reverse-fold.
10
Fold a layer in half
while folding down.
11
Fold and unfold.
12
Reverse-fold.
13
14
Repeat steps 8–13
on the right.
15
16
Fold and unfold to
unlock the layers
at the small arrow.
17
18
Repeat steps 16–17
on the right.

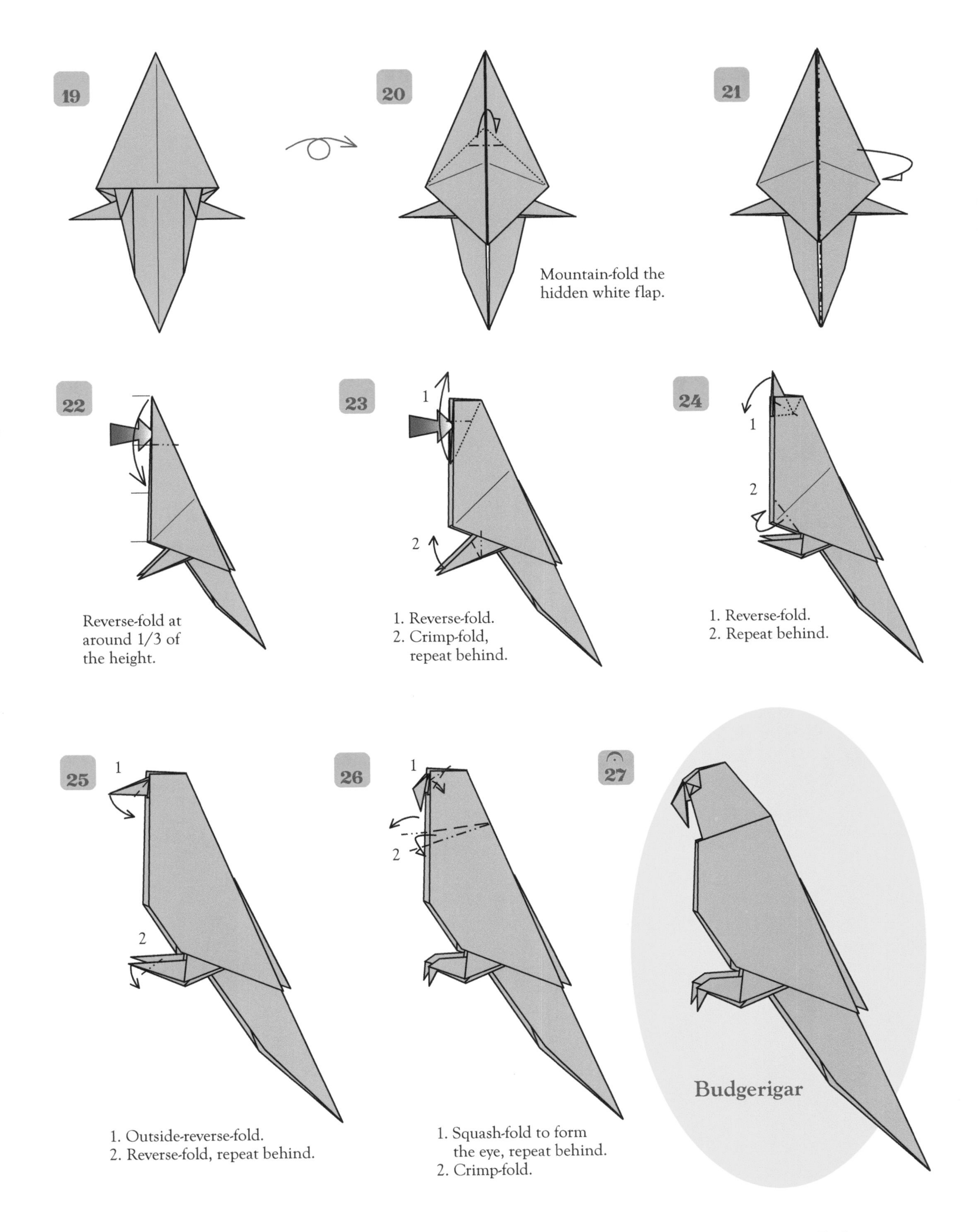
19
20
21
Mountain-fold the
hidden white flap.
22
23
24
1
2
1
2
Reverse-fold at
around 1/3 of
the height.
1. Reverse-fold.
2. Crimp-fold,
repeat behind.
1. Reverse-fold.
2. Repeat behind.
25
26
27
1
2
1
2
1. Outside-reverse-fold.
2. Reverse-fold, repeat behind.
1. Squash-fold to form
the eye, repeat behind.
2. Crimp-fold.
Budgerigar

White-faced Heron

A common bird in Australia and New Zealand, these herons have a grey body, white head and yellow legs. They can sometimes be found perching on fence posts and rooftops and primarily eat small aquatic creatures such as frogs and fish.

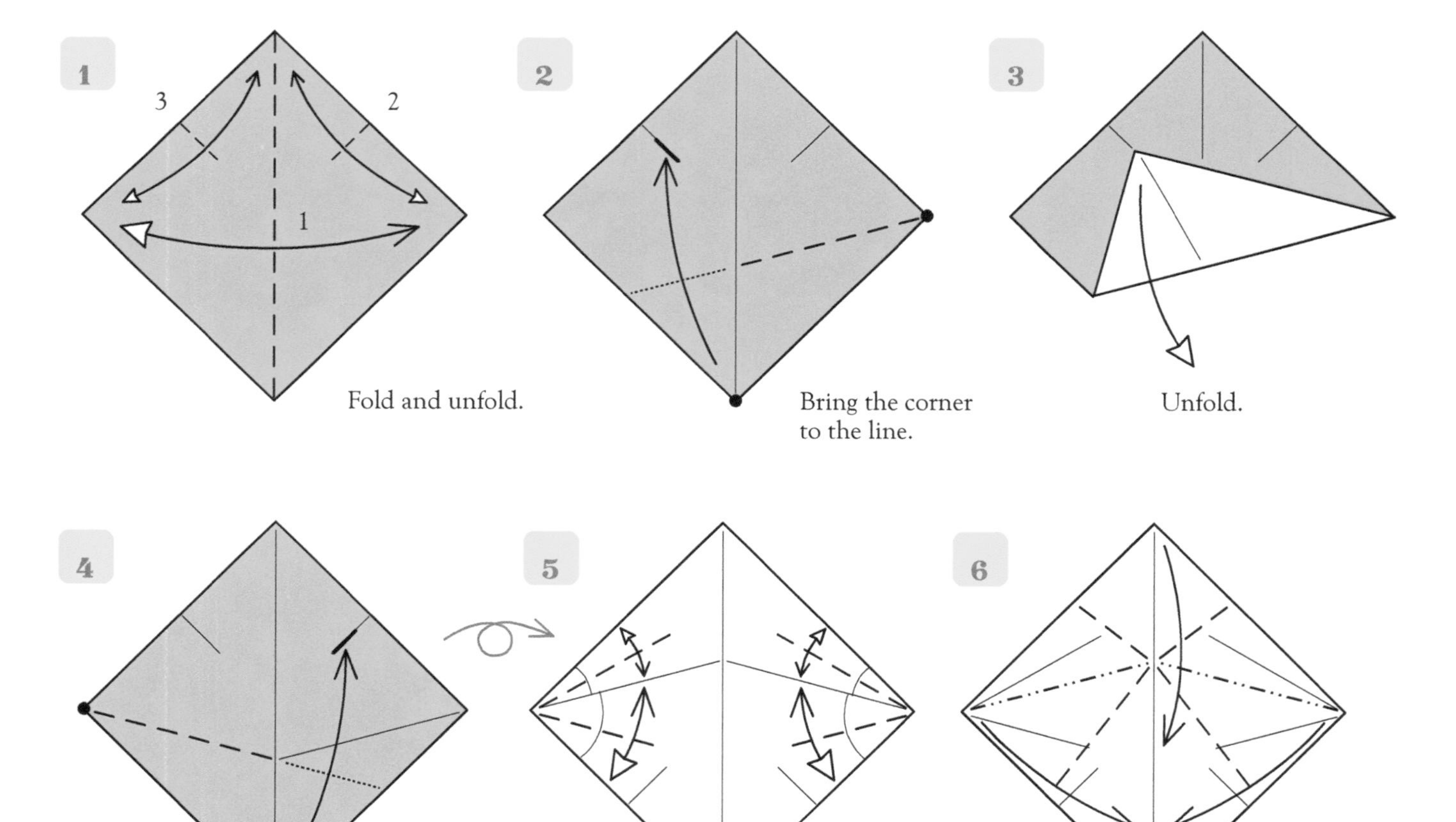

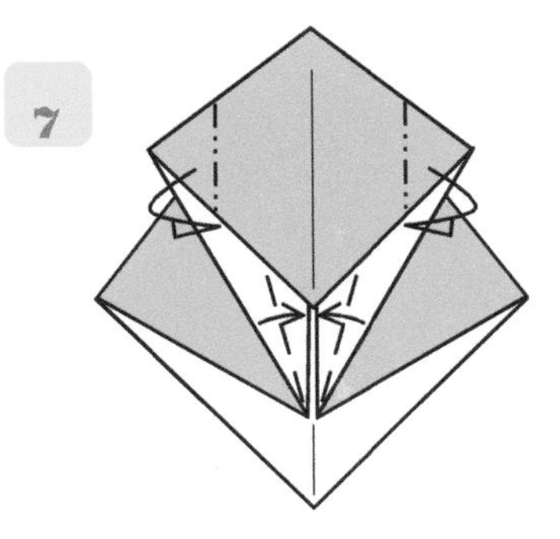

Make reverse folds. Valley-fold along the creases. The mountain fold lines are vertical.

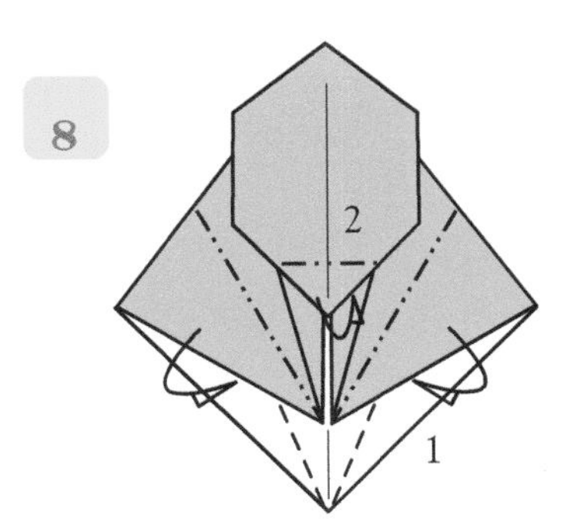

1. Make reverse folds. Mountain-fold along the creases.
2. Mountain-fold.

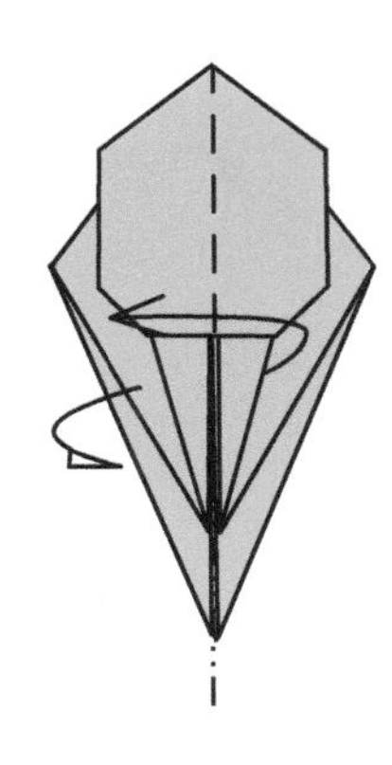

Rotate 90°.

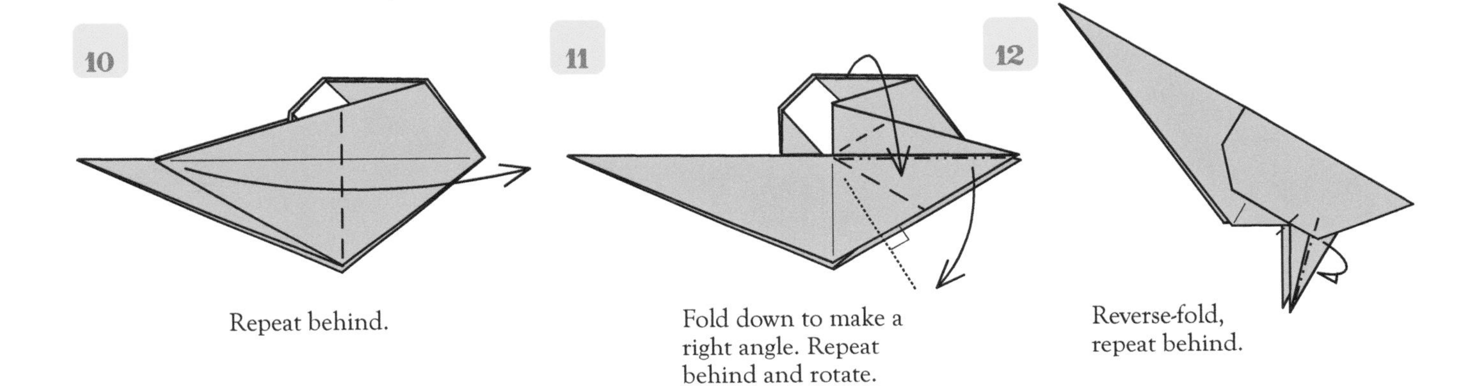

Repeat behind.

Fold down to make a right angle. Repeat behind and rotate.

Reverse-fold, repeat behind.

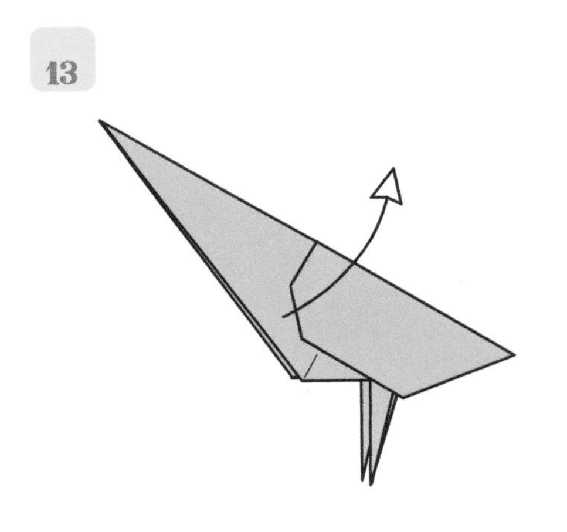

Unfold and rotate.

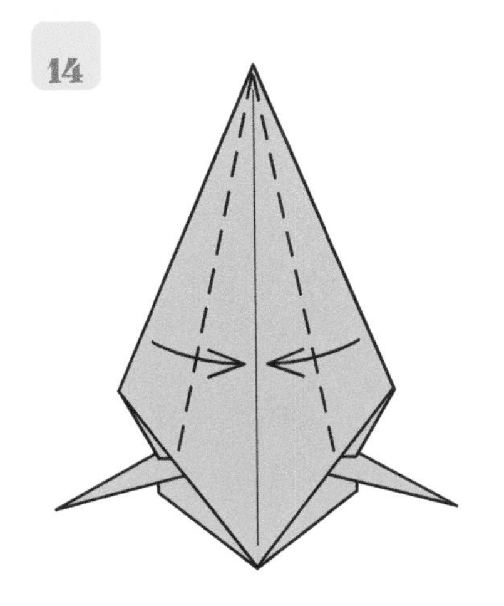

Fold to the center.

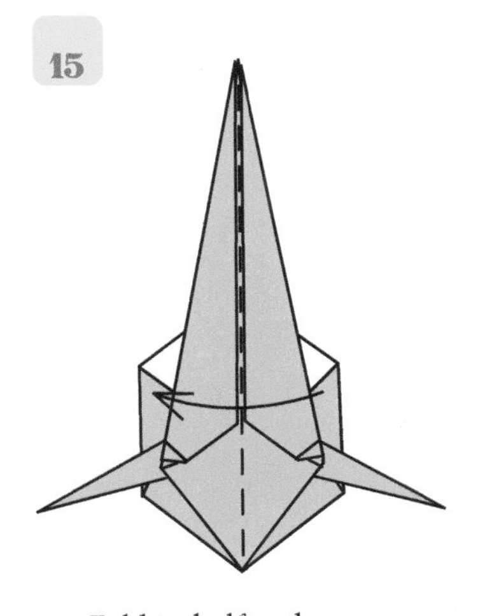

Fold in half and rotate.

16

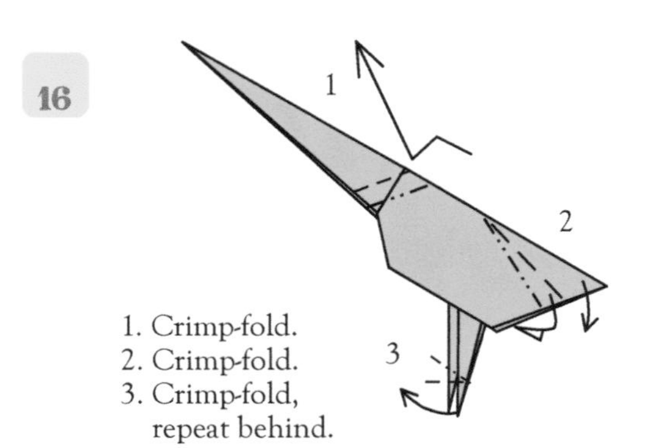

1. Crimp-fold.
2. Crimp-fold.
3. Crimp-fold, repeat behind.

17

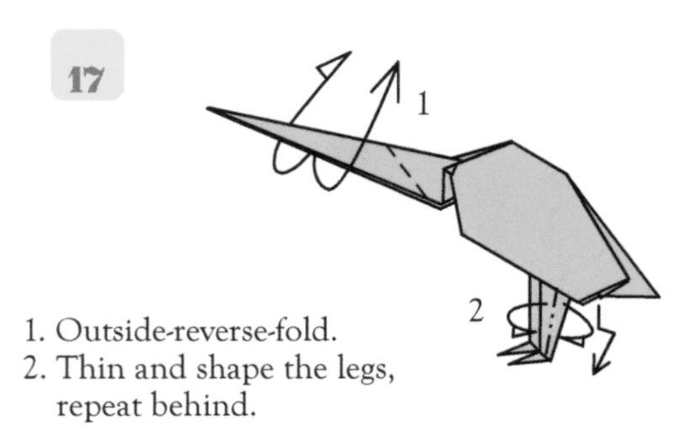

1. Outside-reverse-fold.
2. Thin and shape the legs, repeat behind.

18

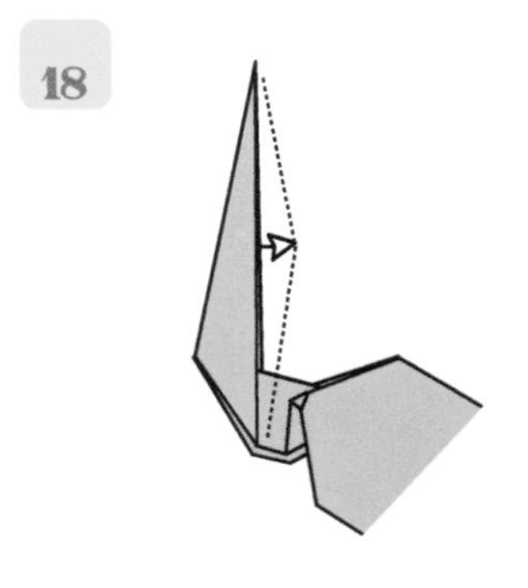

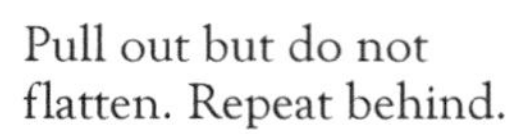

Pull out but do not flatten. Repeat behind.

19

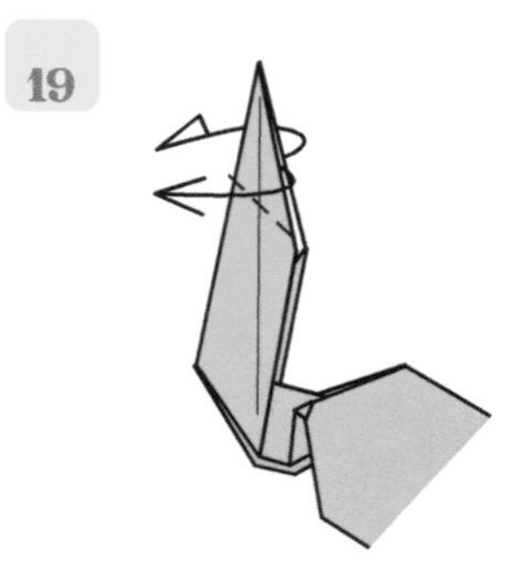

Outside-reverse-fold.

20

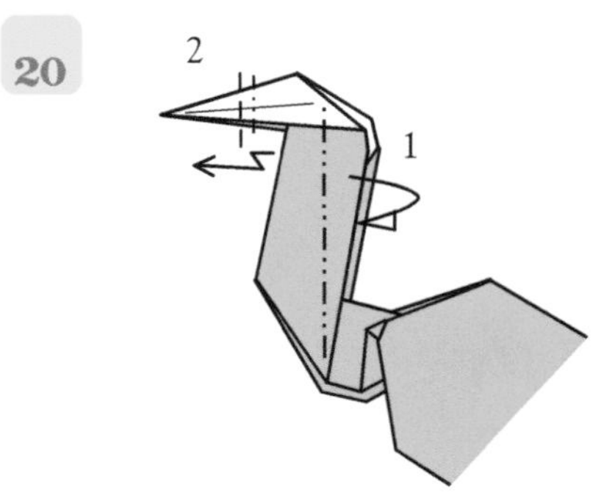

1. Slide the paper back inside, repeat behind.
2. Crimp-fold.

21

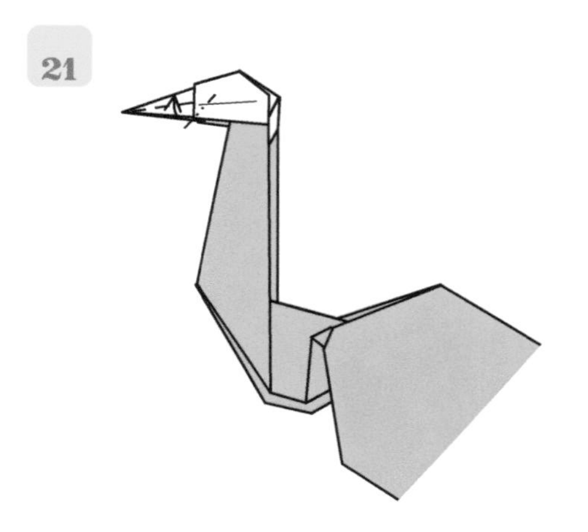

Fold up, repeat behind.

22

White-faced Heron

Australian Magpie

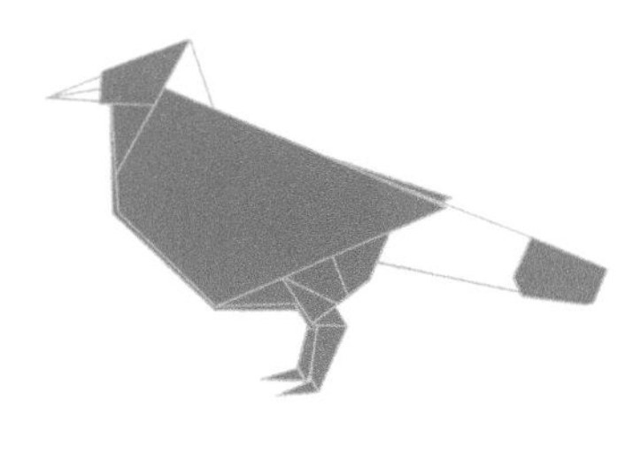

Sporting black and white pulmage, these birds can recognize individual humans and are also fine songbirds. They will eat insects and small invertebrates such as beetles and earthworms. They are intelligent and have been seen to engage in problem solving behavior.

1

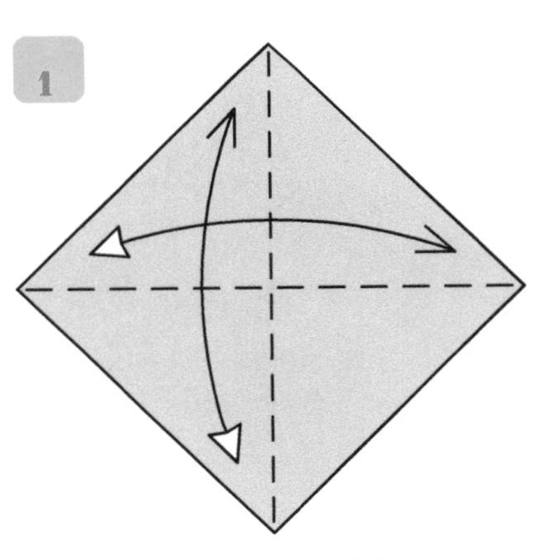

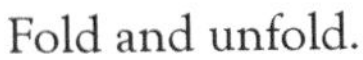
Fold and unfold.

2

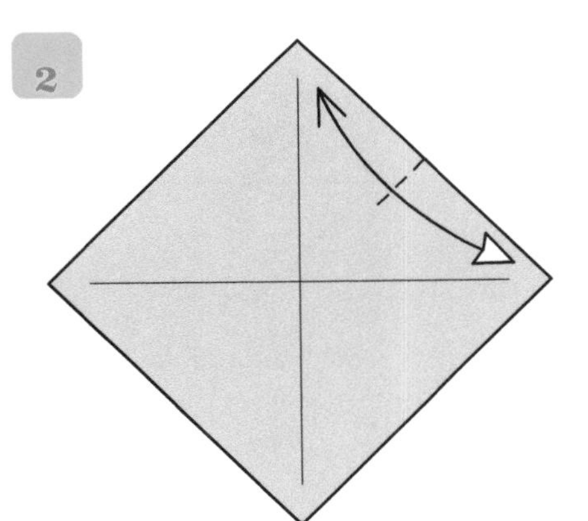

Fold and unfold on the edge.

3

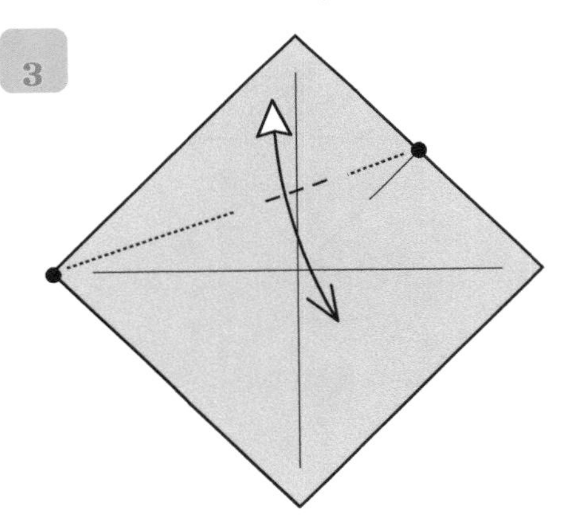

Fold and unfold on the diagonal.

4

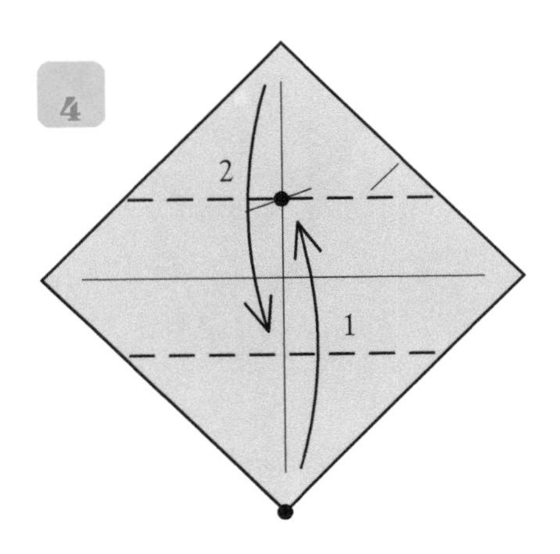

5

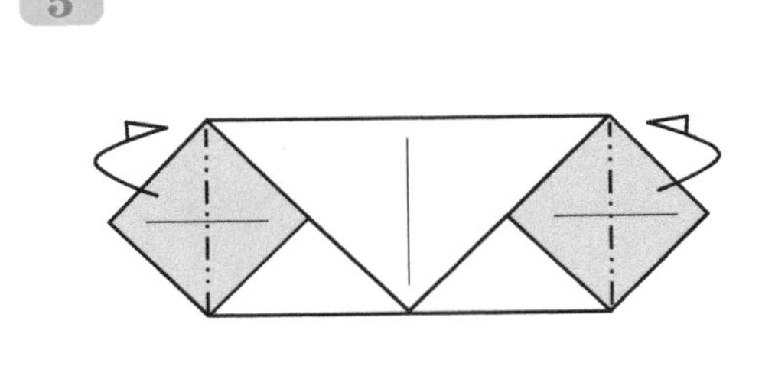

6

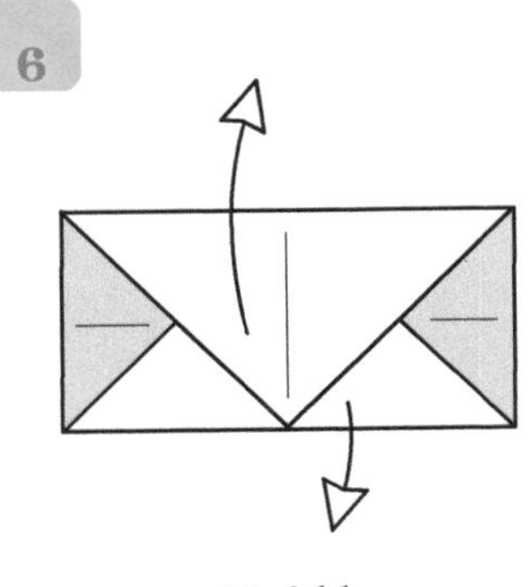

Unfold.

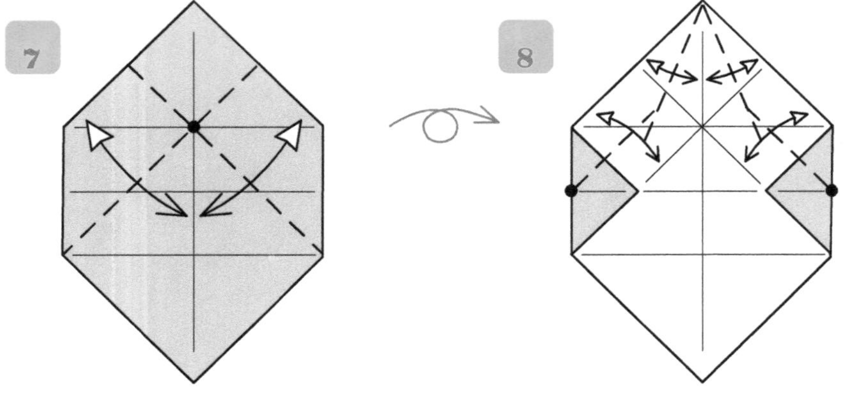

Fold and unfold.

Fold and unfold.

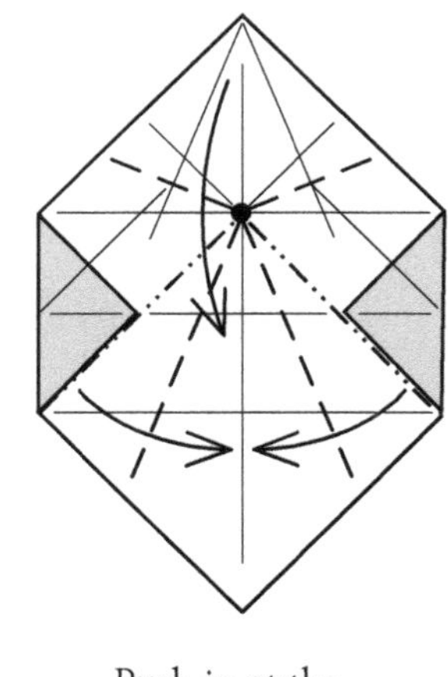

Push in at the dot and flatten.

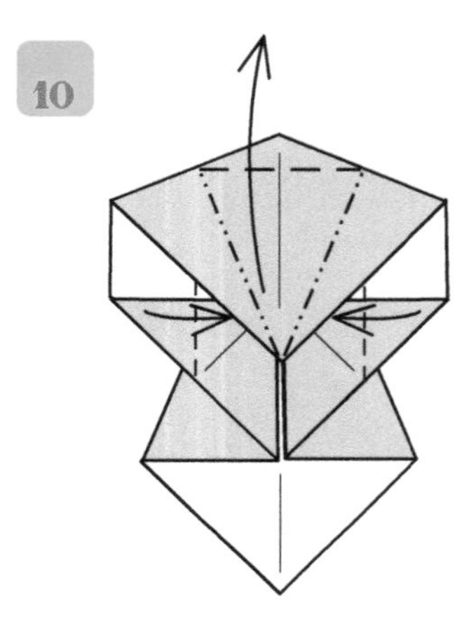

Petal-fold.

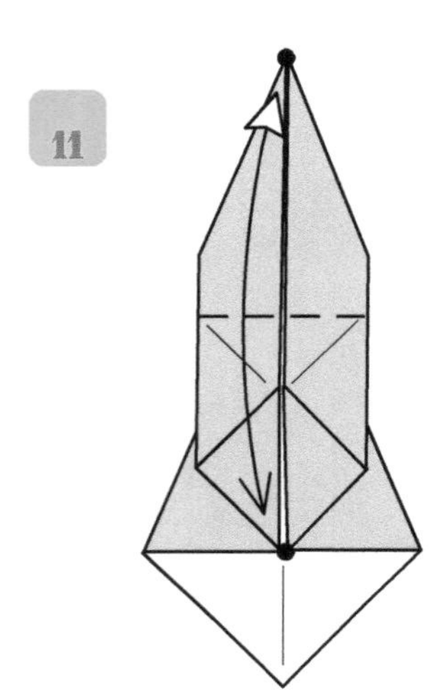

Fold and unfold.

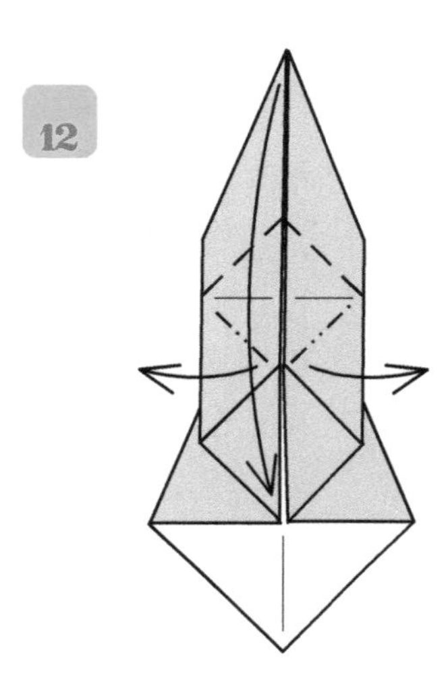

Pull out from the center and fold down.

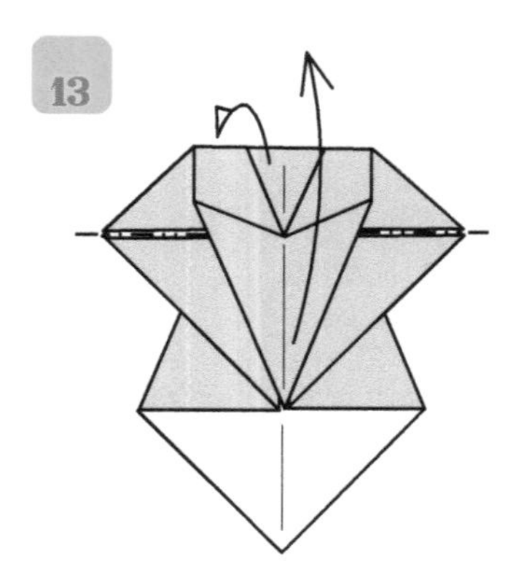

14

Make reverse folds.

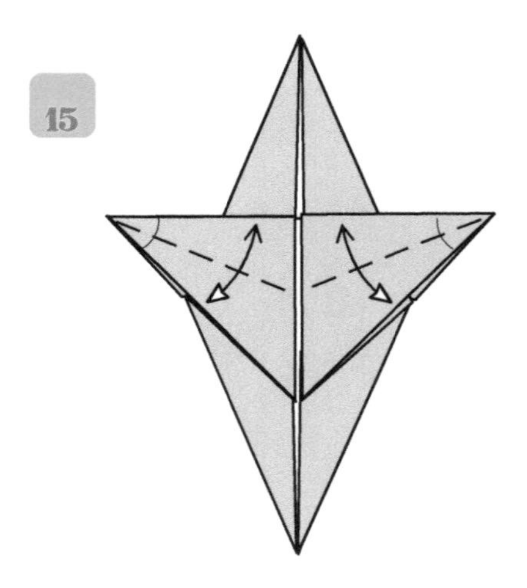

Fold and unfold the top flap.

16

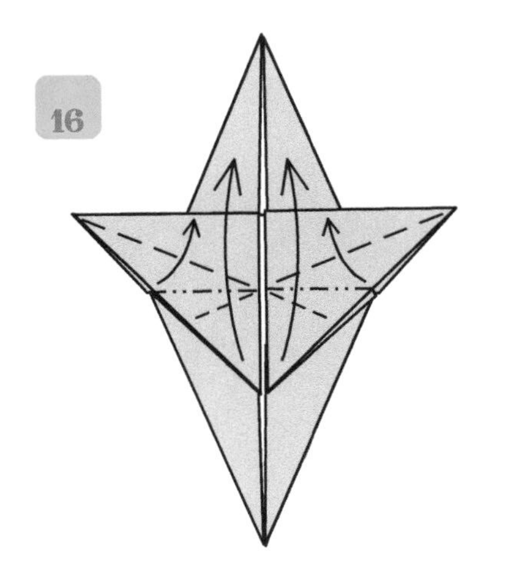

17

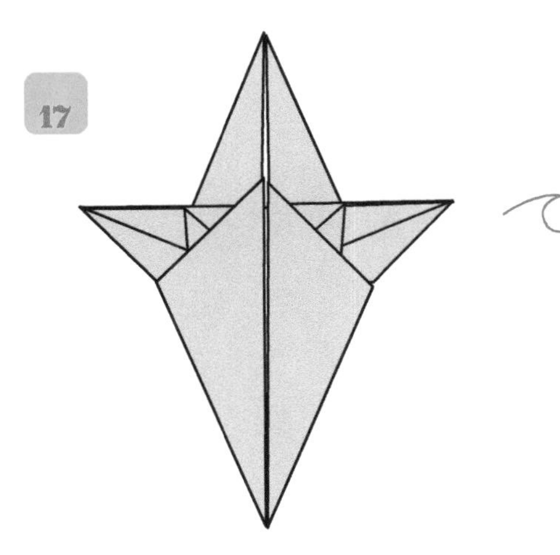

18

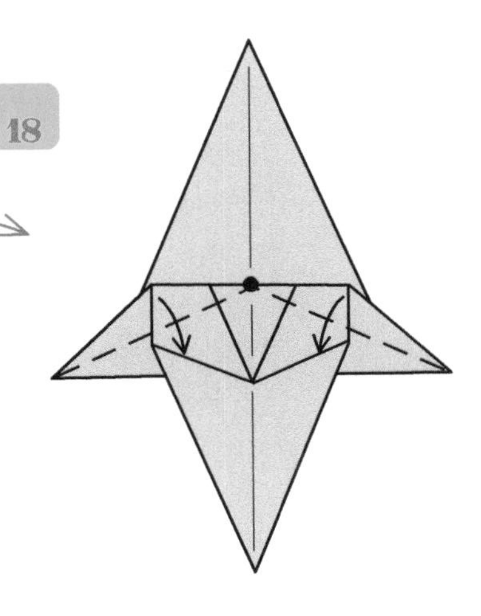

Rotate 180°.

19

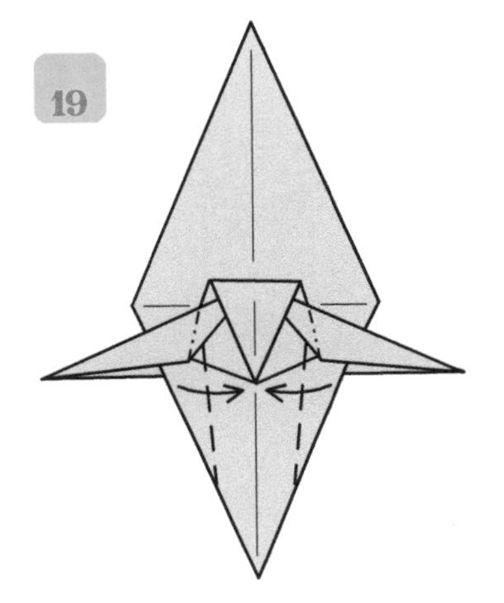

Make reverse folds.

20

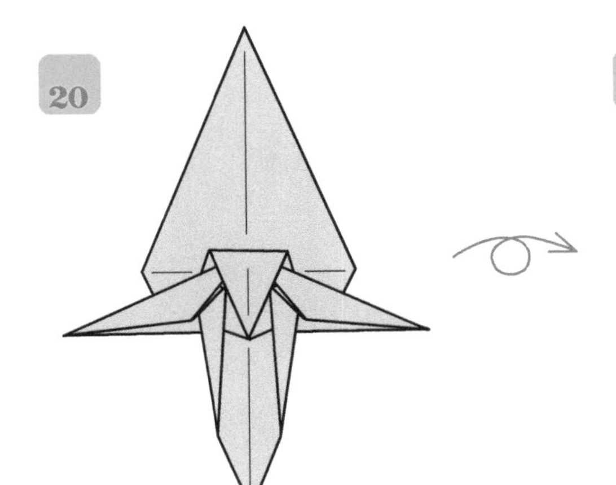

21

Unfold on the left and right and fold up at the bottom.

22

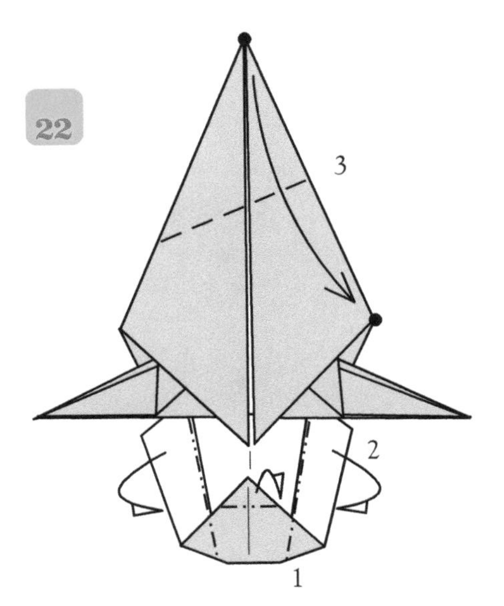

1. Fold behind.
2. Fold behind.
3. The dots will meet.

23

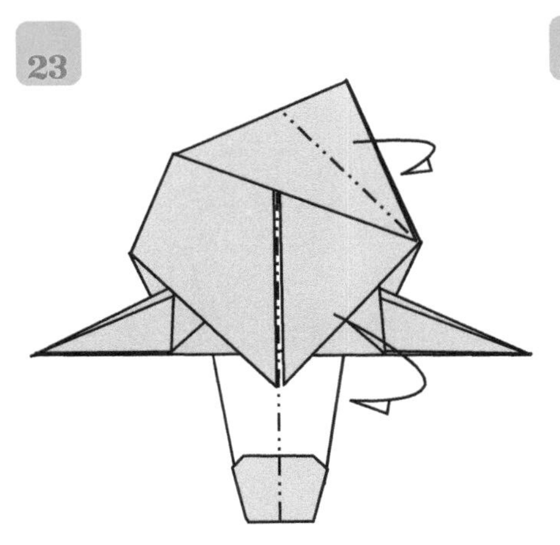

Fold in half and rotate.

24

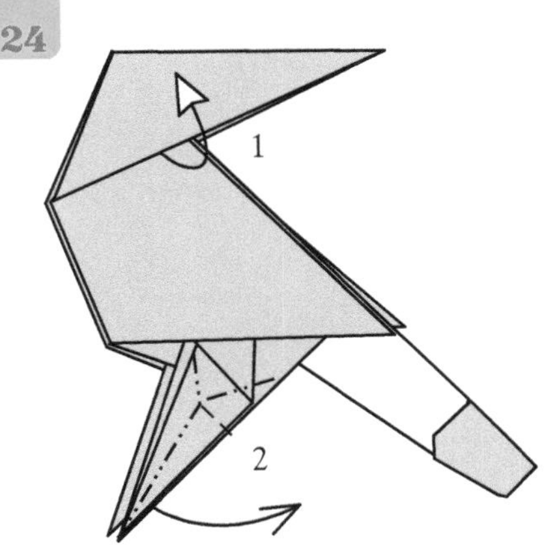

1. Wrap around.
2. Double-rabbit-ear.
Repeat behind.

25

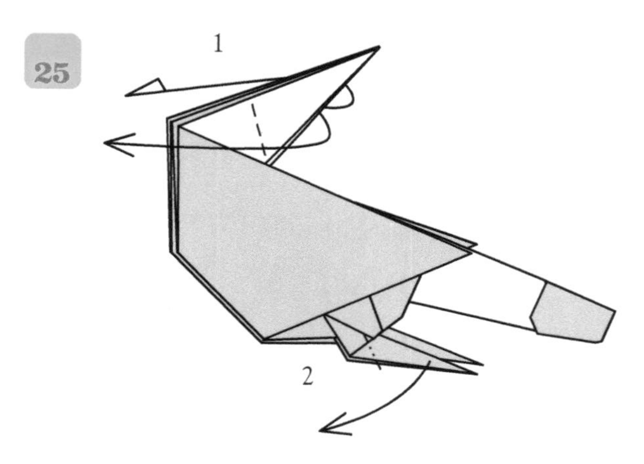

1. Outside-reverse-fold.
2. Reverse-fold, repeat behind.

26

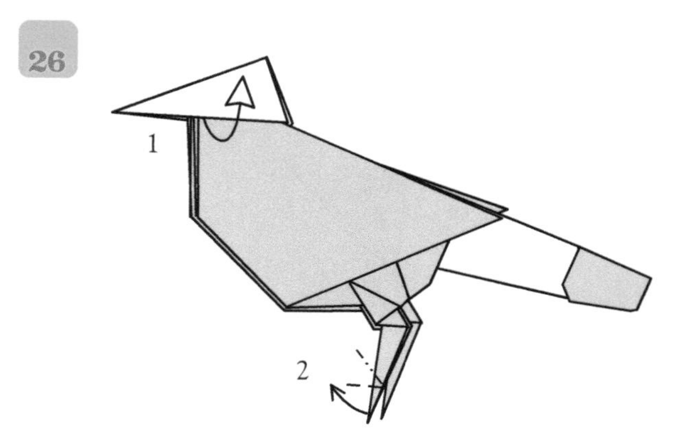

1. Wrap around.
2. Crimp-fold.
Repeat behind.

27

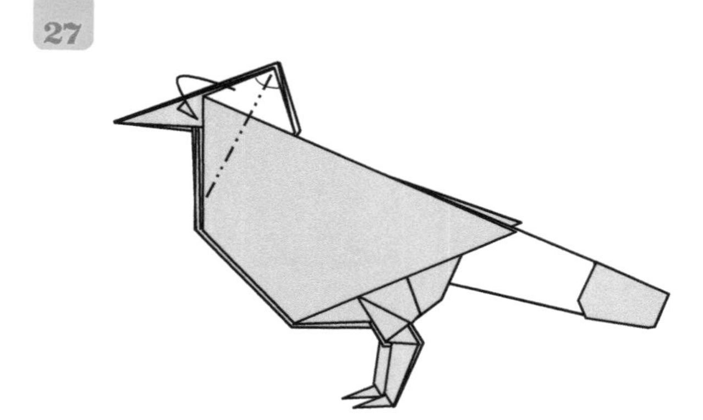

Repeat behind.

28

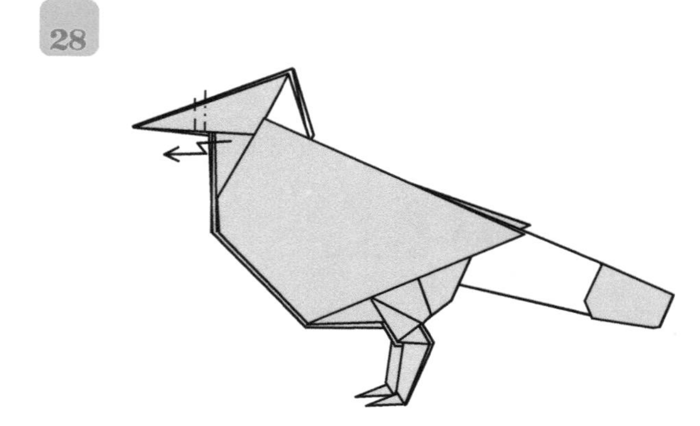

Crimp-fold.

29

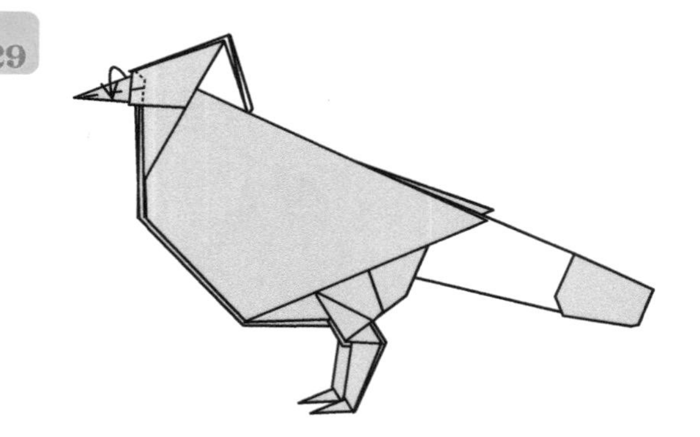

Fold the top layer in half. Repeat behind.

30

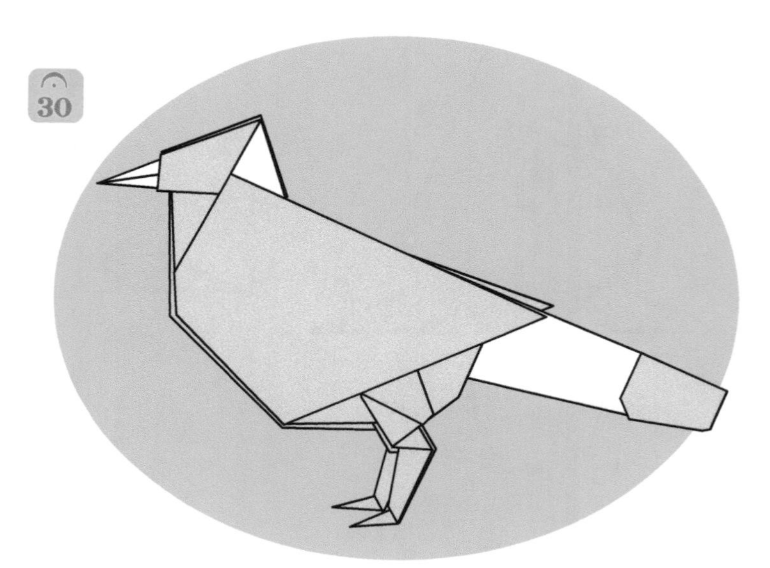

Australian Magpie

Third Movement

Minuet of Colorful Cubes with a Trio of Shapes Based on Cubes

As a basic shape, the cube is ornamented with color-change patterns. Here is a collection of a cube with five colorful cubes. Sporting complex patterns, each can be folded in under 25 steps. These cubes make elegant stands to display the mammals, birds, and bugs from the other movements. The trio shows more shapes based on the cube.

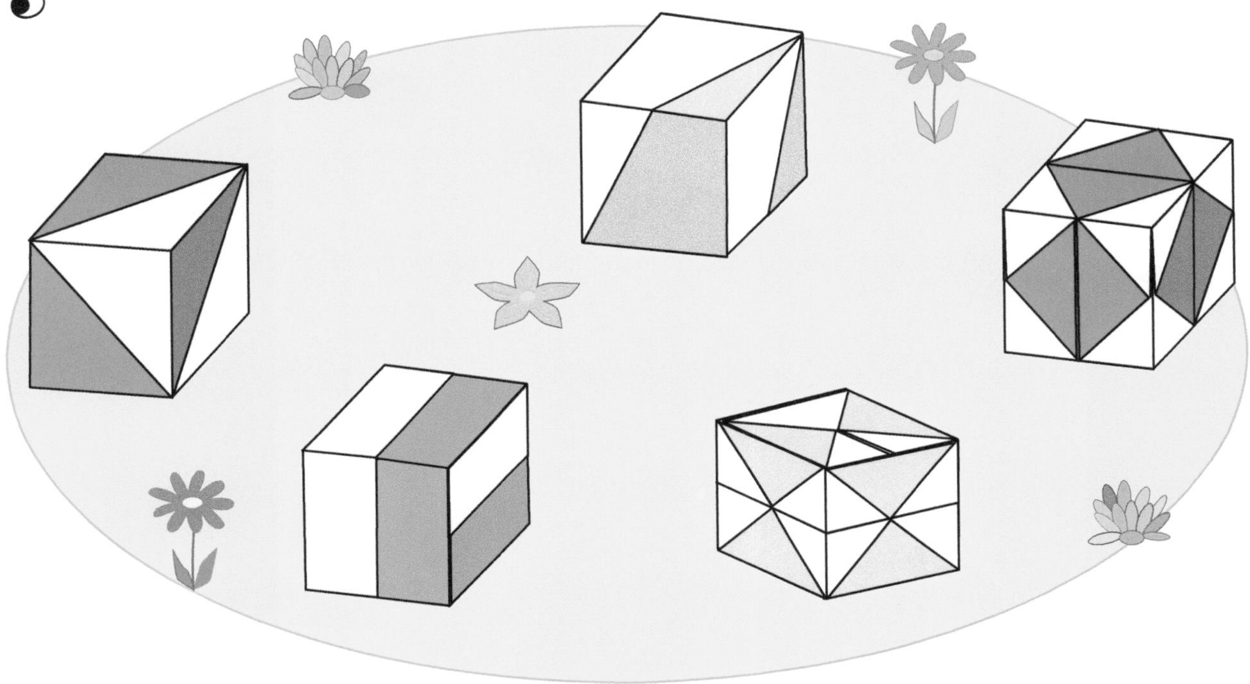

Cube

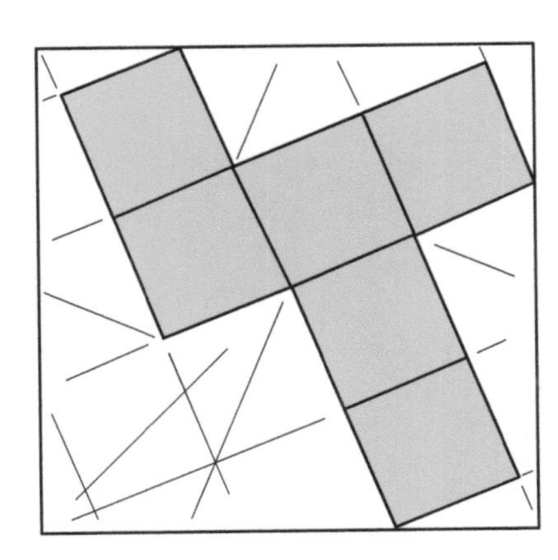

As one of five Platonic Solids, Plato believed the Cube represented Earth becuase of its stability. This folding method produces a larger cube than the traditional waterbomb cube. The crease pattern shows 3/4 square symmetry.

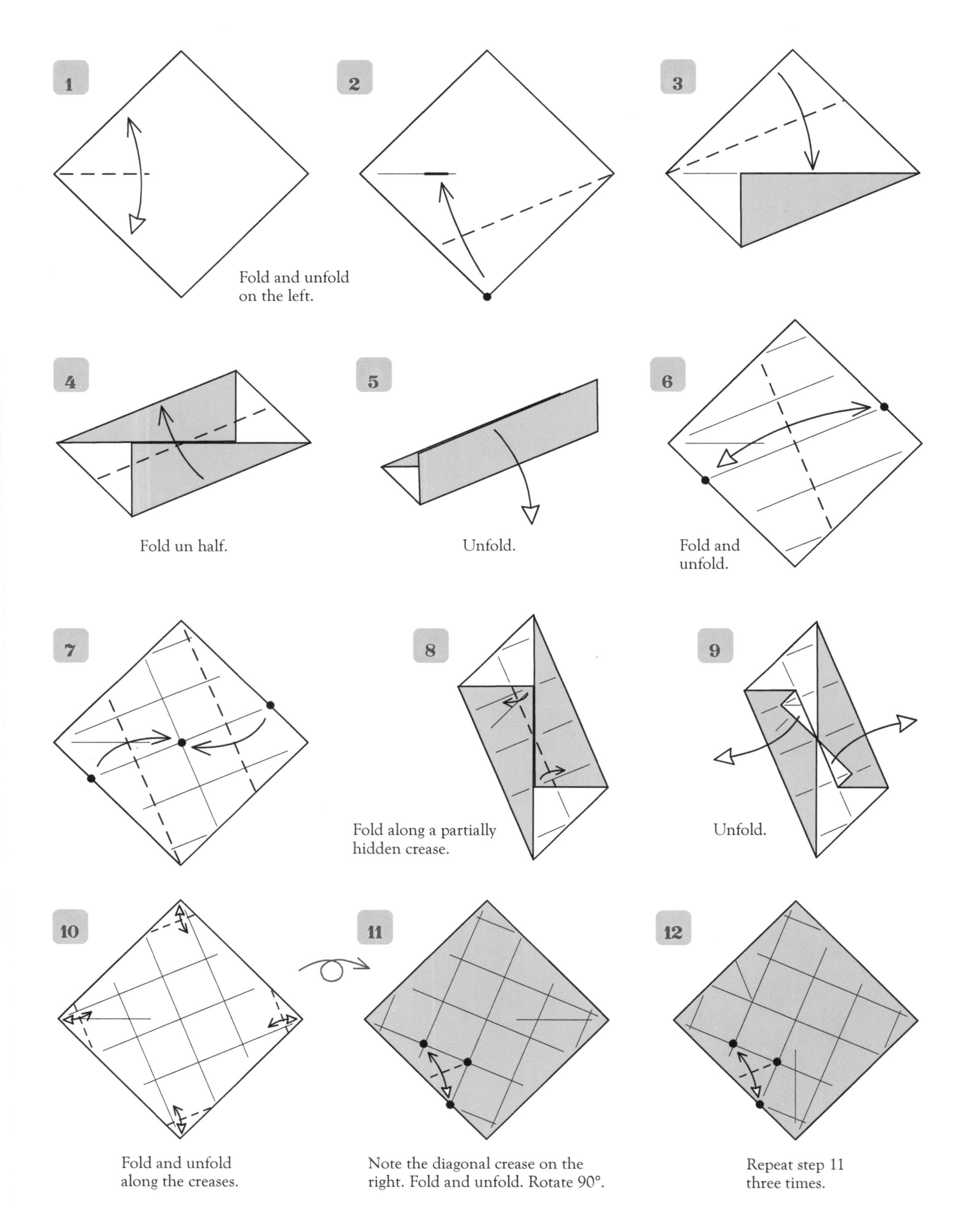
1
Fold and unfold
on the left.
2
3
4
Fold un half.
5
Unfold.
6
Fold and
unfold.
7
8
Fold along a partially
hidden crease.
9
Unfold.
10
Fold and unfold
along the creases.
11
Note the diagonal crease on the
right. Fold and unfold. Rotate 90°.
12
Repeat step 11
three times.

13

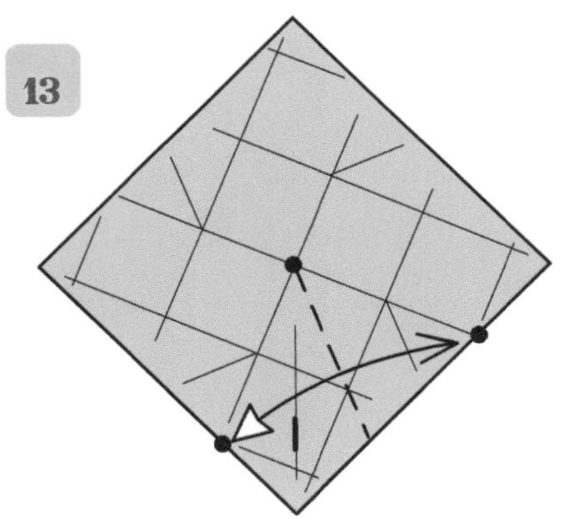

Note the orientation of the vertical crease by the bottom. Fold and unfold.

14

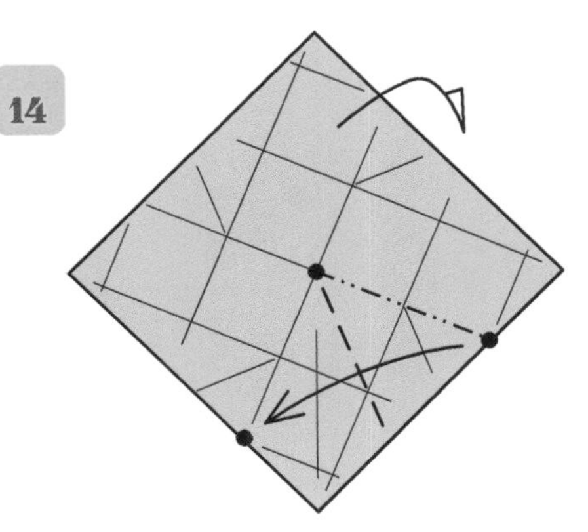

Puff out at the dot in the center as the model becomes 3D.

15

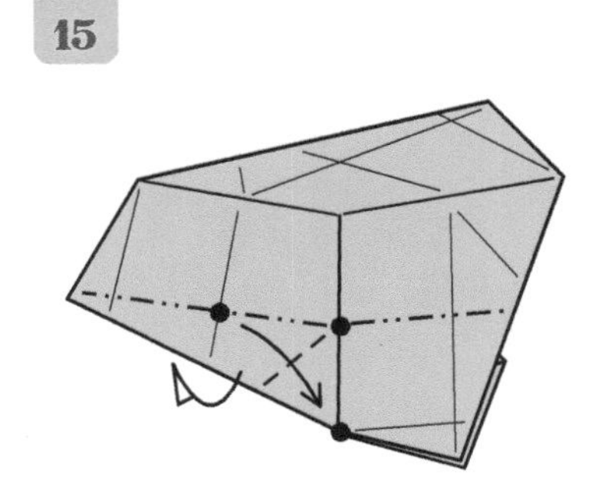

Puff out at the dot in the center and flatten inside.

16

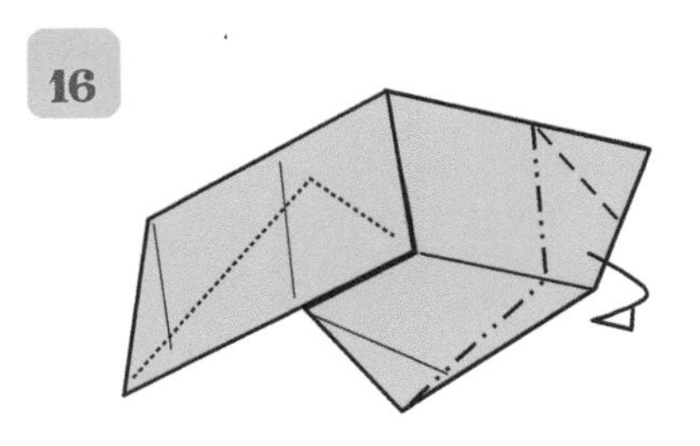

Flatten the inside paper shown with the x-ray lines. Repeat step 15 two times. Rotate the loose corners to the top. One side has more layers.

17

Fold and unfold. Repeat on the other two flaps.

18

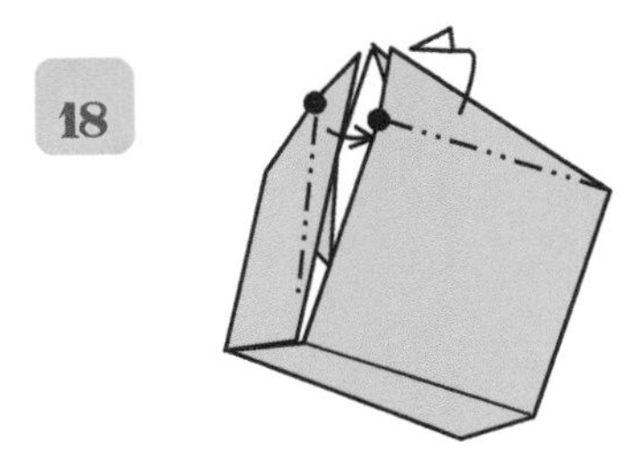

Interlock the three tabs to close and lock the model. Two of three dots are shown. The dots will meet.

19

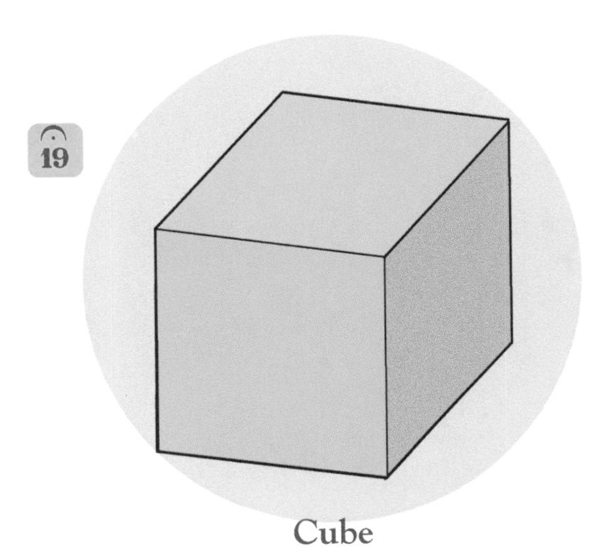

Cube

Cube of Triangles

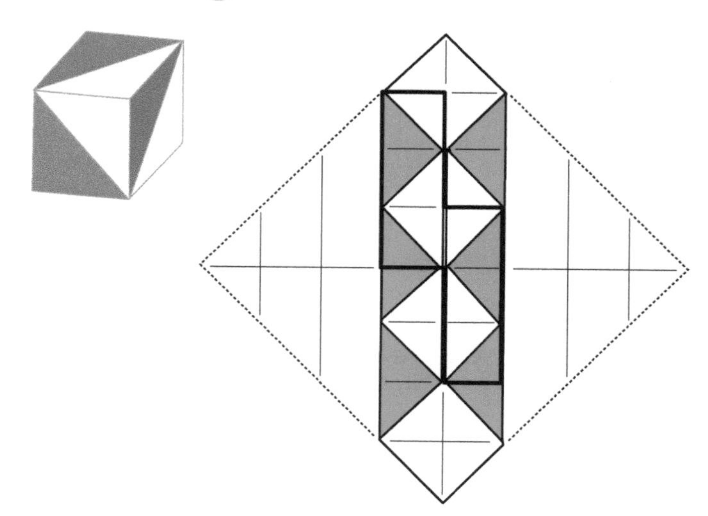

Each of the six faces of this cube show two triangles of different colors. Two bands of three squares are used in the layout. This is close to odd symmetry. In only 14 steps, this color-change cube takes fewer steps than the first cube.

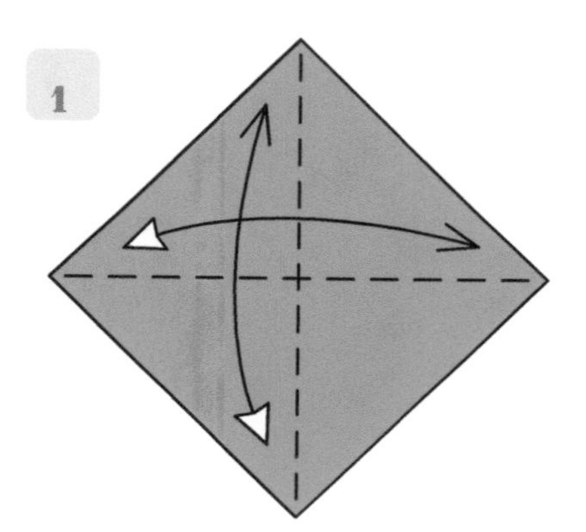

Fold and unfold.

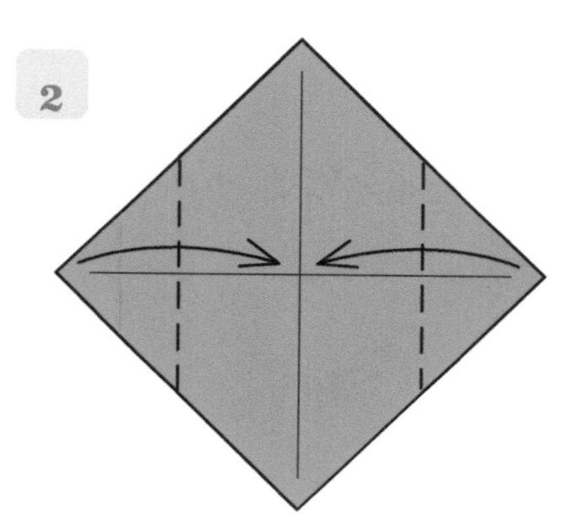

Fold to the center.

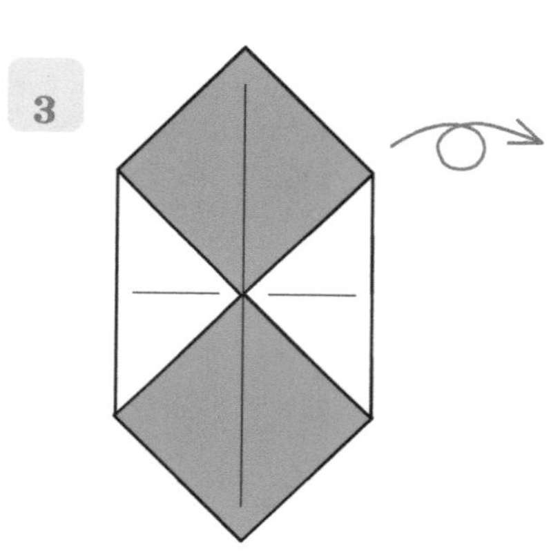

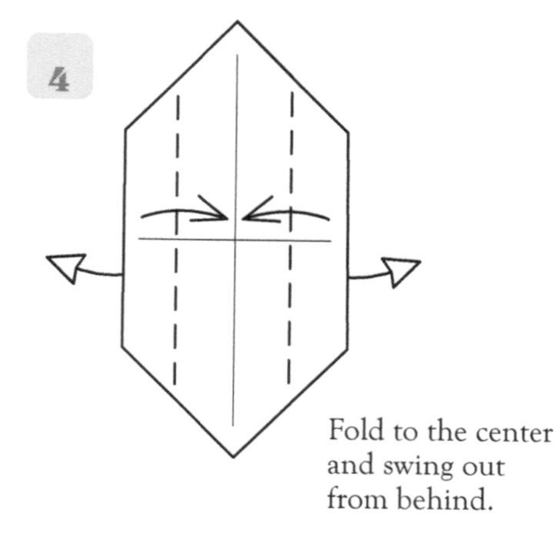

Fold to the center and swing out from behind.

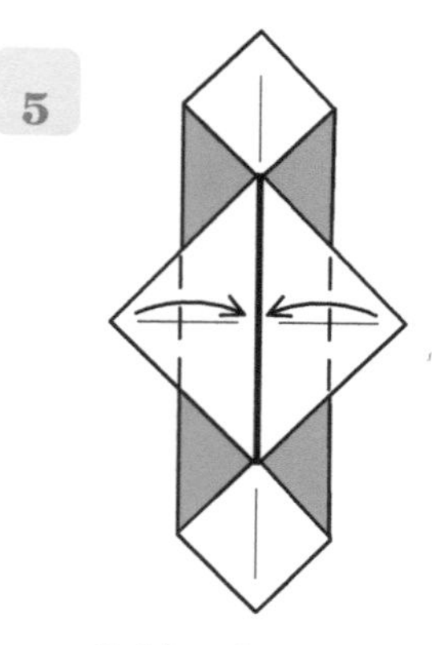

Fold to the center.

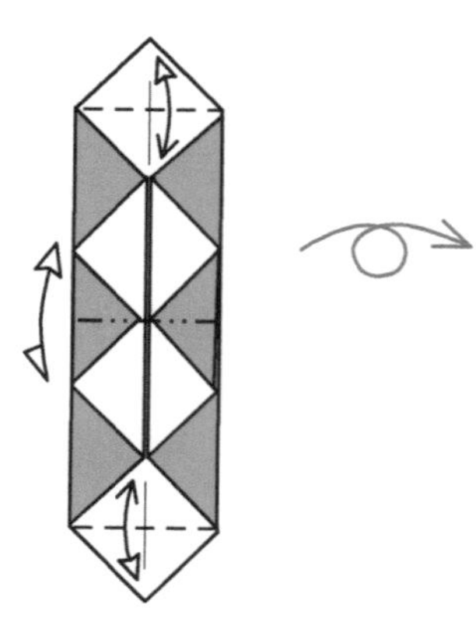

Fold and unfold.

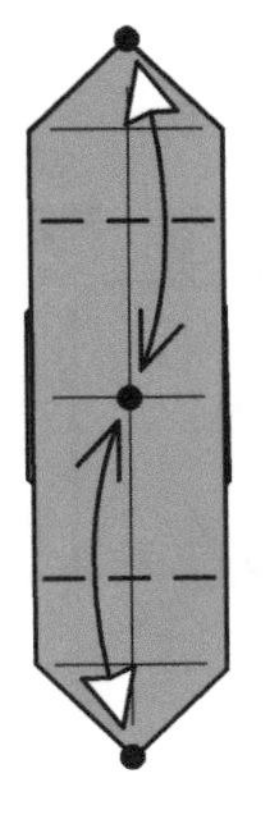

Fold and unfold.

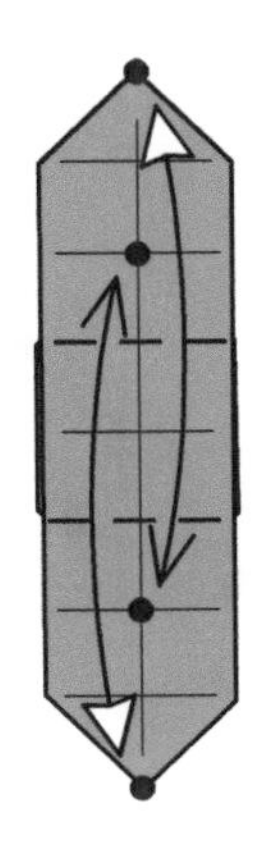

Fold and unfold.

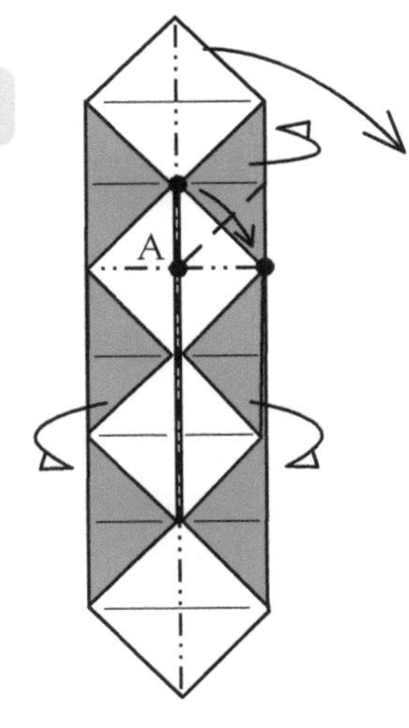

Puff out at dot A. The model will become 3D.

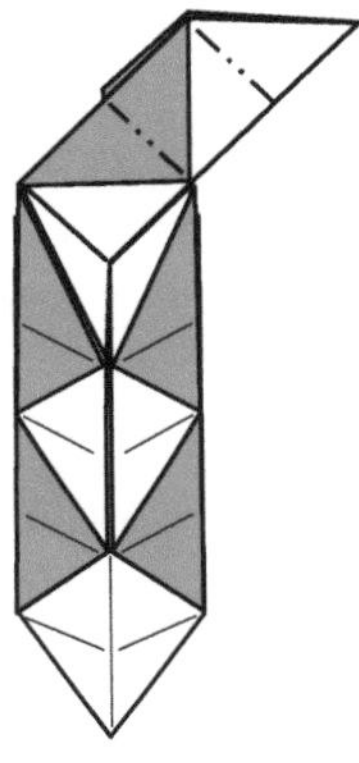

Fold and unfold along the creases. Rotate the top to the bottom.

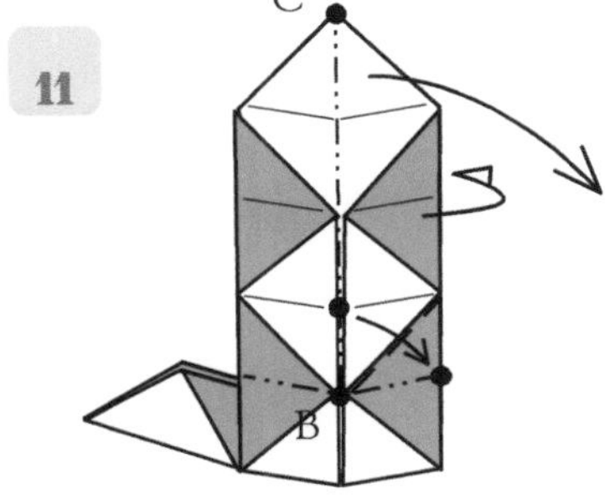

Puff out at dot B. Rotate so dot C goes to the top.

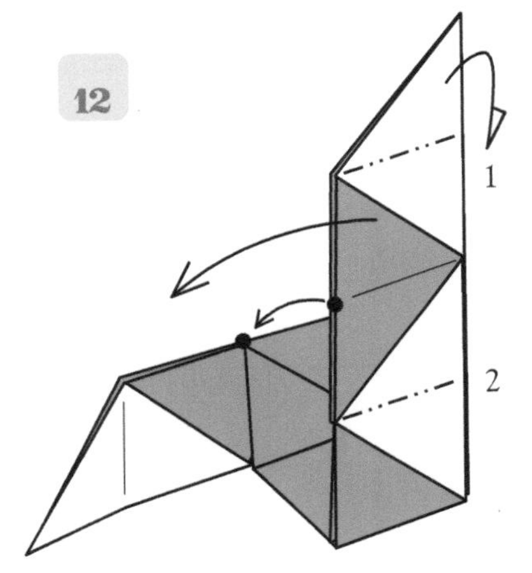

1. Fold behind.
2. The dots will meet.

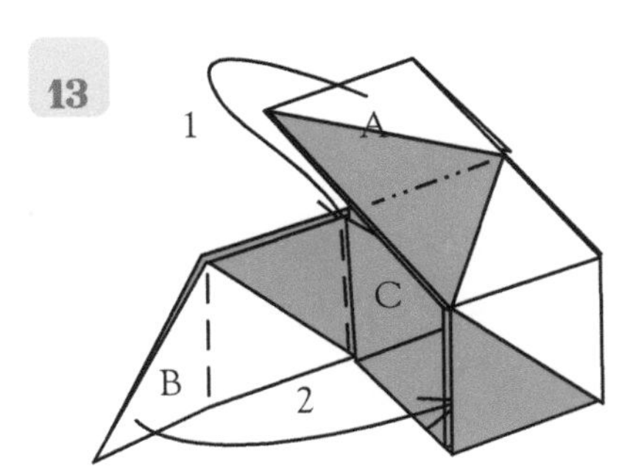

1. Tuck A into the pocket behind C.
2. Tuck B into the pocket.

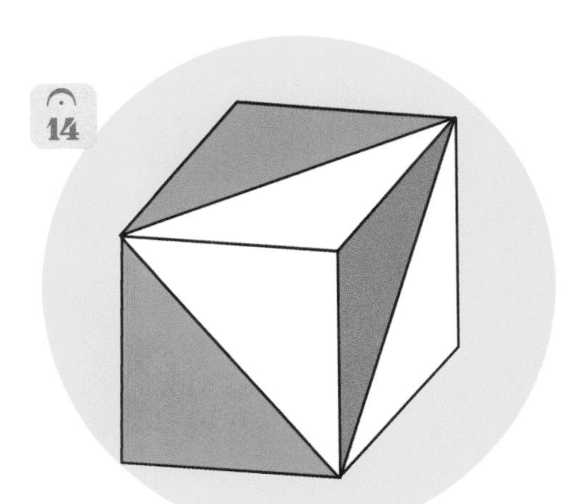

Cube of Triangles

Marble Cube

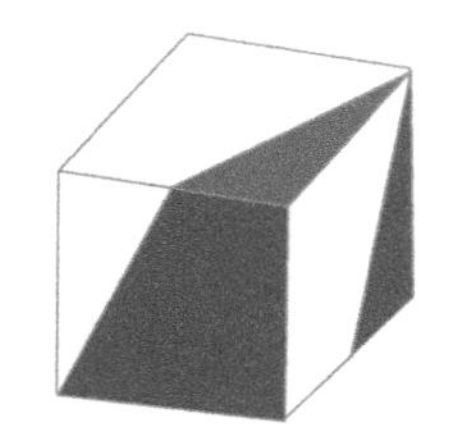

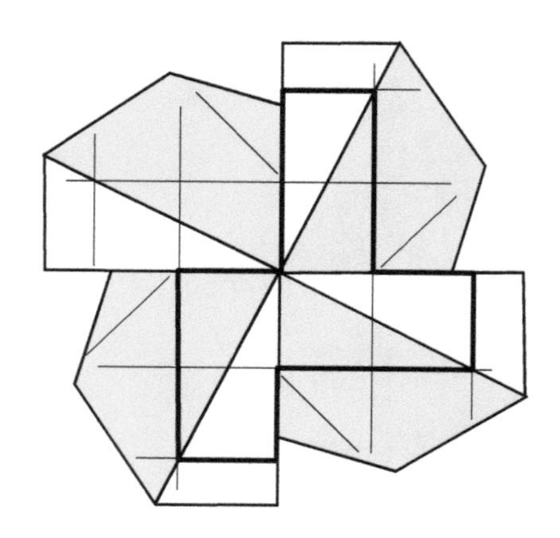

A pinwheel is formed to show both sides of the paper, with just the correct angles so a diagonal covers two squares, starting from the center of the paper. The model uses 3/4 square symmetry and uses a similar method as the first cube in this minuet.

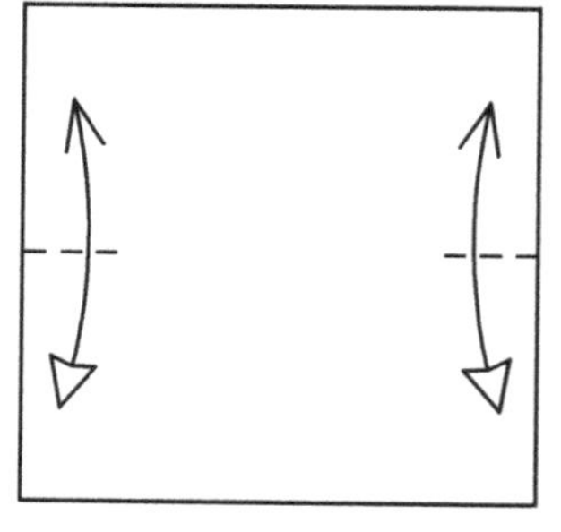

Fold and unfold on the left and right.

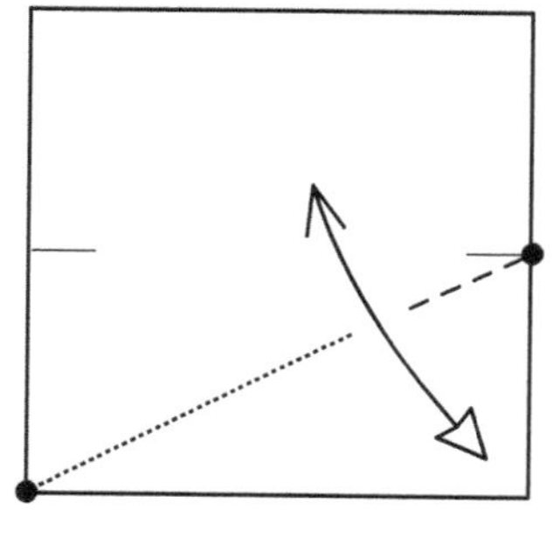

Fold and unfold on the right.

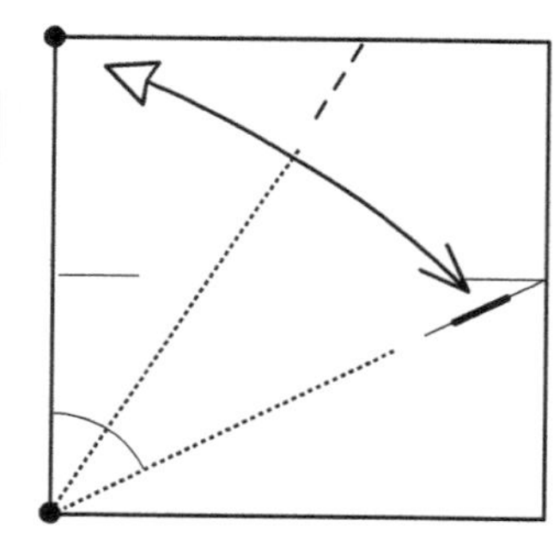

Bisect the angle. Fold and unfold on the top. Rotate 180°.

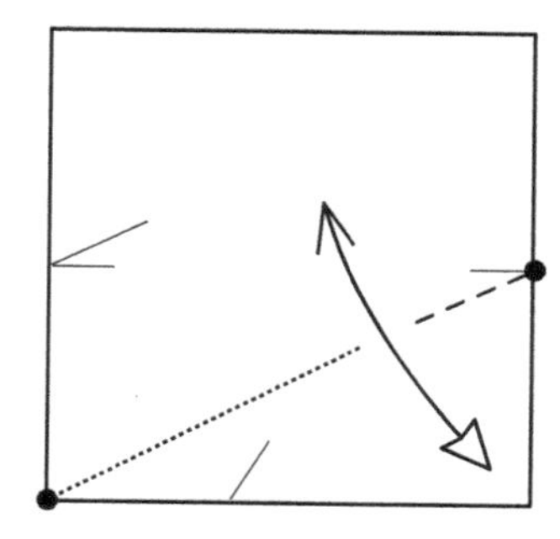

Repeat steps 2–3.

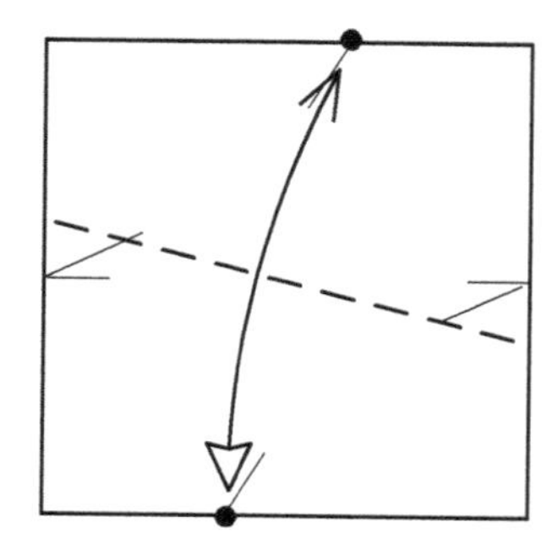

Fold and unfold. Rotate 90°.

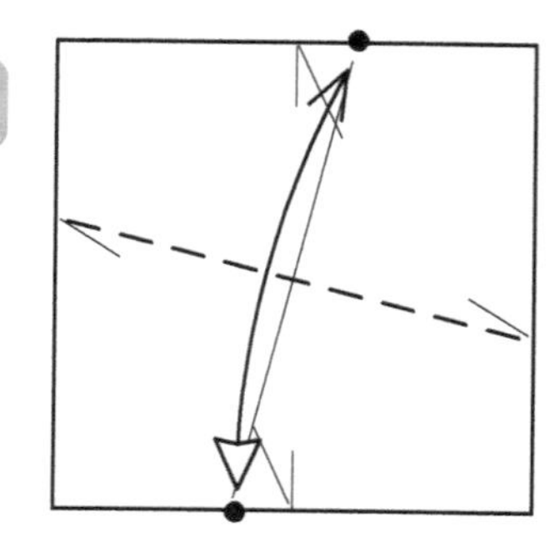

Fold and unfold.

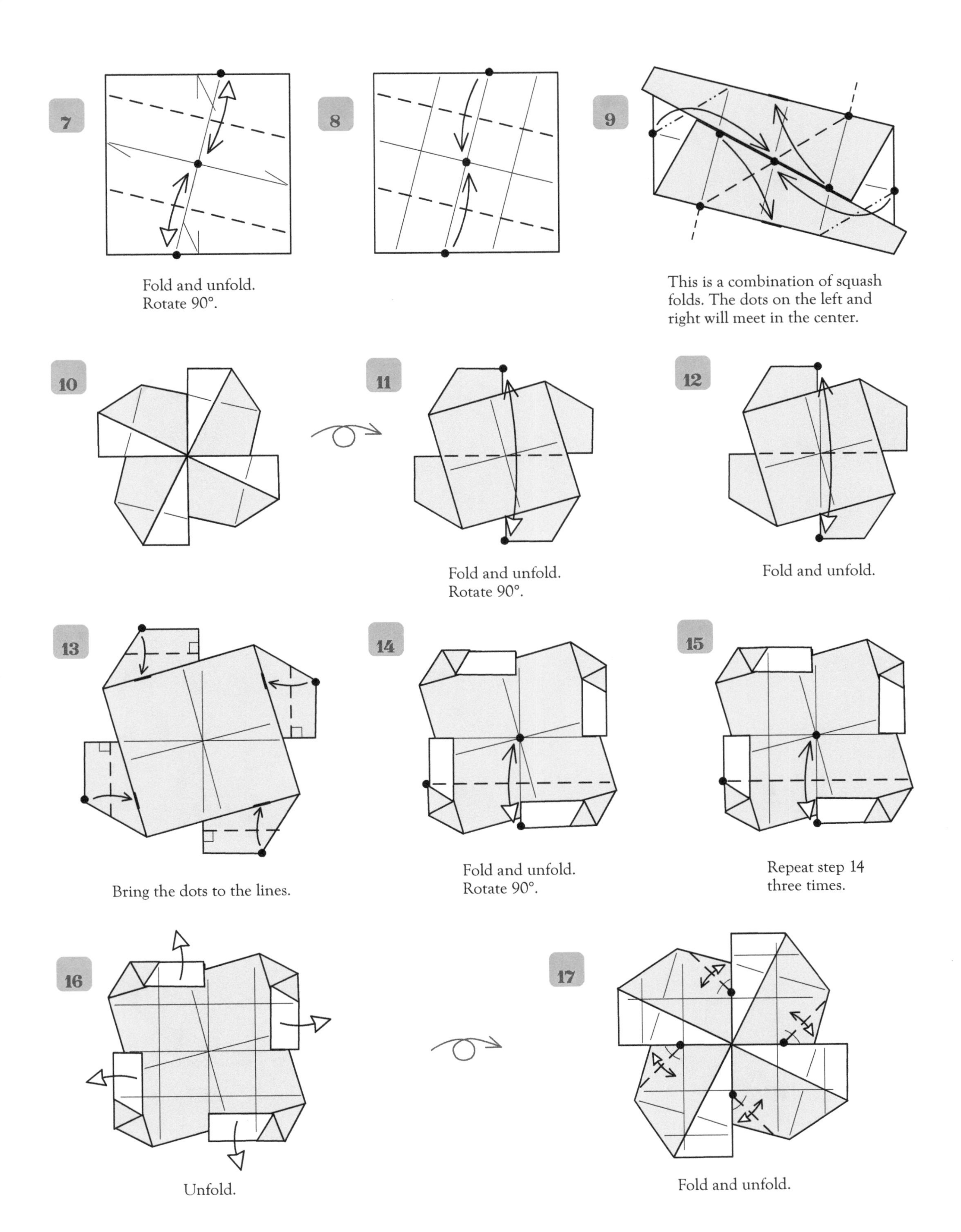
7
Fold and unfold.
Rotate 90°.
8
9
This is a combination of squash folds. The dots on the left and right will meet in the center.
10
11
Fold and unfold.
Rotate 90°.
12
Fold and unfold.
13
Bring the dots to the lines.
14
Fold and unfold.
Rotate 90°.
15
Repeat step 14 three times.
16
Unfold.
17
Fold and unfold.

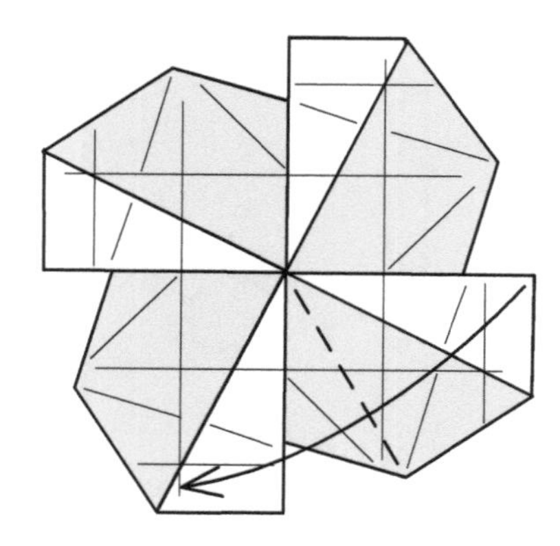

19

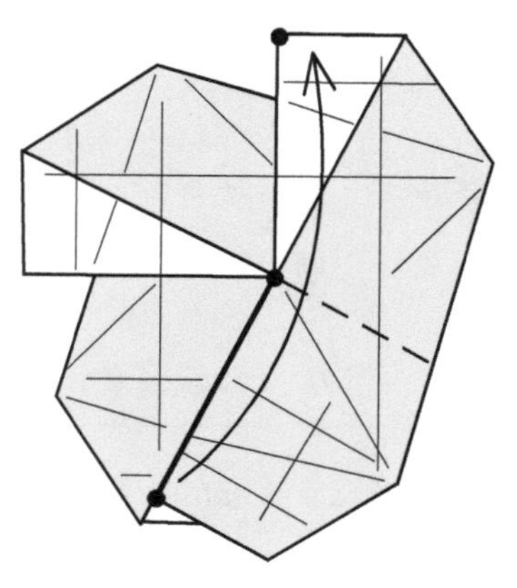

Puff out at the center dot. The other two dots will meet at the top. Rotate the center dot to the bottom.

20

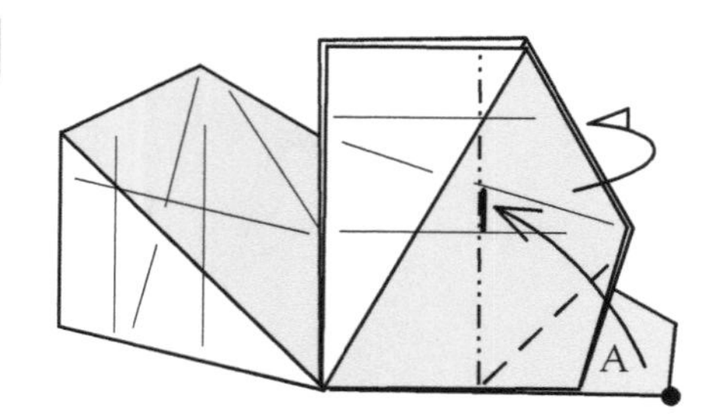

Fold behind along the creases and flatten inside. The dot on flap A will meet the bold line.

21

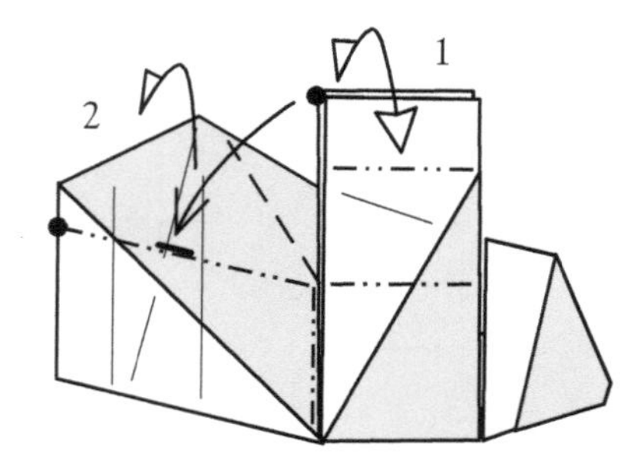

1. Fold and unfold.
2. Repeat step 20 on the left. Rotate so the dot on the left goes to the top.

22

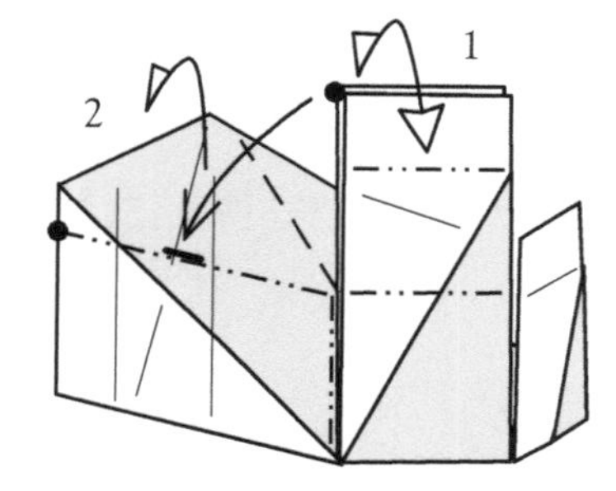

Repeat step 21.

23

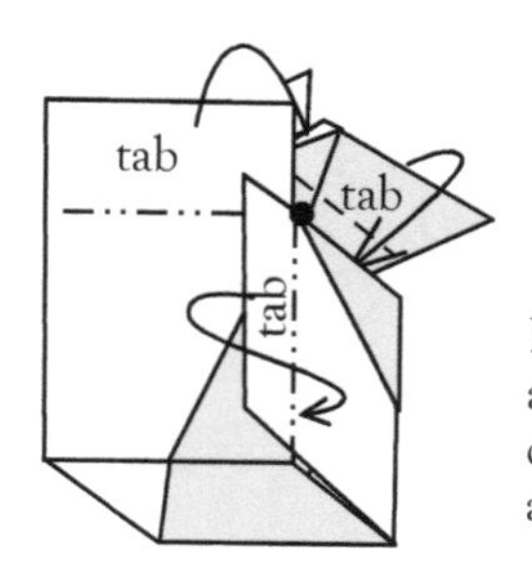

Fold each tab inside at a 90° angle. The tabs meet at the dot and the model closes with a three-way twist lock.

24

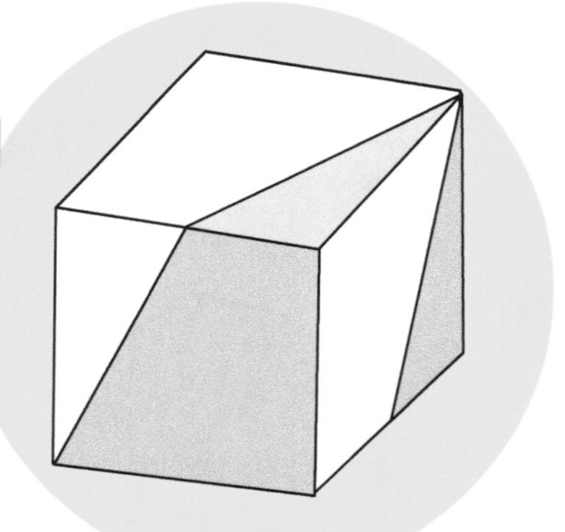

Marble Cube

Banded Cube

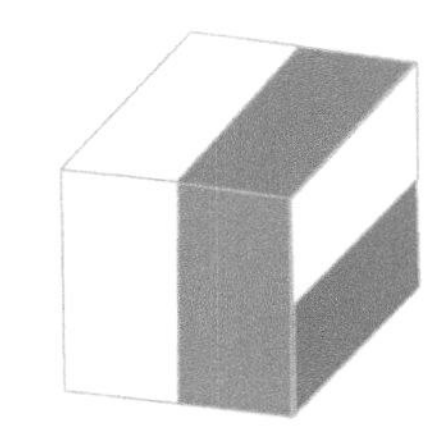

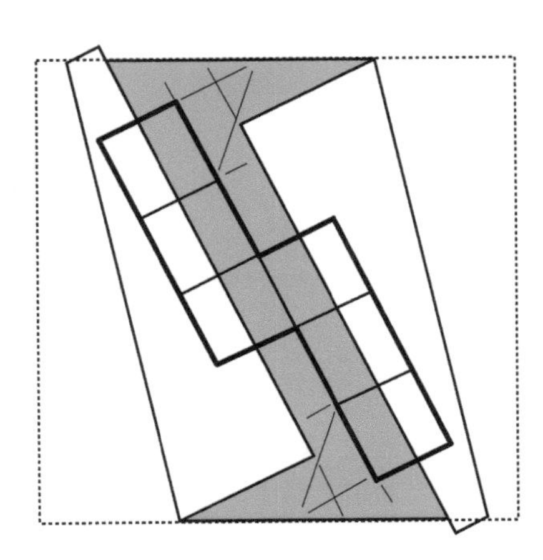

By folding two edges toward the center, a layout with stripes is formed. Placing the six square faces in two rows with three per row is an unusual way to contruct a cube. Odd symmetry is used.

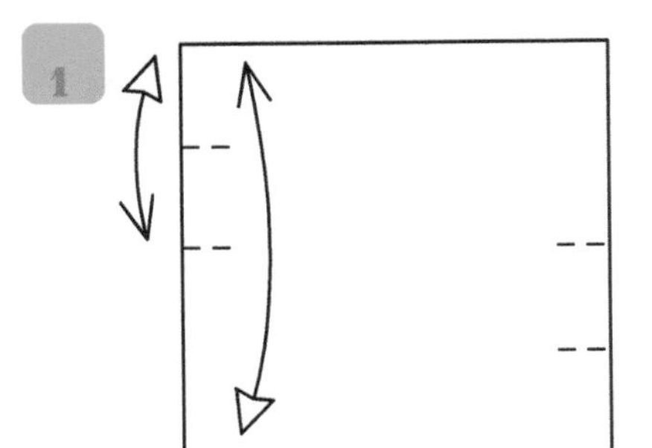

Make small marks by folding and unfolding in quarters.

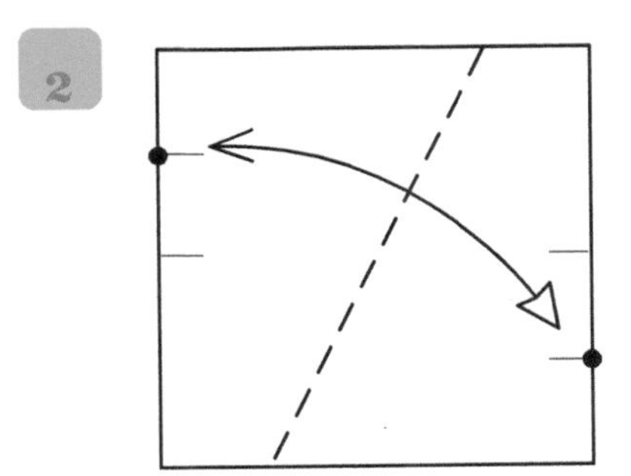

Fold and unfold.

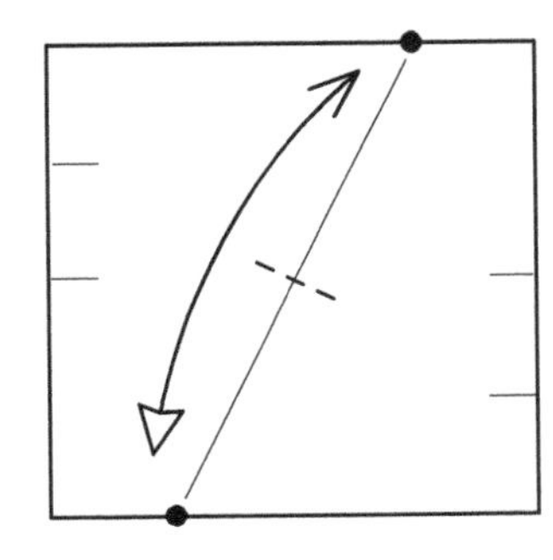

Fold and unfold in the center.

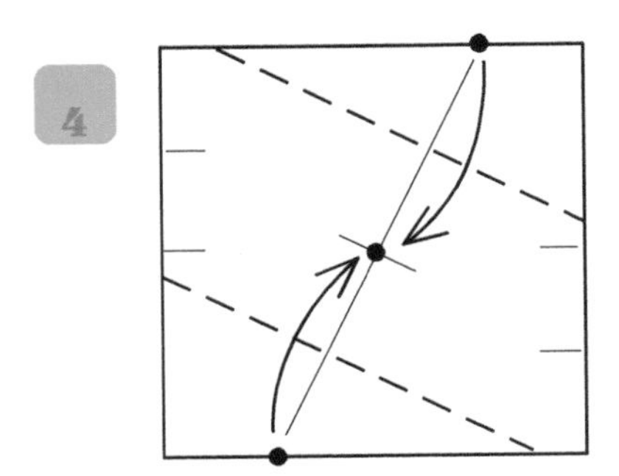

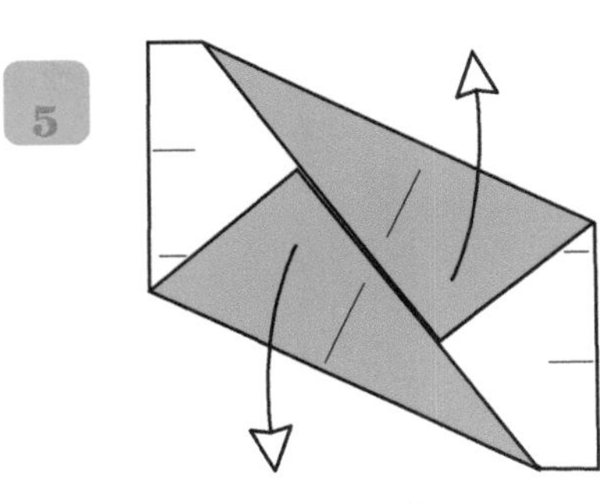

Unfold.

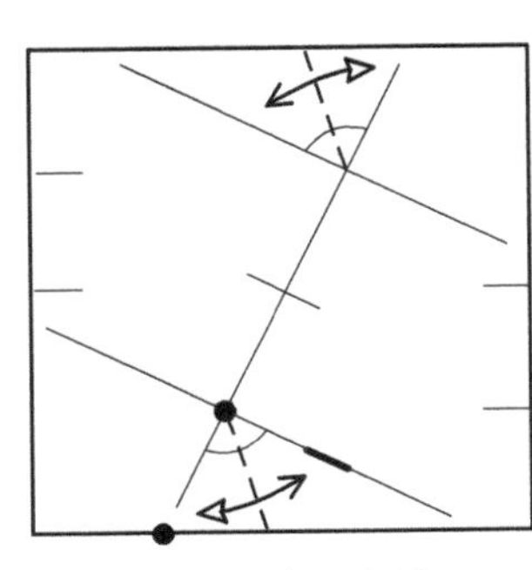

Fold and unfold.

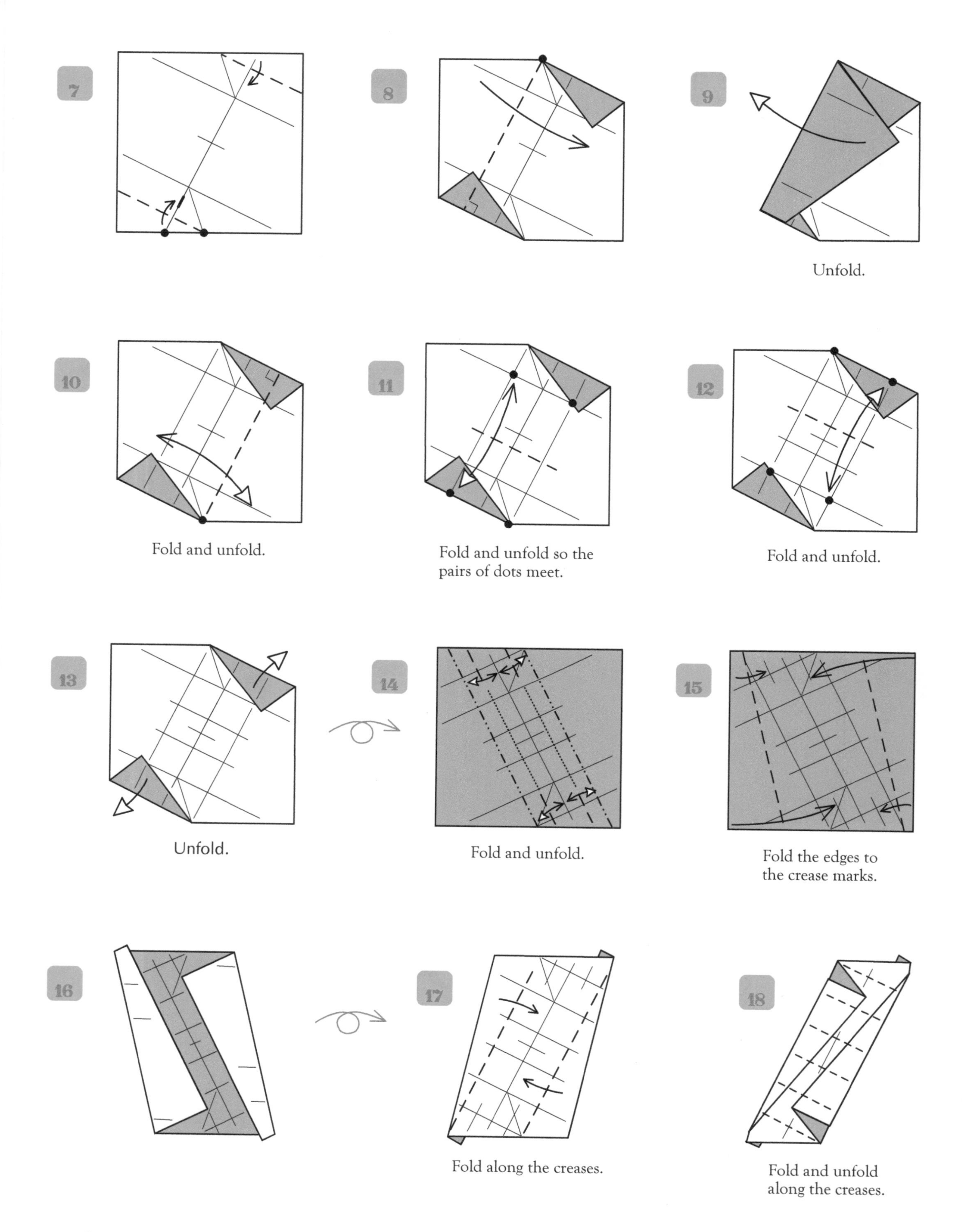
7
8
9
Unfold.
10
Fold and unfold.
11
Fold and unfold so the pairs of dots meet.
12
Fold and unfold.
13
Unfold.
14
Fold and unfold.
15
Fold the edges to the crease marks.
16
17
Fold along the creases.
18
Fold and unfold along the creases.

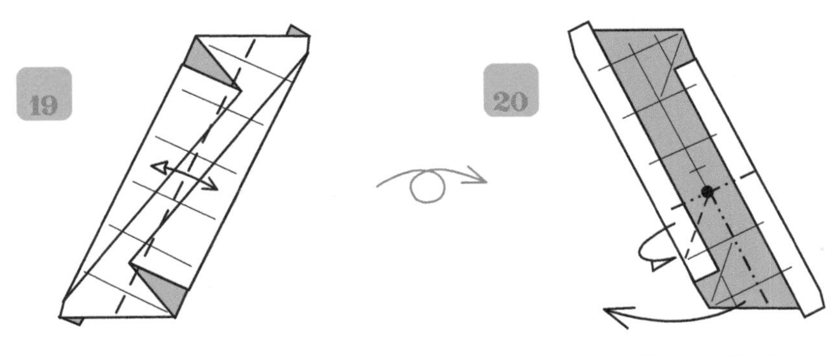

Fold and unfold.

Puff out at the dot.

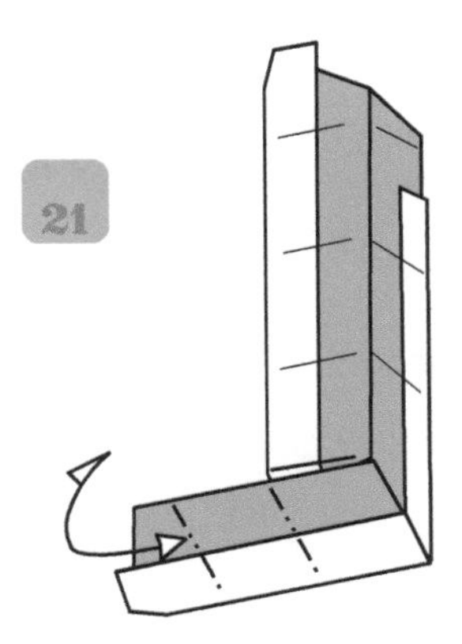

Fold and unfold along the creases. Rotate.

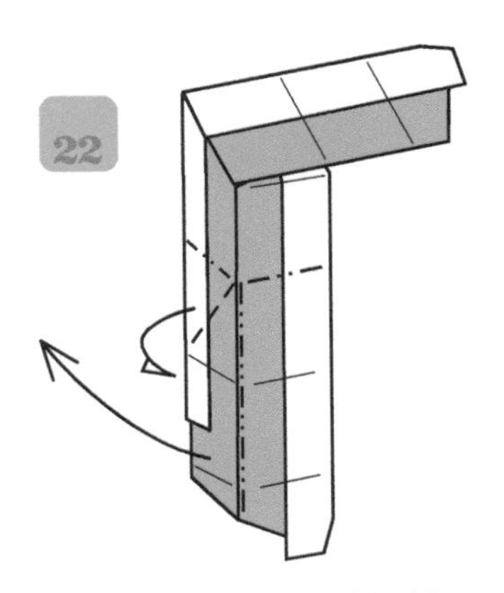

Repeat steps 20–21.

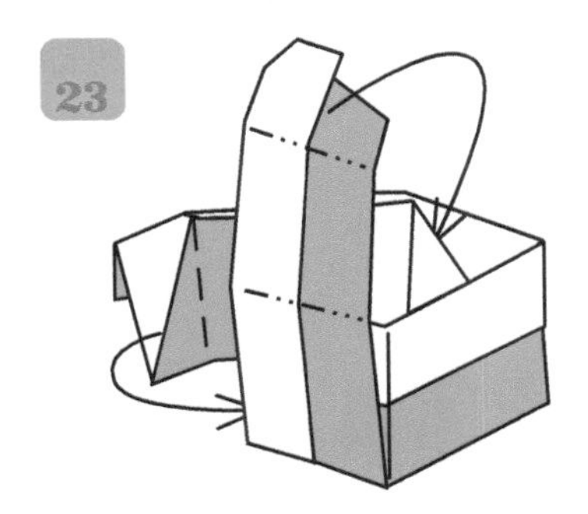

Tuck inside.

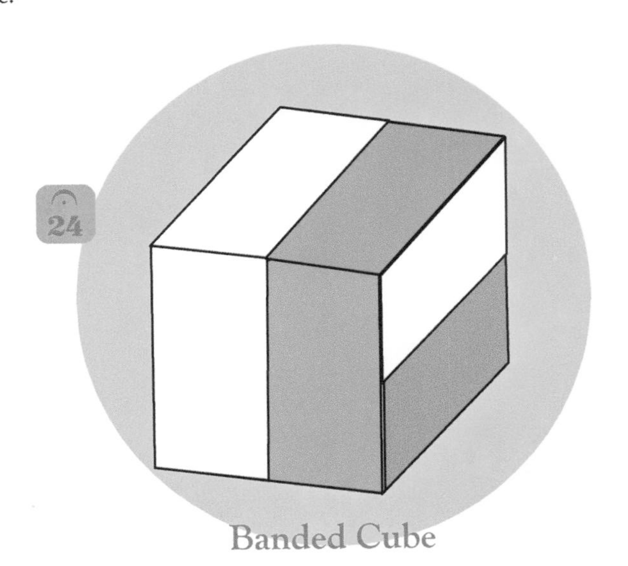

Banded Cube

Fancy Cube

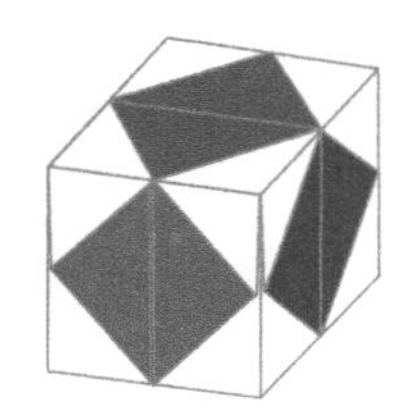

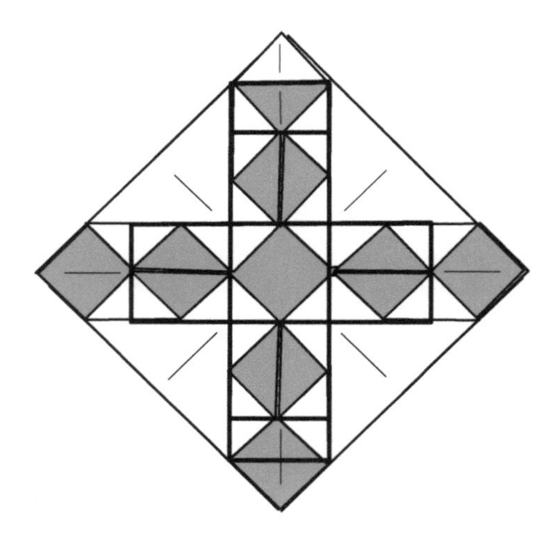

Each face of this cube has a diamond color pattern. The paper is divided into ninths. Square symmetry is used.

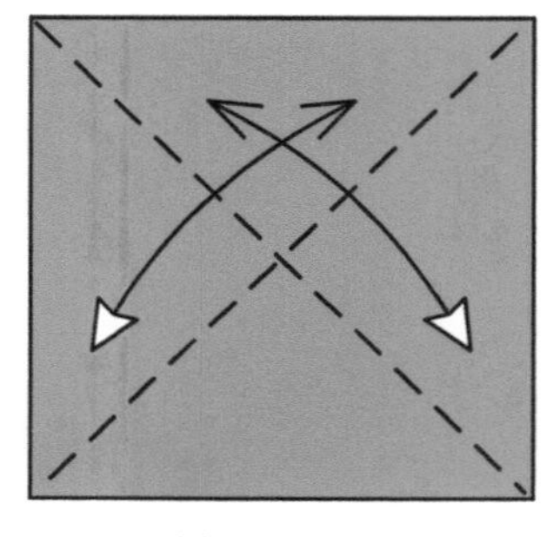

Fold and unfold.

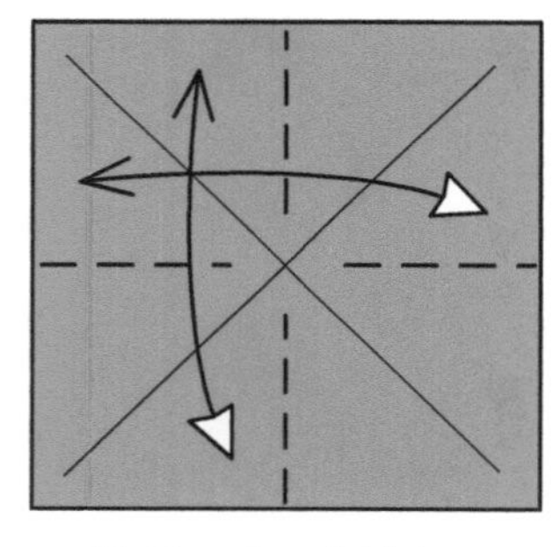

Fold and unfold but not in the center.

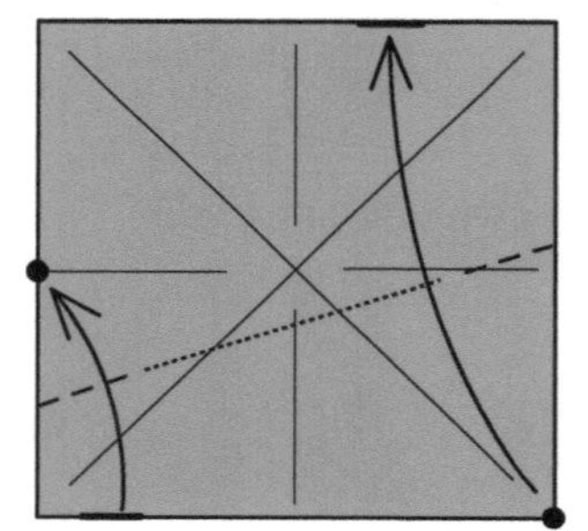

Bring the lower right corner to the top edge and the bottom edge to the left center. Crease on the left and right.

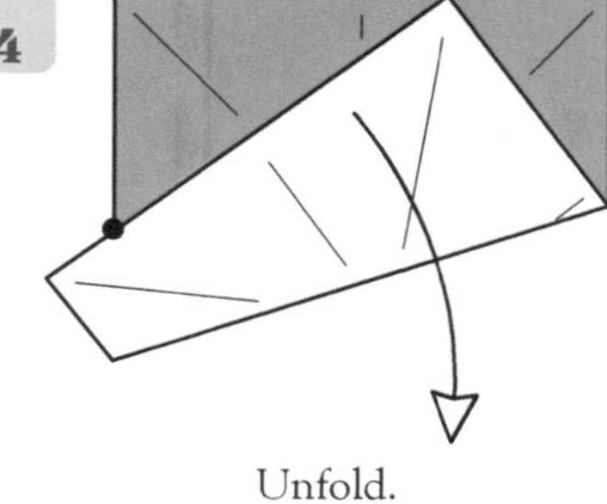

Unfold.

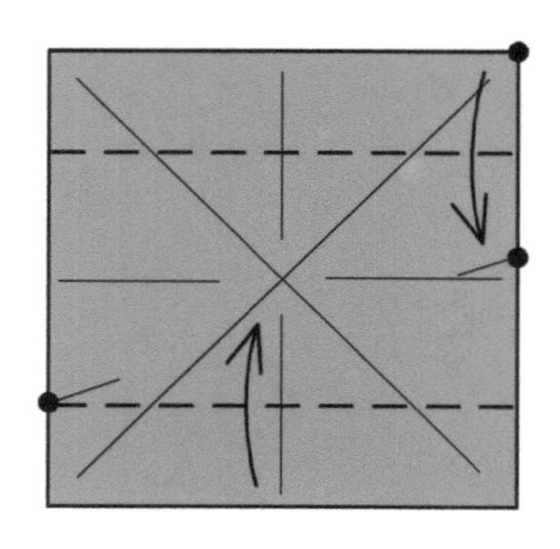

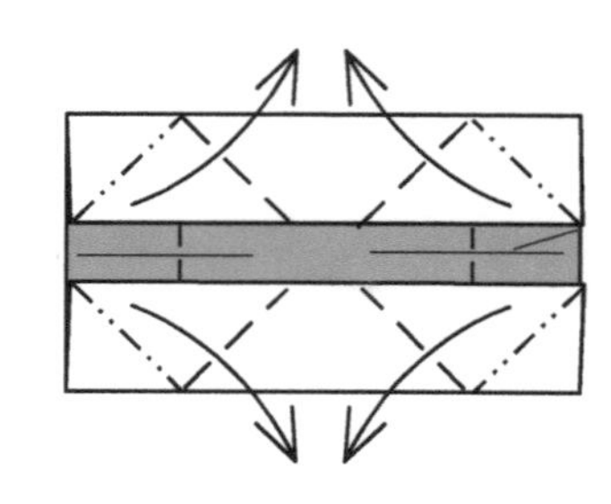

Make four squash folds.

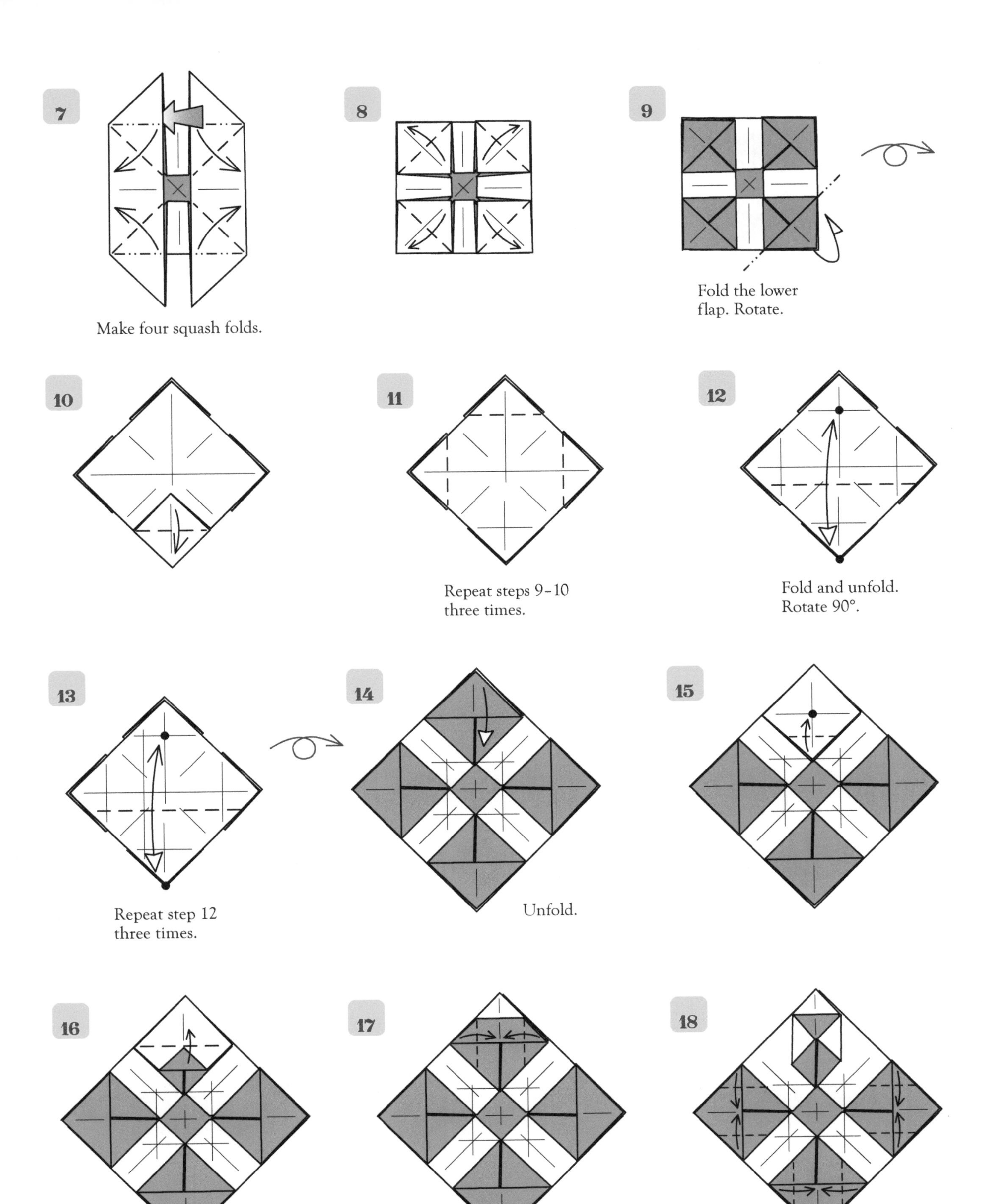
7
Make four squash folds.
8
9
Fold the lower flap. Rotate.
10
11
Repeat steps 9–10 three times.
12
Fold and unfold. Rotate 90°.
13
Repeat step 12 three times.
14
Unfold.
15
16
17
18

19

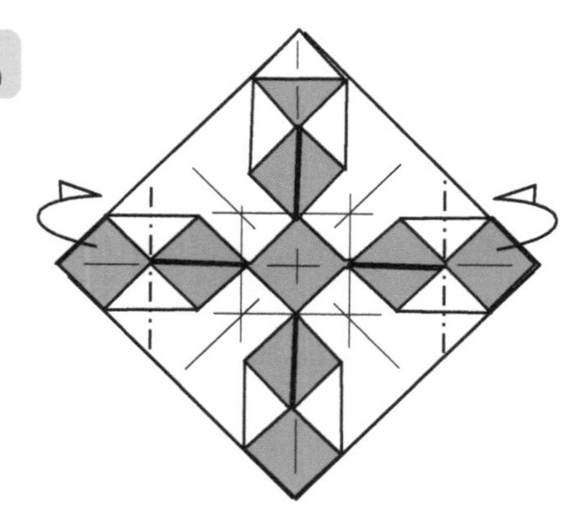

20

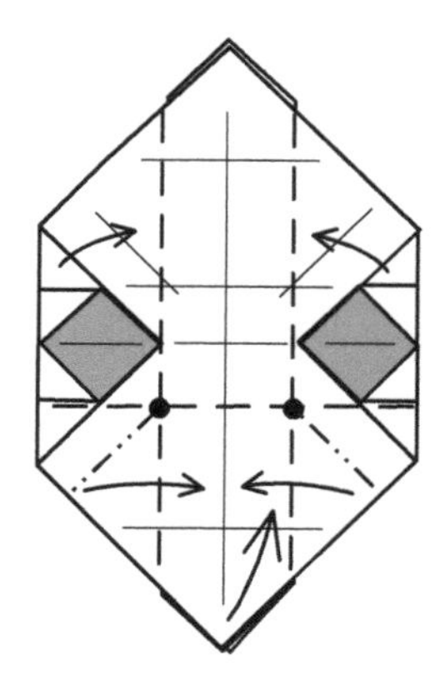

Push in at the dots. Rotate.

21

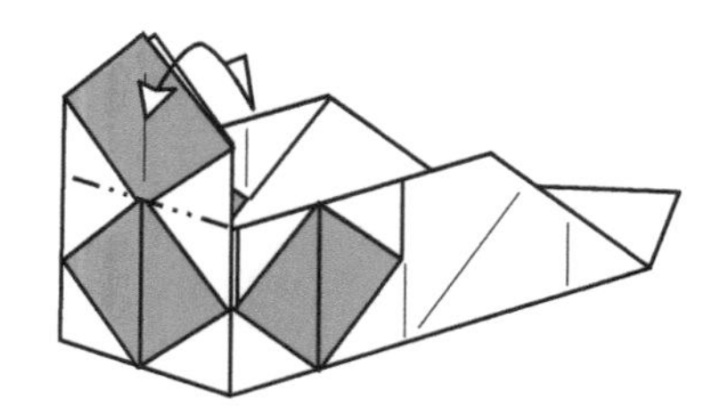

Fold and unfold.

22

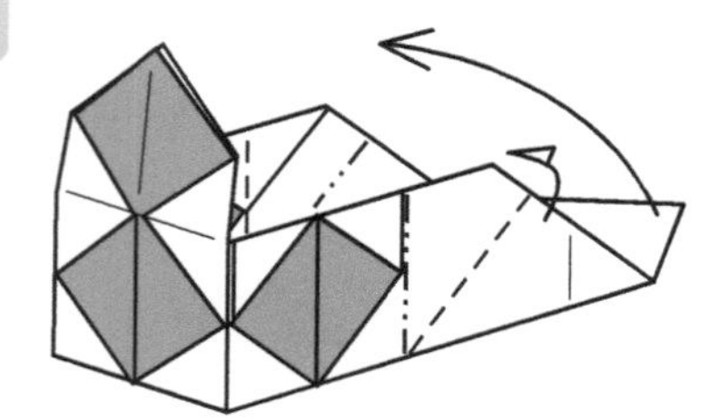

Repeat steps 20–21
on the right.

23

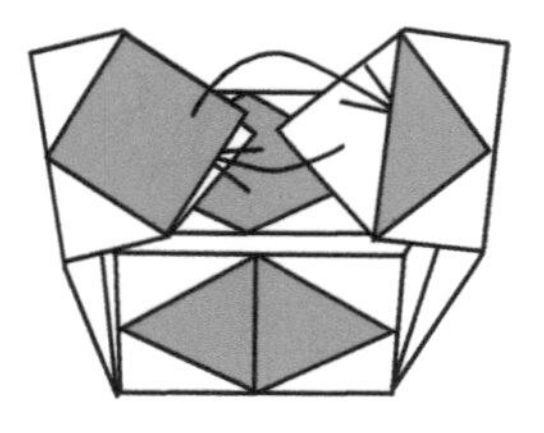

This is a view from the top.
Tuck the layers inside.

24

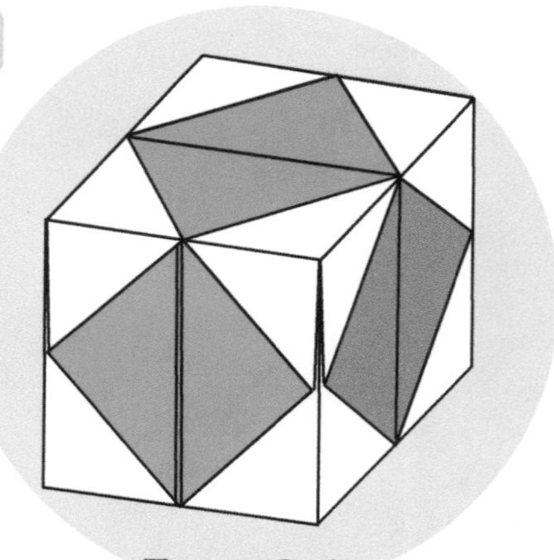

Fancy Cube

Kaleidoscopic Cube

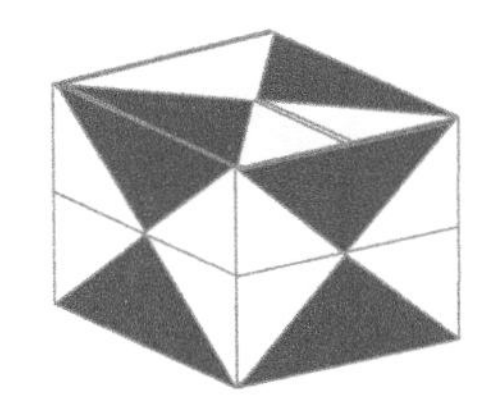

This cube has complex color-change patterns on all sides yet is folded in only 19 steps. To achieve a good result, the model must be folded carefully and will challenge the folder and the paper.

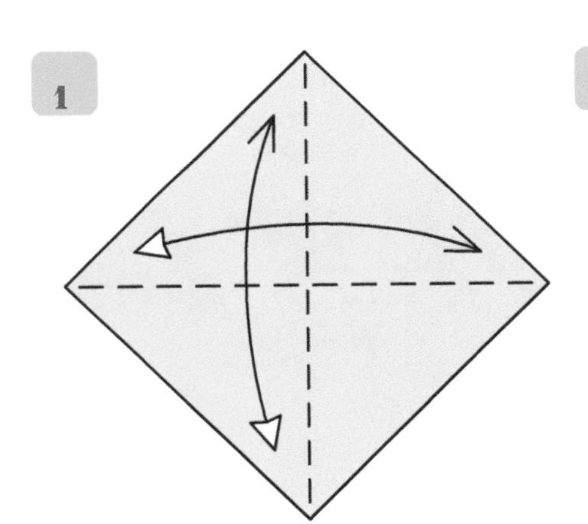

Fold and unfold.

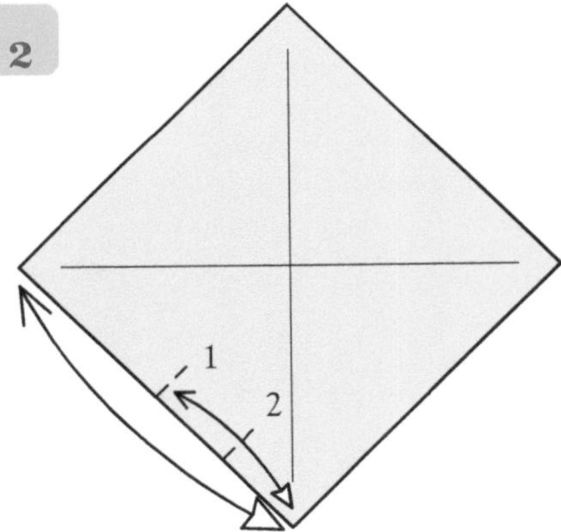

Fold and unfold on the edge to find the quarter mark.

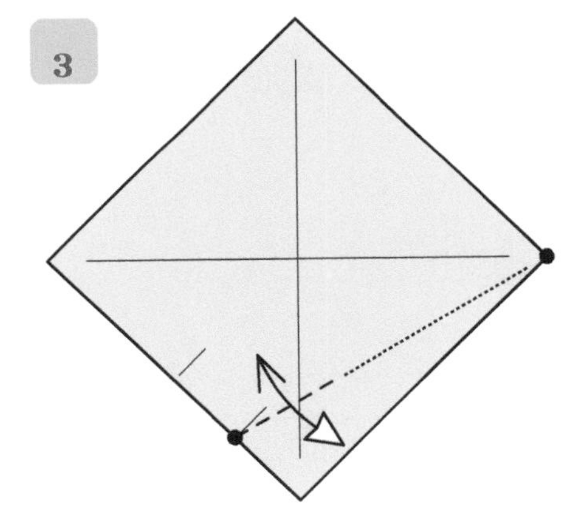

Fold and unfold.

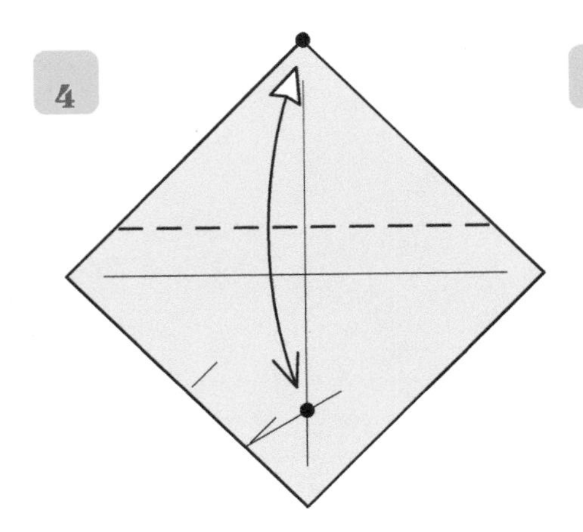

Fold and unfold.

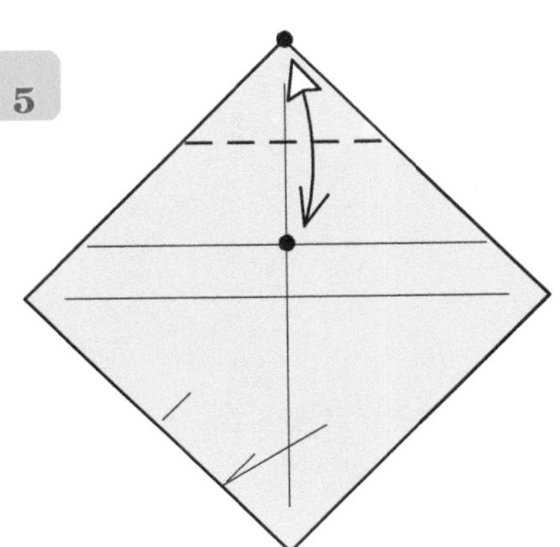

Fold and unfold.

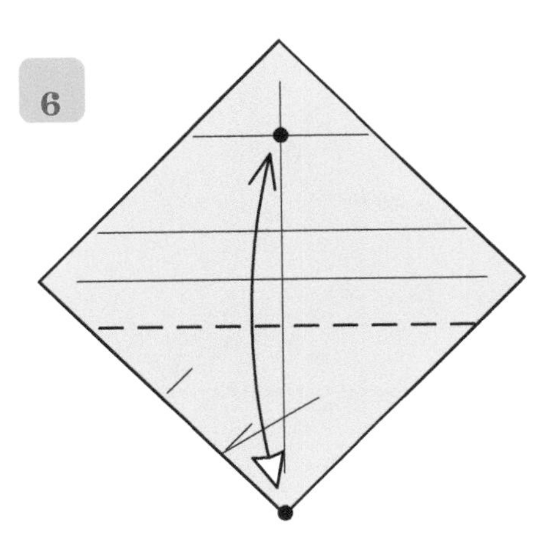

Fold and unfold.

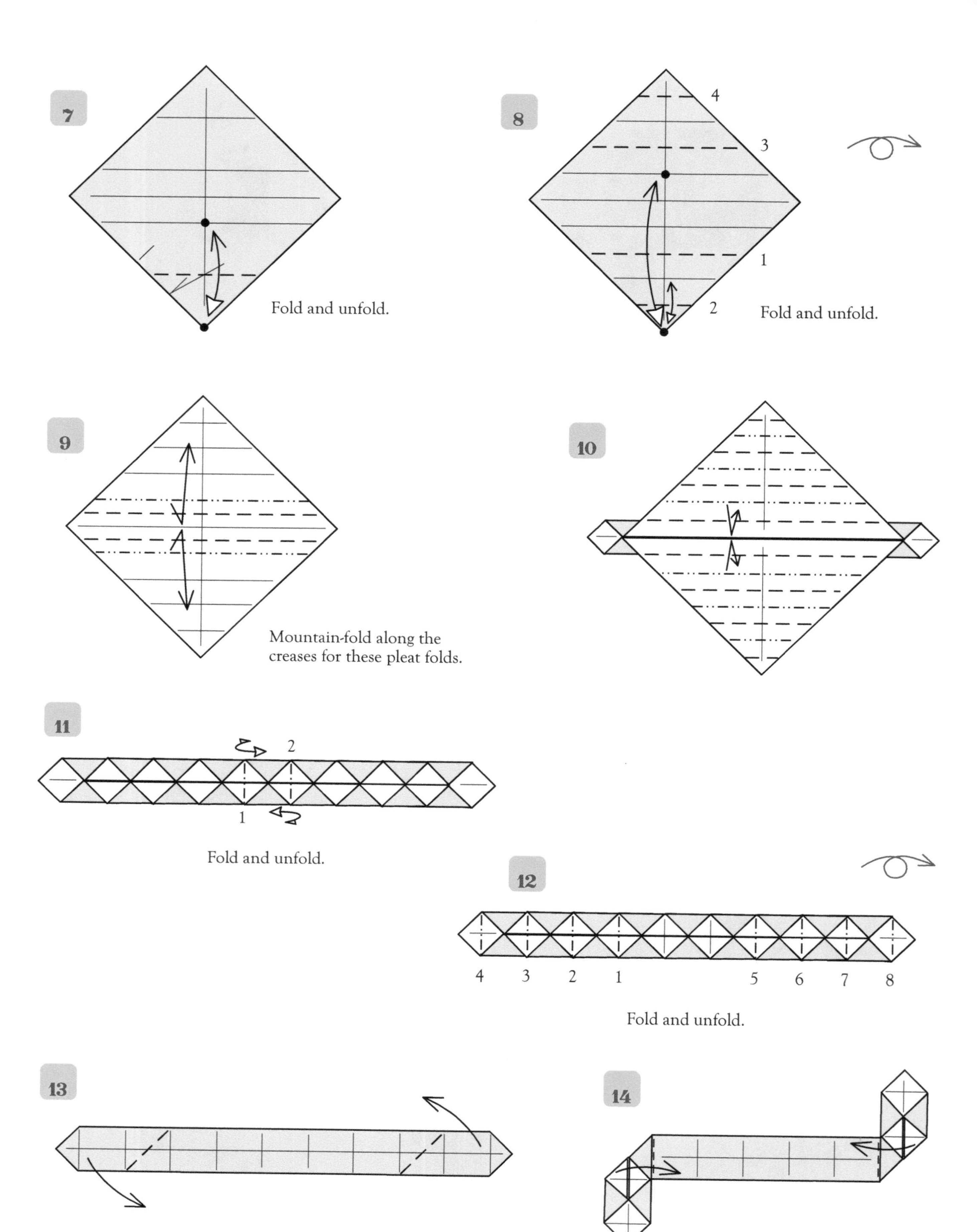
7
Fold and unfold.
8
4
3
1
2
Fold and unfold.
9
Mountain-fold along the
creases for these pleat folds.
10
11
2
1
Fold and unfold.
12
4
3
2
1
5
6
7
8
Fold and unfold.
13
14

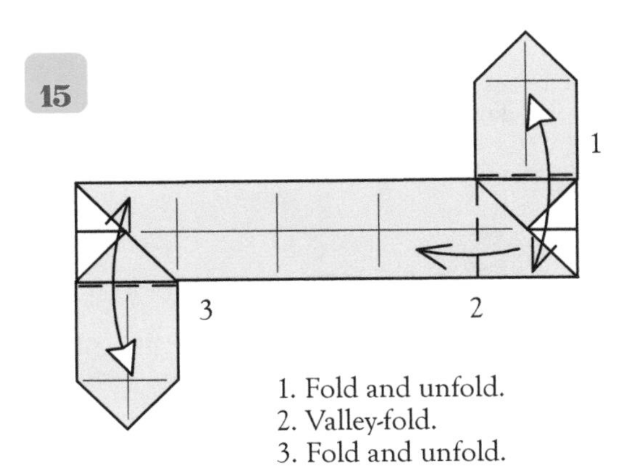

1. Fold and unfold.
2. Valley-fold.
3. Fold and unfold.

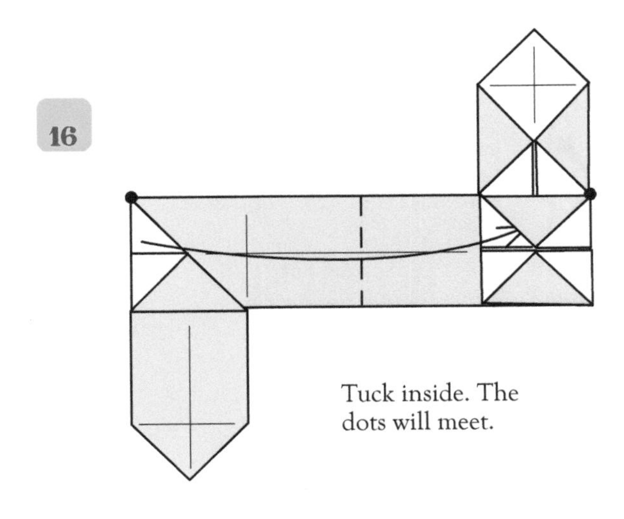

Tuck inside. The dots will meet.

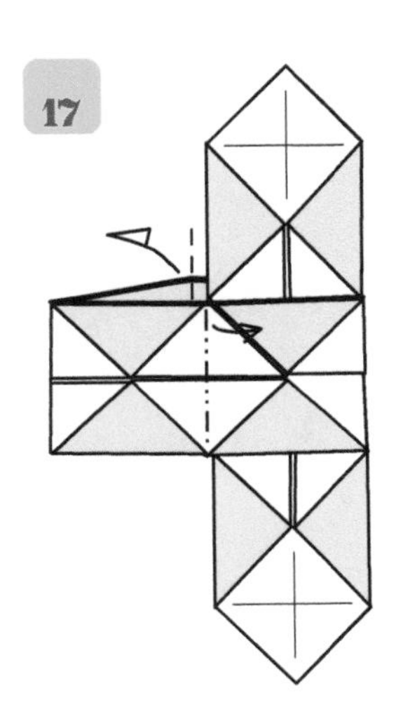

Begin to shape the cube. The bold lines will form a square.

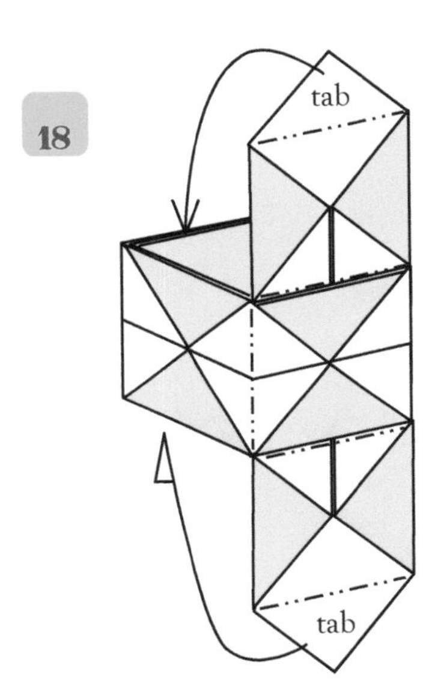

Tuck the tabs into the pockets. There are several choices for the pockets, choose wisely.

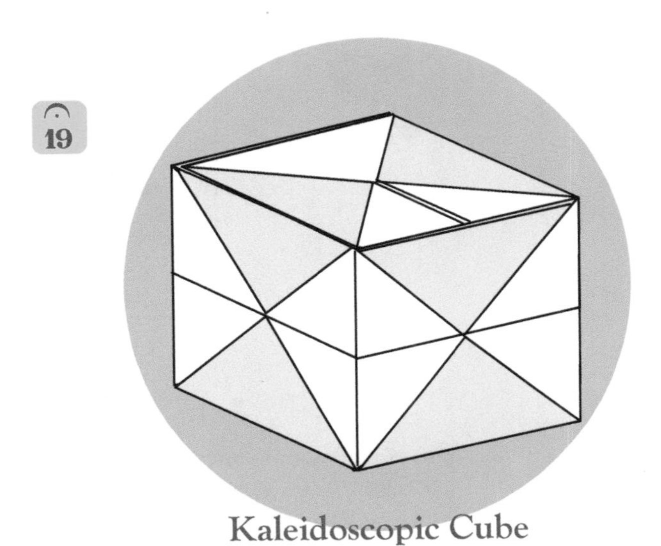

Kaleidoscopic Cube

Trio of Shapes Based on Cubes

The cube can be used as a base to form more complex shapes. The Dimpled Truncated Cube and Cubehemioctahedron are formed by sinking the corners of the the cube. The Stella Octangula is also related to the cube. Each of these models is based on square symmetry: the folds on one side of the square will be repeated on all sides, simplifying the folding.

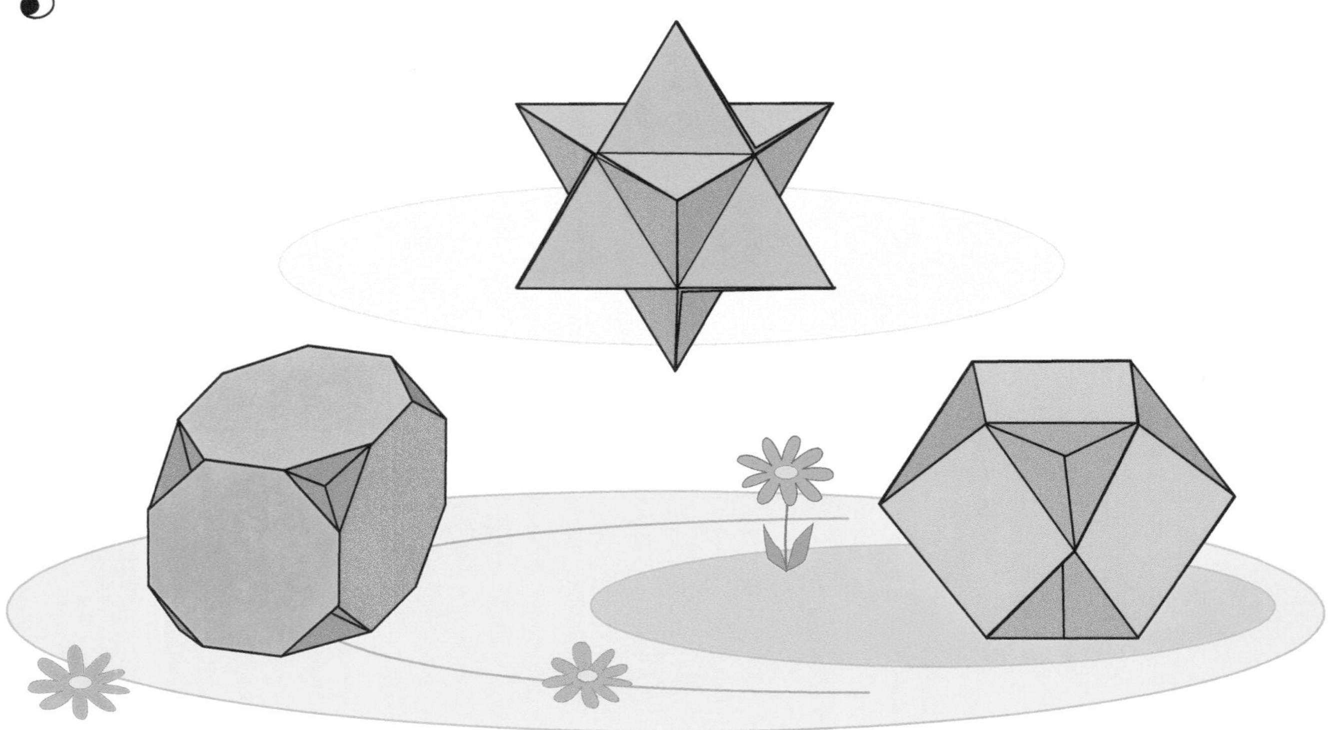

Dimpled Truncated Cube

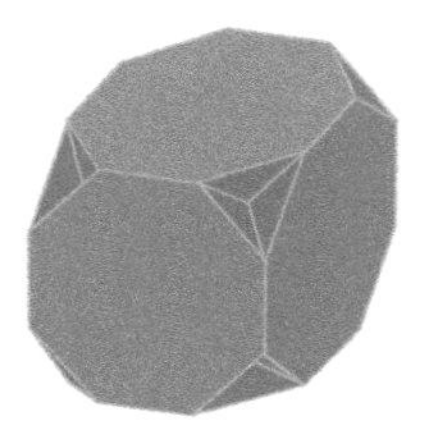

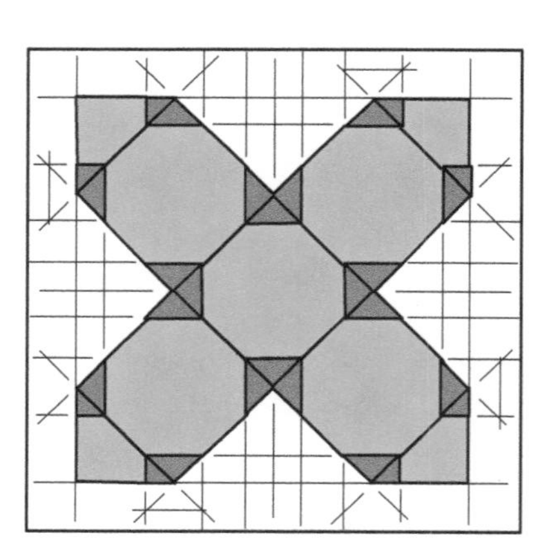

This polyhedron is composed of six octagons and eight sunken triangular sides. The layout shows this design is based on square symmetry. The shape is that of a cube with sunken corners at just the right lengths so the squares of the cube become octagons.

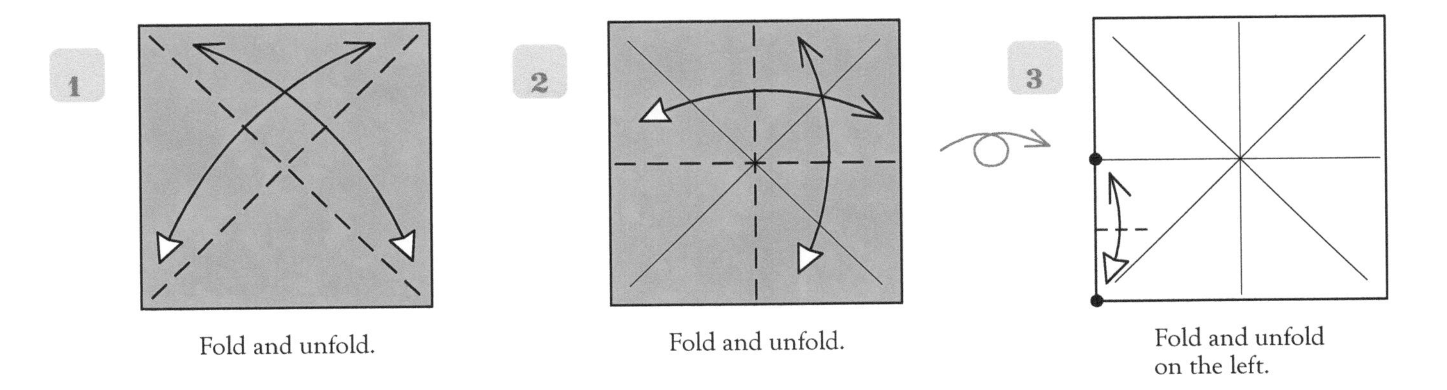

Fold and unfold.

Fold and unfold.

Fold and unfold on the left.

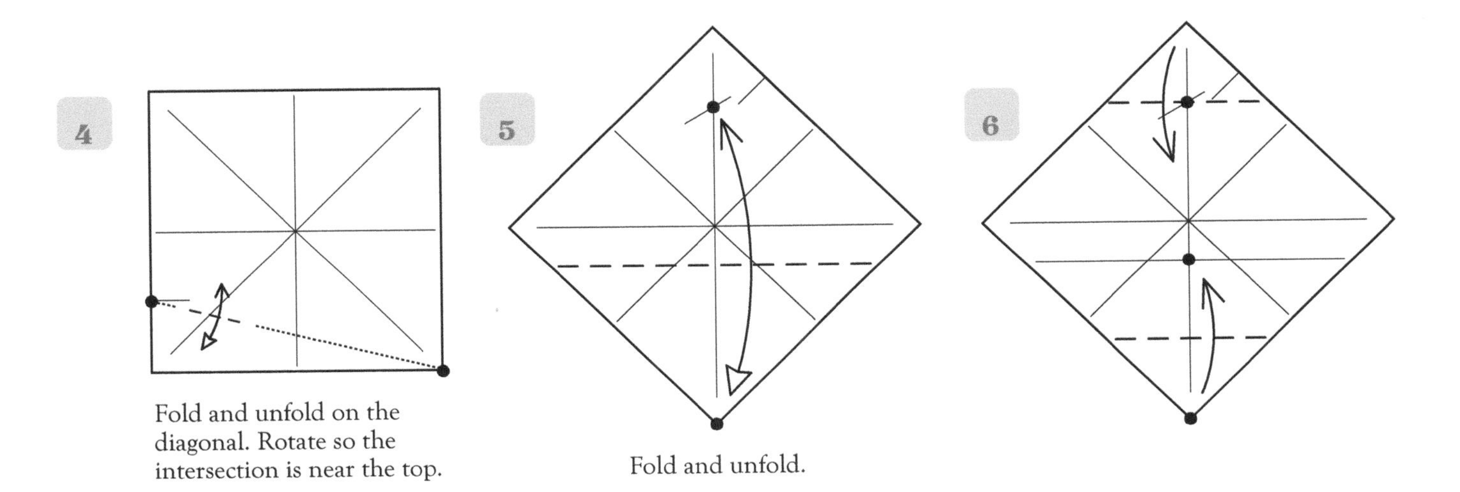

Fold and unfold on the diagonal. Rotate so the intersection is near the top.

Fold and unfold.

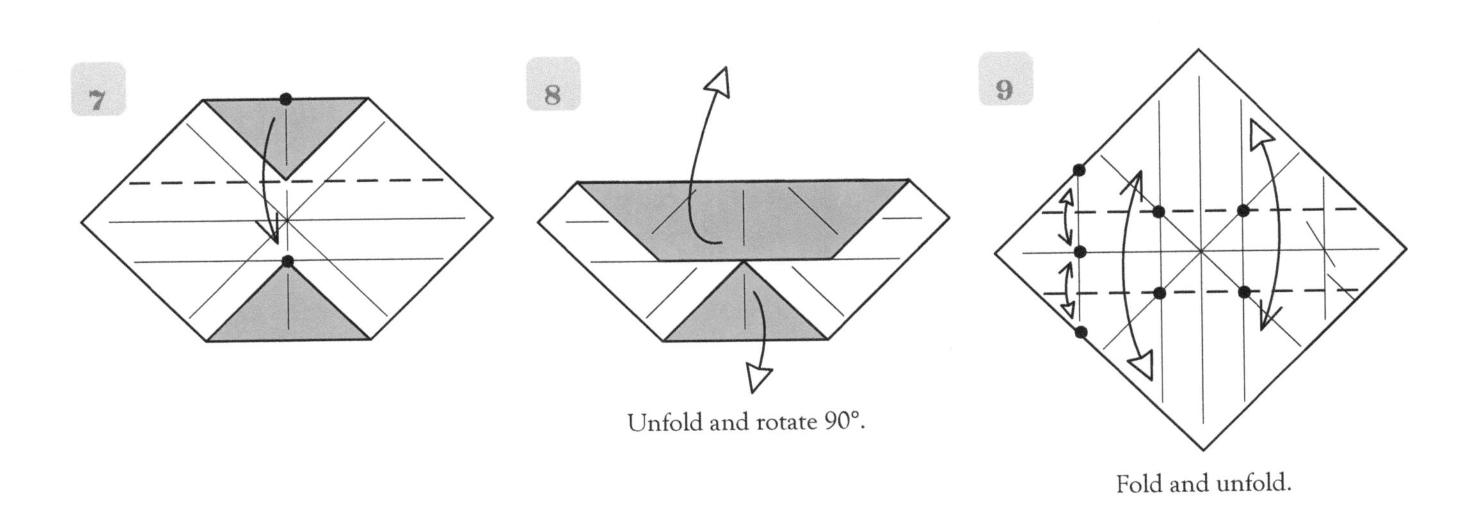

Unfold and rotate 90°.

Fold and unfold.

10

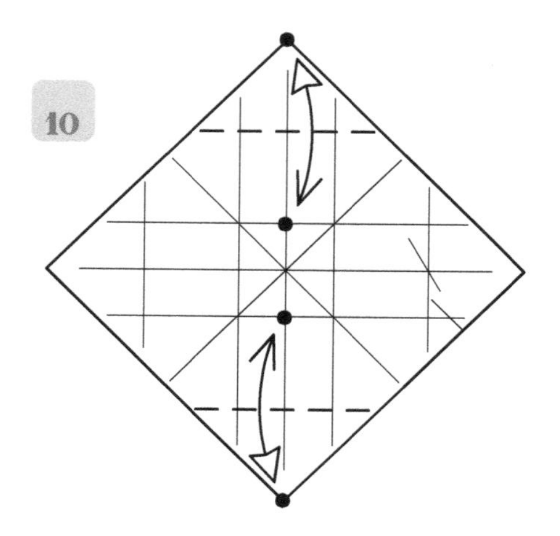

Fold and unfold. Rotate.

11

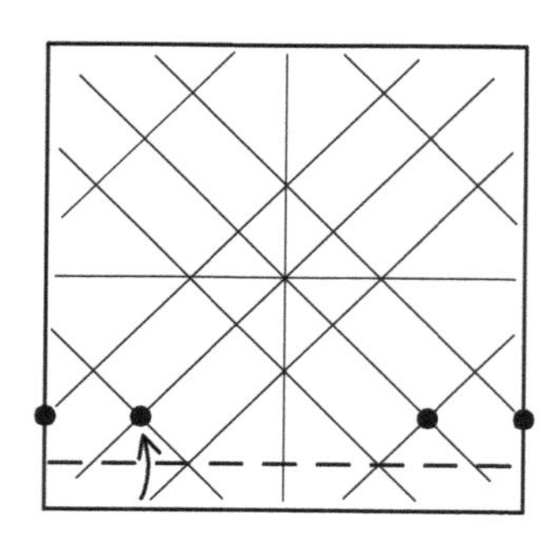

Fold up to the dots.

12

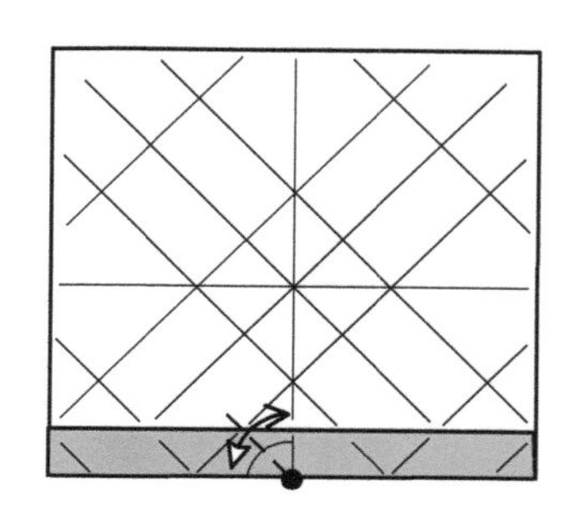

Fold and unfold.

13

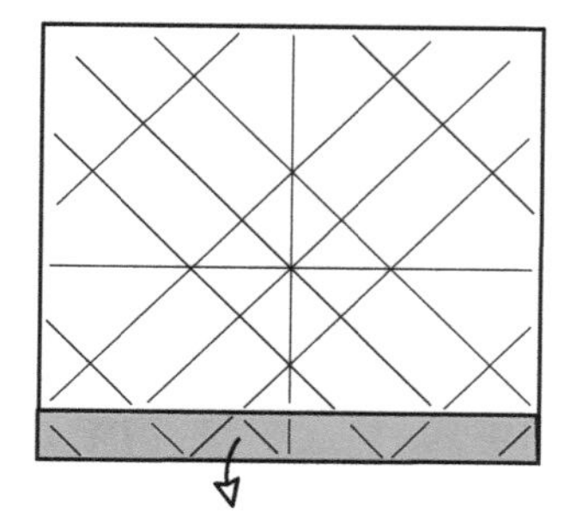

Unfold and rotate 90°.

14

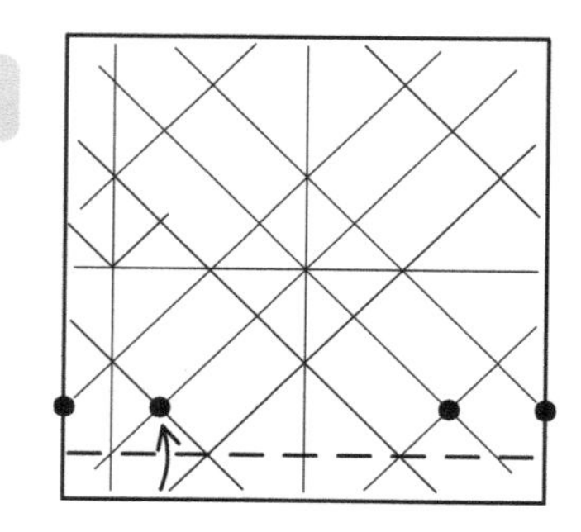

Repeat steps 11–13 three times.

15

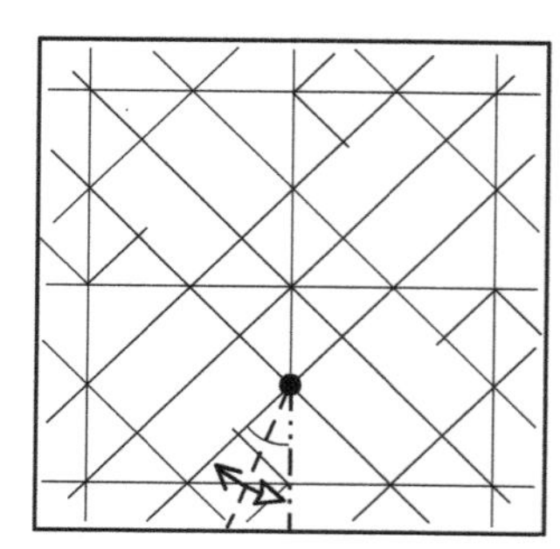

Push in at the dot and bisect the angle. Fold and unfold.

16

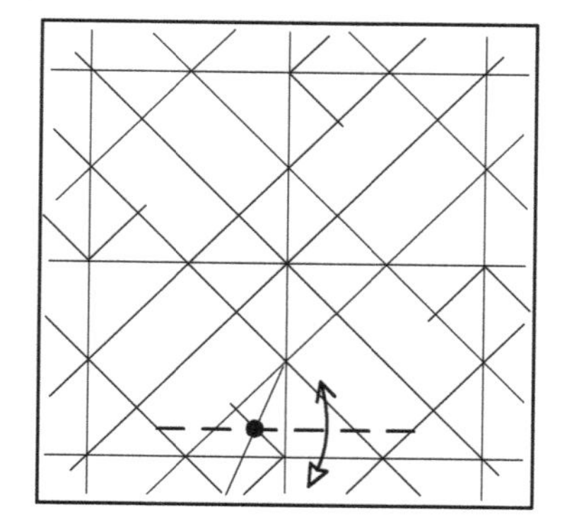

Fold and unfold.

17

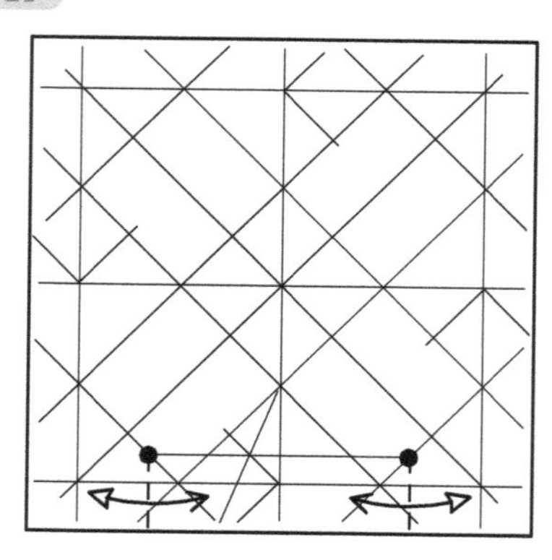

Fold and unfold.

18

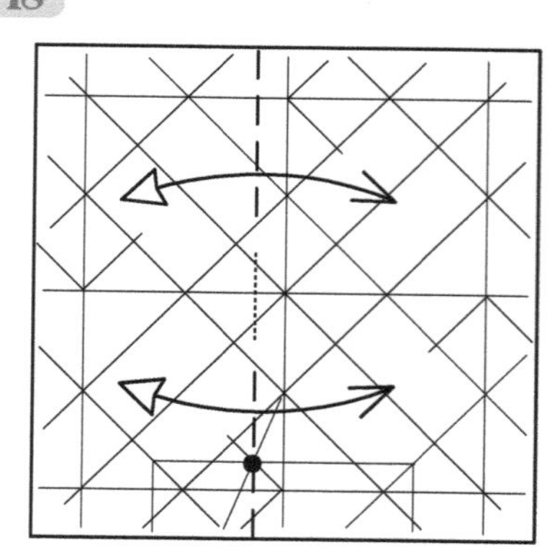

Fold and unfold but not in the center.

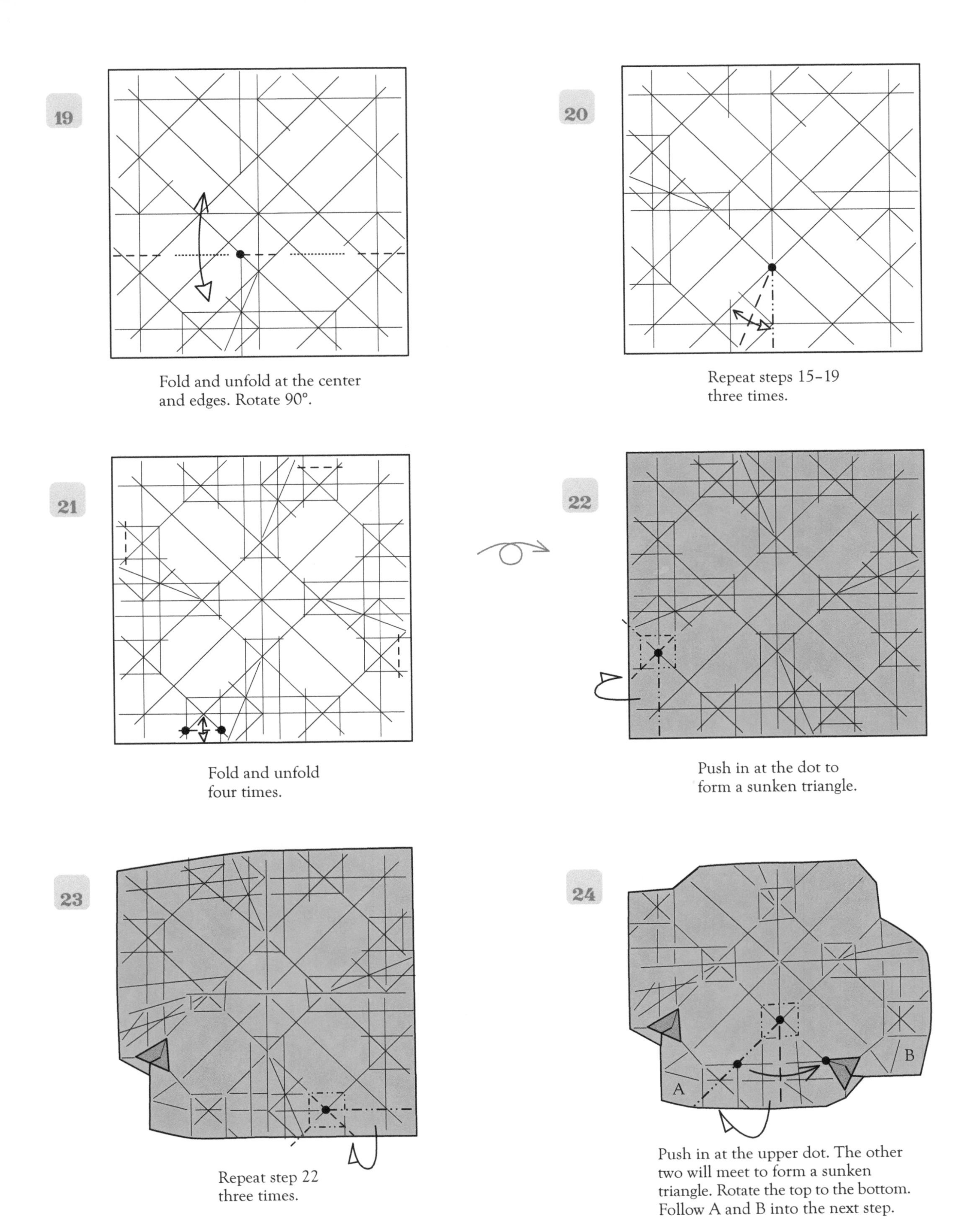

Fold and unfold at the center and edges. Rotate 90°.

Repeat steps 15–19 three times.

Fold and unfold four times.

Push in at the dot to form a sunken triangle.

Repeat step 22 three times.

Push in at the upper dot. The other two will meet to form a sunken triangle. Rotate the top to the bottom. Follow A and B into the next step.

25

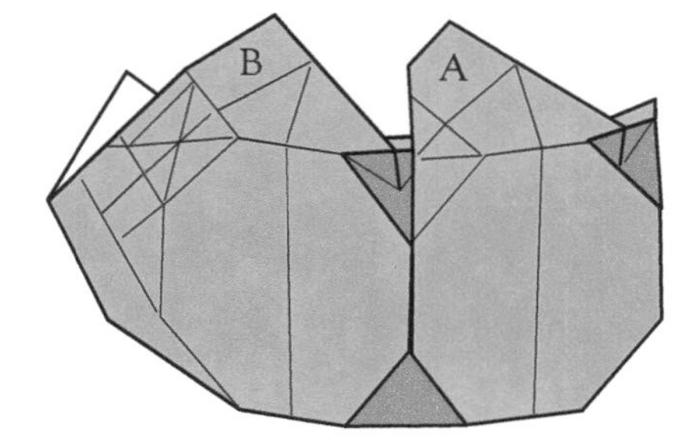

Repeat step 24
three times.

26

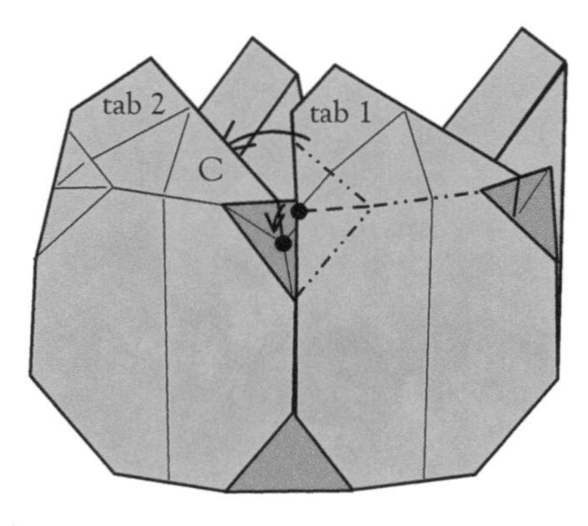

There are four tabs at the top, two are shown. Push in at the upper dot and tuck tab 1 under C so the dots meet. Continue all around.

27

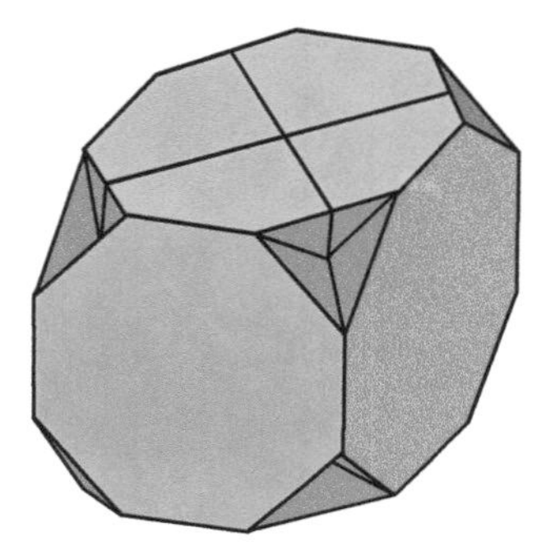

Rotate the top
to the bottom.

28

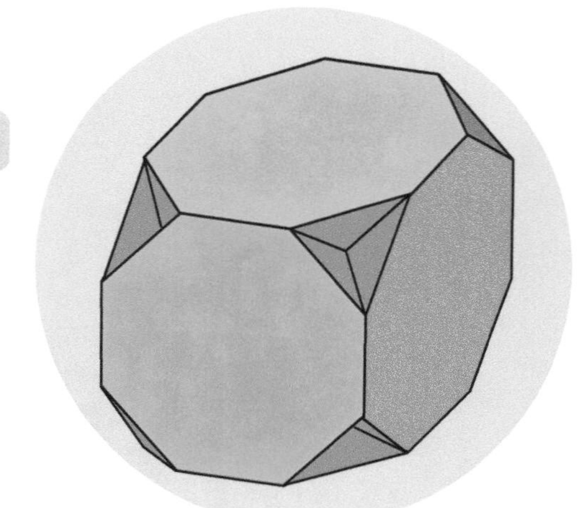

Dimpled
Truncated Cube

Cubehemioctahedron

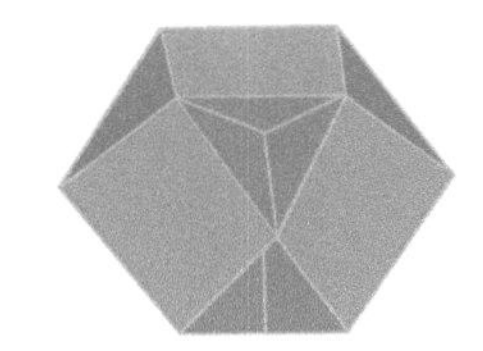

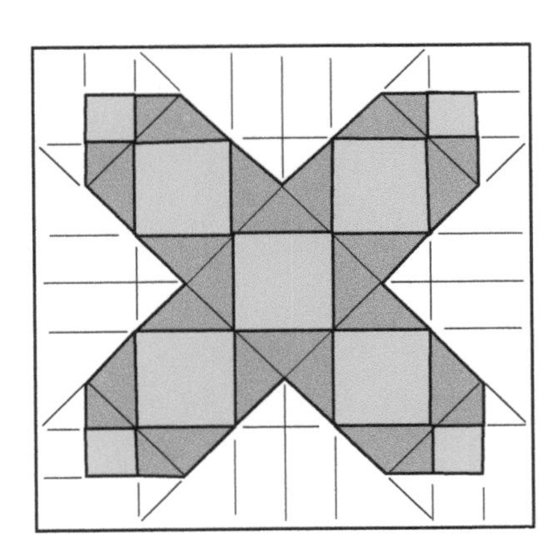

The cubehemioctahedron is basically a cube with sunken corners. This model uses square symmetry. The darker paper in the crease pattern shows the sunken sides. The paper is divided into fifths.

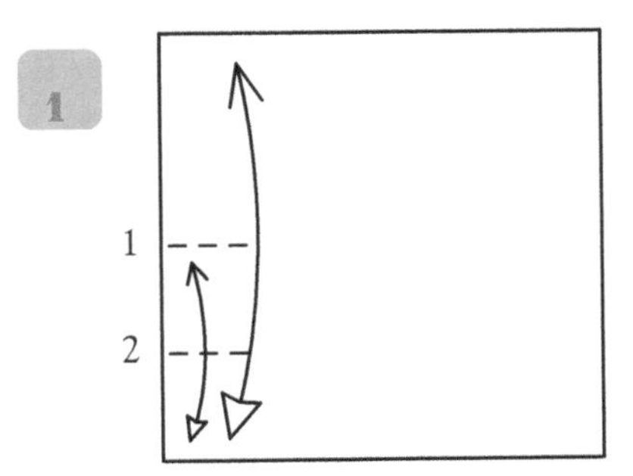

Fold and unfold on the left.

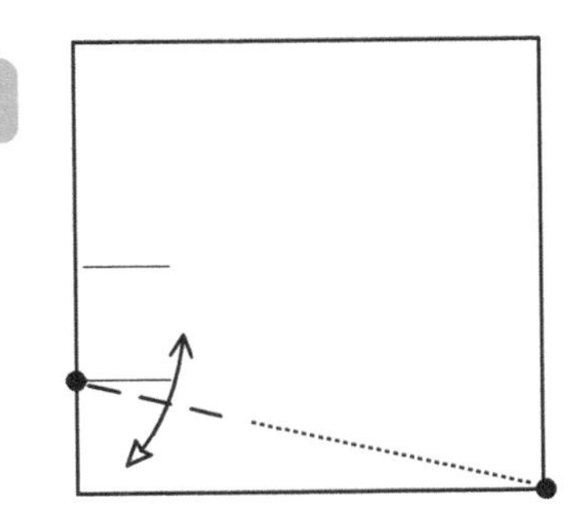

Fold and unfold.

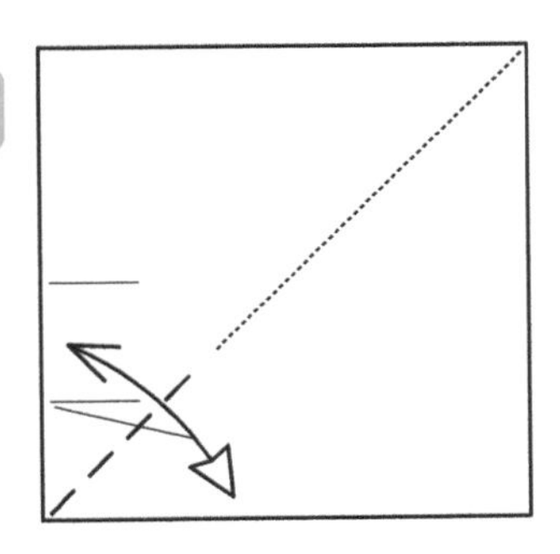

Fold and unfold.

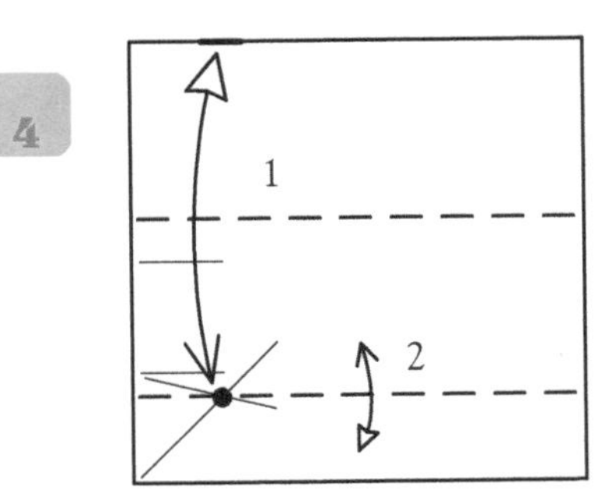

Fold and unfold.

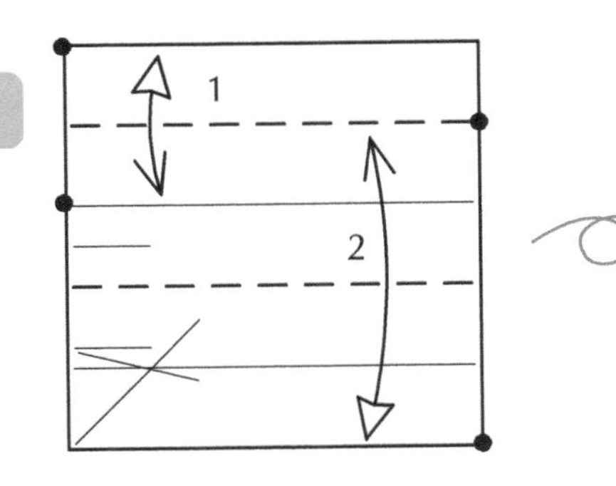

Fold and unfold.

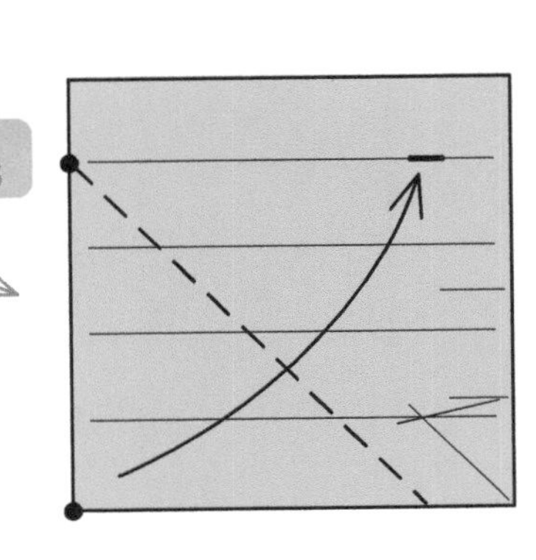

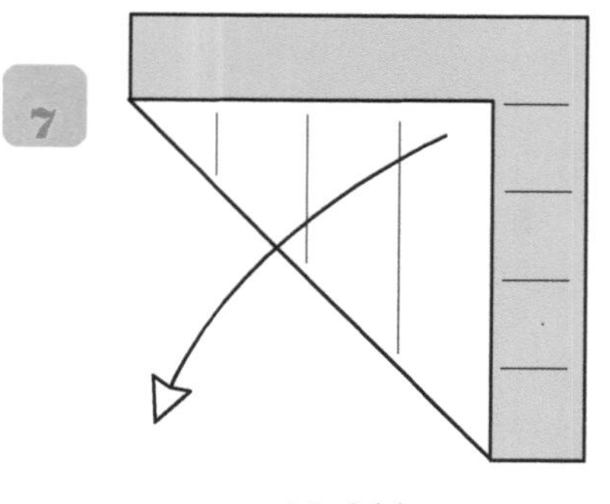

Unfold.

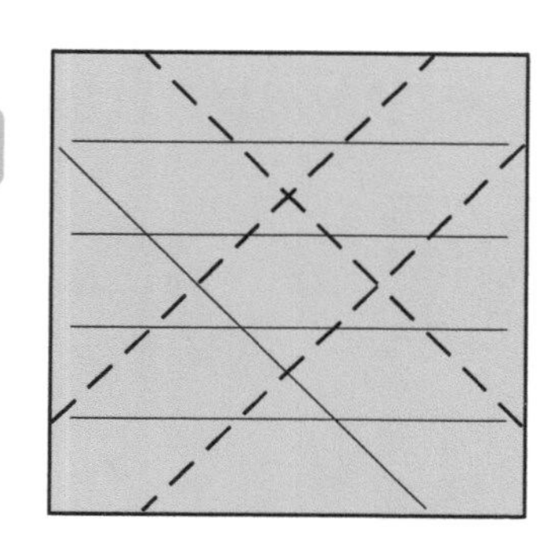

Fold and unfold three times.

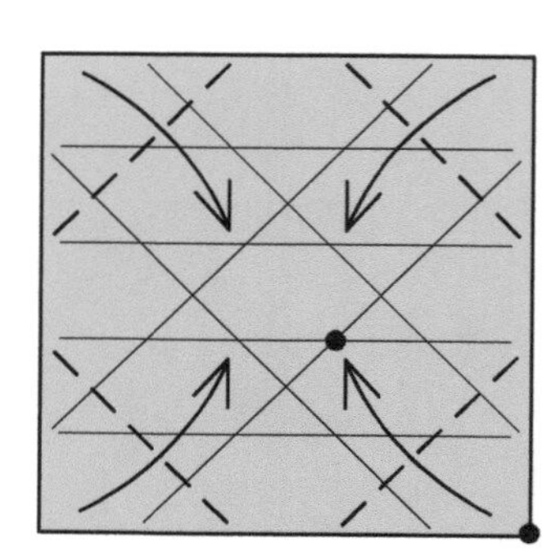

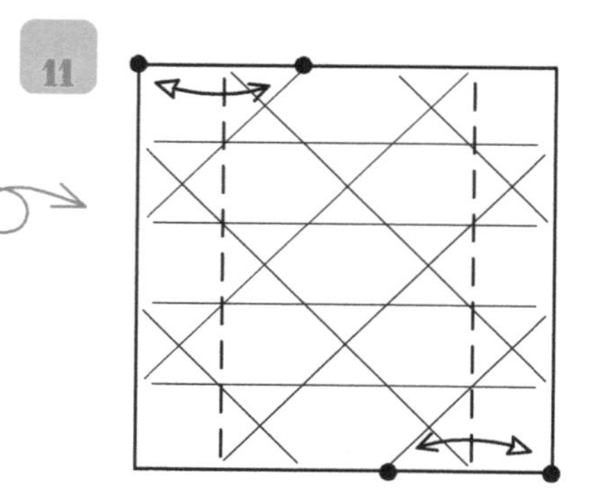

Unfold.

Fold and unfold.

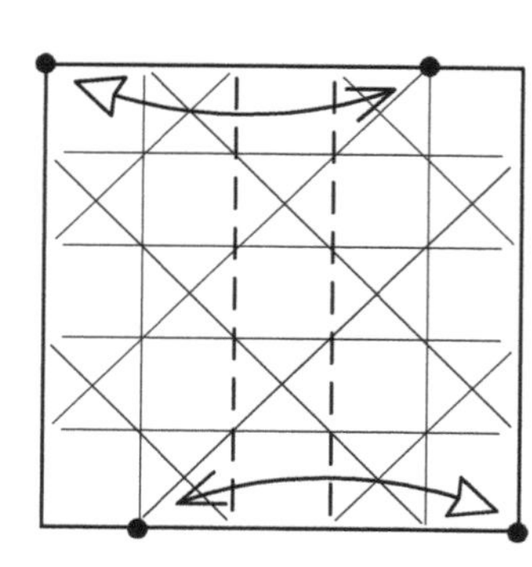

Fold and unfold.

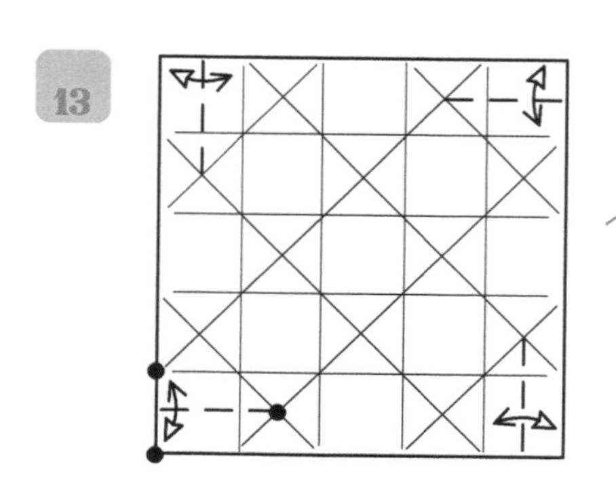

Fold and unfold.

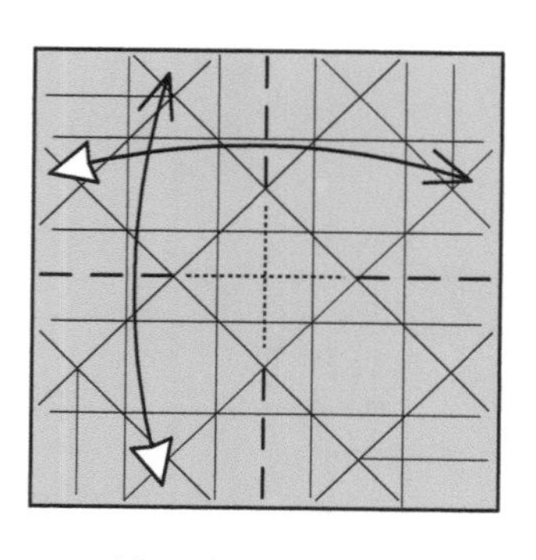

Fold and unfold in half but not in the center.

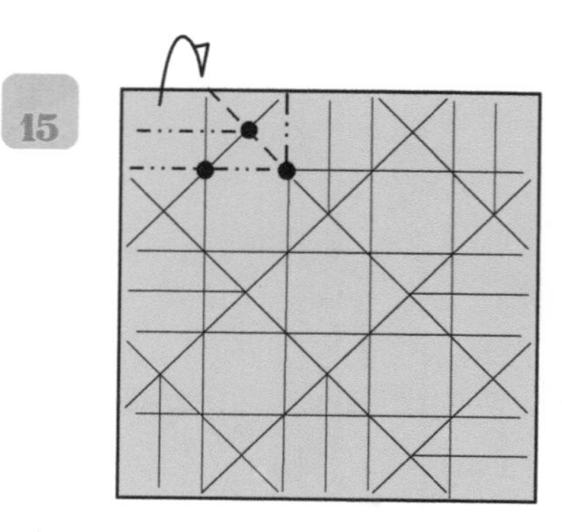

Push in at the upper dot and puff out at the two lower dots, to make a sunken triangle.

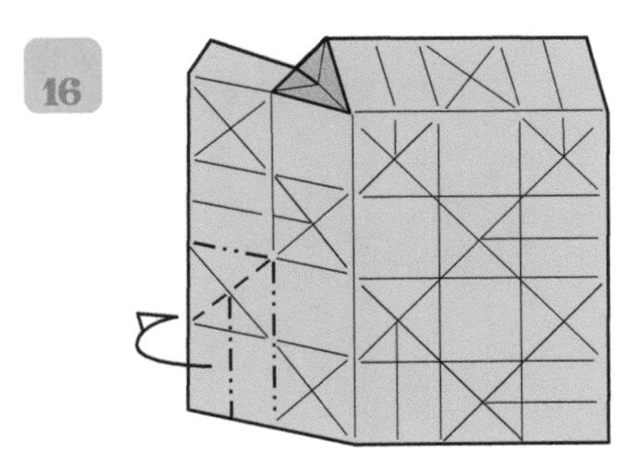

Repeat step 15 three times.

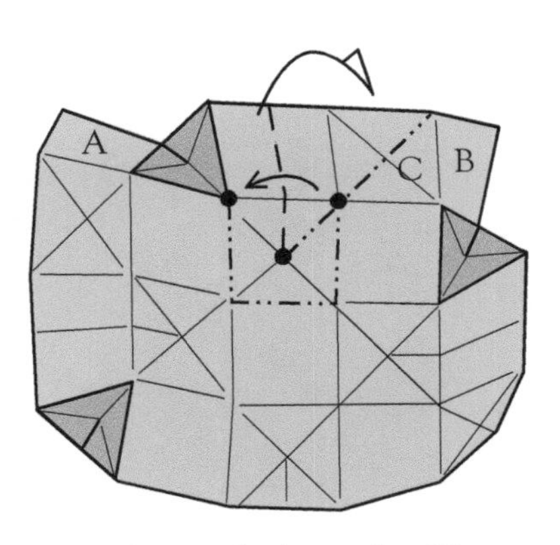

Push in at the lower dot. The other two will meet to form a sunken triangle. Follow A, B, and C into the next step.

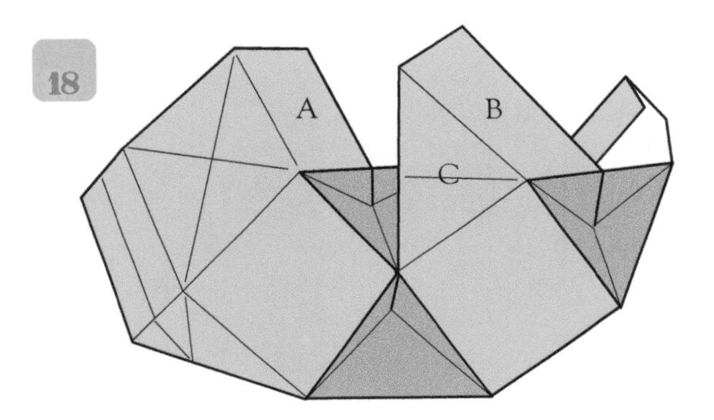

Repeat step 17 three times.

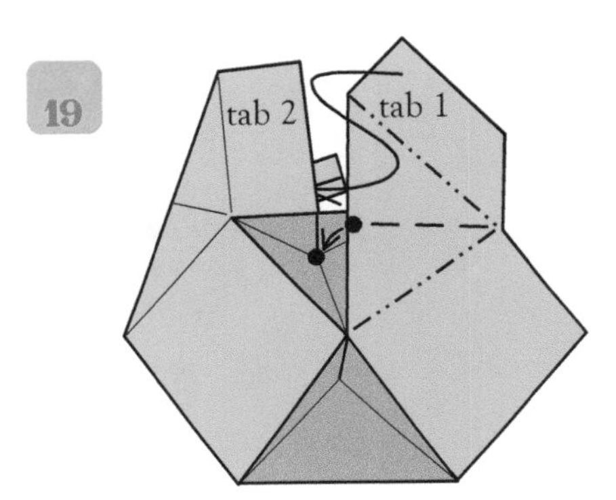

There are four tabs at the top, two are shown. Tuck tab 1 under tab 2 so the dots meet. Continue all around.

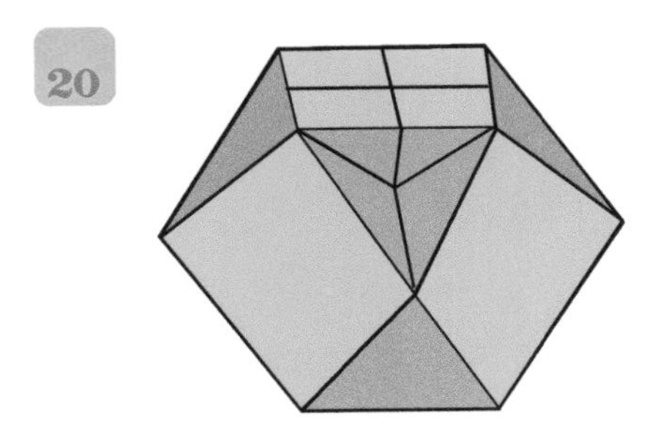

Rotate the top to the bottom.

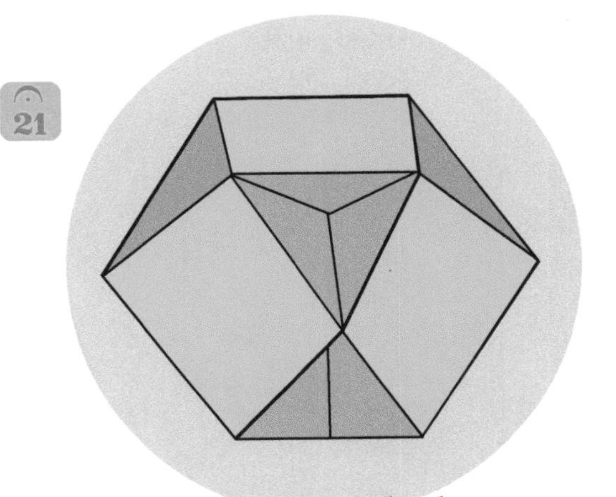

Cubehemioctahedron

Stella Octangula

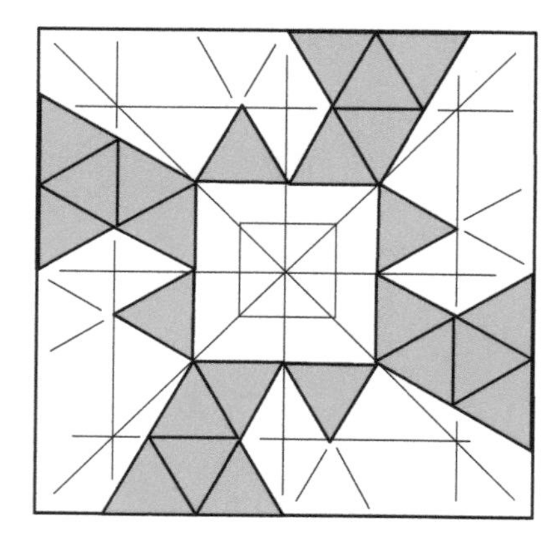

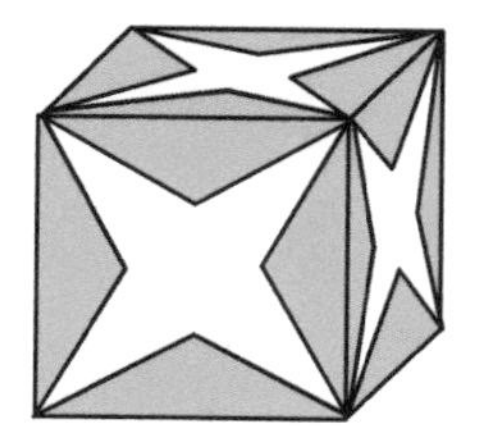

All the sides of this eight-pointed star are equilateral triangles. It can be formed by taking a cube and collapsing along an "X" on each side. However, this design uses a different approach. The model holds its shape well without any locks or tabs. I hope you like the last few steps as the model takes shape in a surprising manner. Square symmetry simplifies the folding method.

1

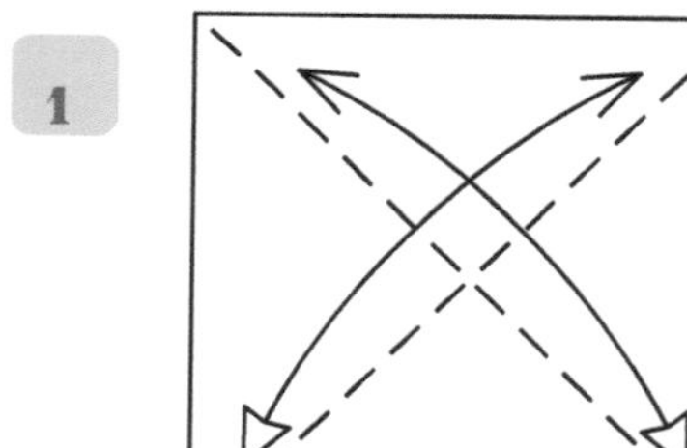

Fold and unfold.

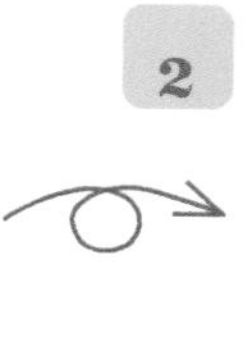

2

Fold and unfold.

3

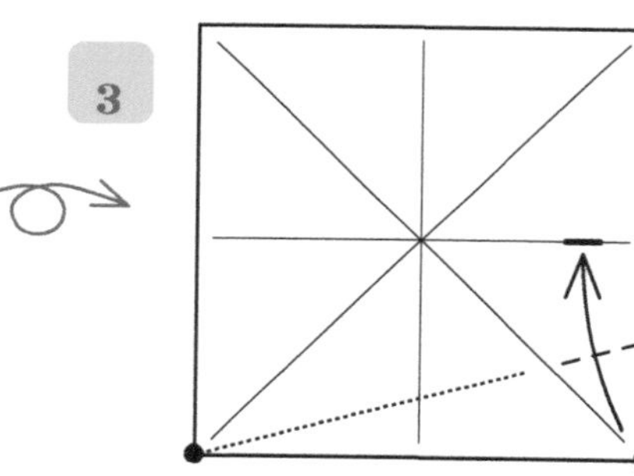

Bring the corner to the line.

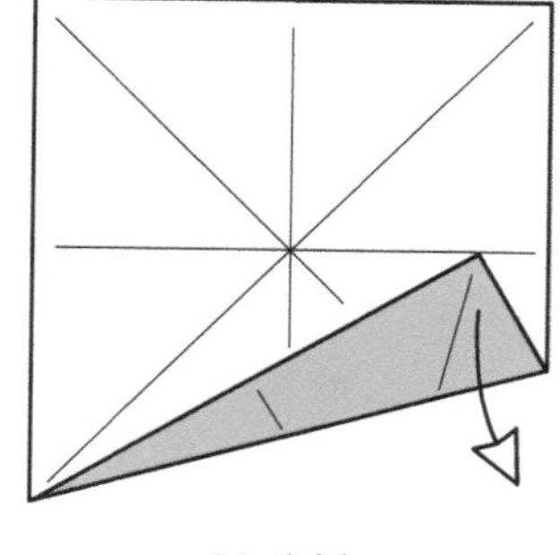

Unfold.

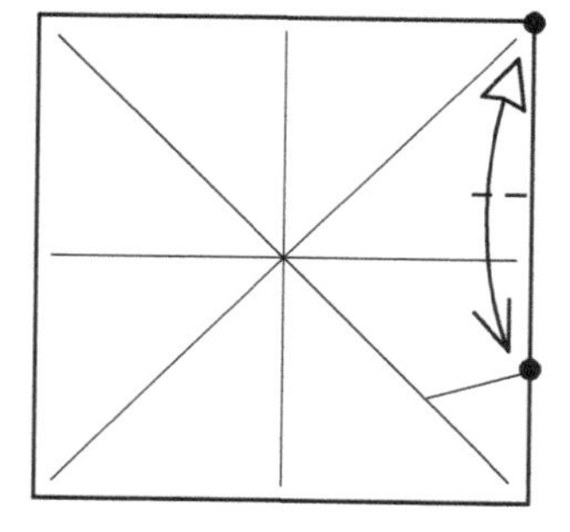

Fold and unfold on the right.

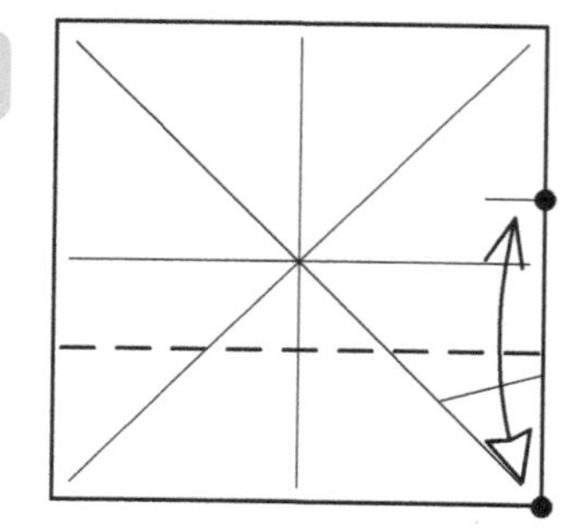

Fold and unfold. Rotate 180°.

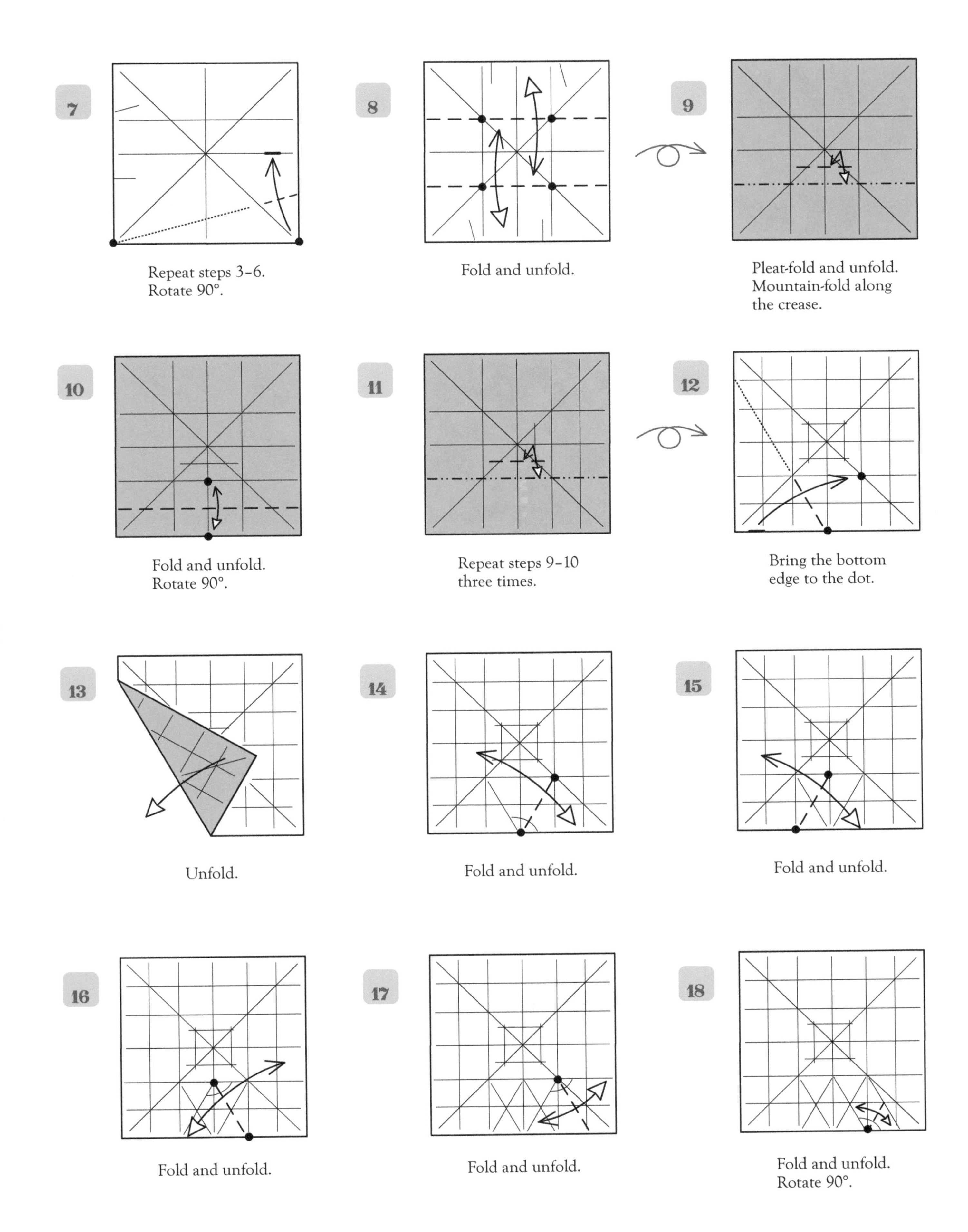

7. Repeat steps 3–6. Rotate 90°.

8. Fold and unfold.

9. Pleat-fold and unfold. Mountain-fold along the crease.

10. Fold and unfold. Rotate 90°.

11. Repeat steps 9–10 three times.

12. Bring the bottom edge to the dot.

13. Unfold.

14. Fold and unfold.

15. Fold and unfold.

16. Fold and unfold.

17. Fold and unfold.

18. Fold and unfold. Rotate 90°.

19

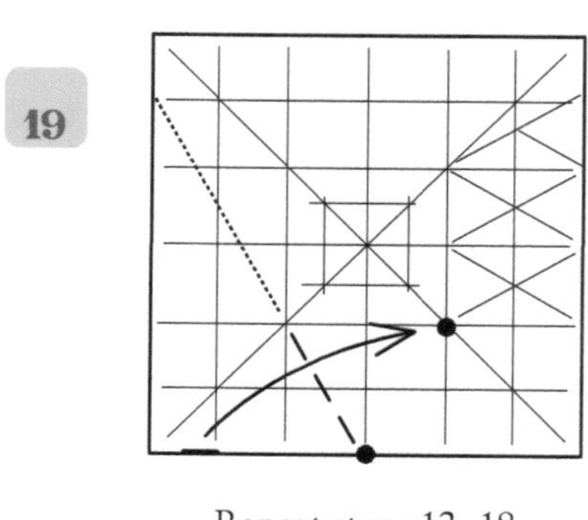

Repeat steps 12–18
three times.

20

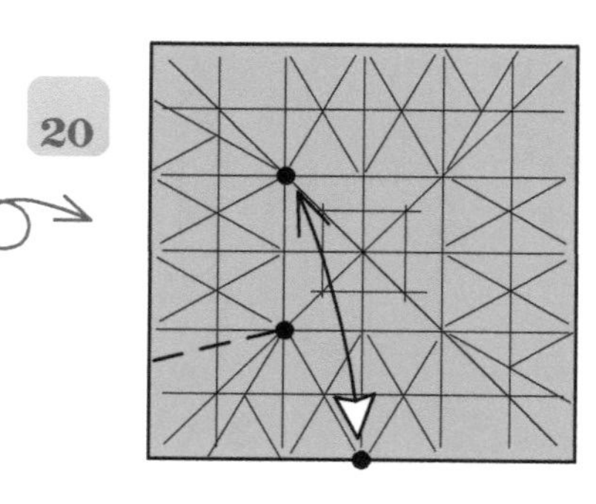

Fold and unfold.
Rotate 90°.

21

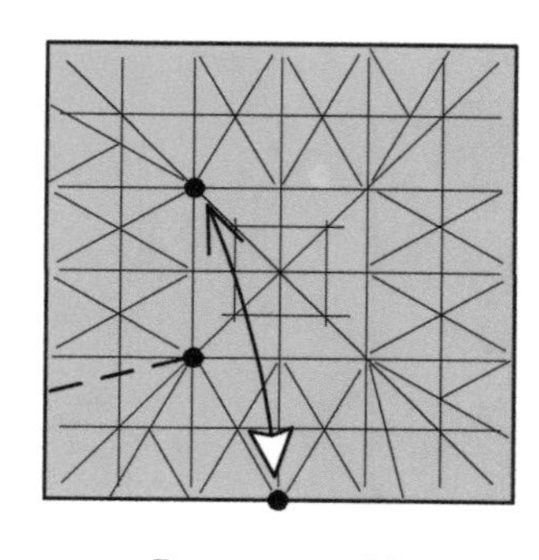

Repeat step 20
three times.

22

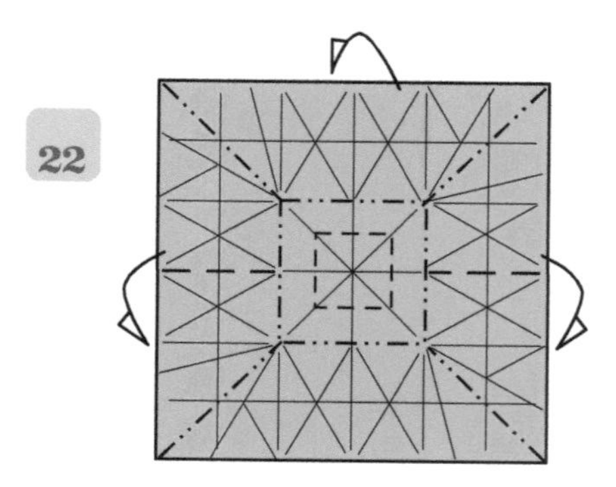

This is similar to making a
sunken waterbomb base.

23

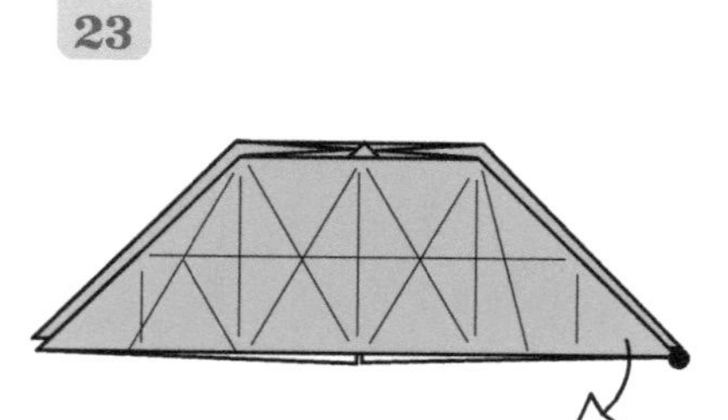

Spread the paper and rotate
the top to the bottom so the
dot goes to the top.

24

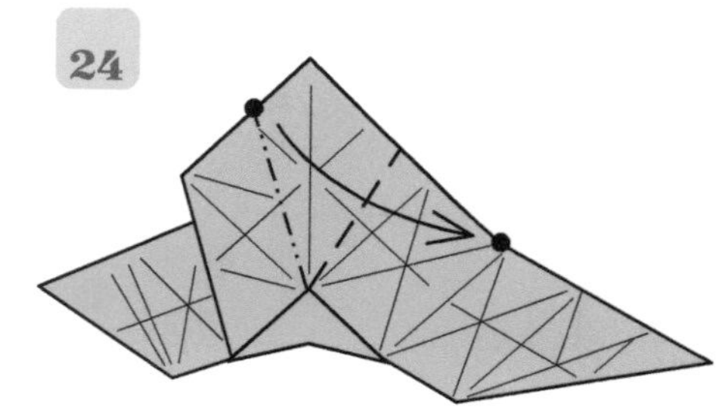

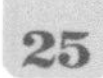

25

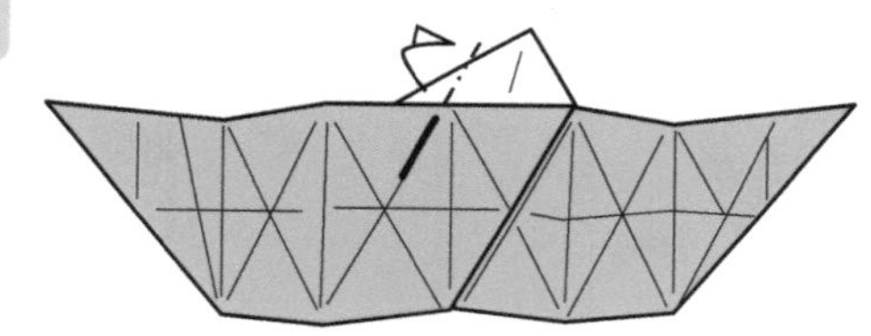

Fold behind the bold line.

26

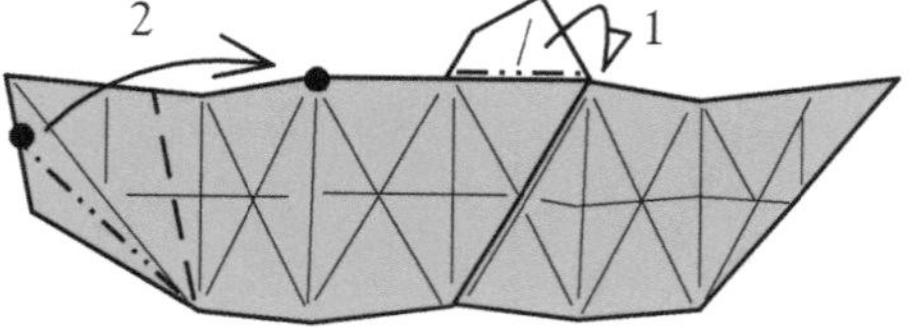

1. Wrap around.
2. Repeat steps 24–26
   three times.

27

1. Push in so the dots meet.
   The dark region will be
   hidden.
2. Bend along the crease at 2.
3. Repeat 1 and 2 three times,
   going around.

28

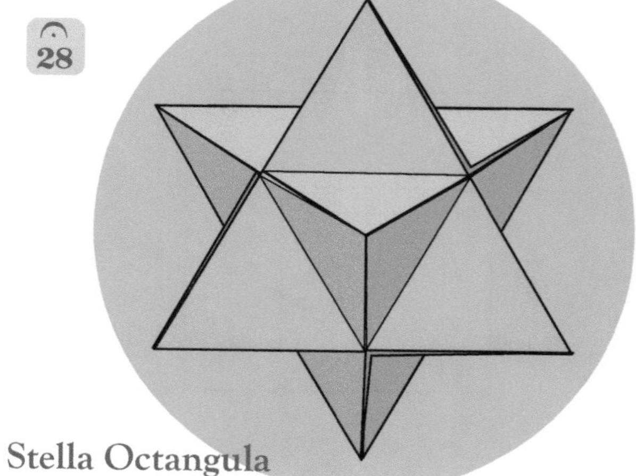

Stella Octangula

Fourth Movement

Allegro: The Buzzing of Backyard Bugs

8va

Backyard bugs are all around to entertain you. Whether the Mosquito finds you attractive, the Hornet scares you, or the Katydid simply displays its beauty, they will demand your attention. Fold carefully to bring these small creatures to life and enjoy their high-pitched songs. From the wingless Ant to the Dragonfly with four wings, these complex creatures add enjoyment and mystery.

Ant

As one of the smartest insects, ants teach each other by their interactions. They evolved about 130 million years ago and started agriculture long before people did. They can carry objects over 50 times their own weight. Working together, they carry leaves and twigs to their nest. The females do not have wings and are the workers in colonies. Males have wings so they can search for mates. Some ants link legs together to act as a raft as they float in rivers.

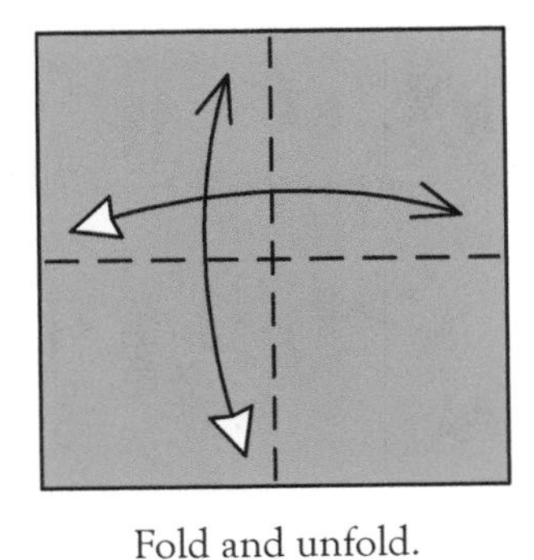

Fold and unfold.

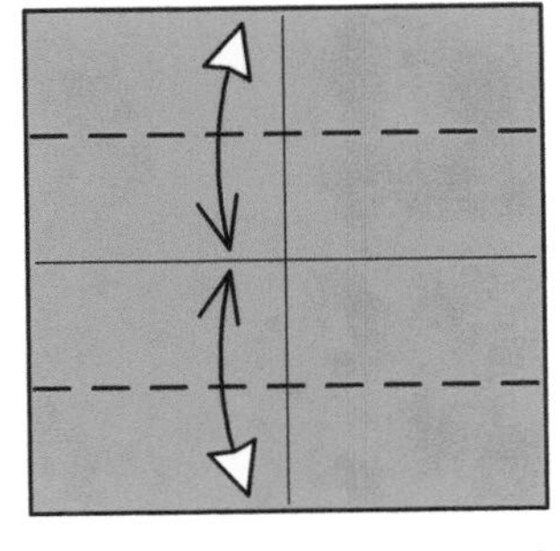

Fold to the center and unfold.

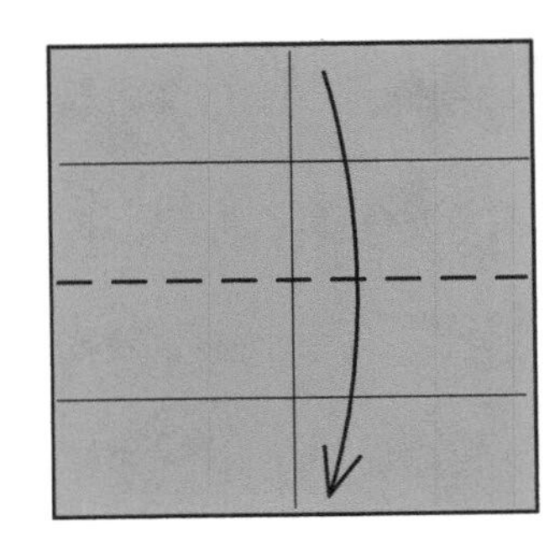

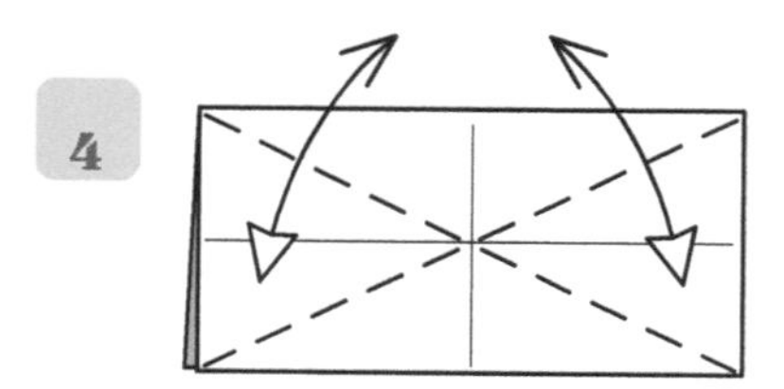

4

Fold and unfold the top layer. Repeat behind.

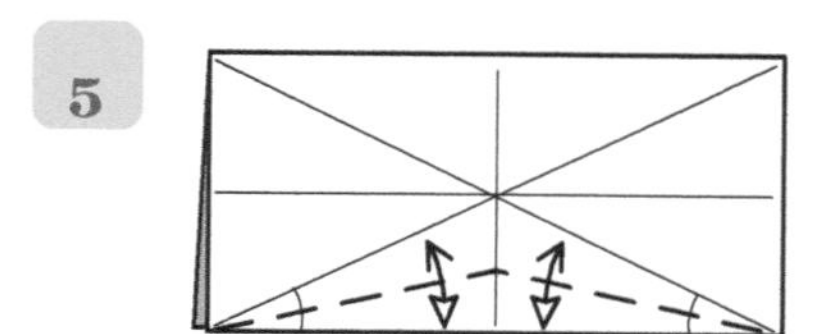

5

Fold and unfold the top layer. Do not repeat behind.

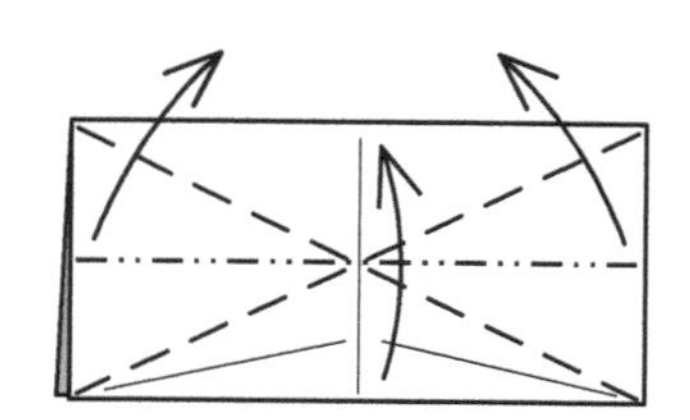

6

Fold along the creases. Repeat behind.

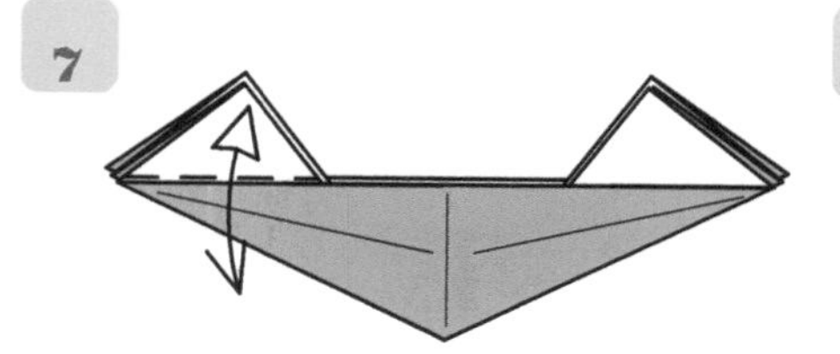

7

Fold and unfold the top flap.

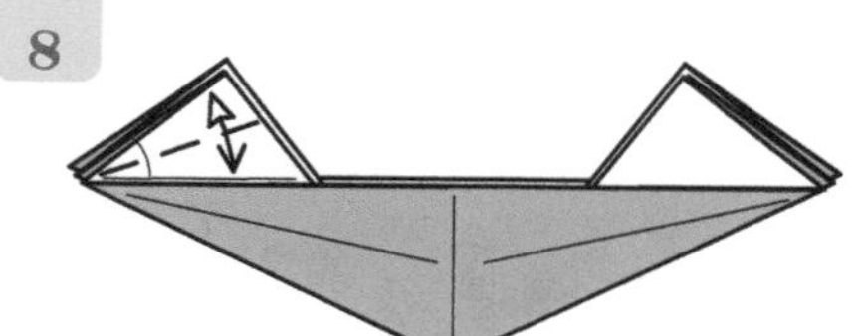

8

Fold and unfold the top flap.

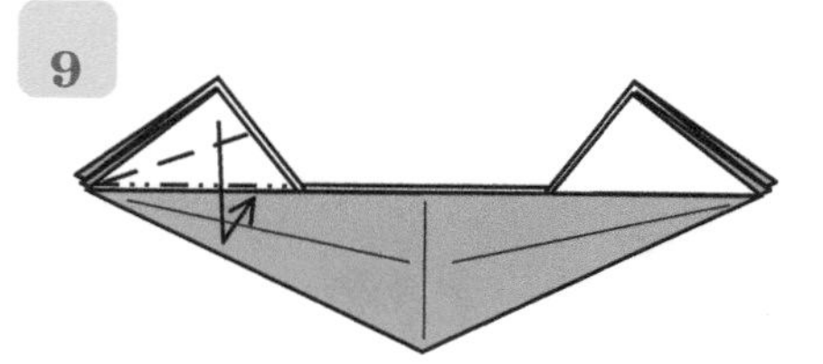

9

Crimp-fold.

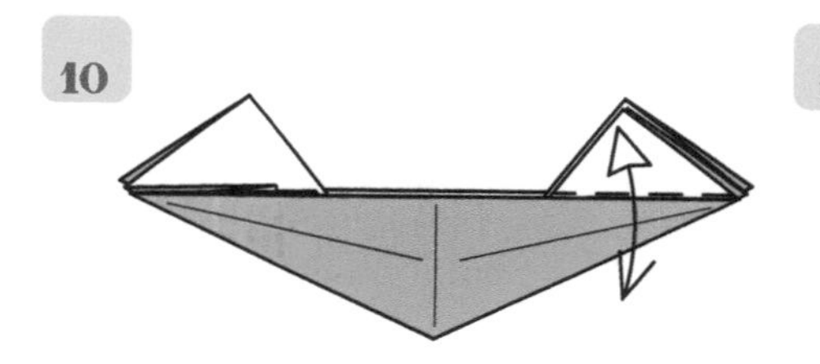

10

Repeat steps 7–9 three times, on the right and behind.

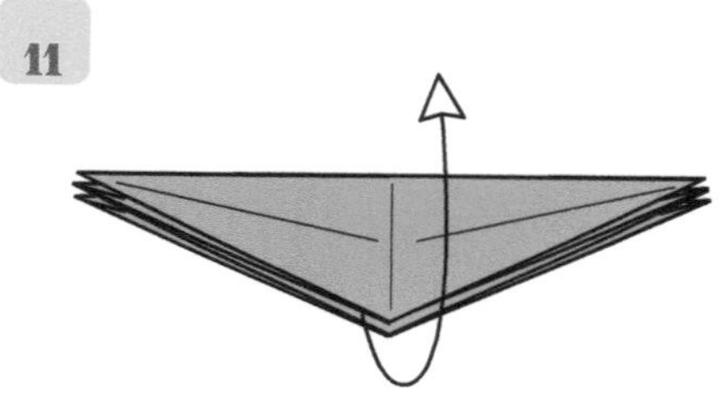

11

Unfold.

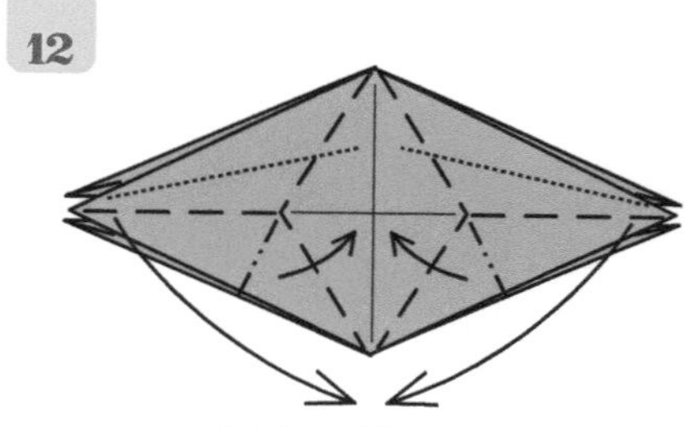

12

Make rabbit ears.

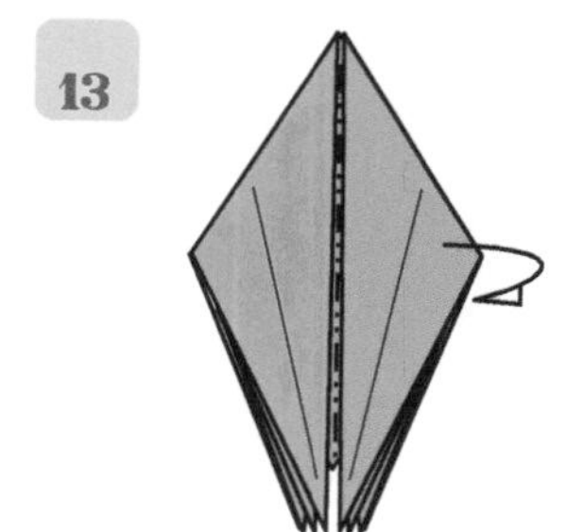

13

Fold in half and rotate.

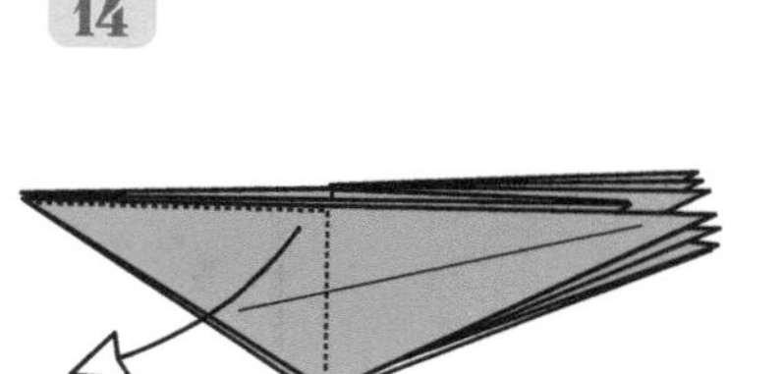

14

Pull out the paper from inside.

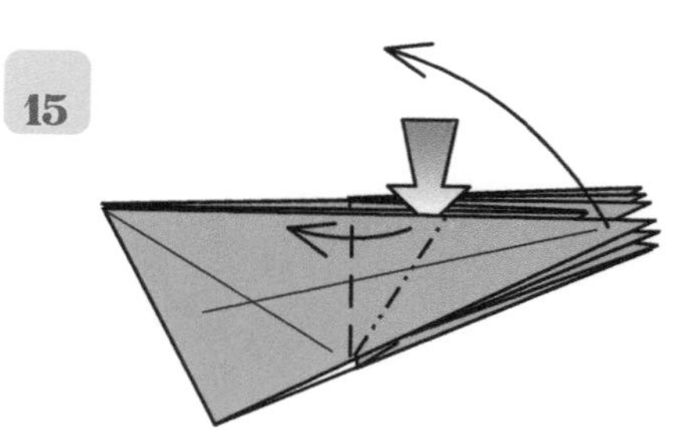

15

Squash-fold three flaps together. Repeat behind.

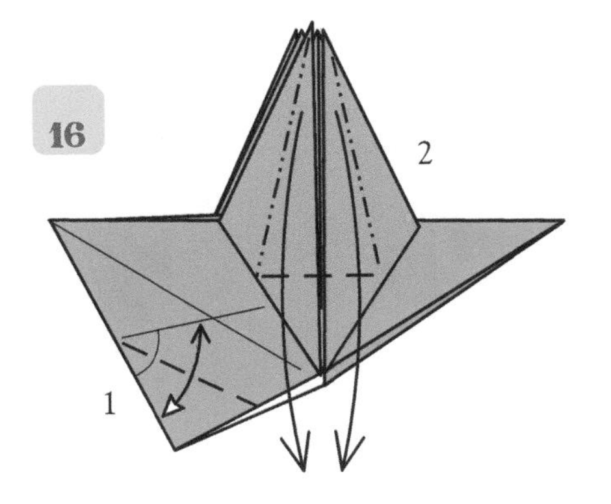

1. Fold and unfold.
2. Petal-fold all the layers, repeat behind.

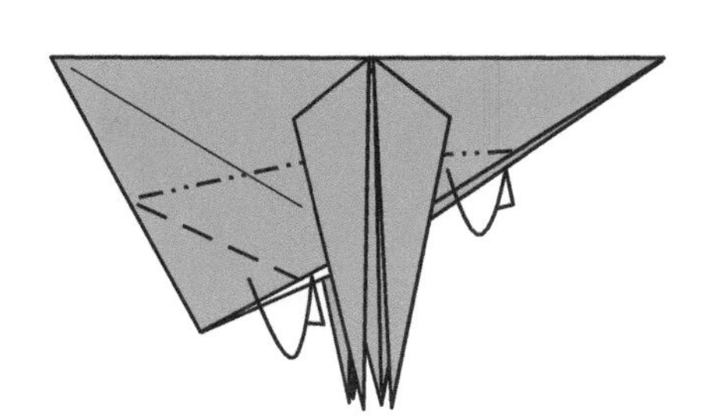

This is similar to a crimp fold. Fold inside along the creases on the left.

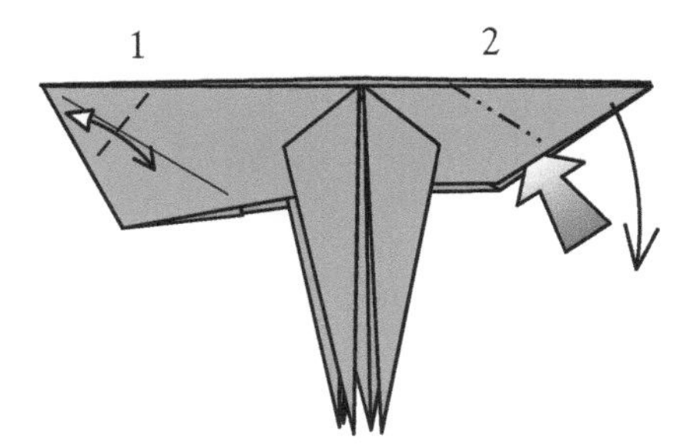

1. Fold and unfold.
2. Reverse-fold.

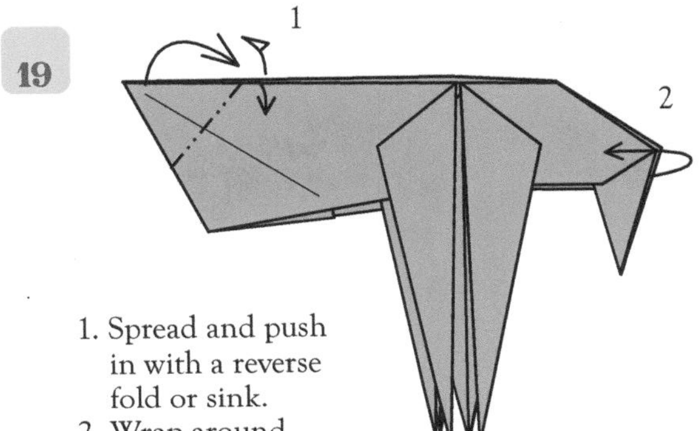

1. Spread and push in with a reverse fold or sink.
2. Wrap around, repeat behind.

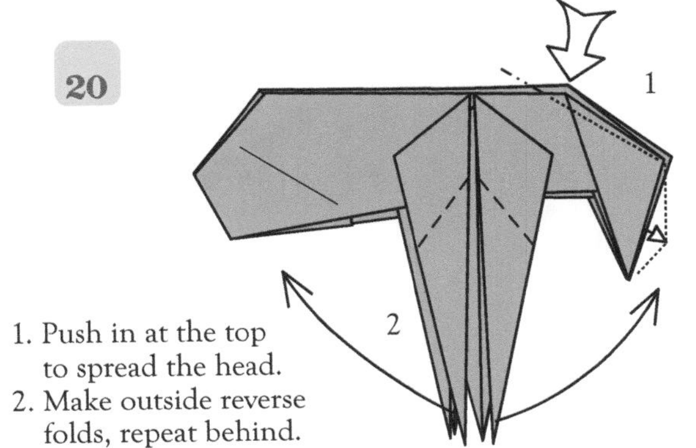

1. Push in at the top to spread the head.
2. Make outside reverse folds, repeat behind.

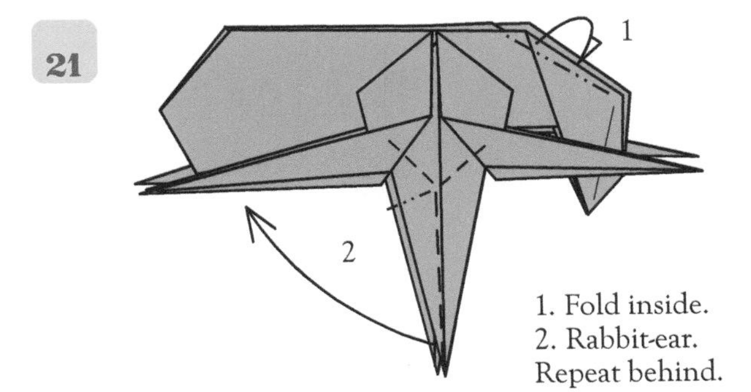

1. Fold inside.
2. Rabbit-ear.
Repeat behind.

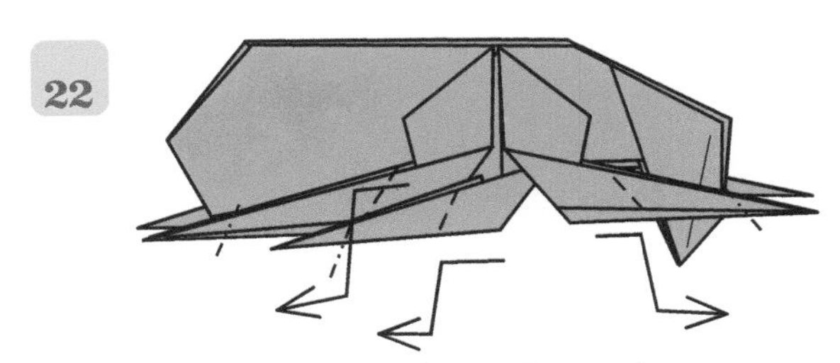

Bend the legs with outside reverse folds. Repeat behind

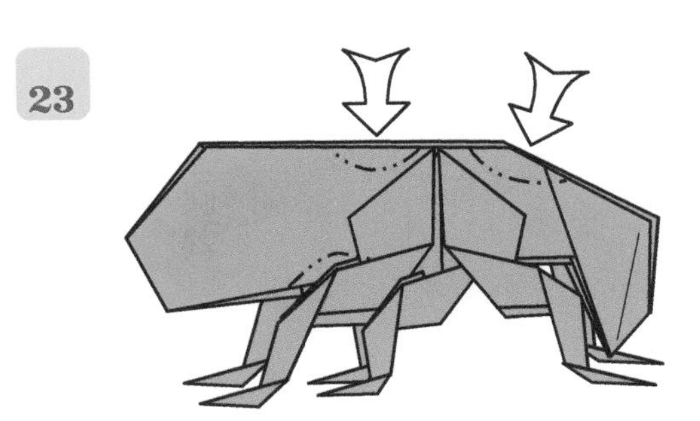

Shape the head, thorax, and body.

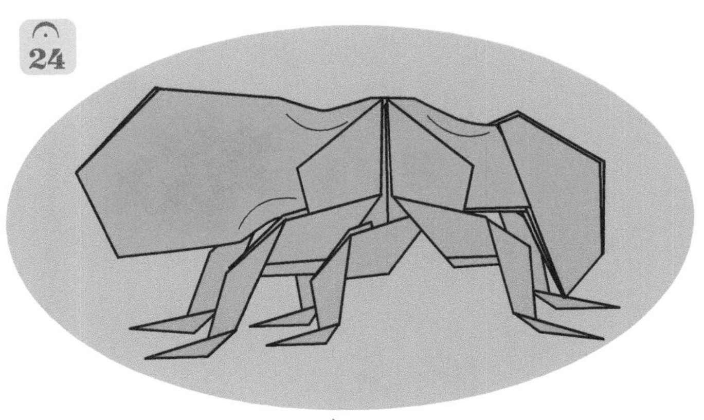

Ant

Mosquito

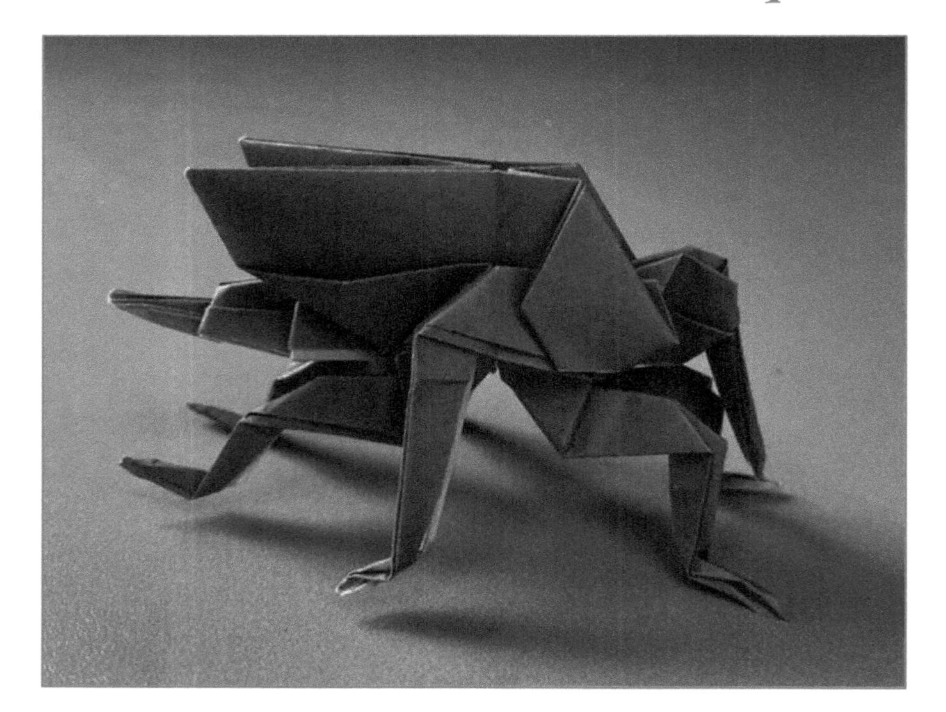

Mosquitoes are a variety of fly and are named by the Spanish word for "little fly". They lived with dinosaurs during the Triassic Period 400 million years ago. Only the females bite and though they prefer horses and cattle, we will do just fine. Annoying as they are, they are part of the food chain for frogs, spiders, dragonflies, fish, and other animals. The adults stay close to their larval grounds and live for about two months.

1

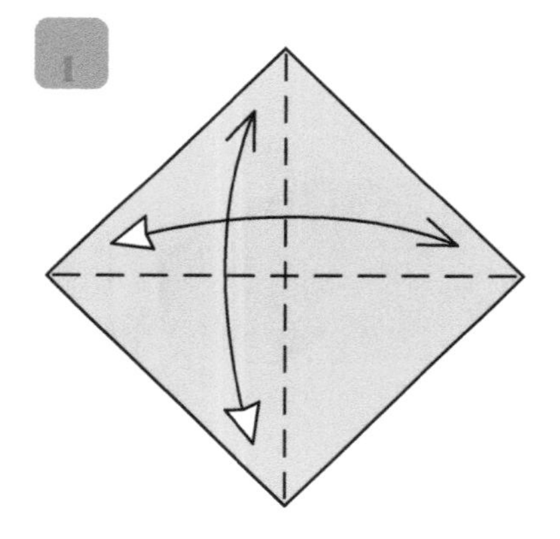

Fold and unfold.

2

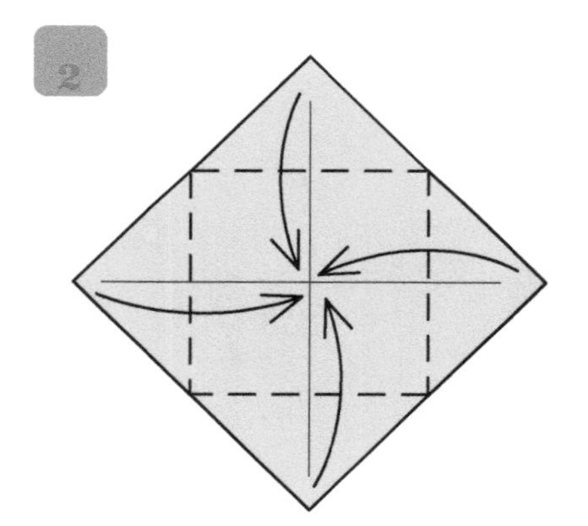

Fold the corners to the center.

3

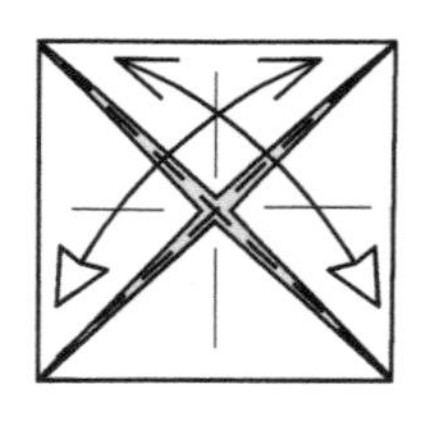

Fold and unfold. Rotate.

4

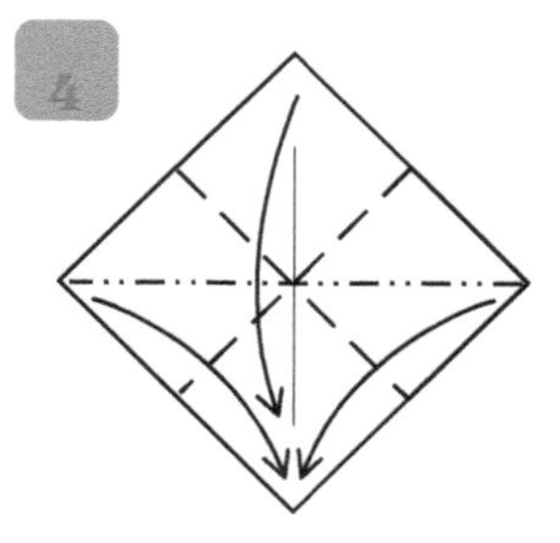

This is the same as the Preliminary Fold.

5

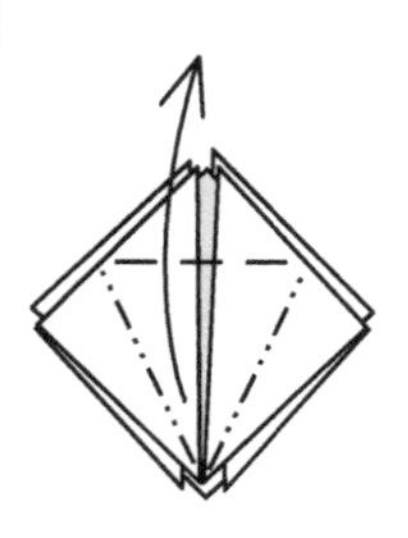

Petal-fold, repeat behind.

6

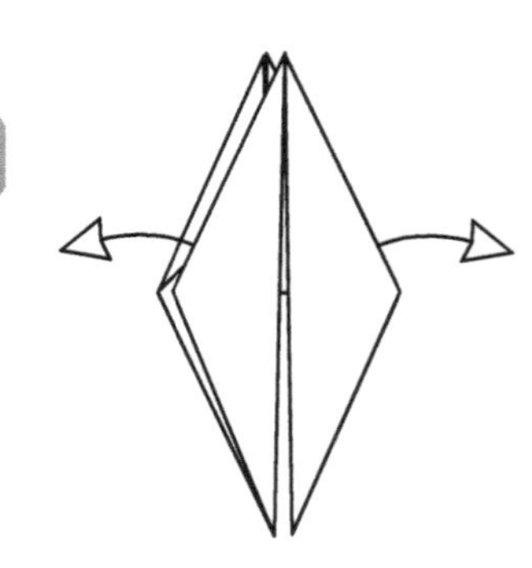

Pull out the hidden corners, repeat behind.

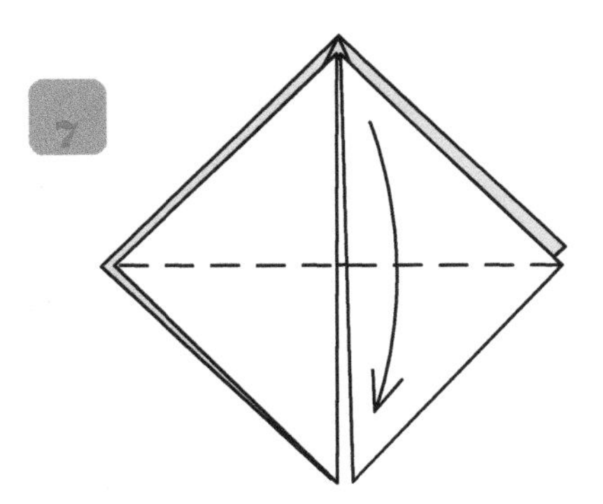

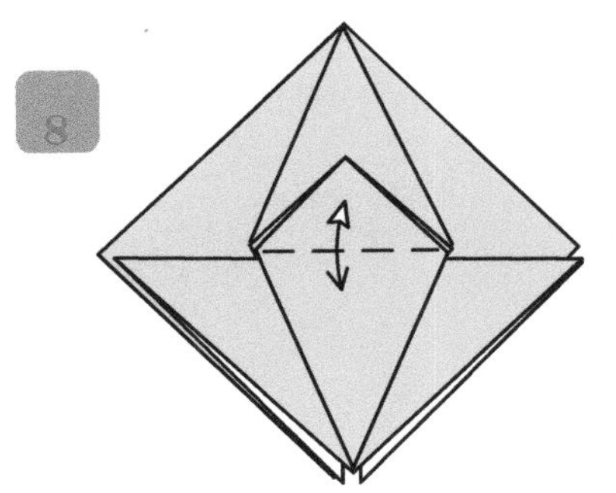

Fold and unfold.

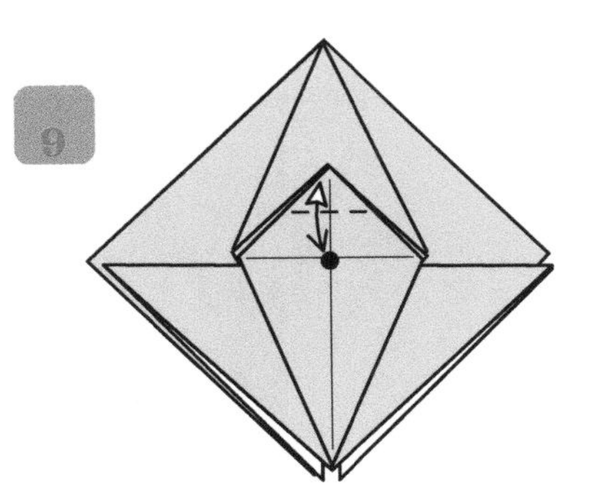

Fold and unfold.

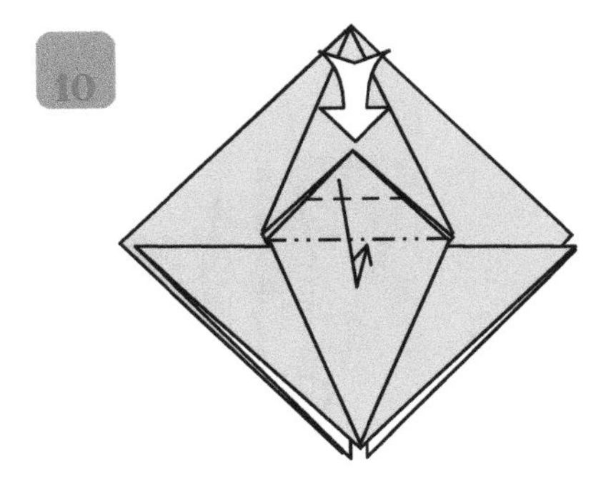

Sink down and up.

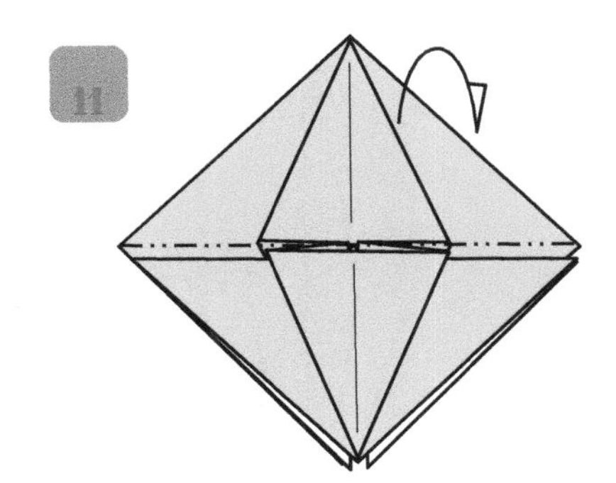

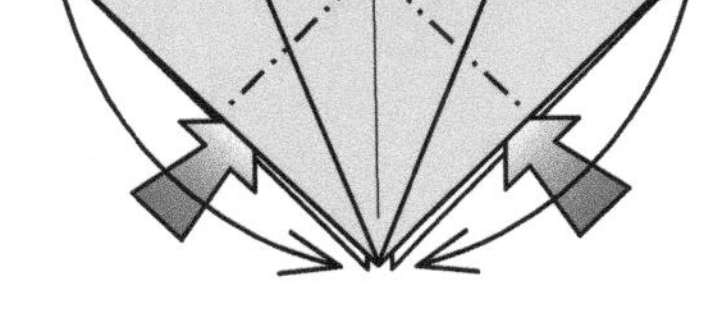

Make reverse folds.
Repeat behind.

Fold and unfold
the top flaps.

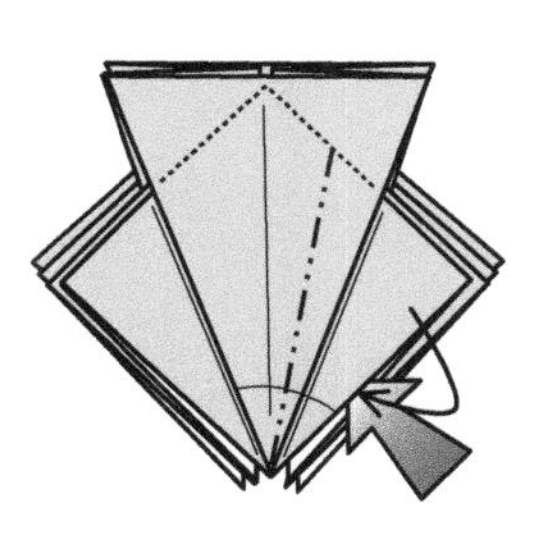

Reverse-fold.

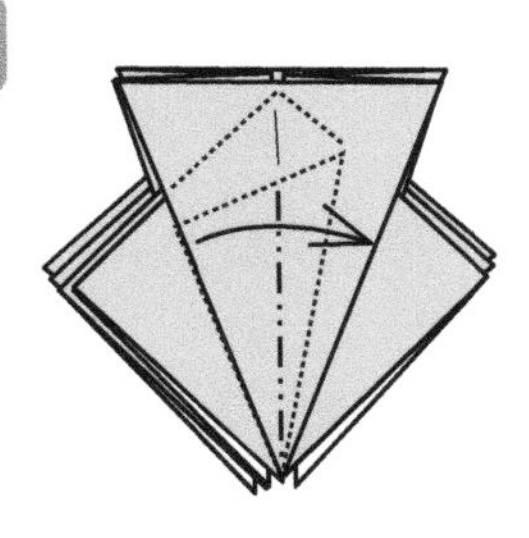

Reverse-fold the
hidden flap.

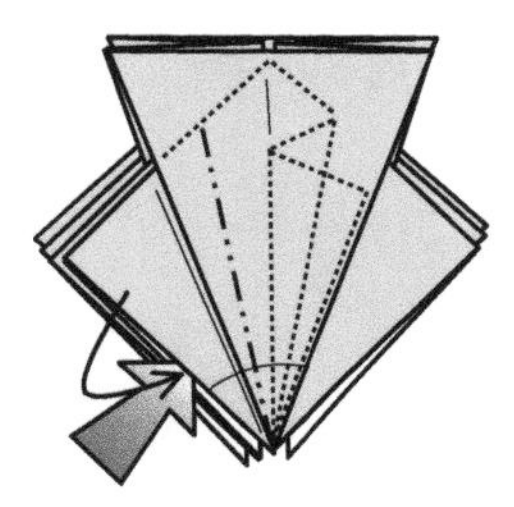

Repeat steps 14–15
on the left.

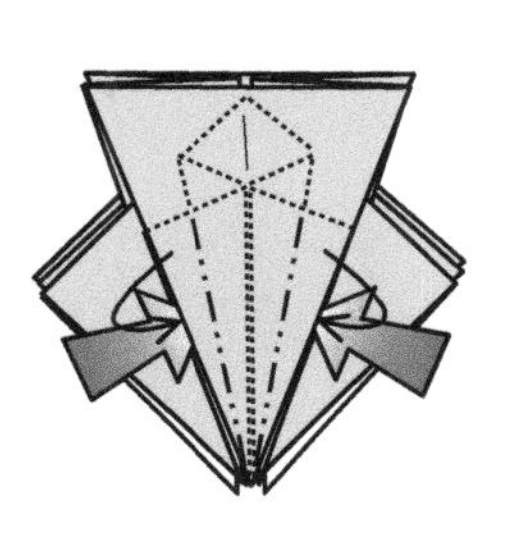

Make reverse folds.

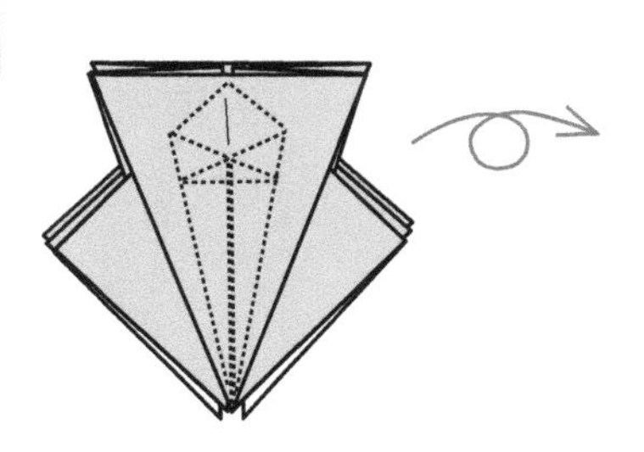

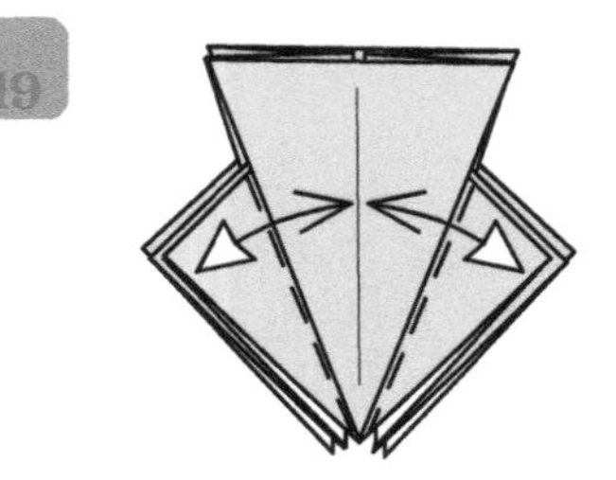

Repeat steps 13–18.

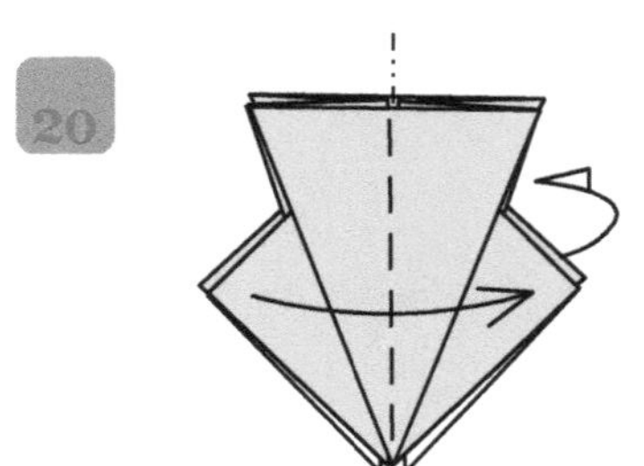

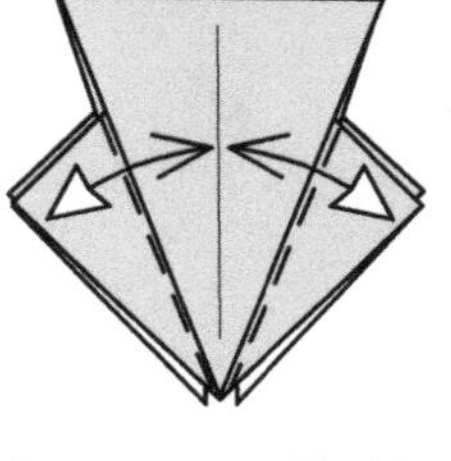

Repeat steps 13–19.

22

Repeat behind.

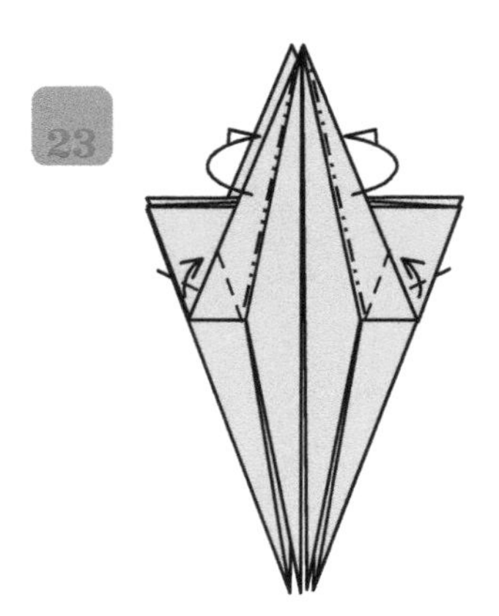

Repeat behind.

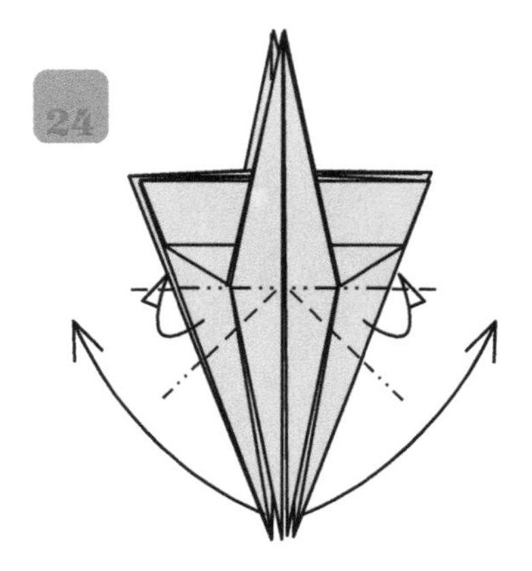

Make crimp folds.

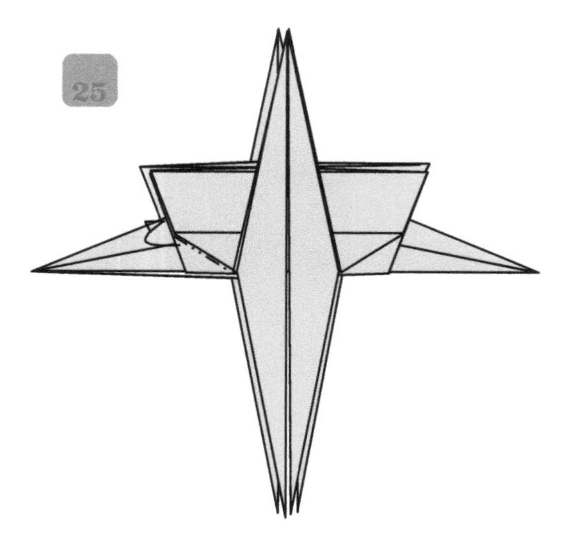

Slide the paper.
Repeat behind.

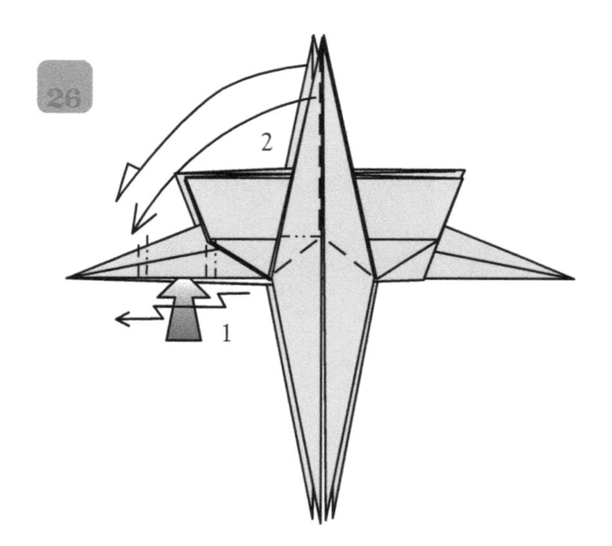

1. Make crimp folds.
2. Rabbit-ear, repeat behind.

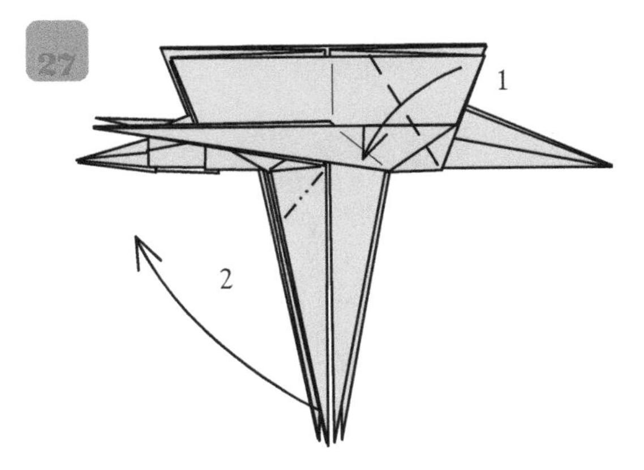

1. Fold down.
2. Reverse-fold.
Repeat behind.

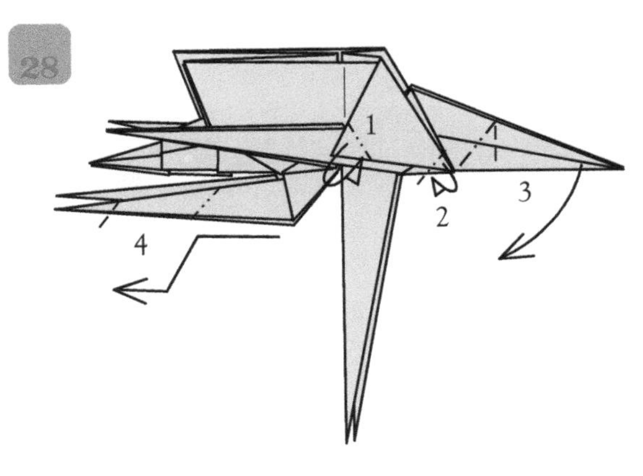

1. Mountain-fold.
2. Mountain-fold.
3. Crimp-fold.
4. Make reverse folds.
Repeat behind at 1, 2, and 4.

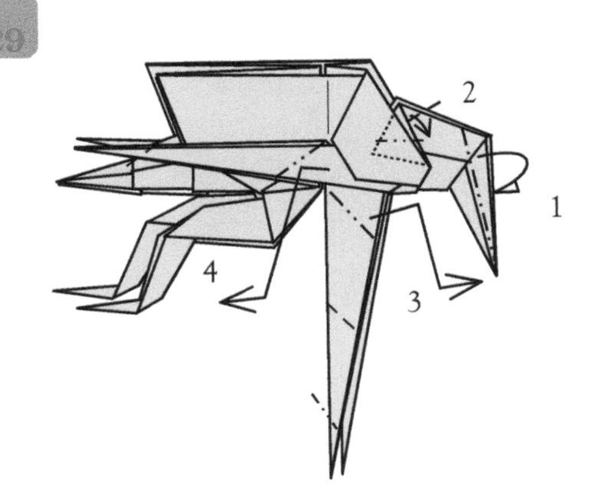

1. Fold inside.
2. Reverse-fold.
3. Make reverse folds.
4. Make reverse folds.
Repeat behind.

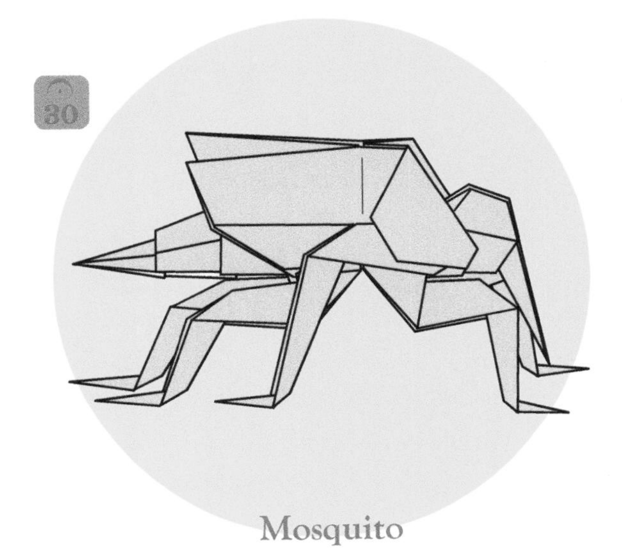

Cicada

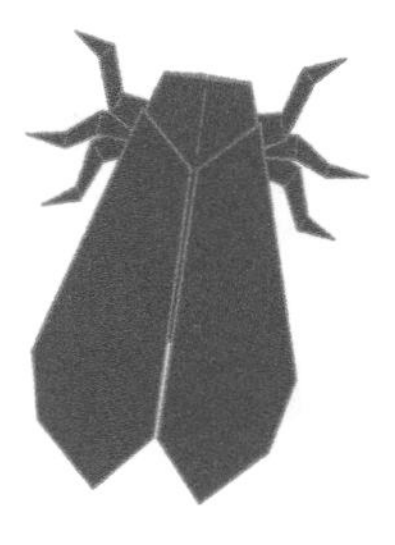

Cicadas live a longer life than most bugs, spending 13 or 17 years underground as nymphs. They feed off of trees. At the right yearly cycle and when the temperature eight feet below the ground is exactly 64° F, they emerge and climb on trees. First, they shed their skin. Since they are clumsy flyers, they are easy targets for birds and other animals to feast upon. Huge choruses of male cicadas sing very loud buzzing songs.

1

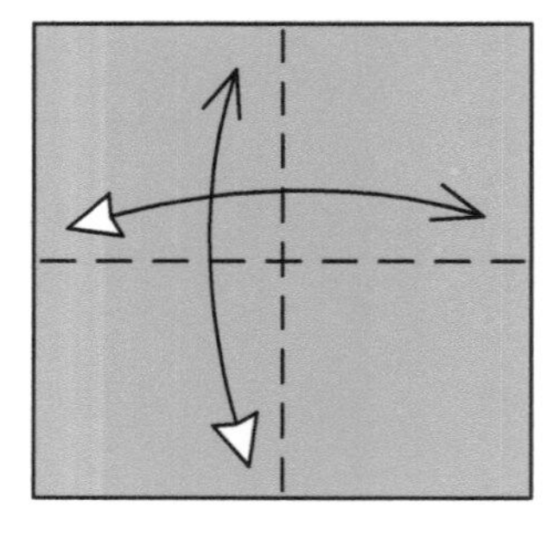

Fold and unfold.

2

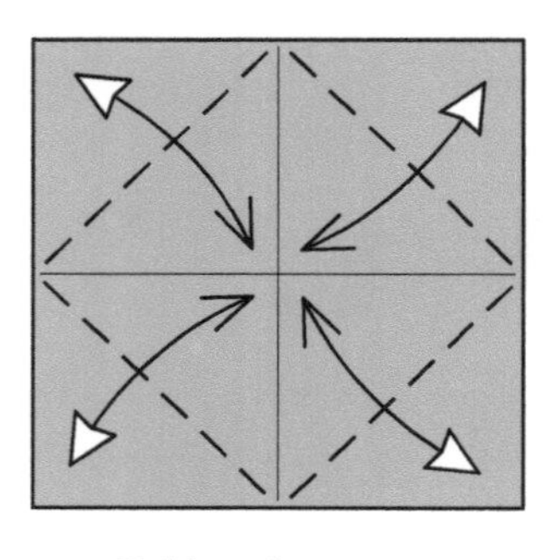

Fold to the center and unfold.

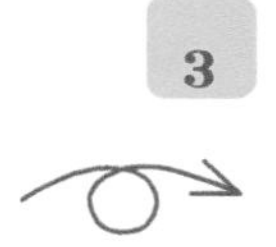

3

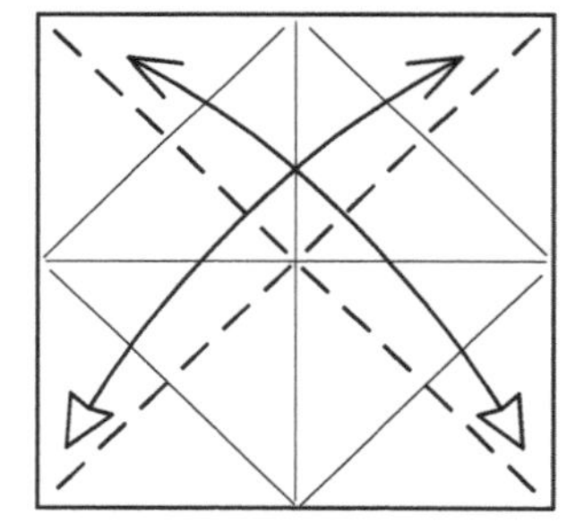

Fold and unfold.

4

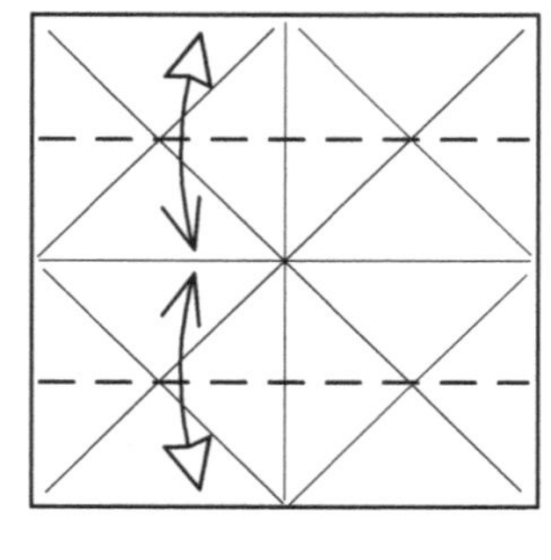

Fold to the center and unfold.

5

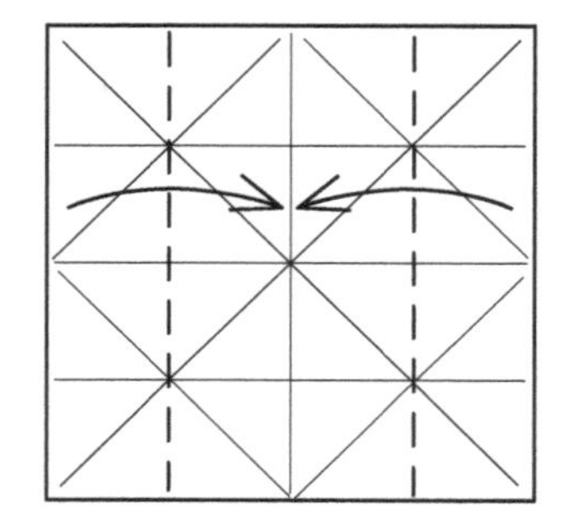

Fold to the center.

6

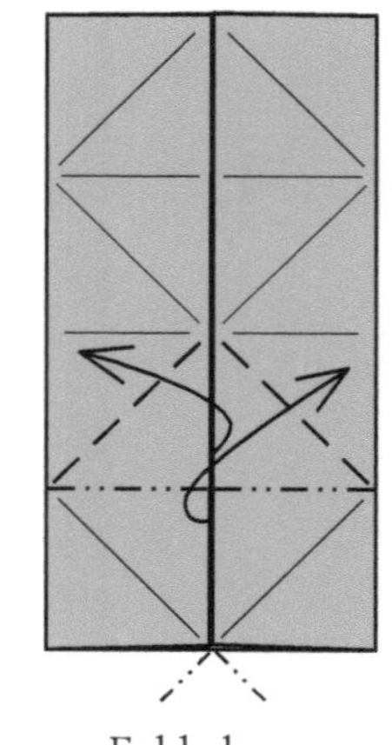

Fold along the creases.

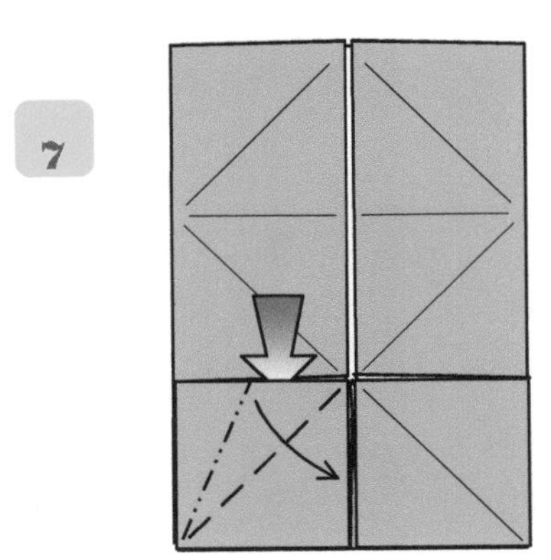

Squash-fold.

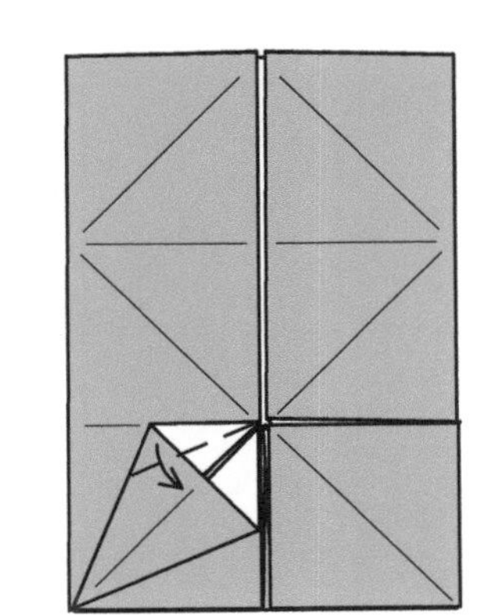

9

Wrap around
and tuck inside.

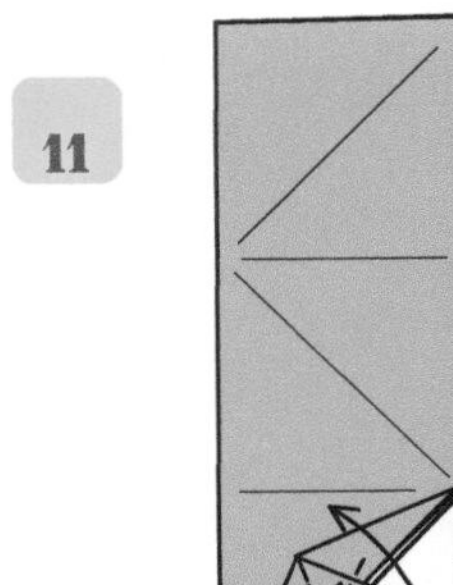
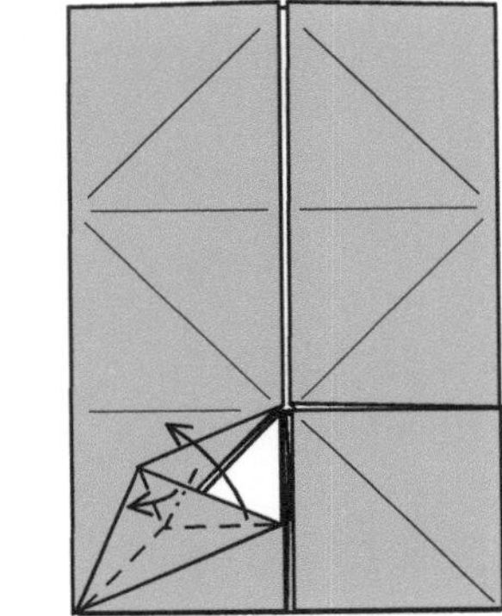

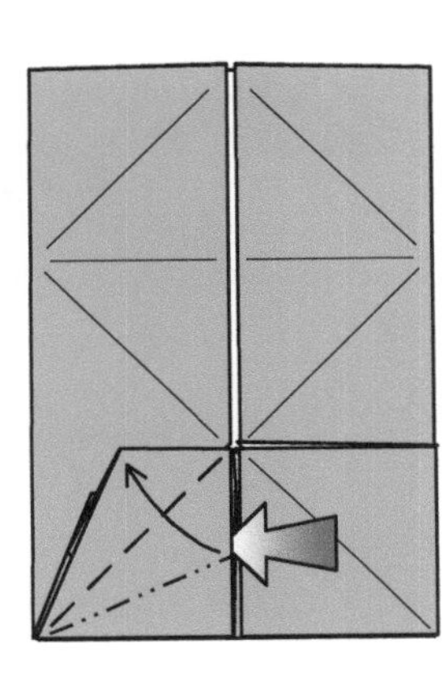

Repeat steps 7–11 in
the opposite direction.

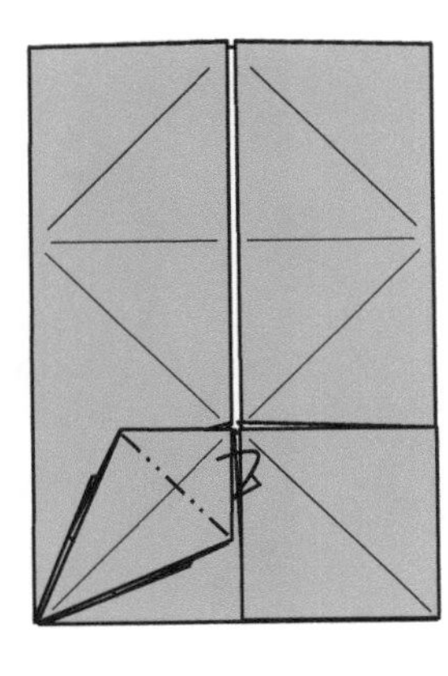

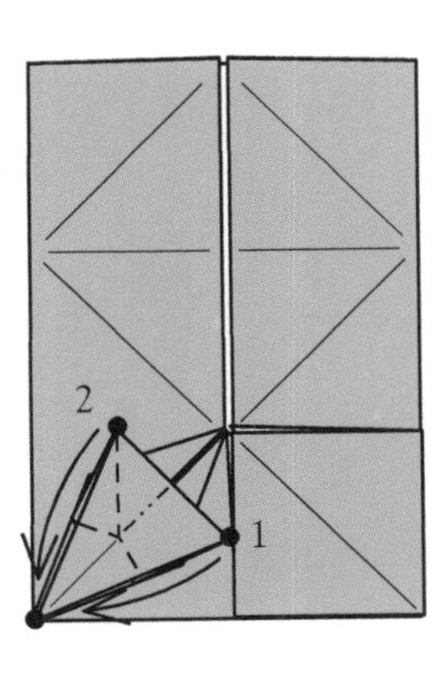

Fold in order.

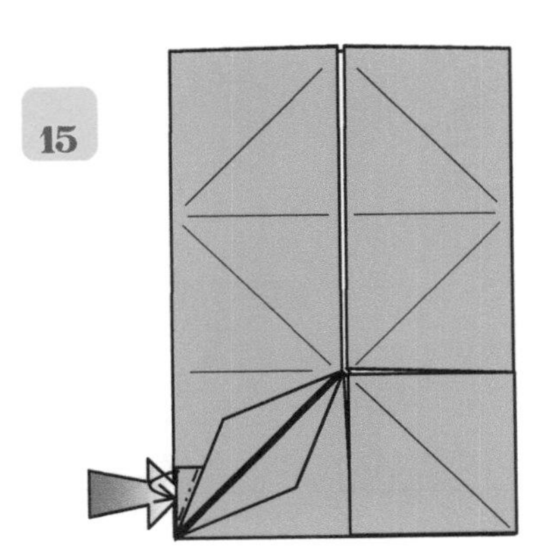

Reverse-fold.

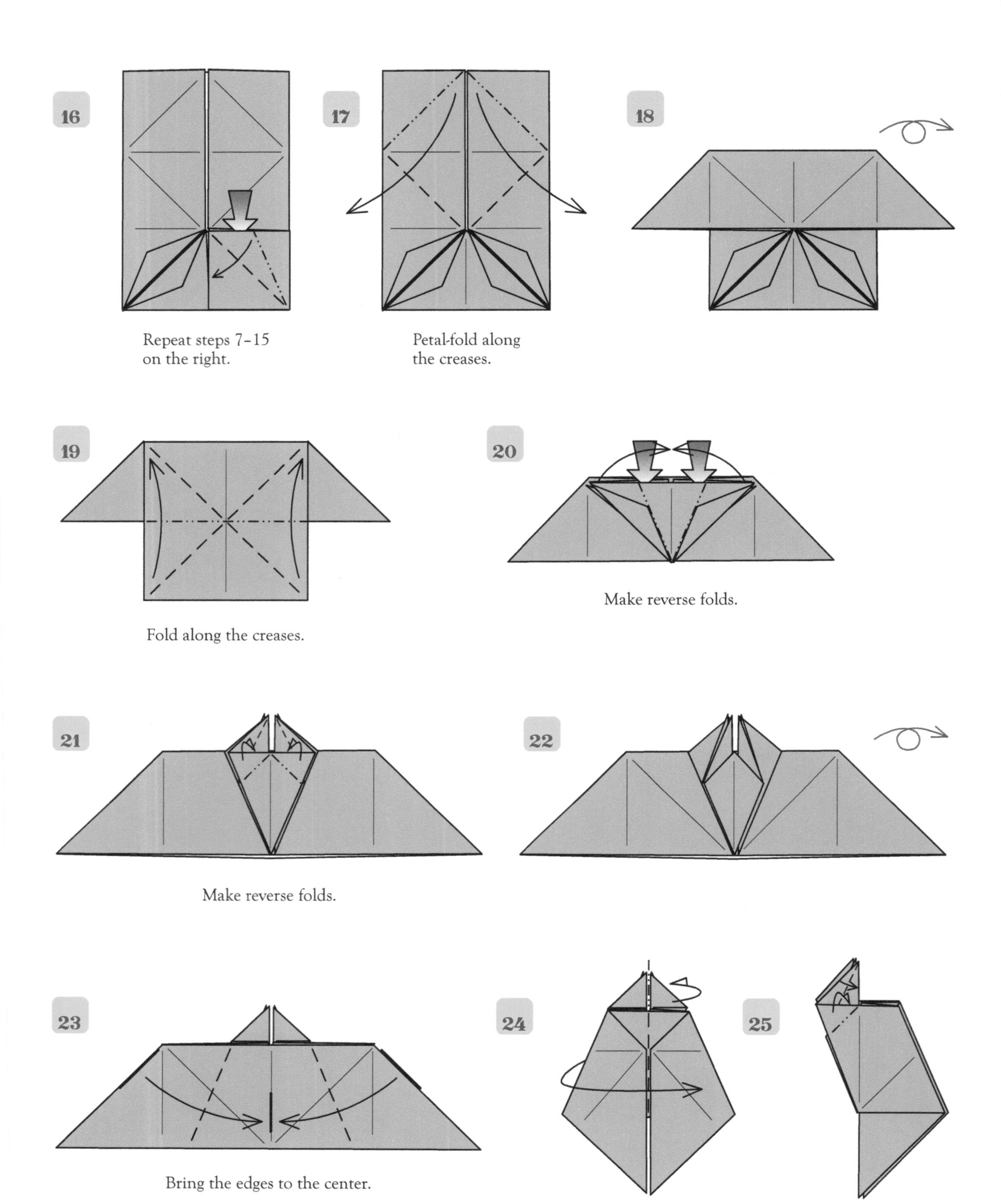
16
Repeat steps 7–15
on the right.
17
Petal-fold along
the creases.
18
19
Fold along the creases.
20
Make reverse folds.
21
Make reverse folds.
22
23
Bring the edges to the center.
24
25
Reverse-fold,
repeat behind.

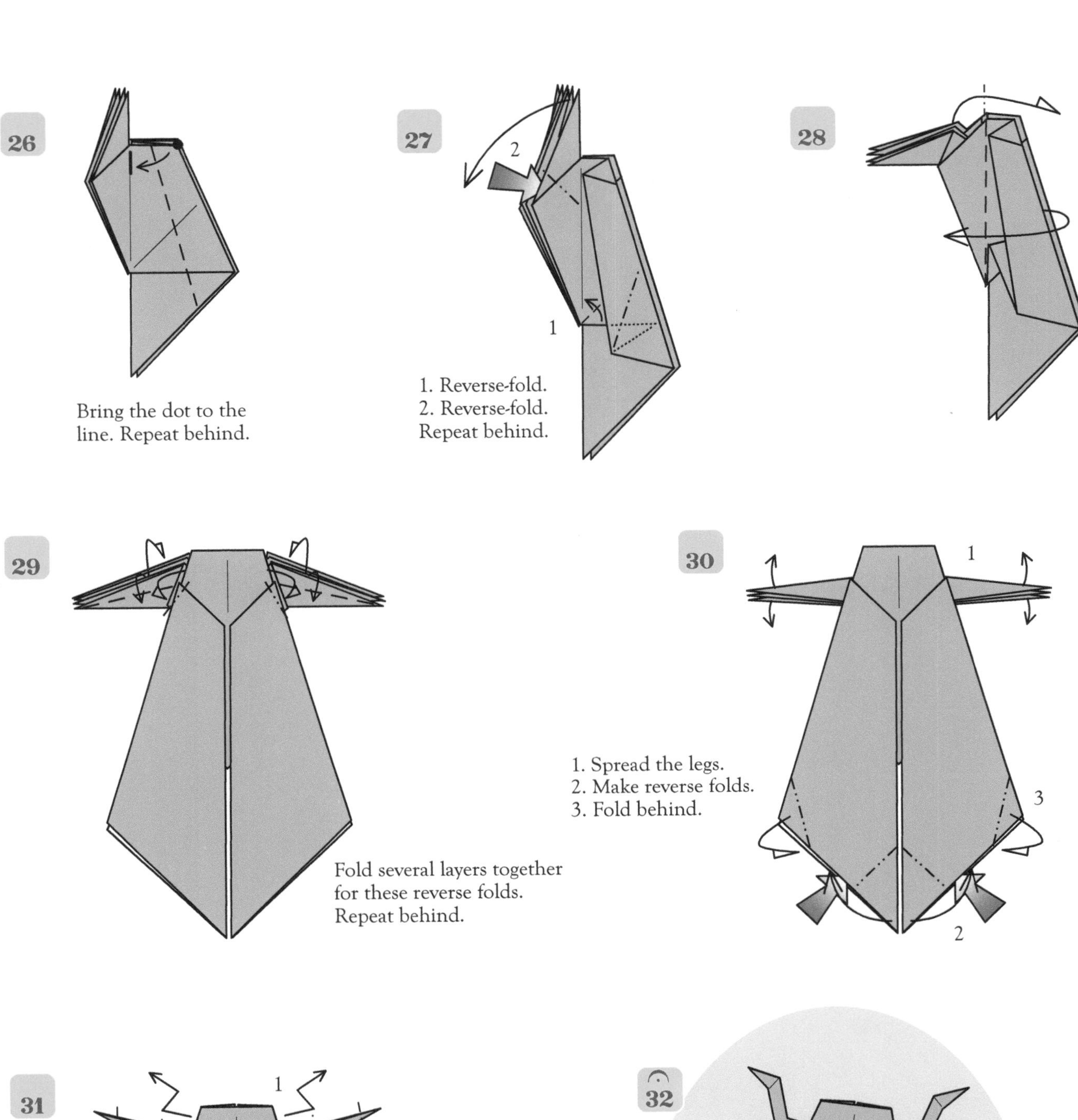

Bring the dot to the line. Repeat behind.

1. Reverse-fold.
2. Reverse-fold.
Repeat behind.

Fold several layers together for these reverse folds. Repeat behind.

1. Spread the legs.
2. Make reverse folds.
3. Fold behind.

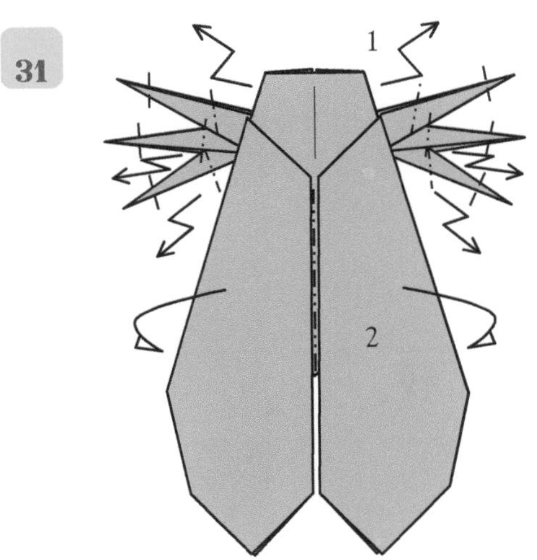

1. Shape the legs.
2. Fold in half, lightly.

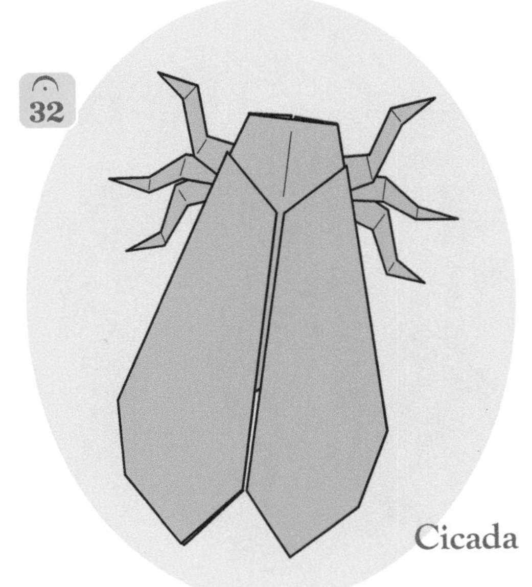

Cicada

Katydid

Katydids are nocturnal insects that like to eat leaves, fruit, snails, and other bugs. Their wings look like detailed leaves. Since they are usually green, they rest on twigs and camouflage into the tree by looking like leaves. Even with large wings, they cannot fly. They sing trilling songs that sound like "katy-did".

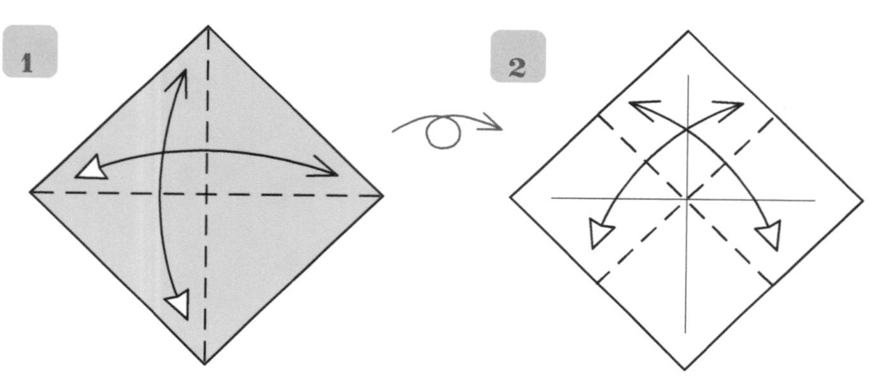

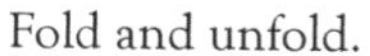

Fold and unfold.

Fold and unfold.

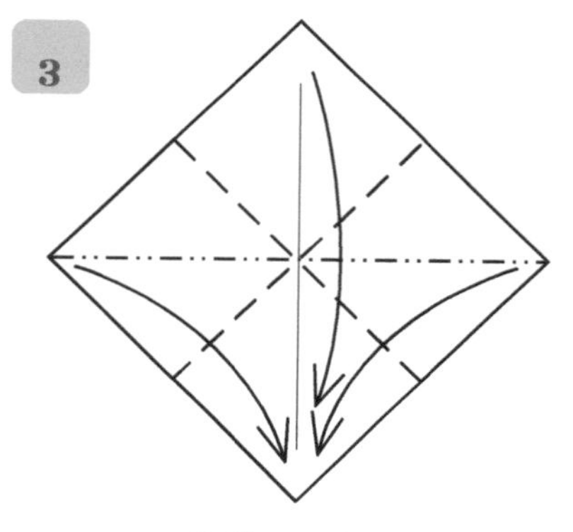

Collapse along the creases.

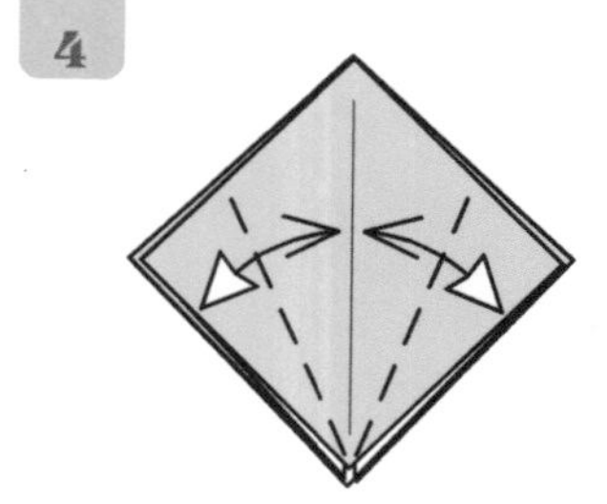

Fold to the center and unfold, repeat behind.

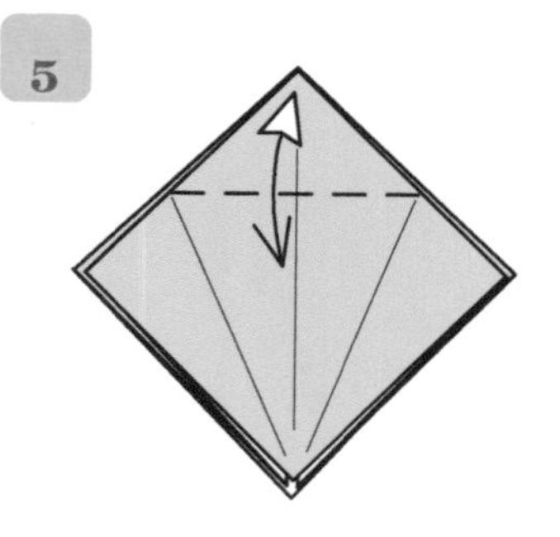

Fold and unfold.

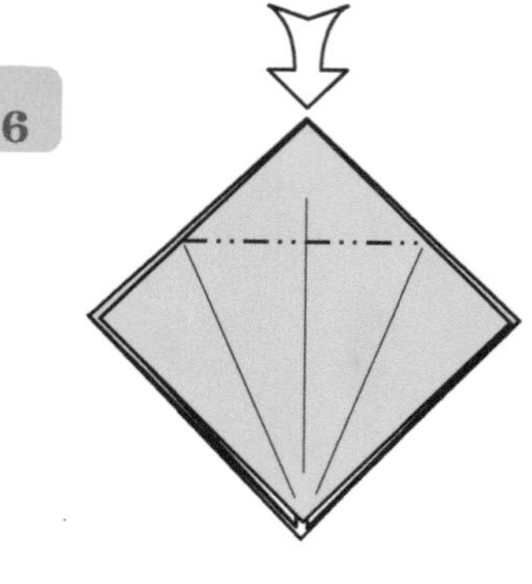

Sink.

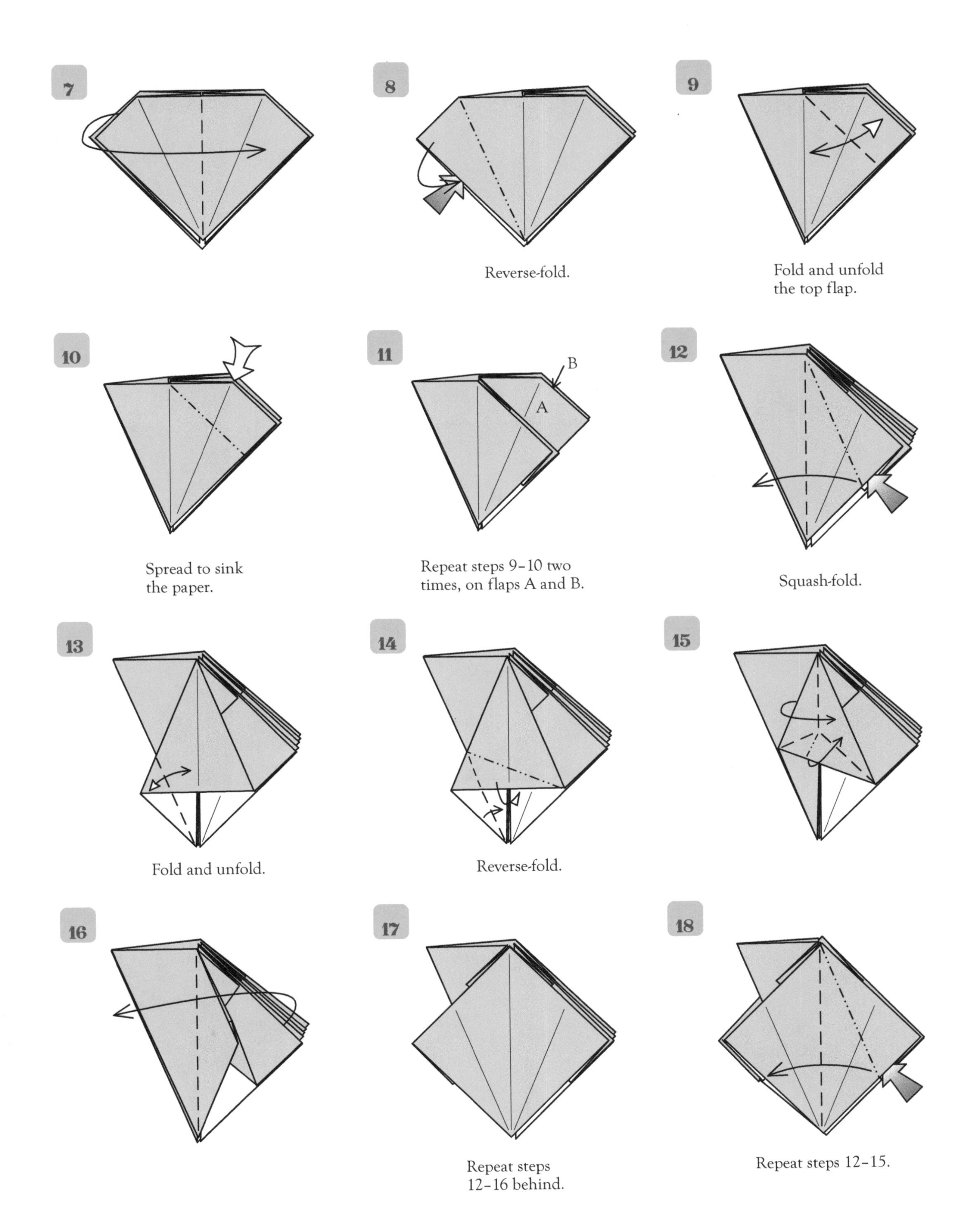

Reverse-fold.

Fold and unfold the top flap.

Spread to sink the paper.

Repeat steps 9–10 two times, on flaps A and B.

Squash-fold.

Fold and unfold.

Reverse-fold.

Repeat steps 12–16 behind.

Repeat steps 12–15.

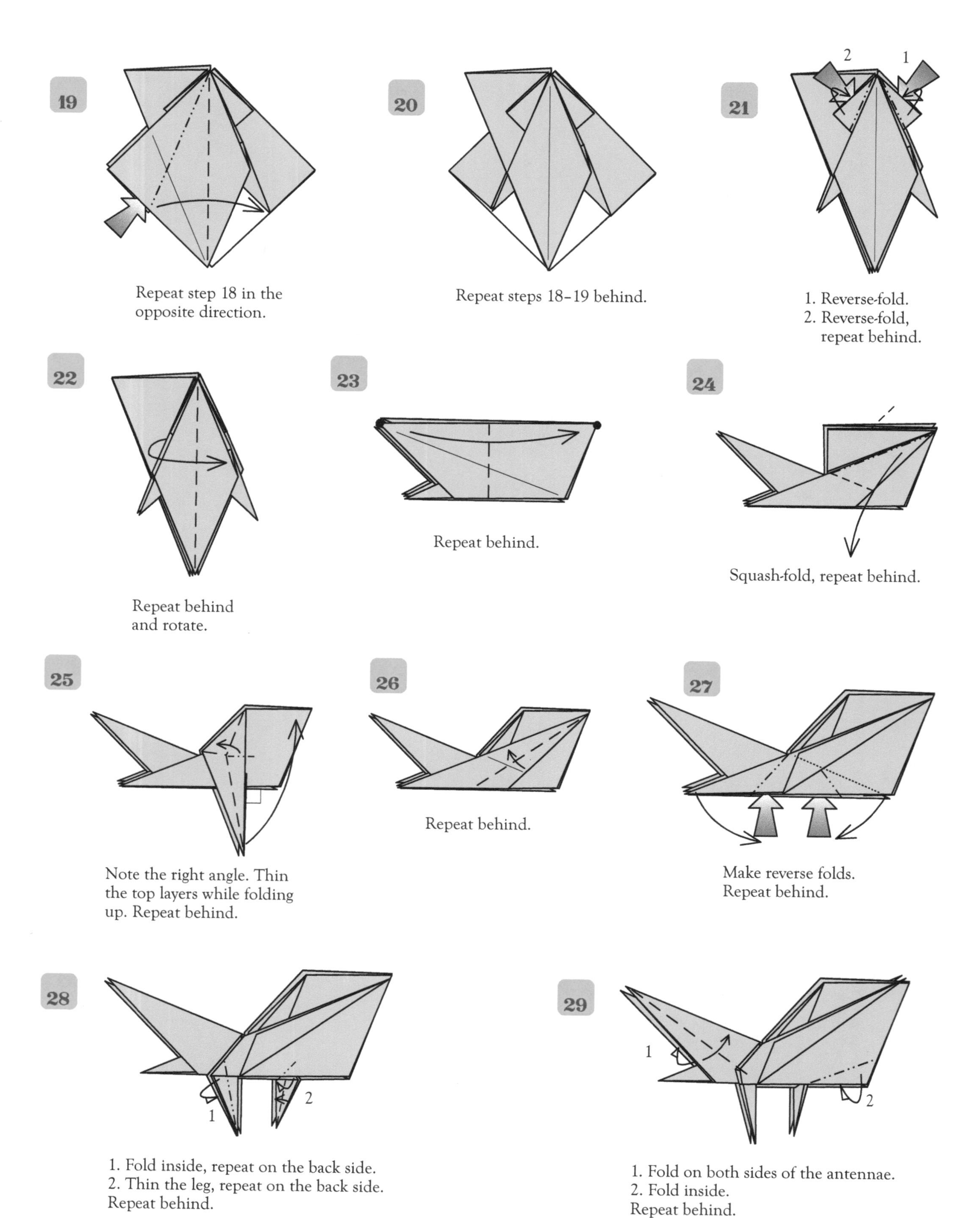
19
Repeat step 18 in the opposite direction.
20
Repeat steps 18–19 behind.
21
2
1
1. Reverse-fold.
2. Reverse-fold, repeat behind.
22
Repeat behind and rotate.
23
Repeat behind.
24
Squash-fold, repeat behind.
25
Note the right angle. Thin the top layers while folding up. Repeat behind.
26
Repeat behind.
27
Make reverse folds. Repeat behind.
28
1
2
1. Fold inside, repeat on the back side.
2. Thin the leg, repeat on the back side.
Repeat behind.
29
1
2
1. Fold on both sides of the antennae.
2. Fold inside.
Repeat behind.

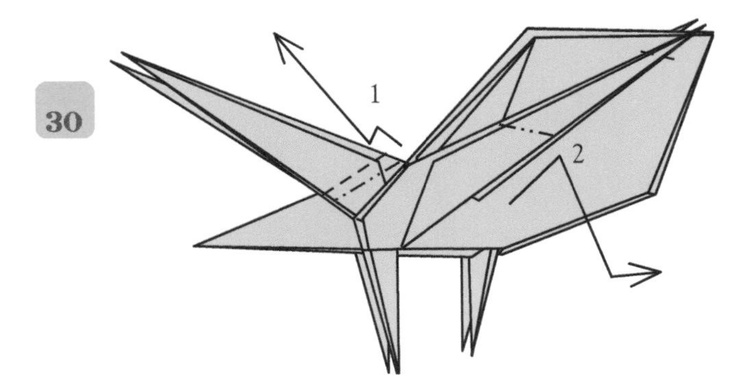

1. Crimp-fold.
2. Make reverse folds.
Repeat behind.

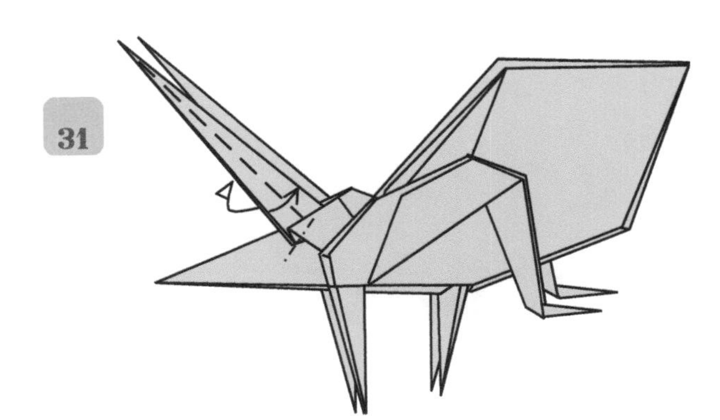

Thin the antennae on the front and back. Repeat behind.

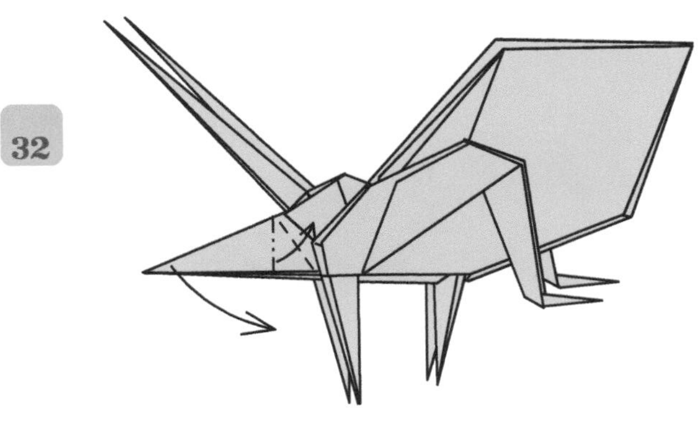

Crimp-fold.

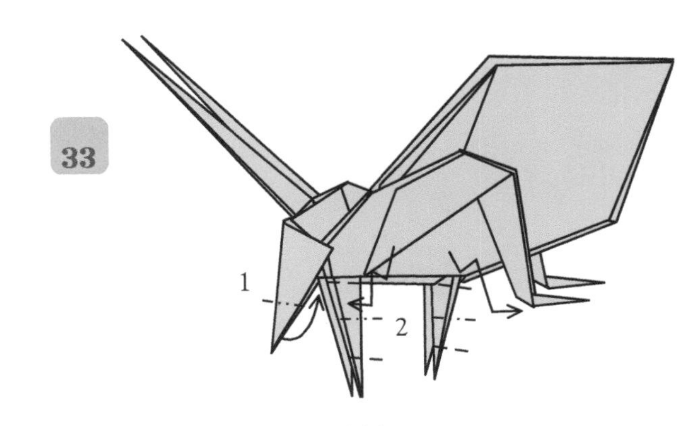

1. Reverse-fold.
2. Shape the legs, repeat behind.

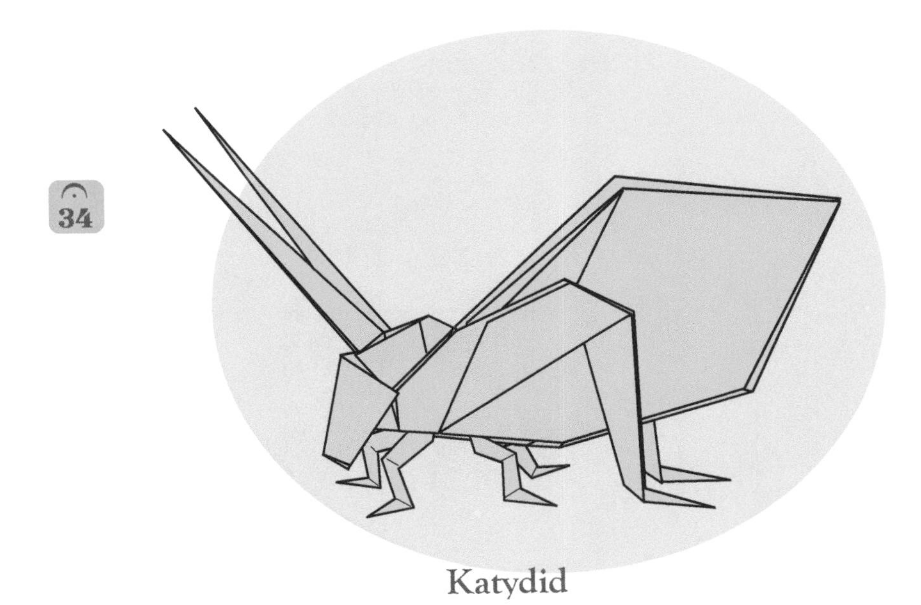

Katydid

Hornet

Hornets are about one to two inches larger than wasps. They are less aggressive than wasps and only sting when threatened. They build large paper nests in high places such as treetops and roofs. Living in large colonies, they help farmers by feeding on other insects like grasshoppers. Hornets are important pollinators and are attracted to bright colors, especially yellow.

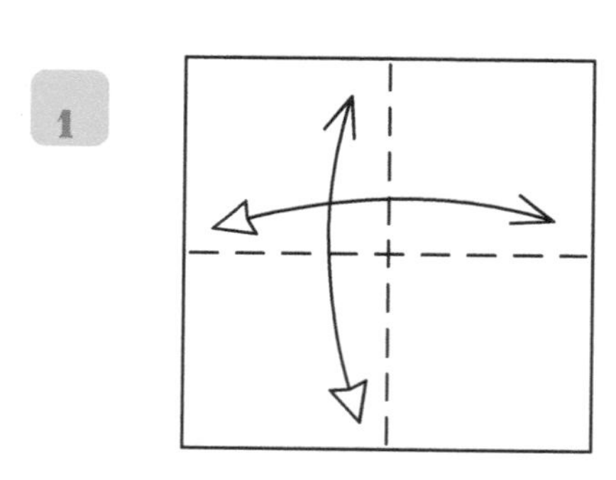

Fold and unfold.

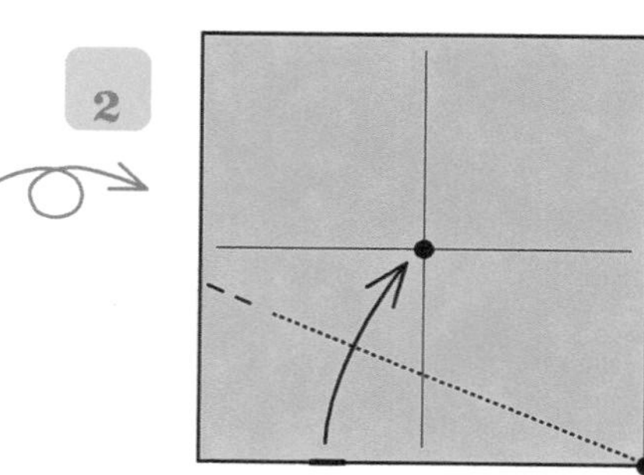

Bring the edge to the center. Crease on the left.

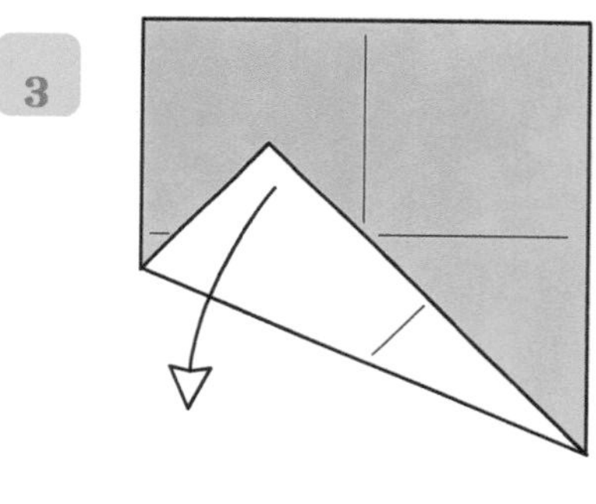

Unfold.

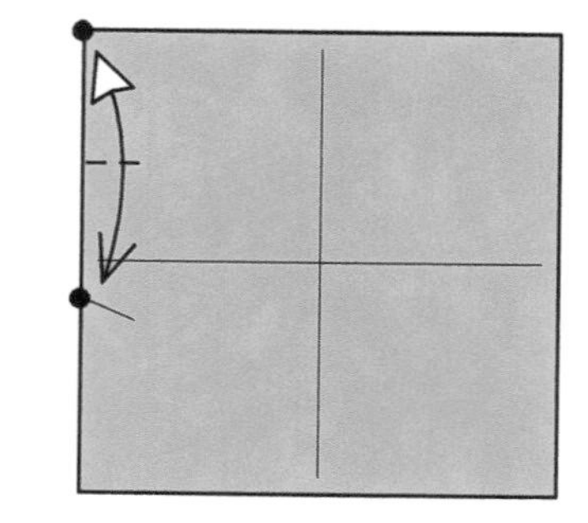

Fold and unfold on the left.

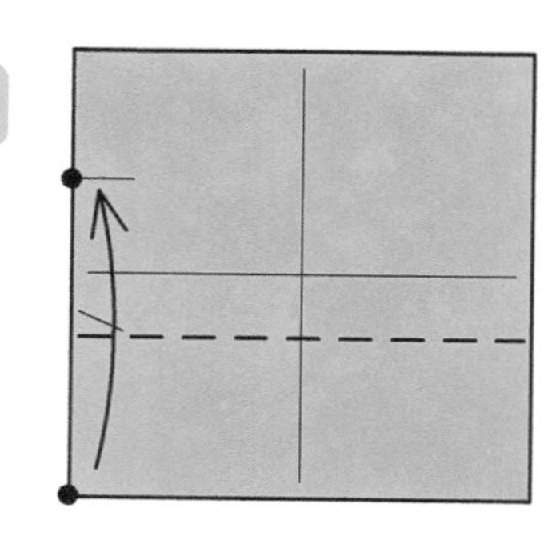

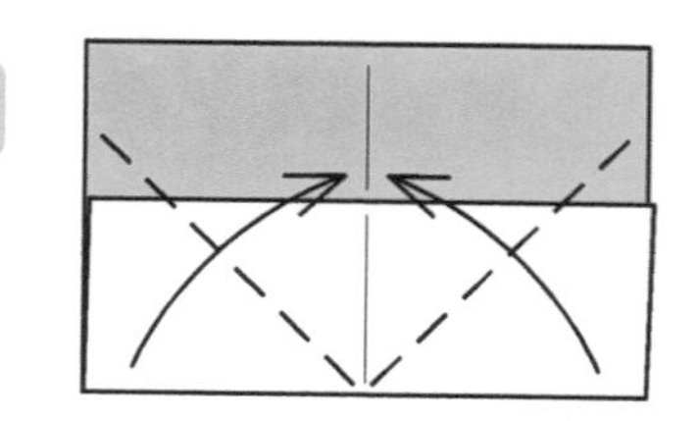

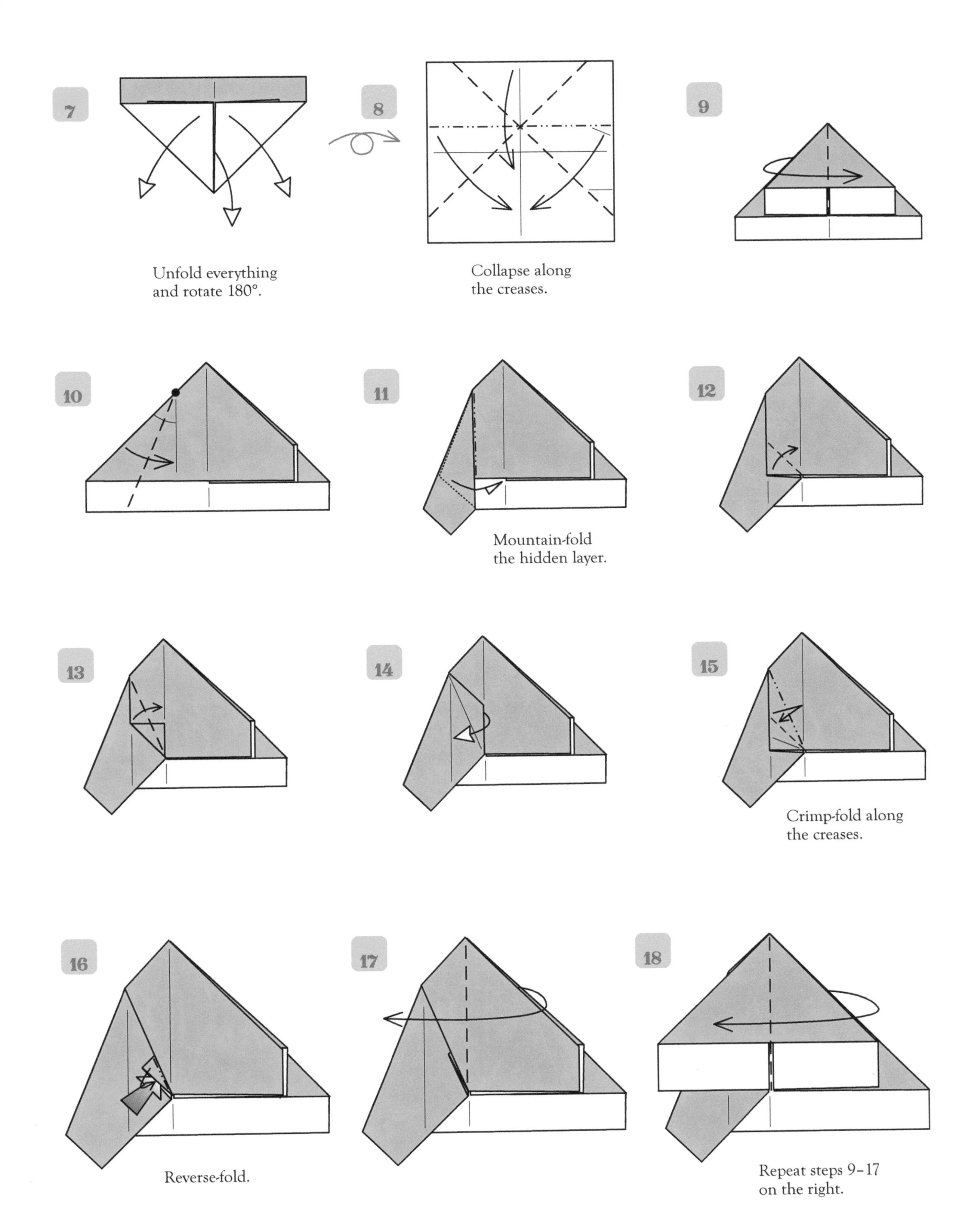

Unfold everything and rotate 180°.

Collapse along the creases.

Mountain-fold the hidden layer.

Crimp-fold along the creases.

Reverse-fold.

Repeat steps 9–17 on the right.

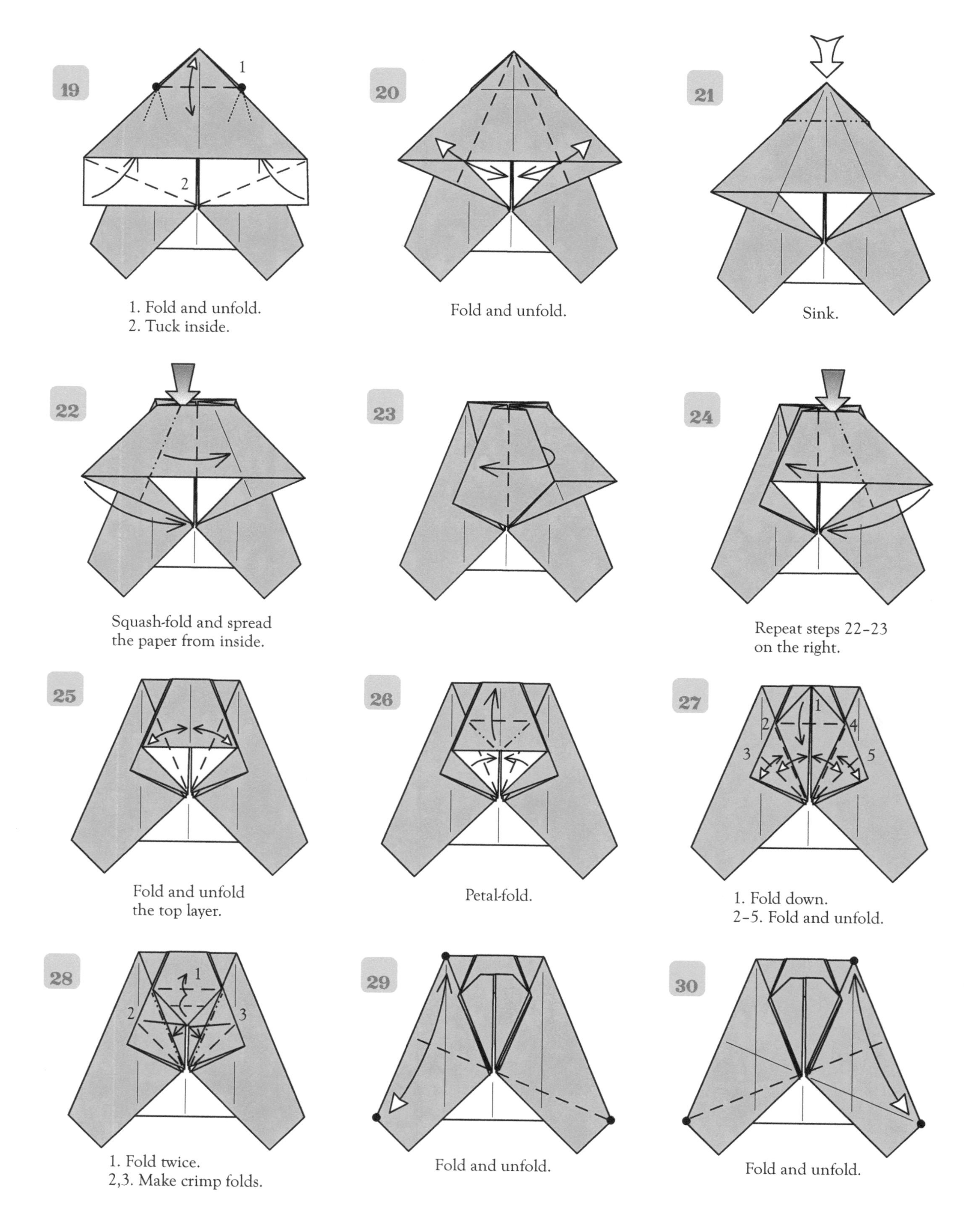
19
1
2
1. Fold and unfold.
2. Tuck inside.
20
Fold and unfold.
21
Sink.
22
Squash-fold and spread
the paper from inside.
23
24
Repeat steps 22–23
on the right.
25
Fold and unfold
the top layer.
26
Petal-fold.
27
1
2
4
3
5
1. Fold down.
2–5. Fold and unfold.
28
1
2
3
1. Fold twice.
2,3. Make crimp folds.
29
Fold and unfold.
30
Fold and unfold.

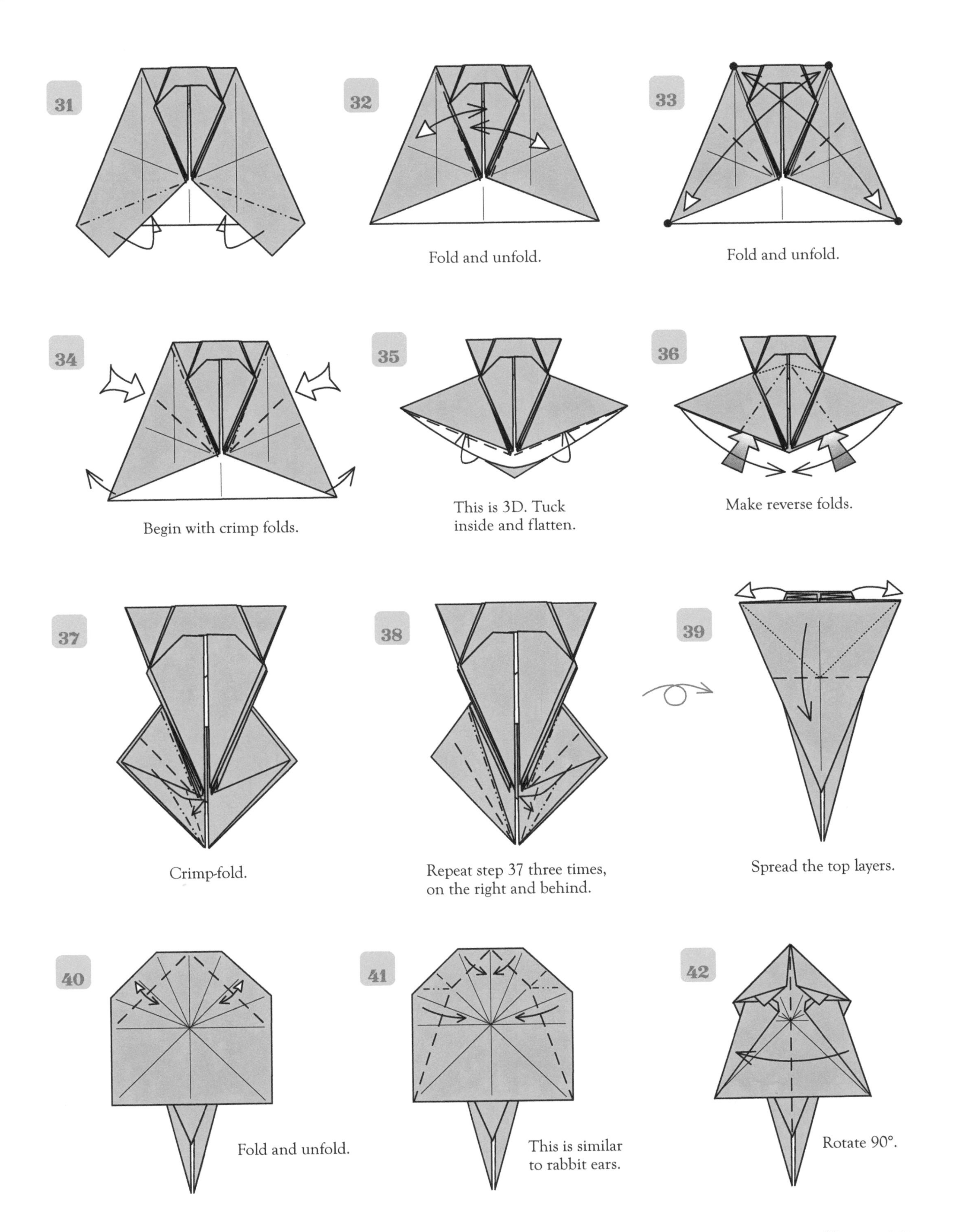
31
32
Fold and unfold.
33
Fold and unfold.
34
Begin with crimp folds.
35
This is 3D. Tuck inside and flatten.
36
Make reverse folds.
37
Crimp-fold.
38
Repeat step 37 three times, on the right and behind.
39
Spread the top layers.
40
Fold and unfold.
41
This is similar to rabbit ears.
42
Rotate 90°.

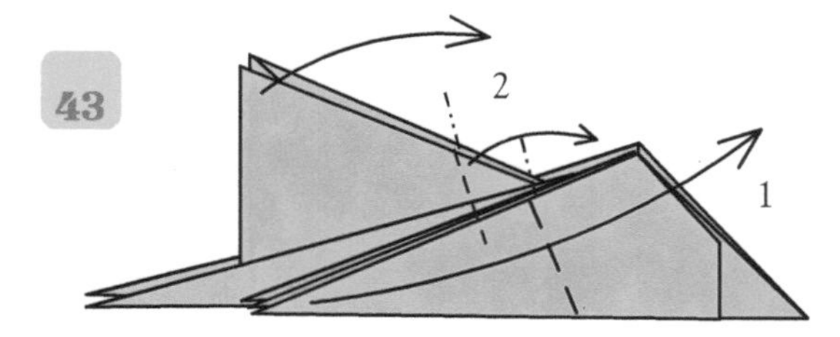

1. Valley-fold, repeat behind.
2. Slide the wings up with a crimp fold.

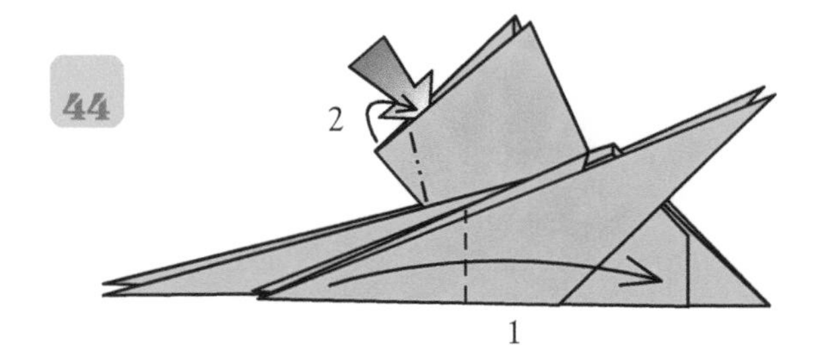

1. Repeat behind.
2. Reverse-fold.

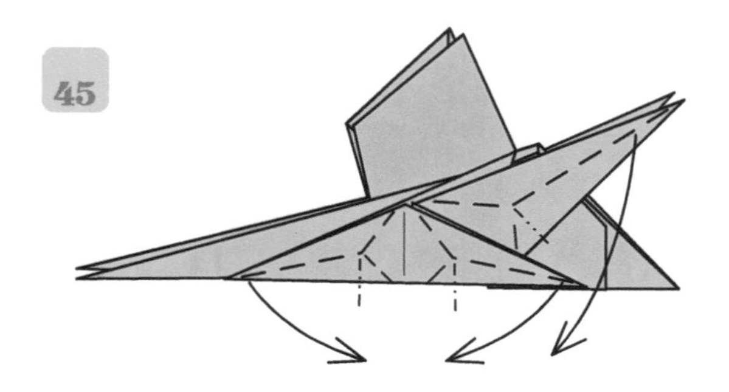

Make rabbit ears.
Repeat behind.

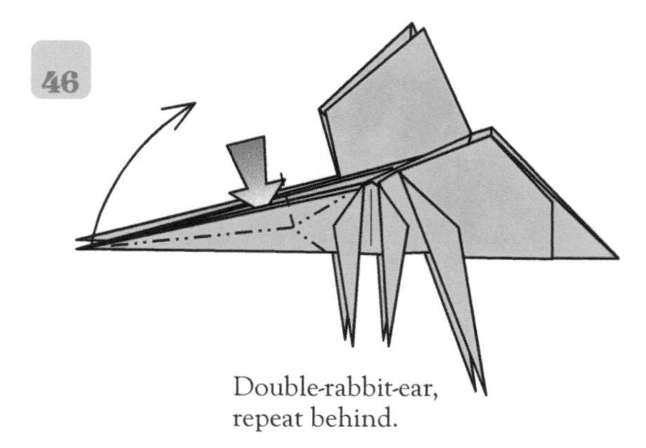

Double-rabbit-ear,
repeat behind.

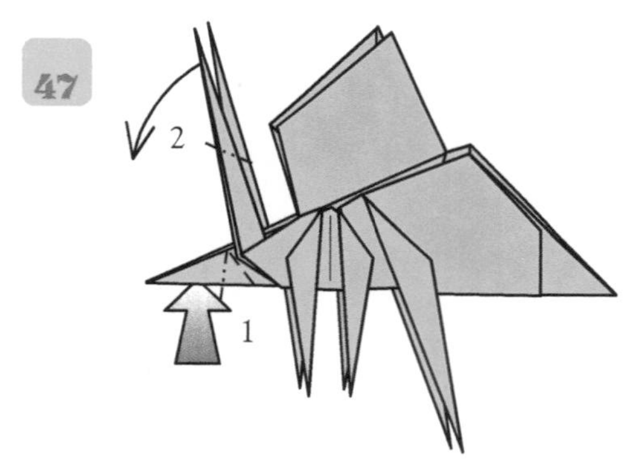

1. Crimp-fold and spread the head.
2. Reverse-fold, repeat behind.

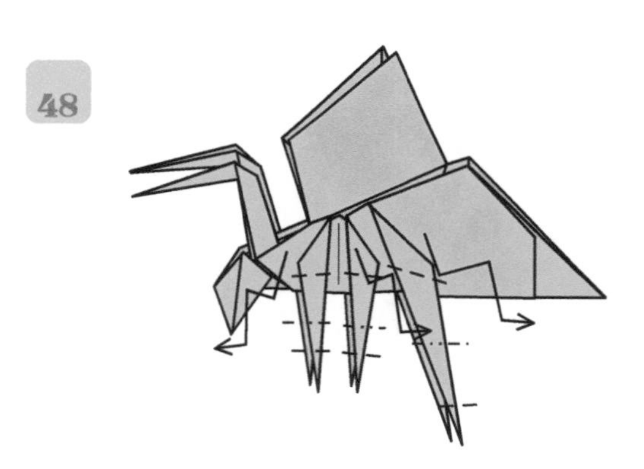

Fold the legs, repeat behind.

Dragonfly

The dragonfly is one of the earliest flying insects to evolve, around 300 million years ago. Their four wings work independently so they can fly like a helicopter. Their large set of compound eyes can see practically all around them. As one of fastest flying insects, they hunt, snatch and eat other insects while flying. They do it so well that their success rate is about 95%. Dragonflies are friendly to people and it brings good luck when they land on you.

1

1. Fold and unfold.
2. Fold and unfold on the top.

2

Fold and unfold on the right.

3

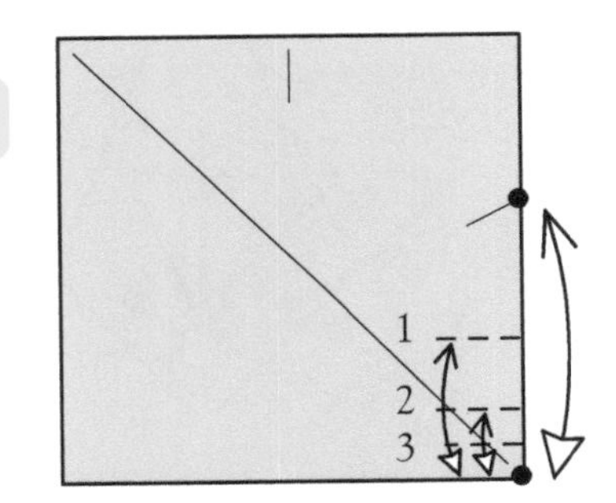

Fold in half three times on the right.

4

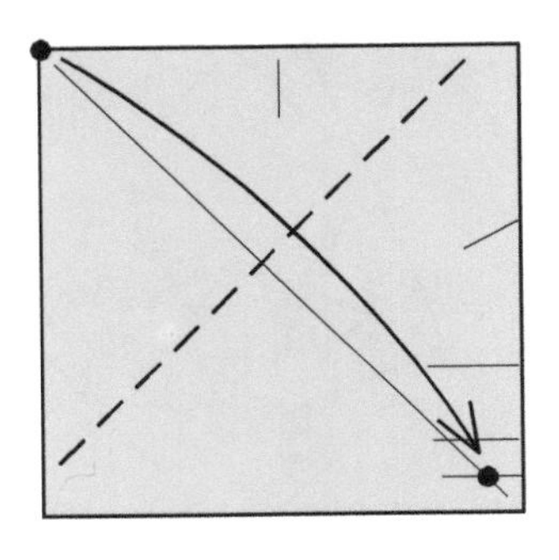

Rotate.

5

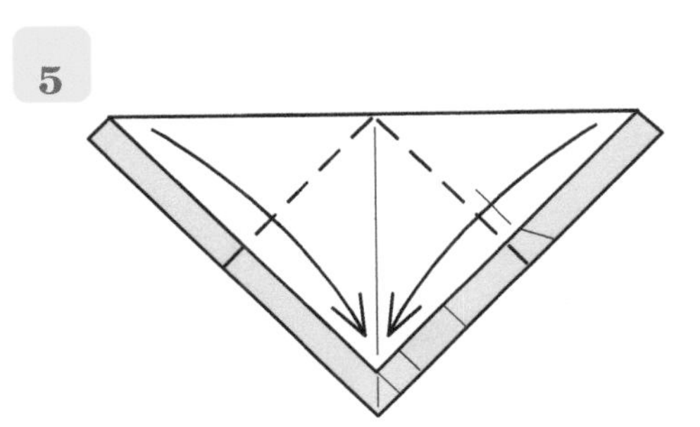

6

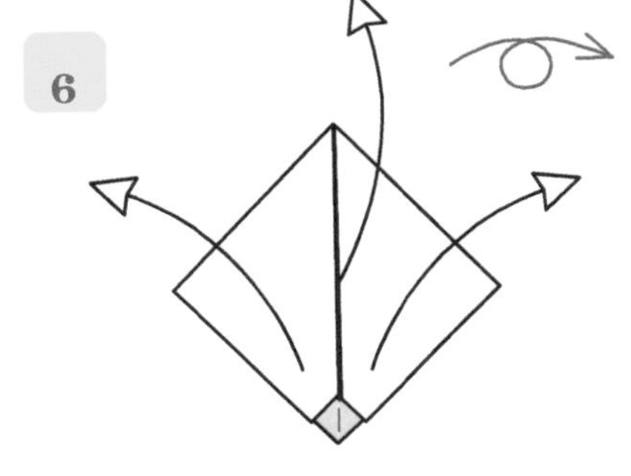

Unfold everything.

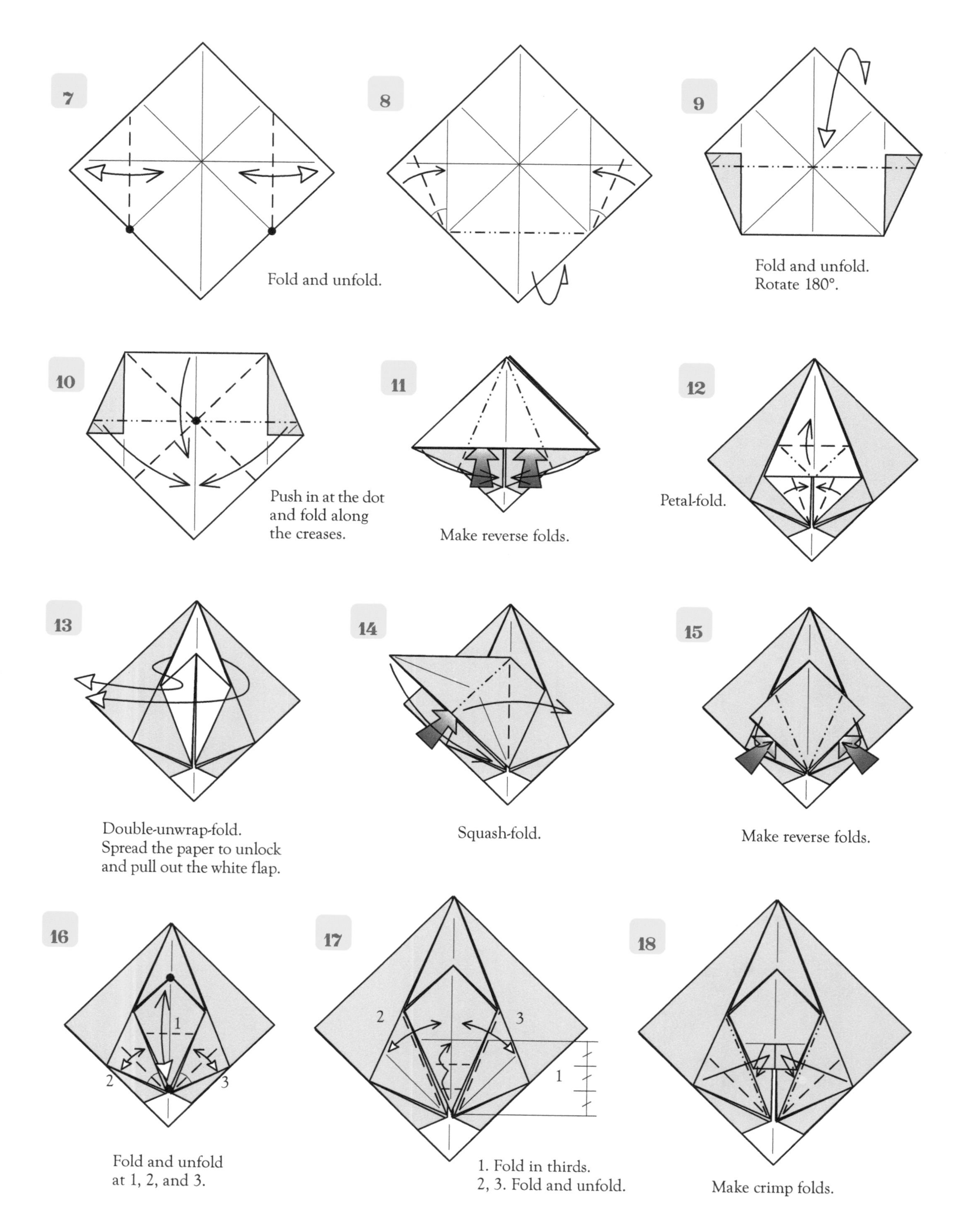
7
Fold and unfold.
8
9
Fold and unfold.
Rotate 180°.
10
Push in at the dot
and fold along
the creases.
11
Make reverse folds.
12
Petal-fold.
13
Double-unwrap-fold.
Spread the paper to unlock
and pull out the white flap.
14
Squash-fold.
15
Make reverse folds.
16
1
2
3
Fold and unfold
at 1, 2, and 3.
17
2
3
1
1. Fold in thirds.
2, 3. Fold and unfold.
18
Make crimp folds.

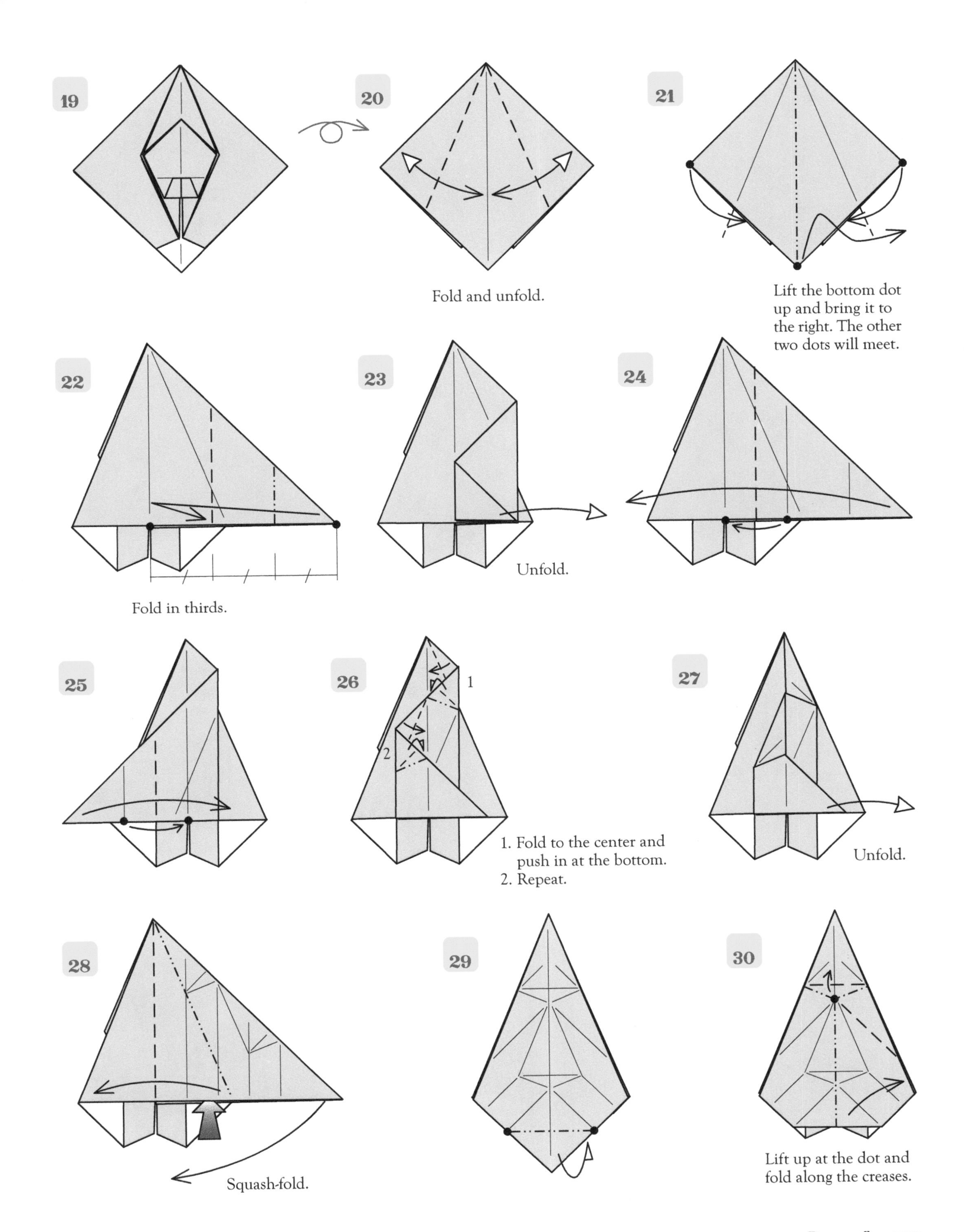
19
20
21
Fold and unfold.
Lift the bottom dot up and bring it to the right. The other two dots will meet.
22
23
24
Unfold.
Fold in thirds.
25
26
1
2
27
1. Fold to the center and push in at the bottom.
2. Repeat.
Unfold.
28
29
30
Squash-fold.
Lift up at the dot and fold along the creases.

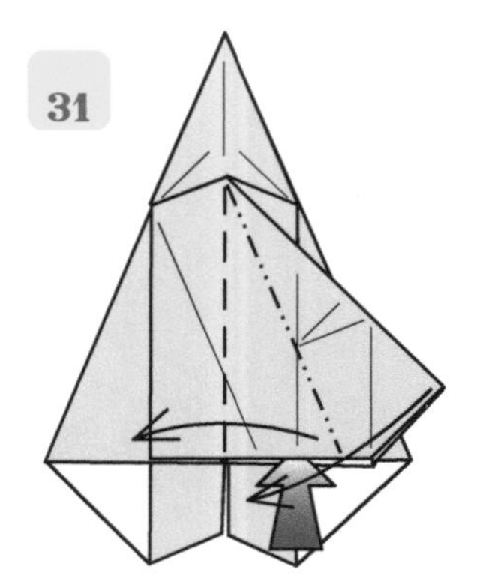

Squash-fold.

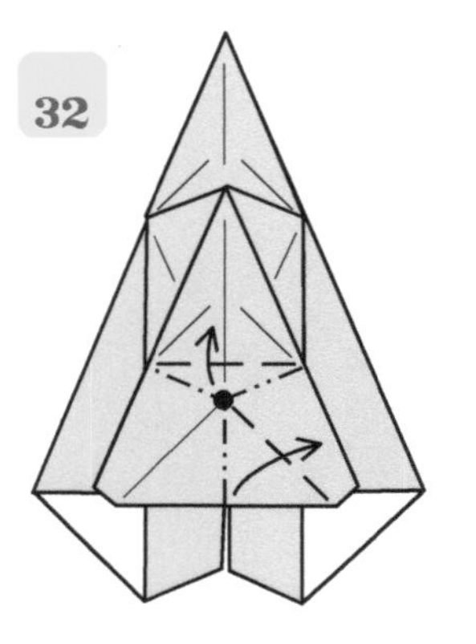

Lift up at the dot and fold along the creases.

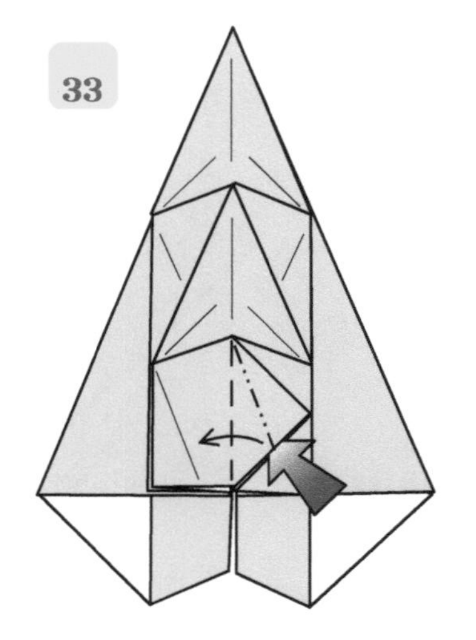

Squash-fold.

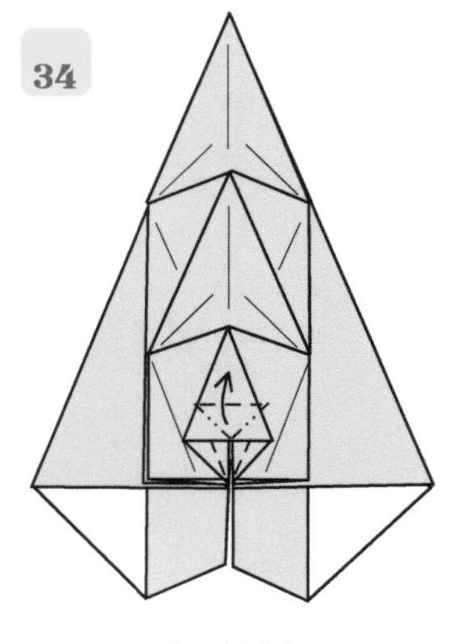

Petal-fold.

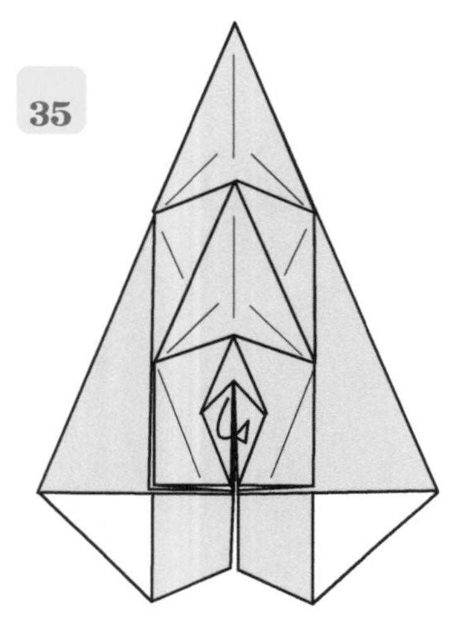

Spread the paper to wrap around and tuck the flap inside.

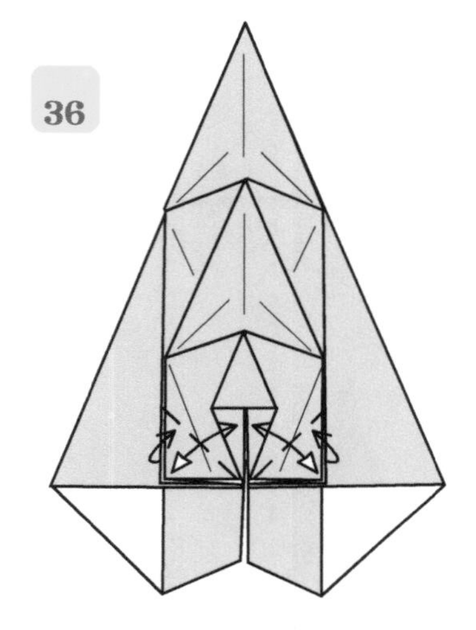

Fold and unfold two flaps on both sides.

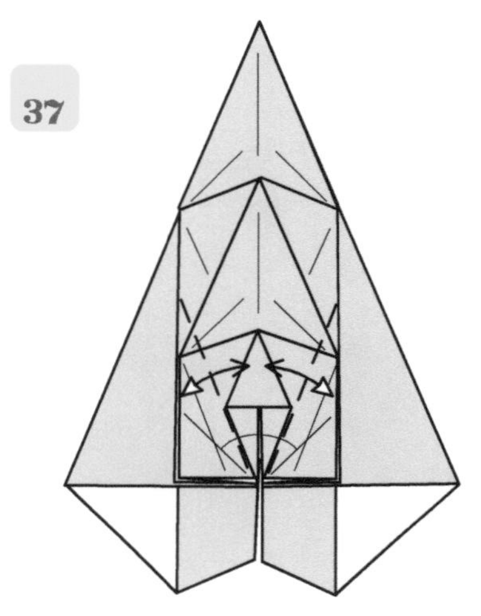

Fold and unfold two flaps on both sides.

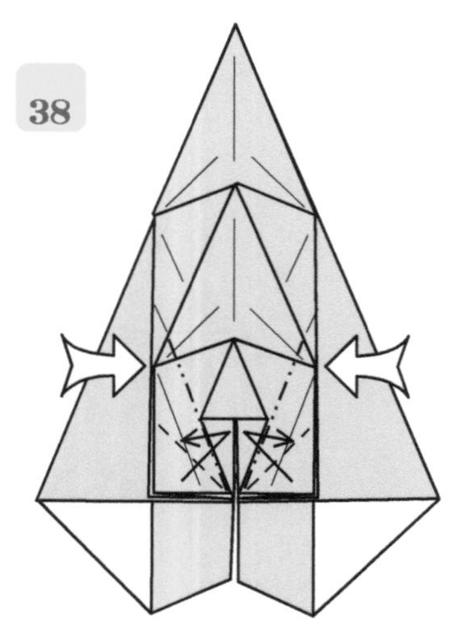

Crimp-fold and sink on both sides.

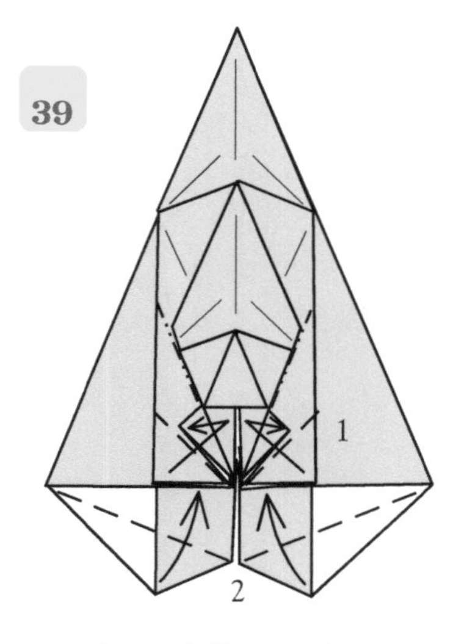

1. Crimp-fold on both sides.
2. Fold up.

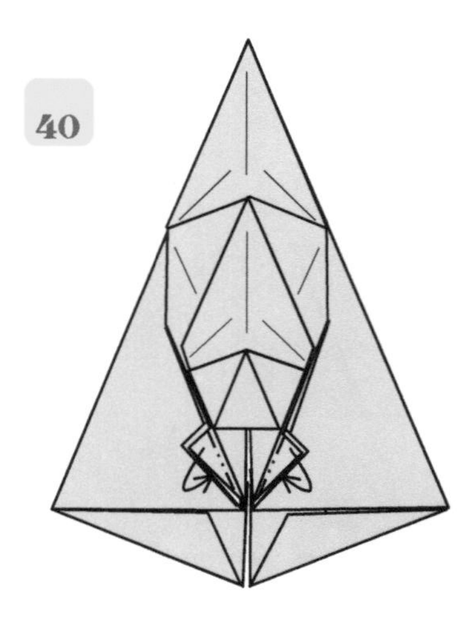

Make four reverse folds.

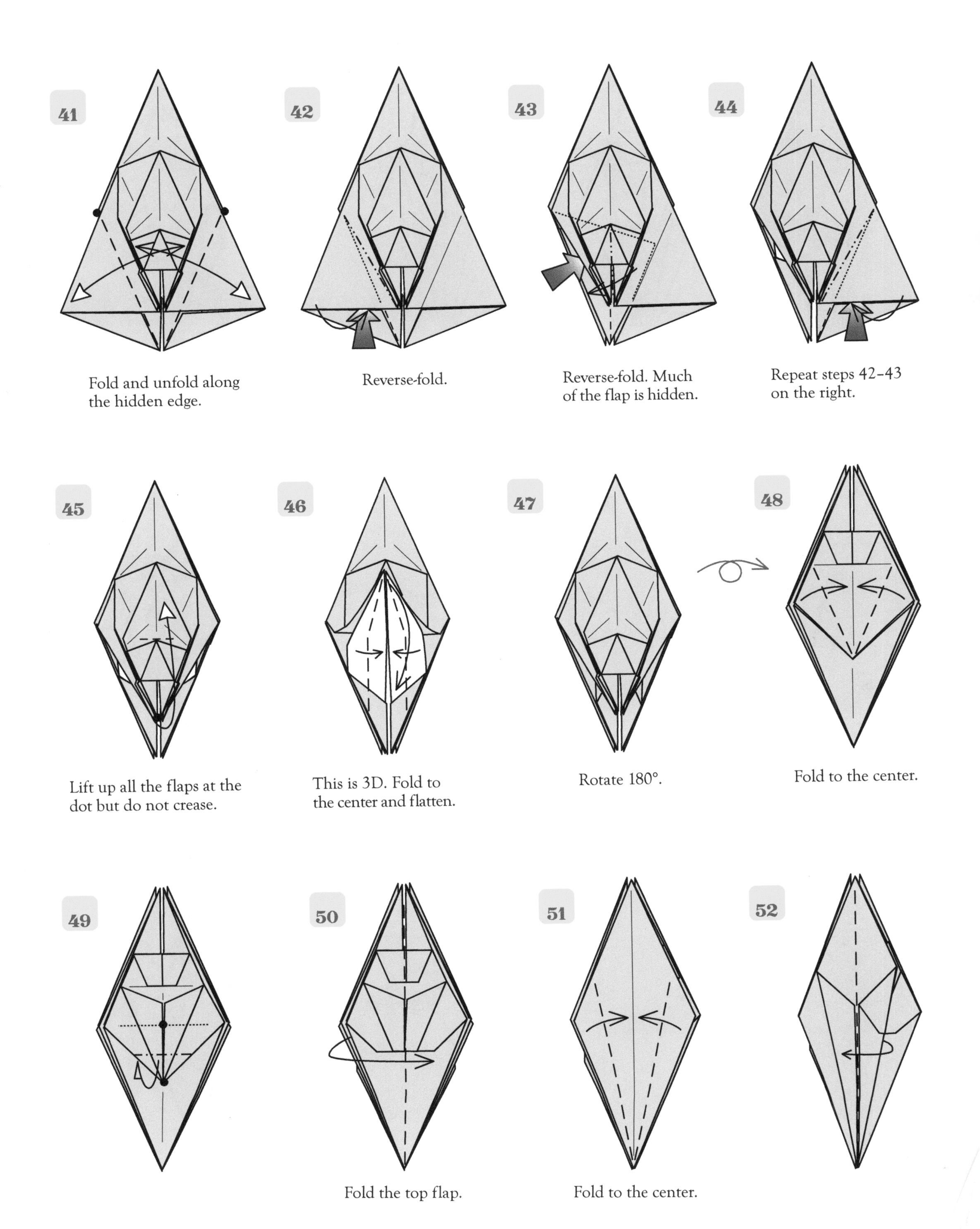

Fold and unfold along the hidden edge.

Reverse-fold.

Reverse-fold. Much of the flap is hidden.

Repeat steps 42–43 on the right.

Lift up all the flaps at the dot but do not crease.

This is 3D. Fold to the center and flatten.

Rotate 180°.

Fold to the center.

Fold the top flap.

Fold to the center.

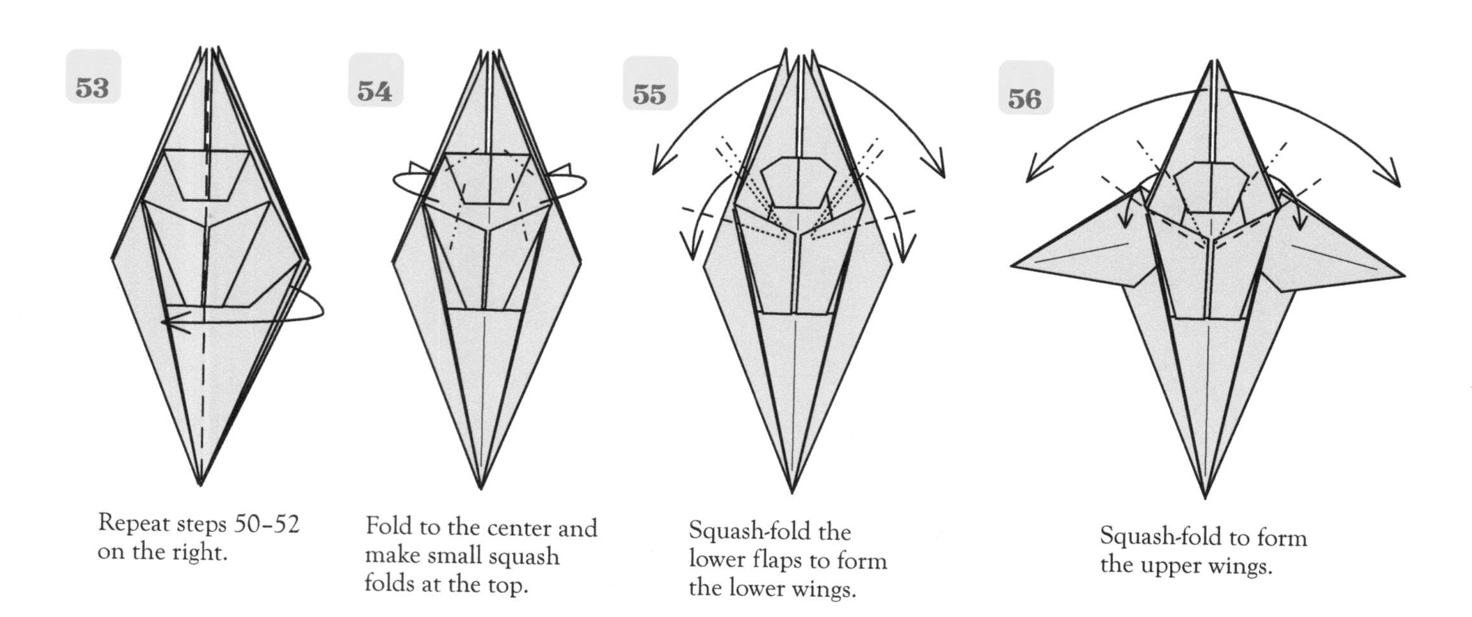

Repeat steps 50–52 on the right.

Fold to the center and make small squash folds at the top.

Squash-fold the lower flaps to form the lower wings.

Squash-fold to form the upper wings.

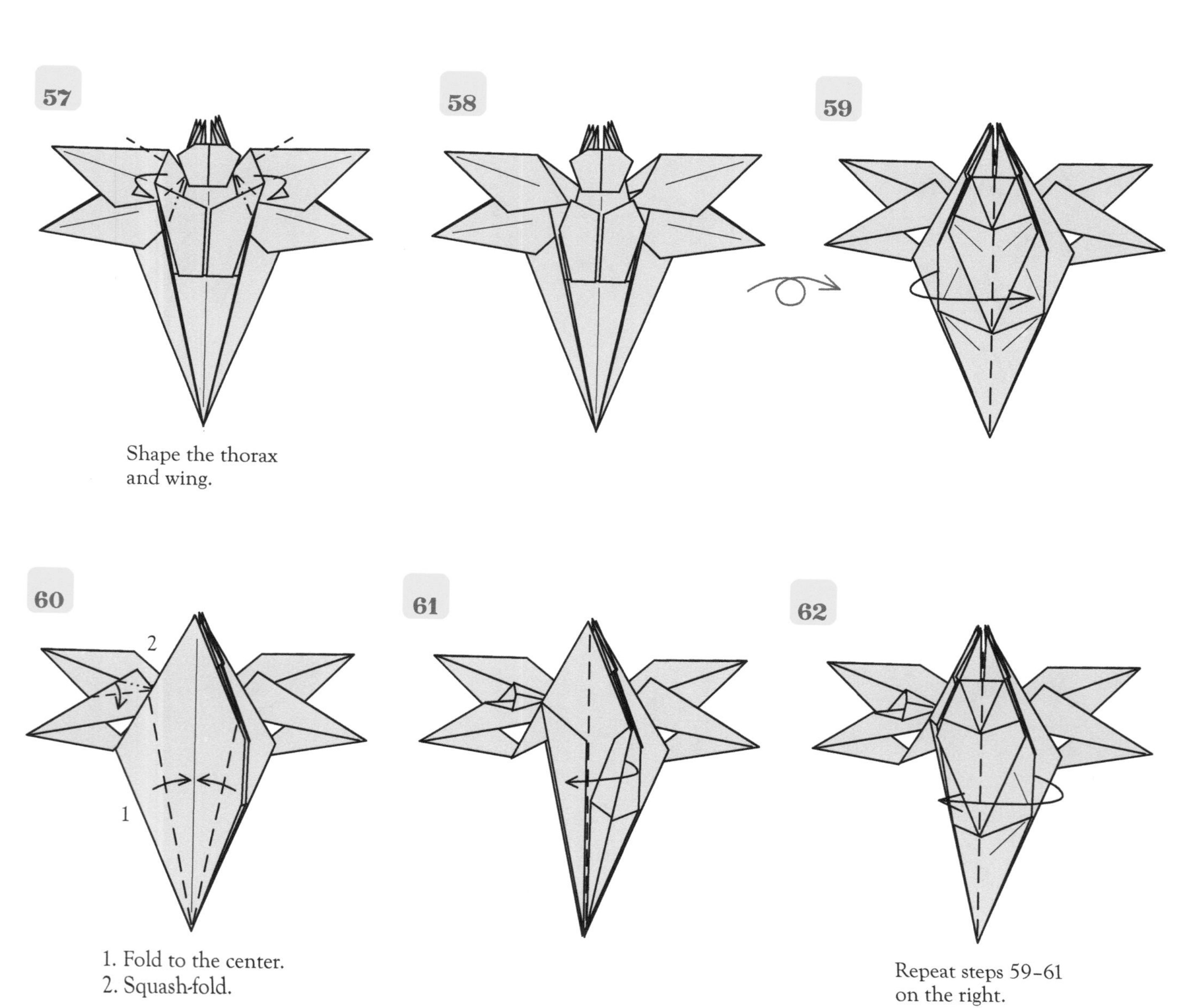

Shape the thorax and wing.

1. Fold to the center.
2. Squash-fold.

Repeat steps 59–61 on the right.

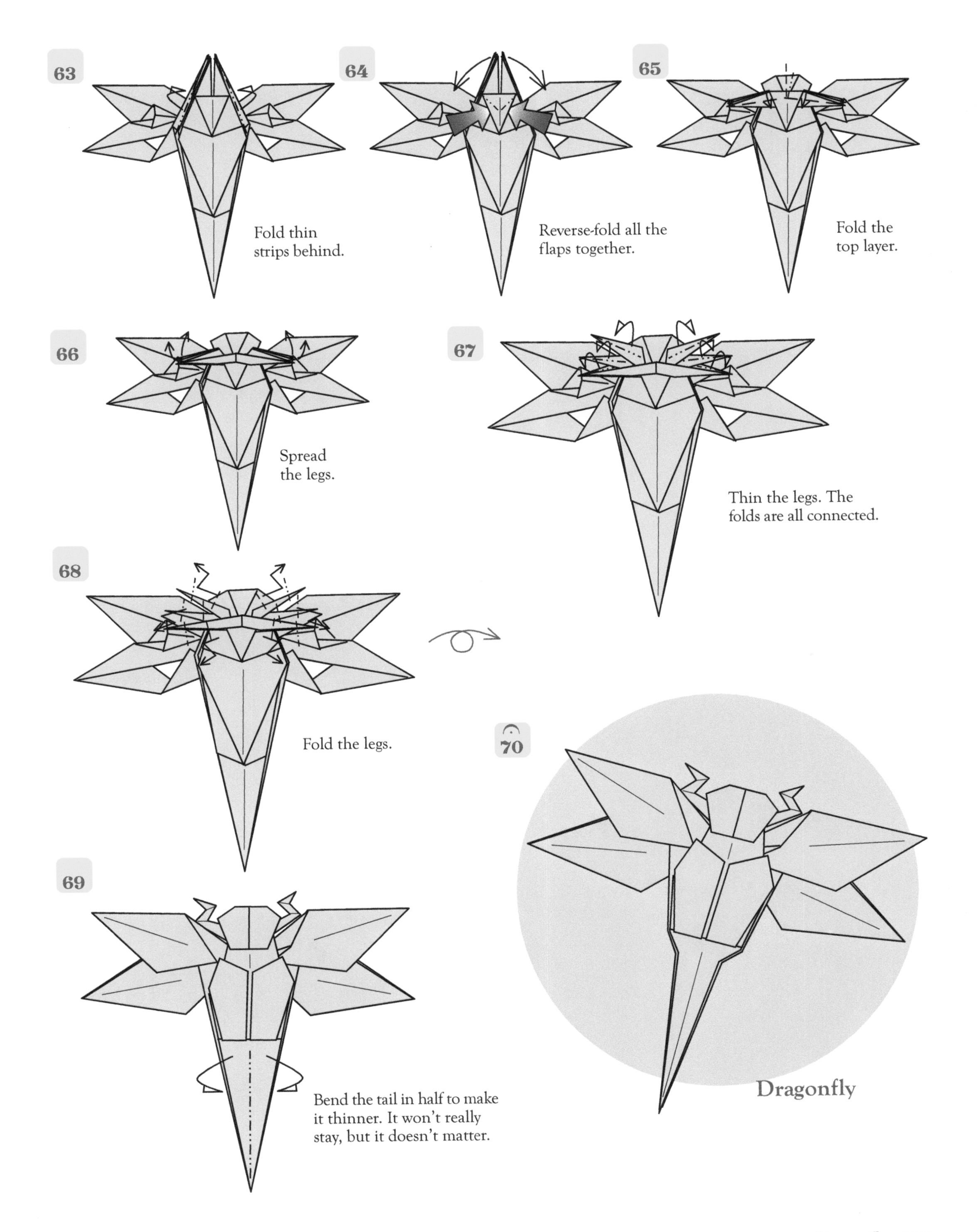
63
Fold thin
strips behind.
64
Reverse-fold all the
flaps together.
65
Fold the
top layer.
66
Spread
the legs.
67
Thin the legs. The
folds are all connected.
68
Fold the legs.
69
Bend the tail in half to make
it thinner. It won't really
stay, but it doesn't matter.
70
Dragonfly

Printed in the USA
CPSIA information can be obtained
at www.ICGtesting.com
LVHW070118291023
762329LV00012B/285